Underwater Photography

Tobias Friedrich

Underwater Photography

rockynook

Tobias Friedrich (www.below-surface.com)

Editor: Joan Dixon
Copyeditor: Jeanne Hansen
Translator: David Schlesinger
Layout: Petra Strauch
Illustrations: Christin Bittner, www.buntundfroehlich.de
Cover Design: Helmut Kraus, www.exclam.de
Printer: Friesens Corporation
Printed in Canada

ISBN 978-1-937538-52-1

1st Edition 2014

Rocky Nook, Inc.
802 East Cota St., 3rd Floor
Santa Barbara, CA 93103

www.rockynook.com

Title of the German original: Die Kunst der Unterwasserfotografie
ISBN: 978-3-86490-103-4

Library of Congress Cataloging-in-Publication Data

Friedrich, Tobias, author.
Underwater photography / by Tobias Friedrich. -- 1st edition.
pages cm
ISBN 978-1-937538-52-1 (softcover : alk. paper)
1. Underwater photography. 2. Photography--Digital techniques. 3. Single-lens reflex cameras. I. Title.
TR800.F72 2014
778.7'3--dc23
2014008843

Distributed by O'Reilly Media
1005 Gravenstein Highway North
Sebastopol, CA 95472

This book is printed on acid-free paper.

For my parents. With love.

Table of Contents

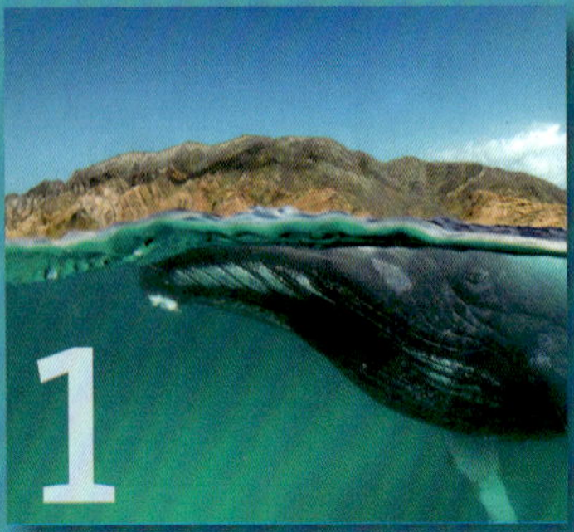

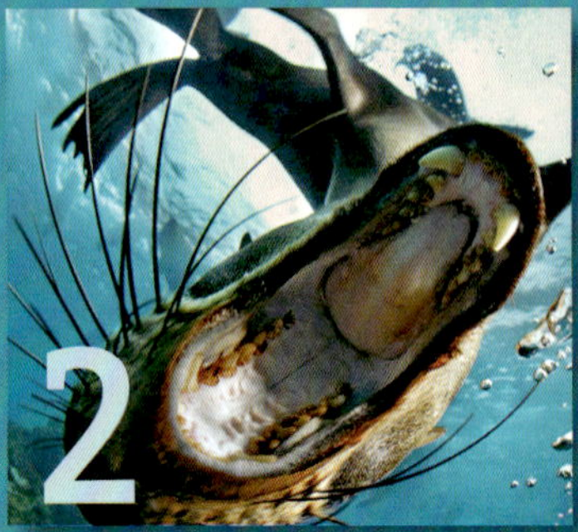

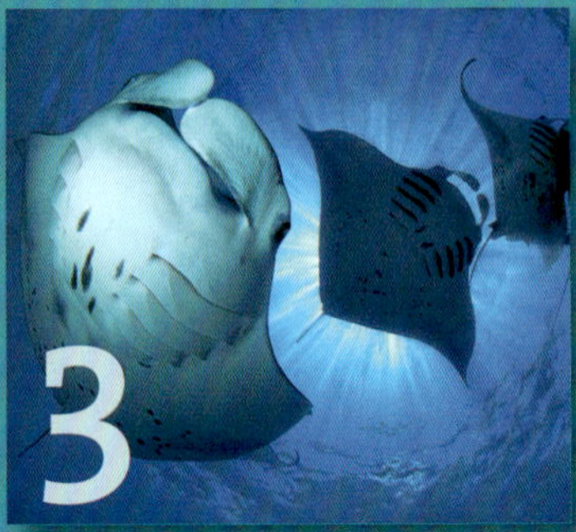

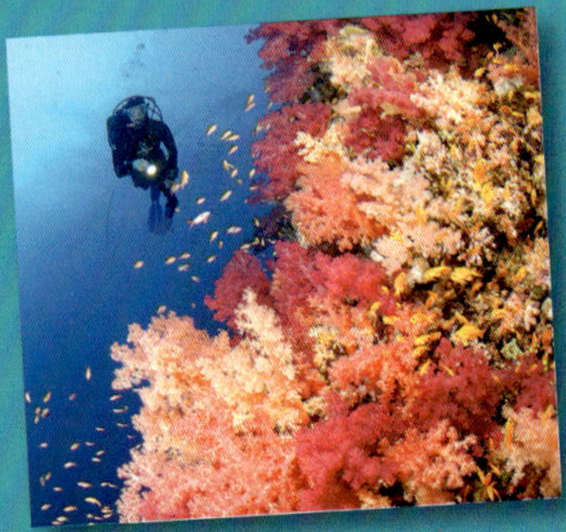

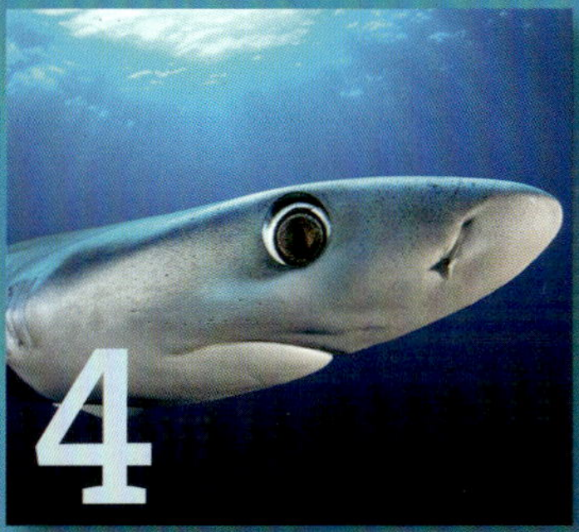
4

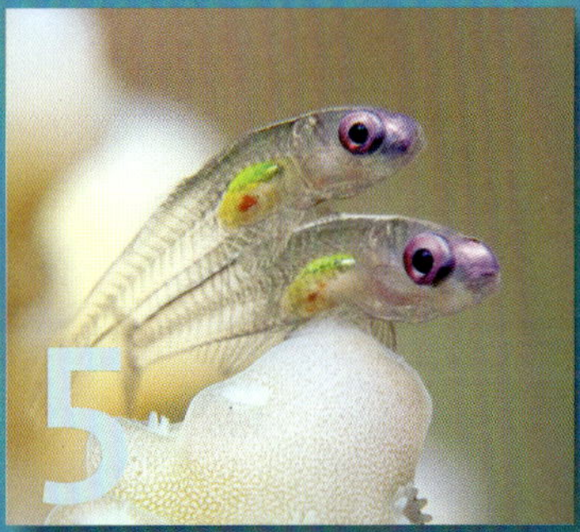
5

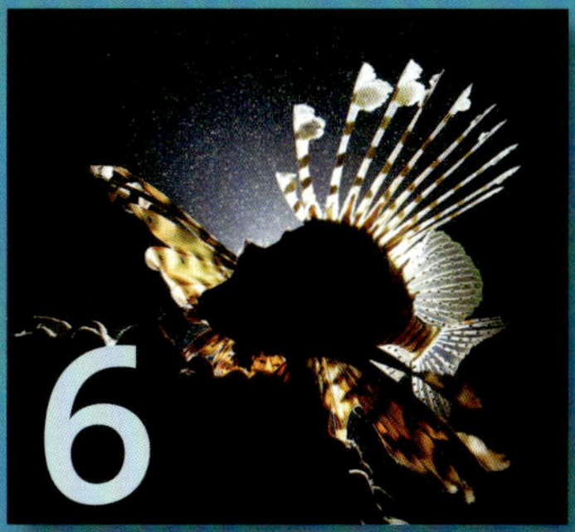
6

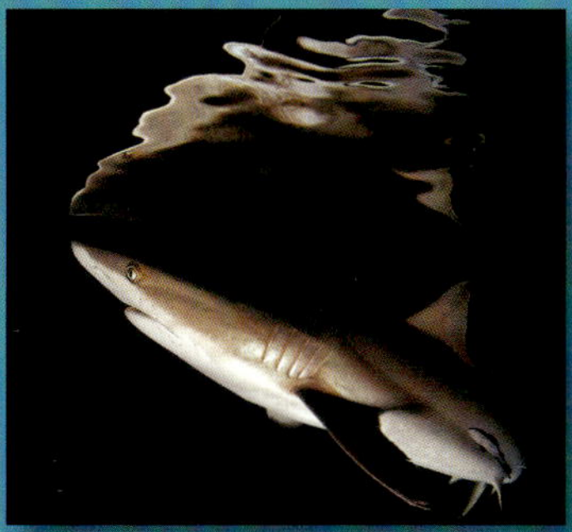

Foreword by Ernie Brooks

This book will take you on a photographic journey that will change the way you envision our unique Water Planet Earth. The young and multi-talented German photographer Tobias Friedrich showcases the quiet beauty of this fascinating world. I am honored to be a witness to his imagery and I admire his ability to capture light and feeling with a reverent style that has received international acclaim in many of the world's magazines and photographic competitions. Every one of his photographs bespeaks his love of the sea, and it is this that has captured my attention in these troubled times for the fragile waters of our planet. Each photograph in the book has a caption that reminds the viewer of the occasion and meaning at the time of the capture on camera.

Tobias has the remarkable ability to instill clarity in all of his images—clarity in the subject's behavior, as in his cover image *The Dark Knight*. It is the dynamic reflection of the shark on the water's surface and the peaceful grace of light cast upon the shark that makes this photograph a living example of Tobias Friedrich's style.

I believe that all artists have mentors who help them to expand their horizons. In my case it was Hans Hass and his *Diving to Adventure* series of films and books from the 1930s through the 1960s. In a world of black-and-white and filled with adventure, Hass opened a vision that I have carried with me for more than 60 years. Being free and weightless in the seas allows the photographer to be as his subjects—on the same plane as the subject or viewing them at an extreme angle that includes scenes below and above the waterline within the same frame.

I believe that one day Tobias will also become a mentor to others and that the message he shares through his photographs will go beyond words and will be understood by all nations, who will carry this message on into the future; that we all must preserve and protect what we love and treasure within this precious Water Planet.

I have hope that this edition will teach a new generation of photographers to produce the highest-quality images, which will allow them to express their own visions of our world.

On his website, Tobias quotes Captain Jacques Yves Cousteau: "From birth, man carries the weight of gravity on his shoulders. He is bolted to Earth. But man has only to sink beneath the surface and he is free." Thank you Tobias for your gift to all, and may your life be filled with the joy of being free from the weight of gravity. I am sure that the Cousteau family today, in the heart of Jean-Michel Cousteau and his organization, Ocean Futures Society, will also treasure your remarkable photography.

Introduction

About the Book

Once you've caught the fever to explore the world under the sea with your camera, there is no cure. Our fascination with underwater realms is deeply rooted in the beginnings of our evolution when we floated in the ocean as single-celled organisms. Interactions with playing dolphins, elegant sharks, and majestic whales will forever live in our memories. When we reach for a diving mask, perhaps a miniscule pygmy sea horse fills us with joy, or maybe a powerful and magnificent whale shark swims past and leaves us covered in goose bumps.

We take pictures of these moments so they are never lost and so we can remember them vividly. Our emotions, passion, and excitement from these undersea encounters become inextricably linked with our digital photo files.

How can you take your photography to the next level to produce something more inviting than simple snapshots? How can you capture brilliant colors and razor-sharp subjects that grip the viewer's attention better than hazy and washed-out photos? This book will bring some light into the darkness.

To get started I cover the types of equipment you'll need and why a digital single-lens reflex (DSLR) camera is better than a compact camera for underwater photography. Then I discuss the fundamentals of shooting—the behavior of light under water and the technical details required for taking successful pictures. A proper exposure alone is not enough—good composition is the basis of an effective image. Things get particularly interesting in the chapters on wide-angle and macro photography, where I discuss exposure values, positioning flash equipment, and shooting techniques. Finally, post-processing is where photos receive their finishing touches, and I discuss how you can use a RAW converter to make the most of your photos.

The chapters include case studies that use example photos giving you detail about each shooting scenario. How did the situation play out? What flash setting was used? Why use aperture f/16 instead of f/8? The answers to all these questions and more are paired with illustrations to tease out some of the finer points of underwater photography.

The best way to read this book is from front to back. The information is presented in a logical order, and any holes will be filled in as you read. Browsing is an option too, of course, and you can pick and choose what interests you. The summaries found at the end of each section throughout the book will help you grasp the basic concepts so you can decide what to explore in greater detail.

Whichever way you approach the content, by purchasing this book you've already made your first step toward improving your skills as an underwater photographer.

I hope you enjoy reading!
Tobias Friedrich

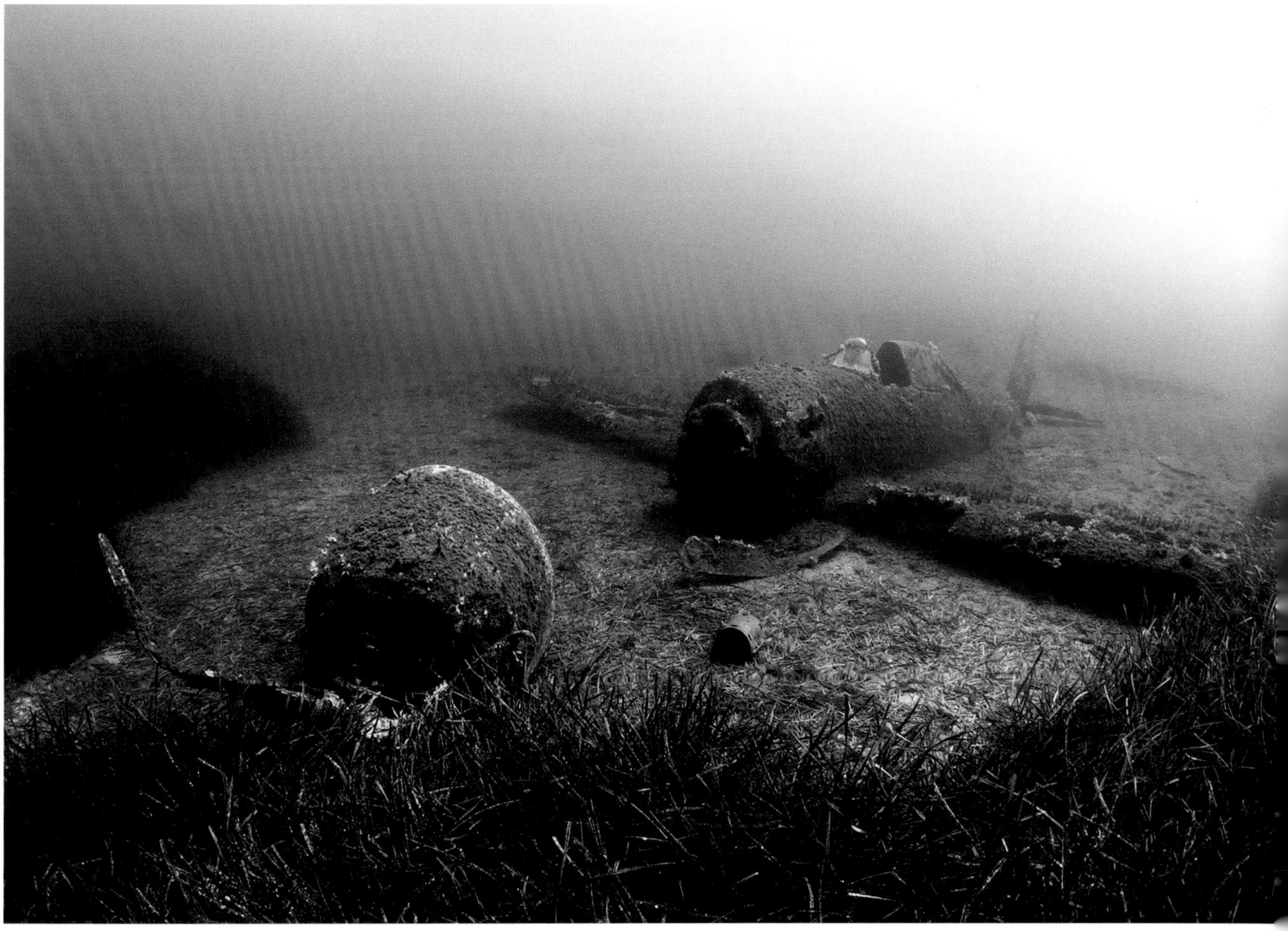

Wreckage of a P-47 Thunderbolt fighter plane off the coast of Corsica, France
Canon EOS 300D • Tokina 10–17mm fisheye lens • 1/60 s • f/7.1 • ISO 200

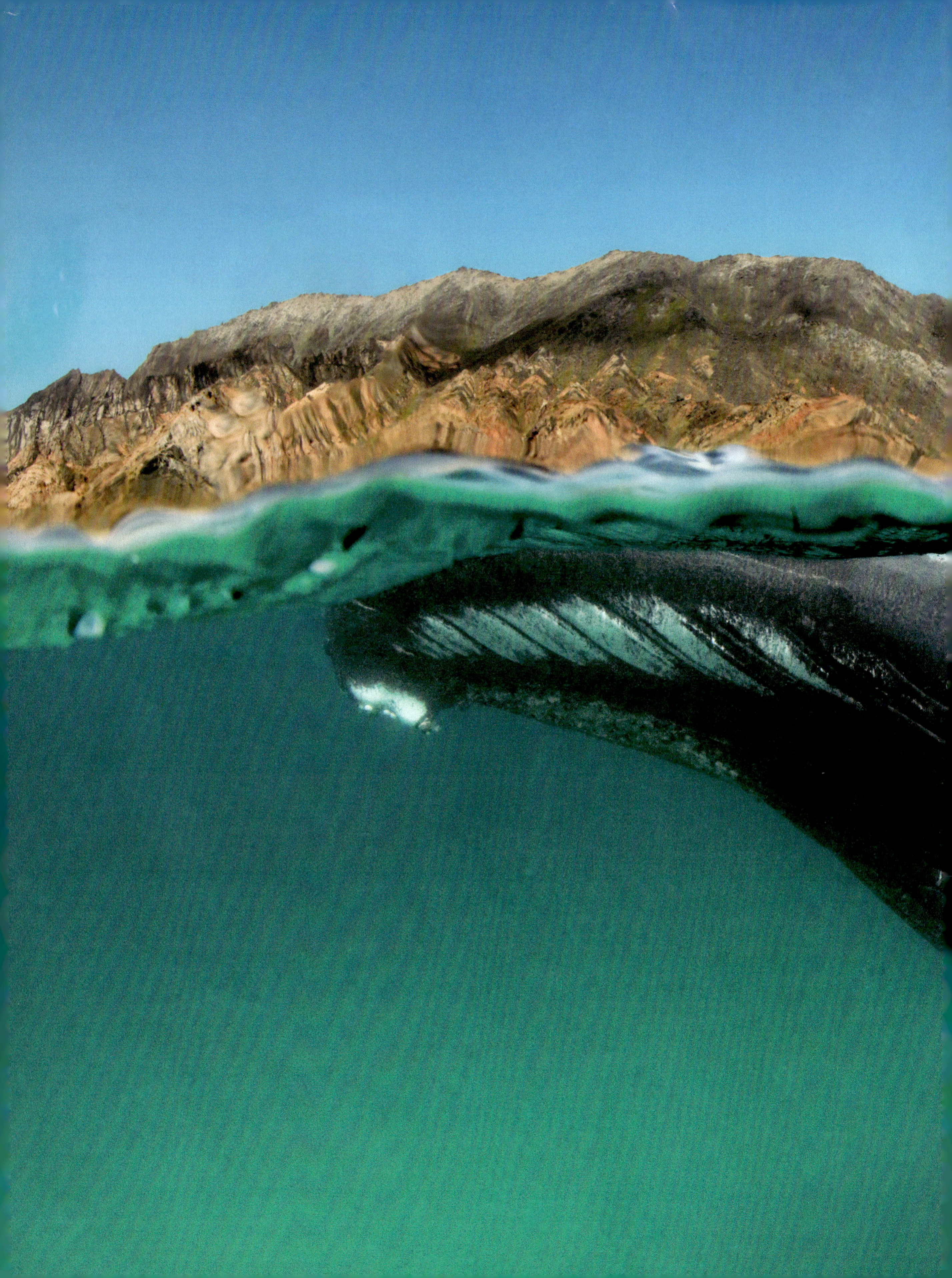

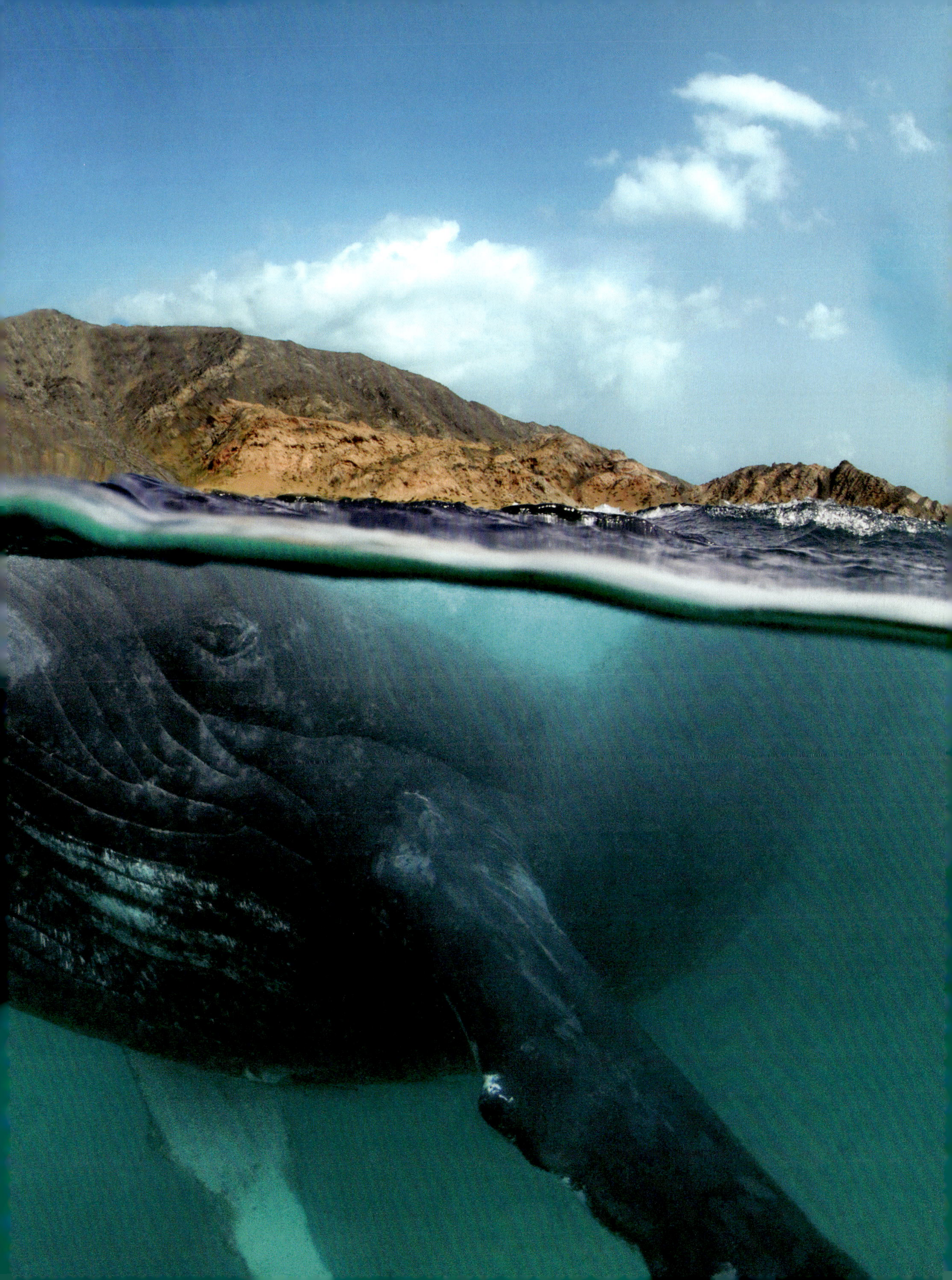

Case Study 1: The Meeting

This photo is a typical example of what you can achieve by altering the perspective of your shot. This encounter with a humpback whale was remarkable because the animal was curious and came closer and closer to the snorkelers. It would have been a waste to simply capture the animal from a traditional perspective below the surface of the water. The best way to find a unique perspective is to try as many angles of view as possible. After I successfully grabbed a few pictures from below the surface, I considered other ways to depict the subject. Because the whale kept swimming right below the surface of the water, I had the option of creating an exposure that was half above and half below the water level; this also allowed me to capture the nearby island in the background.

I needed a high aperture number to make sure the foreground and the background would be sharp. The water was relatively murky and dark so I used a high ISO setting, which allowed me to use a high shutter speed to freeze the animal in place.

Now I just needed to wait for the whale to make an ideal approach. The first and second passes were not great because ill-timed waves obscured my shot and the animal's position wasn't appealing. Patience paid off, though, and the whale swam in a perfect path with the sun at my back. My camera was set to continuous shooting mode, which meant it fired as many shots as possible. Exposures that simultaneously show subjects above and below the water (i.e., split waterline photos) usually produce a lot of poor photos because the changing waves tend to get in the way. Catching the waves when they're flat helps to achieve a successful image, and a large dome port makes the process easier too.

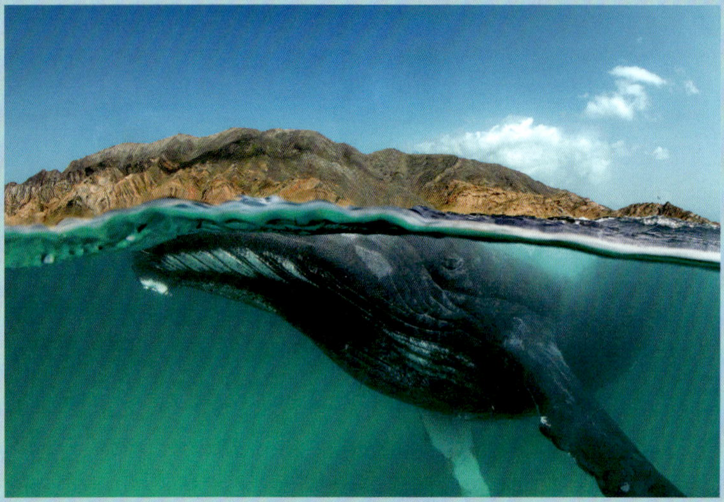

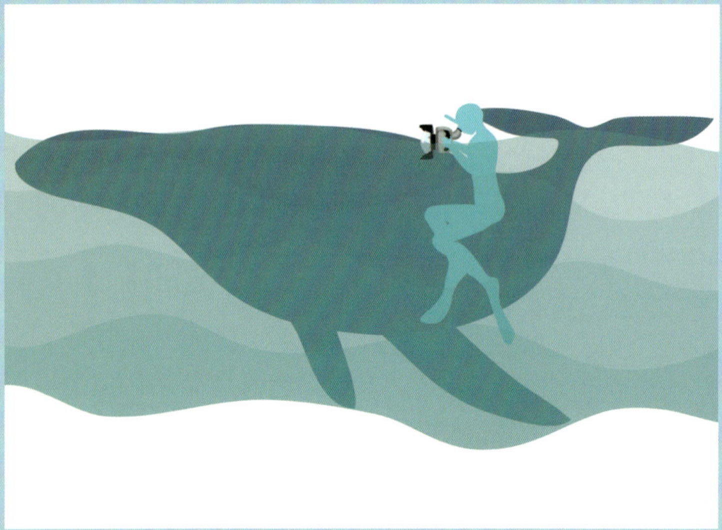

Canon EOS 5D Mark II •
Canon 8–15mm fisheye lens •
no flash • 1/400 s • f/18 • ISO 800

What's particularly attractive about this photo is the repetition of the landform shape above the water's surface and the shape of the whale below. Additionally, the animal's eye is located right in the golden ratio, which further enhances the composition.

The portion of the image that is under water was very dark in the original exposure, so I brightened it up afterward with the help of a RAW converter. I didn't adjust the crop at all, and I didn't use flash because I wanted to remain as agile as possible while I was snorkeling. The penetration of sunlight is usually sufficient just below the surface of the water, which obviates the need for additional artificial lighting (see the section called "Split Waterline Photos" in chapter 4).

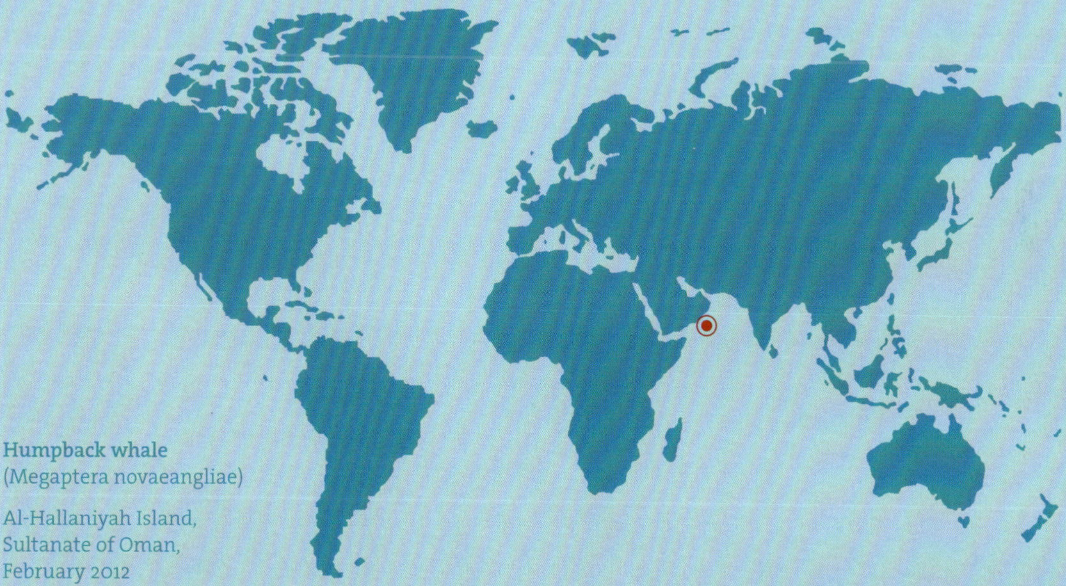

Humpback whale
(Megaptera novaeangliae)

Al-Hallaniyah Island,
Sultanate of Oman,
February 2012

1

Equipment

A compact camera produces passable images above water, but below the surface of water its pictures are dull and boring. The quality of an underwater picture relies considerably on the work of the photographer, but also on the equipment. In contrast to compact cameras, digital single-lens reflex (DSLR) cameras are superior both in their operation and in the results they produce because they have larger image sensors and lenses with superior imaging performance. Furthermore, DSLRs have a much briefer shutter lag than compacts. Most DSLRs allow photographers to snap an image in fractions of a second so they can precisely capture the ideal moment. These reasons make DSLRs indispensable when it comes to underwater photography.

Purchasing such a camera is no trivial matter. A system for underwater photography includes the camera itself, an underwater housing, a wide-angle and a macro lens, a wide-angle and a macro port, a flash arm, and an external flash unit. Entry-level systems can set you back as much as $5,000 to $7,000. A more exhaustive set of equipment might also include a second flash unit, additional lenses and ports, an angle viewfinder, a focus light, closeup lenses, and other accessories that can easily double your investment.

If you are just considering giving underwater photography a try, you should seriously consider if you're ready to grapple with all the technology and equipment that's required. The jump from a compact camera to a DSLR is not only a financial investment; it also requires an investment in time. You won't be able

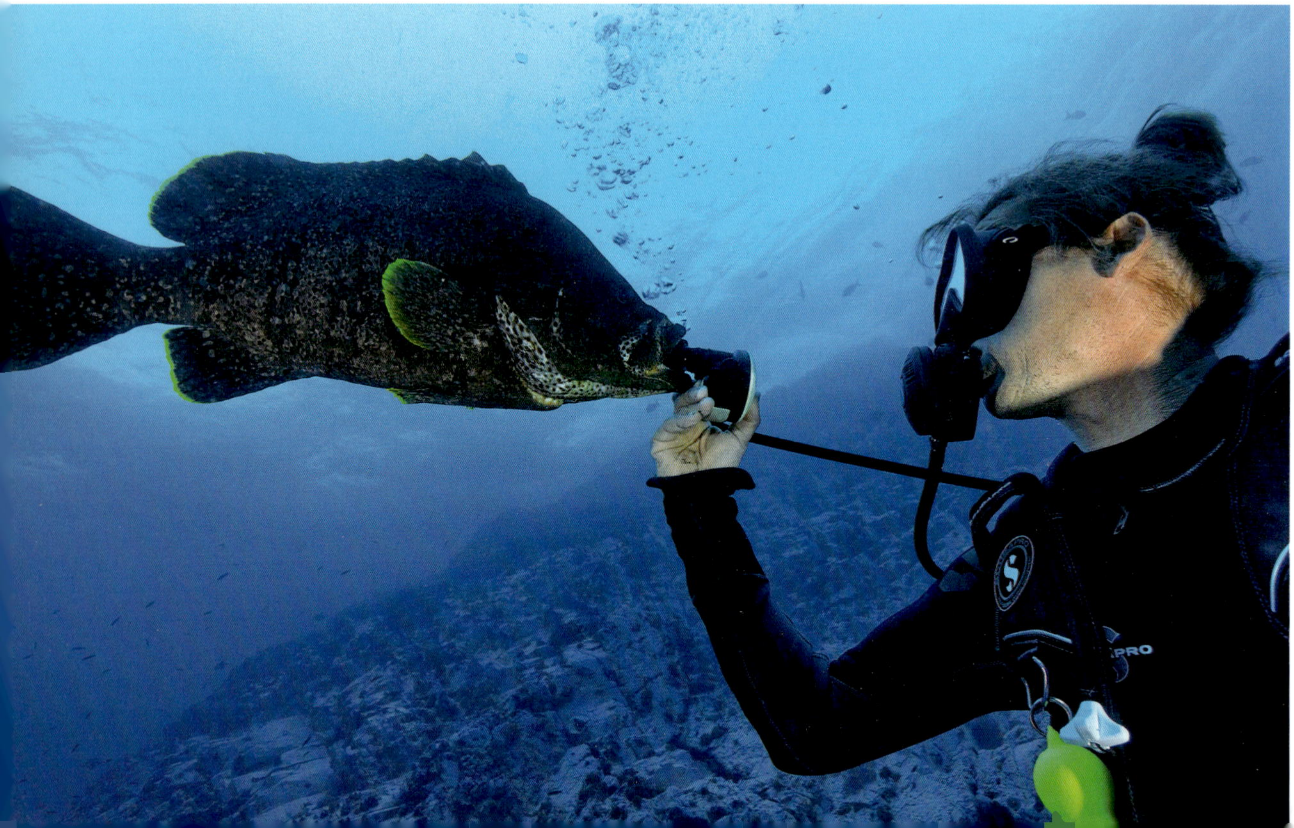

Comical situations will often surprise you during dives. This grouper wanted to try the diver's regulator.

Canon EOS 5D Mark II • Canon 17–40mm wide-angle lens • 1/80 s • f/8.0 • ISO 200 to produce stunning images simply by buying a fancy camera—you'll need to learn the ropes. Spending quality time under water with your camera helps immensely.

1.1 Digital Single-Lens Reflex Cameras

Digital single-lens reflex cameras are commonly known as DSLRs. In simple terms, what makes these cameras unique is the path of light within the camera. Light enters the camera through the lens and is reflected by an internal mirror to reveal an image in the viewfinder. When you press the shutter button, the mirror springs out of the light's path and the shutter opens for the specified length of time, which is usually a mere fraction of a second. This allows the camera sensor, which is positioned behind the shutter, to capture the image. You can view the captured image on the camera's built-in LCD monitor. DSLRs generally have larger sensors and better lenses than compact cameras, which are the main reasons they produce better photos.

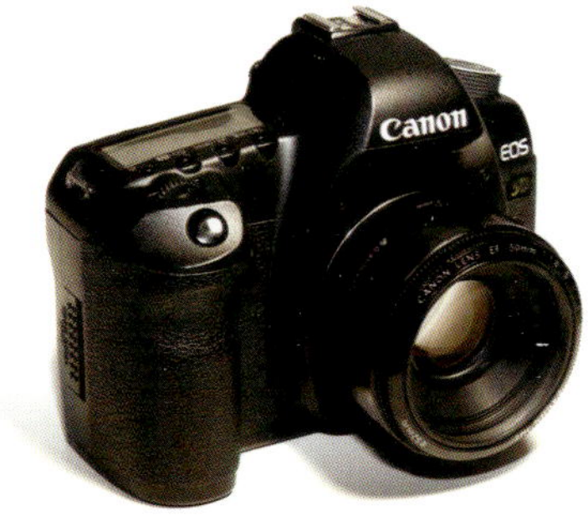

A typical digital single-lens reflex camera (DSLR)

In makes sense to invest in a new DSLR for underwater photography because the underwater housing unit usually costs significantly more than the camera itself. To avoid having to change cameras frequently and doling out gobs of cash for new underwater housings, it's optimal to use each housing for three to five years or more. The longer you use your equipment, the more familiar you'll become with it and the more comfortable you'll be with how it operates. Such familiarity is critical with wildlife photography because you need to react to changing situations in the blink of an eye. If you have to think about how your camera operates, the animal you want to photograph may be gone before you press the shutter release.

When you're shooting under water, manual (M) exposure mode is the best option for producing attractive images. Ignore creative or automatic modes. Shutter-priority and aperture-priority modes have legitimate uses, but those instances are more of an exception than a rule.

SUMMARY:

- DSLRs direct light through the lens, reflect it off a mirror, and guide it to the viewfinder. The mirror springs out of the way as soon as you press the shutter button.
- DSLRs have a clear advantage over compact cameras in terms of image quality.
- Use an up-to-date DSLR for underwater photography so you can use it for a longer period of time.
- In comparison to compact cameras, DSLRs have less shutter lag and faster autofocus.
- When you shoot under water, it's best to use manual (M) exposure mode.

Sensor Sizes

A size comparison of a full-format sensor (left), an APS-C sensor (center), and a Four-Thirds sensor (right). A comparison of compact camera and cell phone camera sensors would show an even more dramatic size reduction.

DSLRs have various sensor sizes. It's generally fair to say that the larger the sensor, the better the image quality, and the more expensive the camera.

Focal lengths for single-lens reflex cameras are based on the 35mm format, which is actually 24 × 36mm. This sensor size is also known as *full frame*. The next smaller sensor is 15 × 23mm. Sensors of this size are called *crop sensors*, and they have roughly half the area of a 35mm sensor. Crop sensors tend to vary slightly among camera models, and different manufacturers refer to them differently; for example, Nikon crop sensors are called DX, and Canon crop sensors are called APS-C. Compact cameras have sensors that are significantly smaller. At approximately 5 × 7mm, these sensors have roughly 5 percent of the area of a full-frame sensor. This disparity goes a long way in explaining the superior image quality produced by DSLRs.

To compare focal lengths for different lenses, a camera's crop factor, which is determined by the diagonal measurement of a sensor, must be considered. A crop camera's diagonal dimension is about two-thirds as long as a full-frame sensor. To accurately compare focal lengths, multiply the focal length of a crop sensor by a factor of 1.5. A 100mm lens is, depending on the crop factor of the camera, roughly equivalent to a 150mm lens when it is paired with a crop sensor, for example. The term *35mm equivalent* is often employed in this case. The crop factor increases even more with smaller sensors. Compact cameras have permanent built-in lenses, and their focal lengths are already expressed as a 35mm equivalent.

Some photographers speak of a *focal length multiplier* when they calculate a crop factor. In the macro and telephoto range, this can often be helpful, but it's not a true extension of the focal length in an actual sense. Rather, the crop factor describes an enlargement of a section of the image area. For example, a 200mm telephoto lens paired with a crop-sensor camera produces an enlarged section detail that approximately corresponds to a 300mm focal length. In contrast, a 300mm lens used with a full-frame sensor will produce better results because the lens is used more optimally.

Crop factors also have to be considered for minimal focal lengths in the wide-angle range. A 17mm lens amounts to roughly a 25mm focal length, which results in a narrower angle of perspective. This is why wide-angle lenses for crop cameras are much smaller than those for full-frame cameras. It's critical to remember the basic principle that a crop factor is not actually an extension of the focal length; it's only an enlargement of detail in an image.

Another issue related to sensor size is depth of field: the larger the sensor, the shallower the depth of field. This means that when you want to work with a small and selective depth of field, you will need a larger sensor. Smaller sensors are adequate for a deep depth of field. This effect impacts macro and

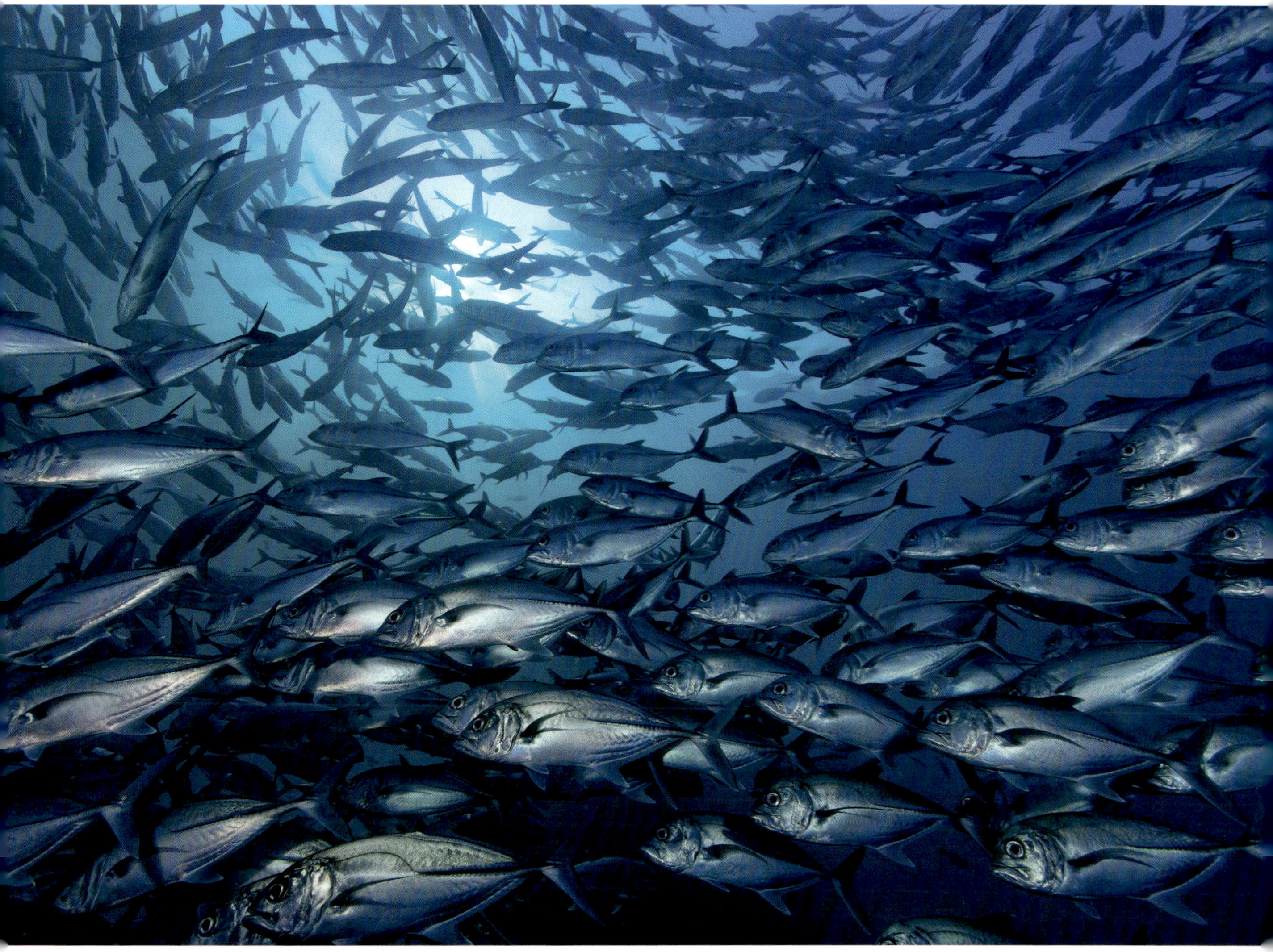

telephoto focal lengths much more than the wide-angle range.

While shooting under water you are likely to find yourself in situations with low light levels—much lower than on land—therefore it's a big help to raise the ISO value, which impacts the light sensitivity of the sensor.

The number of pixels on a sensor, often indicated in megapixels, describes the camera's maximum resolution. Higher resolutions require more pixels to be positioned in a specific area of the sensor. If the pixels have to be crammed very close together, as is likely the case with a crop sensor, they can distort the photo values for adjacent pixels. Accordingly, cameras with larger sensors usually produce less image noise at high ISO values.

Go easy on your flash output when you photograph schools of fish because their scales reflect the light

Canon EOS 5D Mark II • Canon 17–40mm wide-angle lens • 1/200 s • f/10 • ISO 200

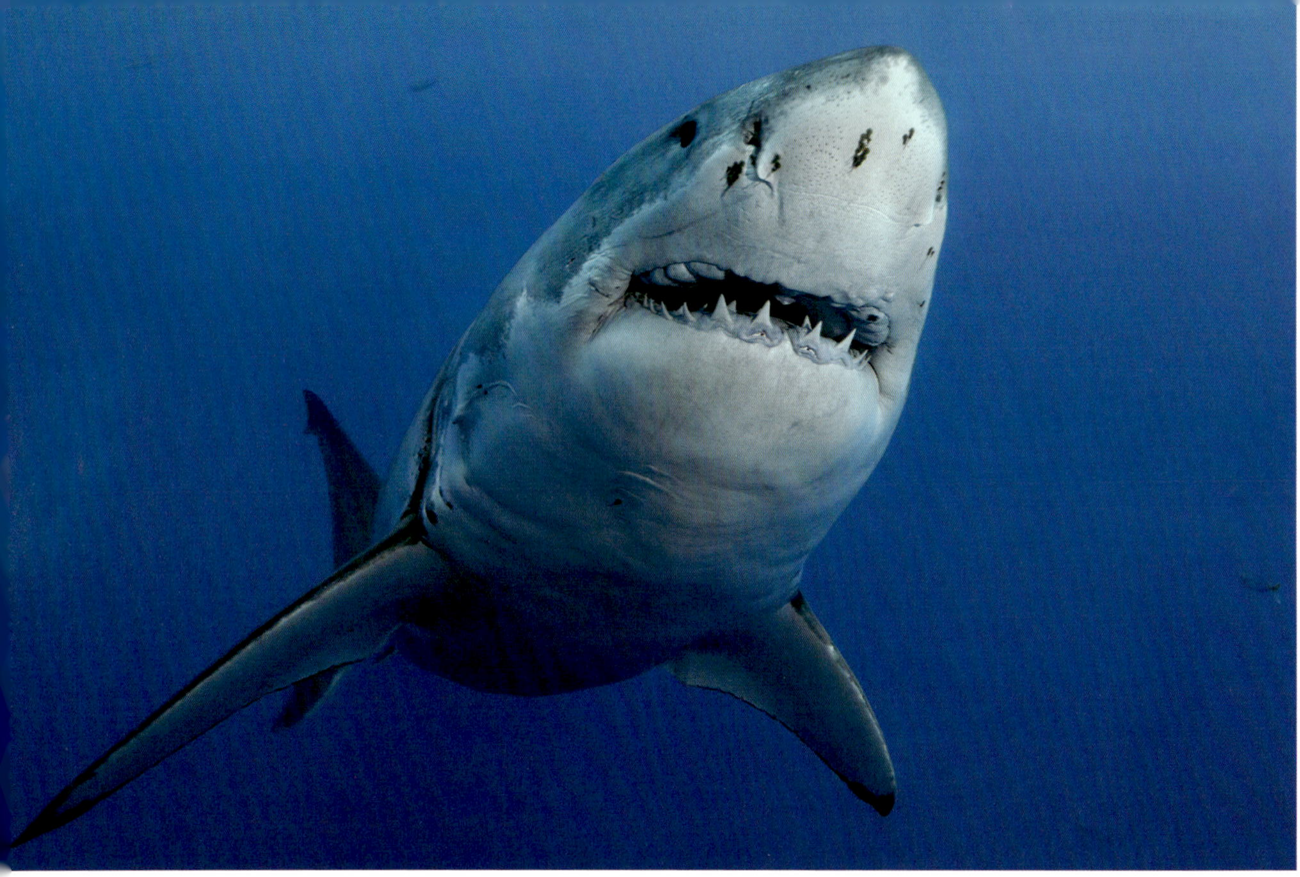

There are only a few places on earth, such as Guadalupe Island in Mexico, where you can take good pictures of great white sharks

Canon EOS 5D Mark II • Canon 17–40mm wide-angle lens • 1/125 s • f/9 • ISO 200

Anyone who loves shooting with wide-angle lenses or who is often out and about in poor weather conditions should choose a full-frame camera. For photographers who prefer the macro realm, a camera with a crop factor may be perfectly adequate.

SUMMARY:

- The larger the image sensor, the better the image quality and the more expensive the camera.
- Focal lengths for DSLR lenses are based on the full-frame sensor size, which has dimensions of 24 × 36mm.
- A camera with a crop sensor produces a reduced image area, and the lens focal length is multiplied by a factor of roughly 1.5.
- A crop factor is not an elongation of the focal length; it simply captures a smaller section of the image that has been enlarged.
- The larger the sensor, the shallower the depth of field.
- Larger image sensors produce better image quality at high ISO values.

Lenses

Three lens types suffice for underwater photography: a wide-angle lens, a fisheye lens, and a macro lens. While telephoto lenses may produce enviable results on land, they are not suitable for underwater photography because they require you to be far away from your subject. When you use a telephoto lens under water, you'll end up with bluish or colorless images because water is about 800 times more dense than air. This means that underwater photographers have to work as close as possible to their subjects. This close proximity exacerbates the challenges of water's relatively high density. A minimal distance between the camera and the subject will produce rich, colorful underwater pictures (see the "Shooting Distance" section in chapter 4).

There are two main classes of camera lenses: fixed focal length (also known as *prime*) and zoom. As the name says, fixed focal-length lenses are permanently set and can't be changed. In contrast, the focal length for zoom lenses is variable and can be changed as needed for a specific situation. Prime lenses generally produce higher quality images, but zoom lenses offer more flexibility when you define your image area.

Standard lenses that are often included with new cameras don't have much functional utility under water. Neither wide-angle nor macro images are possible because these lenses don't have a range of focal lengths that are ideal for underwater use: the longest distances are not far enough, and the minimum focusing distance isn't near enough. The only exception is when you just want to do reef fish portraits on a dive, but then you'll be restricted to do portraits the whole dive as well.

For the best results, underwater photographers should invest in *fast* lenses. Lens speed has important implications for the quality of the lens and the images it produces. It's sensible to choose lenses that are made by the manufacturer of your camera because these lenses will likely have better functionality and produce higher-quality images when they are paired with a camera of the same brand.

SUMMARY:

- Wide-angle and macro lenses have the most utility for underwater photography.
- The high density of water means that photographers need to be as close as possible to their subjects.
- Standard or kit lenses are not practical for underwater use.
- Prime lenses have better quality, but zooms lenses offer more flexibility.

Pygmy sea horses are less than a half inch long and are best photographed with the super-macro method so they appear as large as possible in your images

Canon EOS 5D Mark II • Canon 100mm macro lens • INON UCL-165 closeup lens • 1/30 s • f/16 • ISO 400

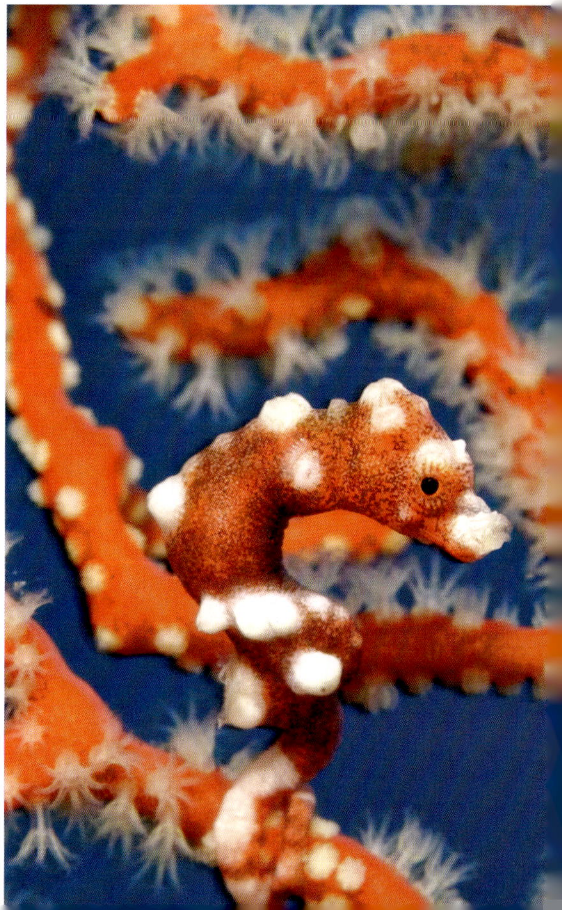

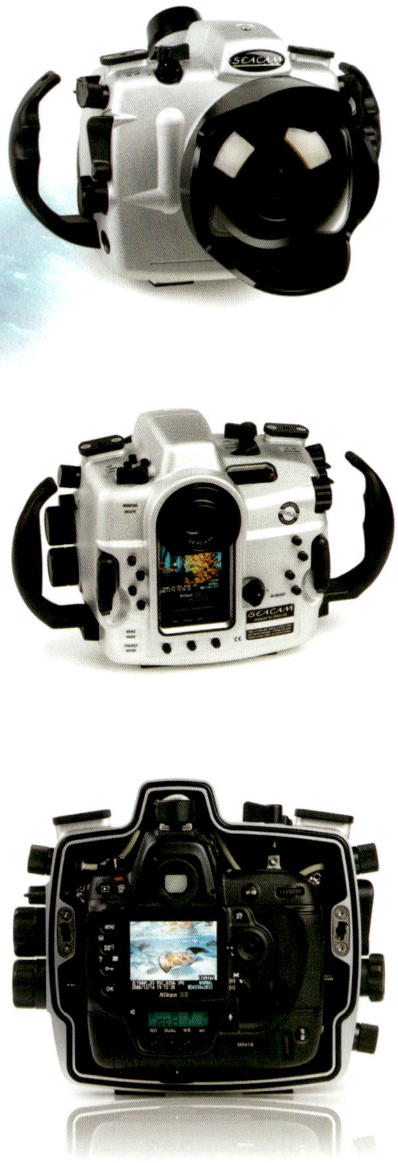

An underwater housing for a DSLR (Photo courtesy of SEACAM)

1.2 Underwater Camera Housings

Choosing an underwater camera housing is one of the most difficult tasks you will face as a beginning underwater photographer. You'll have to consider many factors, including how long you want to be able to use your housing and how much money you're willing to invest. Before you buy a DSLR, you'll need to find out if compatible underwater housings are available. Underwater cases are produced by third-party manufacturers in relatively limited supply and are usually available for only the most popular cameras.

An important consideration when you choose a camera brand is how many accessories are available. Accessories such as front ports and viewfinders aren't usually interchangeable among brands. With the aim of using your equipment for as long as possible and leaving open the possibility of upgrading your camera model later, it usually makes sense to plan on a long-term relationship with the housing manufacturer of your choosing.

Another criterion to consider is what the camera housing is made of. Polycarbonate (plastic), carbon, and aluminum models are available. Polycarbonate cases have the advantage of being relatively light and affordable, and any leaks are readily visible. Polycarbonate housings also have disadvantages: They aren't as durable as aluminum and carbon cases, and they acclimate quickly to the surrounding temperature, which can result in fogging within the case. Silica gel packets are one way of combating unwanted moisture.

Aluminum cases are usually machined out of a block of aluminum, and due to their robustness, they have become the most popular type of housing.

Carbon cases bring together some of advantages of both polycarbonate and aluminum cases. They are light like plastic but strong like aluminum. It can be cumbersome to manufacture and repair carbon cases, though, which is why aluminum has an edge.

Underwater housings have various sockets and levers that allow photographers to use the functions and features of the DSLR.

On a related note, look for a housing that's equipped with a flocked lining. The flocking avoids reflections and can absorb water in the event of water leakage.

Most housings are equipped with a leak alert that notifies the photographer as soon as water is detected. You should always be aware of where the leak detector is located. If you hold your camera at an angle, you might not be aware of a leak until the housing is already filled up. While you're on a dive, it's good to get in the habit of regularly checking for leaks by looking through the front port.

Generally speaking, your underwater housing should be comfortable in your hands and should offer easy access to controls—including aperture, shutter speed, and ISO—so you don't have to take your hands off the grips.

The housing should be neutrally buoyant when it's under water, with neither upward nor downward force. If needed, you can get small floats or weights at photography stores to balance your system. A slight downward force can sometimes be nice because it creates weight in your hands and gives you a better feel for the camera.

The number and type of flash sockets on the housing will dictate the type of flash units you can use. The S6 and N5 (Nikonos V) flash sockets are both great; a housing that has one of these two connectors is ideal.

The general rule applies here too: The more expensive the housing, the better it will usually be. For example: expensive housings have buttons that you can reach easily or that are controllable even when wearing thick gloves. To achieve this functionality, the levers inside the housing, which enable you to activate the buttons, are complicated to develop and install.

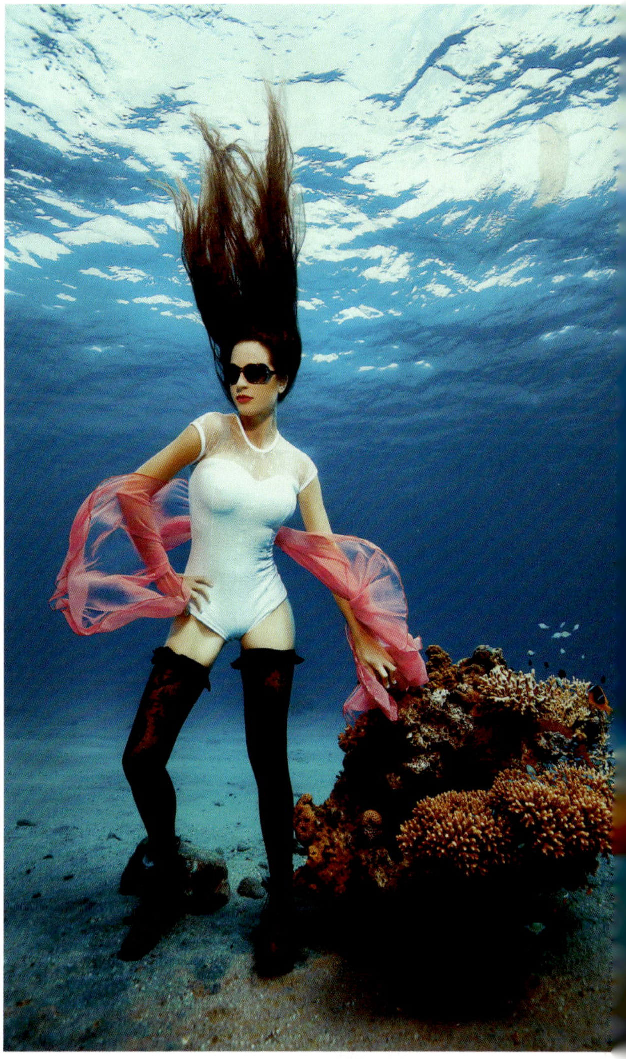

When you photograph a model under water, the top priority is for another diver to ensure the model's safety!

Canon EOS 5D Mark II • Canon 17–40mm wide-angle lens • 1/125 s • f/8 • ISO 200

SUMMARY:

- Before you buy a new camera, check to see if compatible underwater housings are available.
- Choosing a camera manufacturer is a big decision because you'll likely want to continue using your accessories when you upgrade to a new camera model.
- Plastic (polycarbonate) housings are light and affordable, but they can fog up quickly and they're not as robust as aluminum housings.
- Carbon and aluminum housings are robust and durable, but they can cost two or three times as much as plastic housings.
- Sockets and knobs allow most of the functions of a DSLR to work under water.
- Most underwater housings include a leak alarm that alerts photographers to water leakage.
- You can adjust housings that aren't neutrally buoyant by using specially designed floats or weights.
- The S6 or N5 flash connectors are good options—ideally your housing should include both types.
- As a general rule, the more expensive a housing is, the better it is.

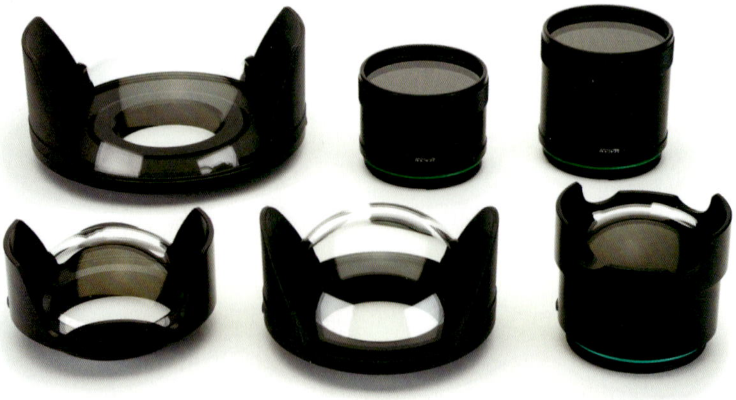

Various front ports that you can mount on an underwater housing, depending on which lens you are using (Photo courtesy of SEACAM)

Front Ports

The lenses of a DSLR are interchangeable. This means that the front side of an underwater housing must accommodate various lens shapes, which is accomplished with ports that attach to the front of the housing with either bayonet mounts or threads.

Flat ports are designed for use with macro and standard lenses. They are cylindrical tubes with a flat disc at the end, and they resemble the shape of a lens. The length of the plan port depends on the lens it is intended to encase. The distance between the end of the lens and the disk at the end of the port should be as short as possible.

The plan port needs to be longer for lenses that are focused externally or that have variable lengths.

It's best to test your equipment at home before you take it on the road. A conical port that tapers toward the front is ideal for macro photography so you can position the flash unit closer to your subject. This is especially important for very close macro photography. Some manufacturers even offer flat ports equipped with a magnetic ring that allows you to focus as you would with a real lens. When you work with a shallow depth of field, this feature can be a huge advantage.

For wide-angle photography the pane of the port resembles a large half sphere. These so called *dome ports* allow for the large image area to be captured without vignetting.

Dome ports can be constructed of either glass or acrylic. Since acrylic is relatively soft, it can suffer superficial scratches easily, but with a bit of effort the scratches can be polished out. Glass domes, in contrast, are more durable, but any scratches are much more difficult to repair.

To prevent sun streaks from ruining photos, dome ports feature lens hoods along their tops and bottoms. These ports are available in various diameters to accommodate different lenses and subjects.

Dome ports are designed to produce good image quality with many different lenses. A standard dome port with a

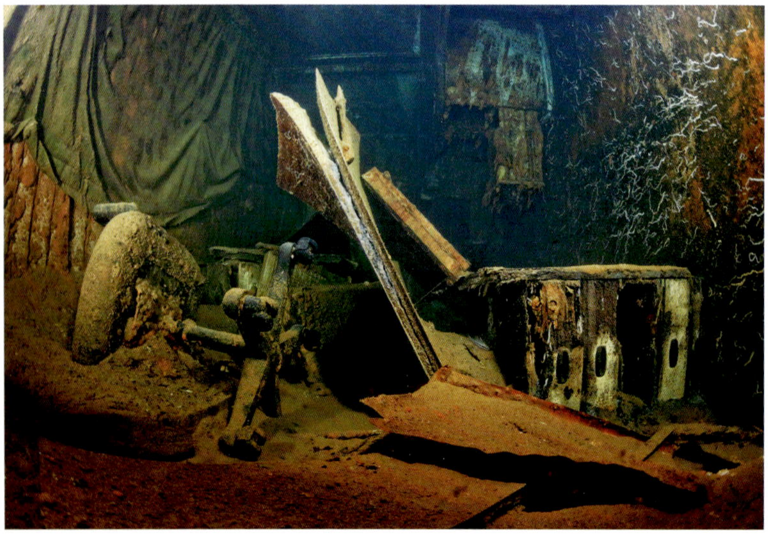

The interior scenes of a shipwreck can be fascinating. It's important to avoid getting floating particles in your shot.

Canon EOS 5D Mark II • Canon 8–15mm fisheye lens • 1/60 s • f/10 • ISO 400

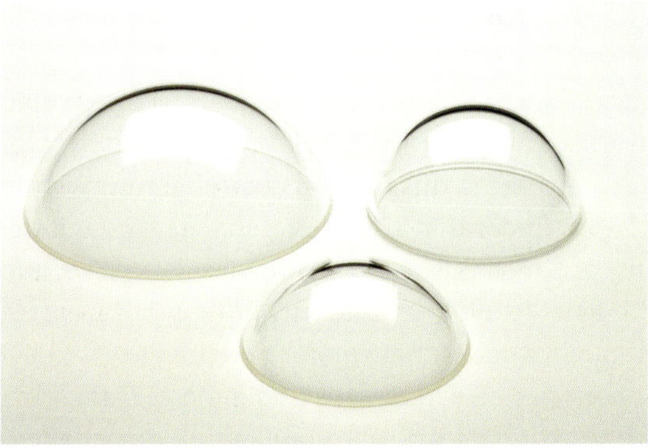

Large dome ports are useful for split waterline photos; conversely, closeup, wide-angle images are best shot with small dome ports (Photo courtesy of SEACAM)

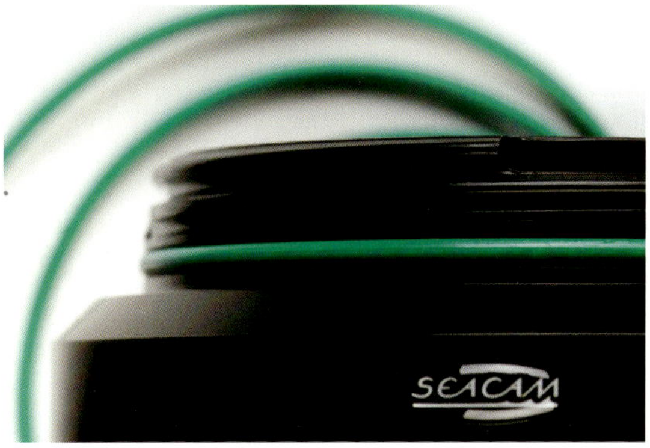

Every front port has an O-ring, which you should diligently care for to minimize the chance of water entering the housing (Photo courtesy of SEACAM)

diameter of 18 cm (7 inches), for example, will work with most fisheye and wide-angle lenses. Each lens, however, requires an adapter ring between the body and the dome port, which positions the port at the correct length. This maximizes image quality and minimizes vignetting.

To optimize the quality of your images, remember that refraction makes the subject appear closer to the camera than it really is. This means that wide-angle lenses have to focus at very short distances, which can lead to out-of-focus corners in some images. To make sure your dome port and lens combination doesn't have this problem, discuss your equipment with a salesperson before you make a purchase. Zoom lenses, which have variable focal lengths, require an additional adapter ring that allows you to control the focal length. A separate zoom ring is required for each lens.

Both a flat port and a dome port are basic equipment for underwater photographers, enabling them to work with both wide-angle and macro lenses.

SUMMARY:

- Ports for camera bodies need to be swapped out, depending on the lens being used.
- Flat ports can be used with macro and standard lenses; they're relatively affordable and have a flat pane at the end.
- Dome ports are used for wide-angle and fisheye lenses, and they're more expensive than flat ports.
- Spacer rings are required to maximize the imaging properties for your port and lens combinations.
- Zoom rings are required so you can set the focal length for zoom lenses.

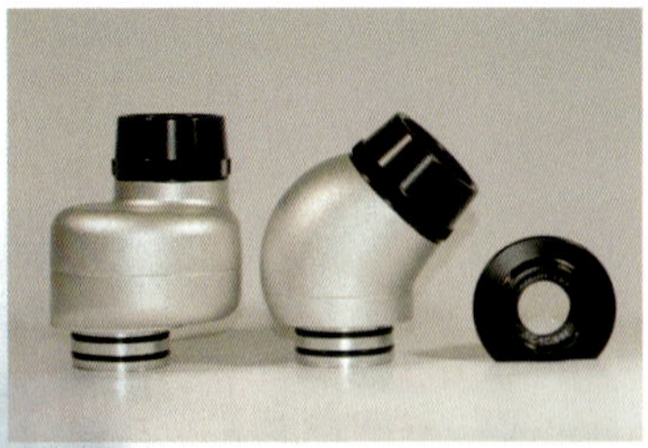

You can attach various viewfinders to your underwater housing. They make it easier for you to examine your photographs and give you more control when you compose your images. (Photo courtesy of SEACAM)

Viewfinders

With your camera encased in an underwater housing and your face protected by a diving mask, the camera's standard viewfinder is too far away for you to have a good look through it. To get around this problem, manufacturers equip the housing with a standard viewfinder that allows you to look through the viewfinder of the actual camera. Sadly, this decreases the size of the picture that you can see through the lens. To avoid this shortcoming you can use a special viewfinder with high-quality optics that enlarges the image.

These specialized viewfinders can be sorted into two general categories: straight and angled. Straight viewfinders will not pose any new challenges for photographers since you simply look through it like a standard viewfinder. Angled viewfinders, however, require a bit of a learning curve because they require you to look down at a certain angle that can make it difficult to find the subject. This problem is most common with macro images. Angled viewfinders have a benefit in macro photography, though: you don't have to get so close to the bottom of the ocean when you photograph subjects near the ocean floor.

Viewfinder attachments are tremendously helpful, but unfortunately they are not cheap. They range in price from about $700 to $1,400 or more. After you try a viewfinder attachment you won't want to be without one because it makes the image area appear substantially larger and it's much easier to examine your subjects with a discerning eye.

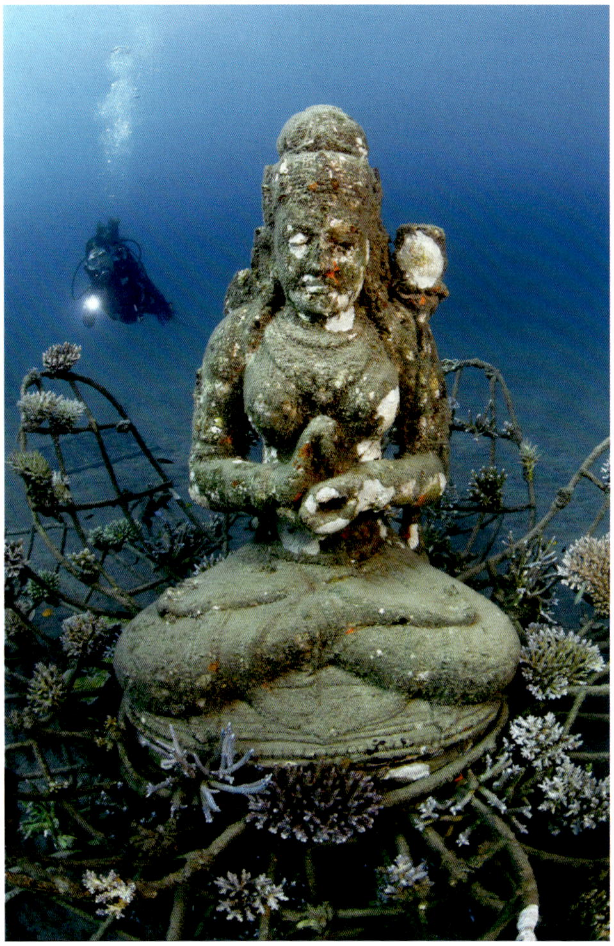

In some pictures, including a diver in the background can be the icing on the cake

Canon EOS 5D Mark II • Canon 8–15mm fisheye lens • 1/160 s • f/13 • ISO 400

SUMMARY:

- An underwater housing causes your camera to be farther from your eye.
- A viewfinder attachment enlarges the otherwise diminished size of the viewfinder image.
- A straight viewfinder attachment makes it easy to find your subject quickly, especially when you shoot macro images.
- An angled viewfinder makes it easy to shoot near the ocean floor, but it can be difficult to get used to when you shoot macro images.
- Enhanced viewfinder optics are not cheap, but they're necessary if you want to evaluate your images underwater.

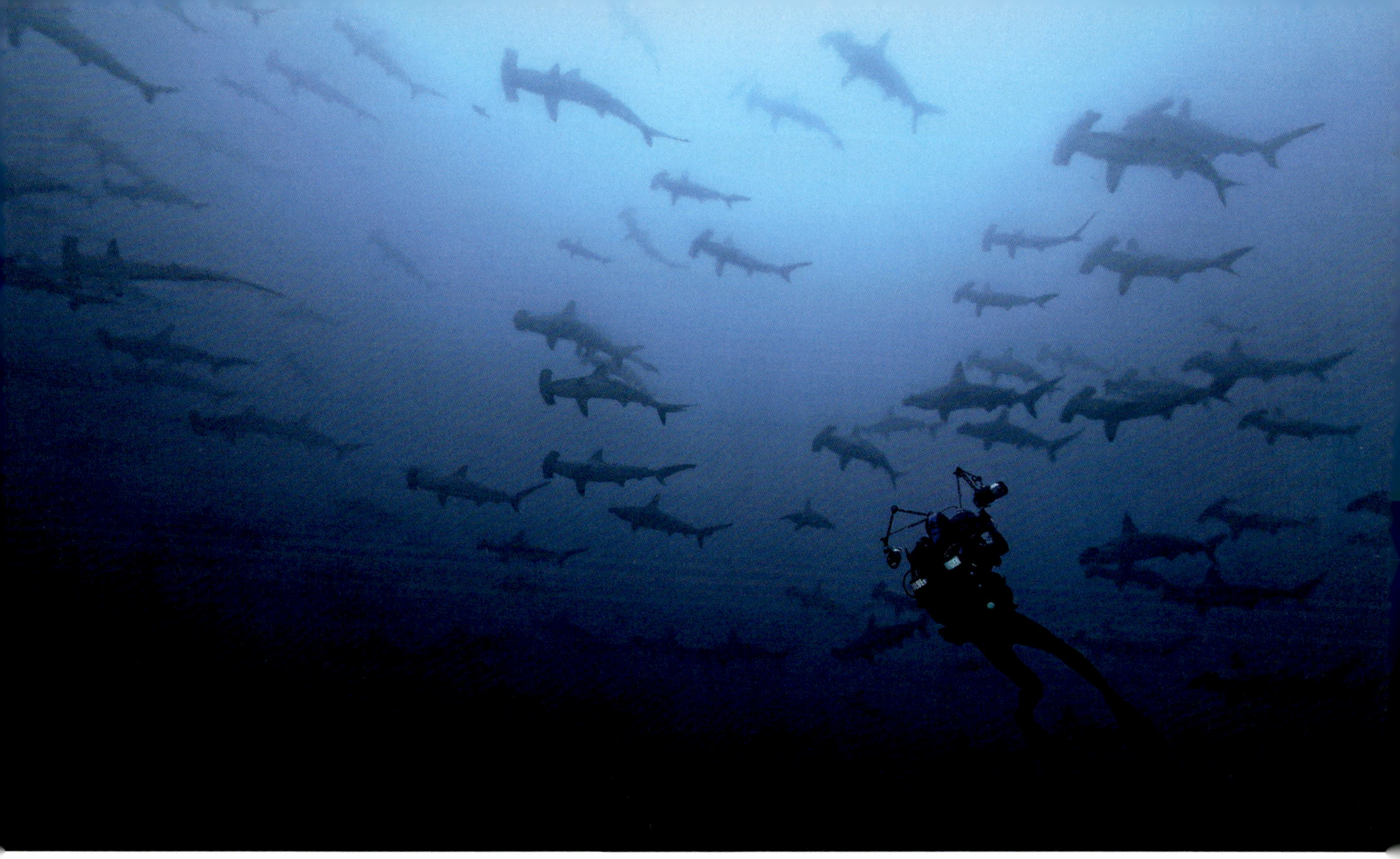

Use a closed-circuit breathing apparatus to photograph hammerheads because exhaled bubbles scare them away

Canon EOS 5D Mark II • Canon 16–35mm wide-angle lens • 1/200 s • f/8 • ISO 400

1.3 Flash Units

With the vast array of flash units on the market, underwater photography beginners often wonder which flash equipment is best for them. The answer is easy: it should be as powerful as possible. All other factors are secondary, and any deficiencies can be more easily overcome. It's better to invest in one powerful flash unit than two weaker flash units because flash output is improved only marginally with a second unit. The advantages of having one really strong flash are most apparent when you shoot backlit scenes or take macro exposures; these two situations need lots of added light.

The advantage of having two flash units is that you can reduce the shadows in a picture. The question of how many flash units to use depends on whether or not you want dramatic contrast in your picture.

The strength of a flash unit is indicated by its guide number, which describes how much brightness it is capable of emitting. The guide number is always measured at ISO 100. A flash unit's output is diminished by approximately half in water. For example, a flash unit with a guide number of 22 produces an output equivalent to a guide number of 11 when used under water. A midlevel flash unit might have a guide number of 12, which is still powerful enough to expose many subjects correctly. The higher the guide number, the more opportunities you'll have to illuminate challenging subjects.

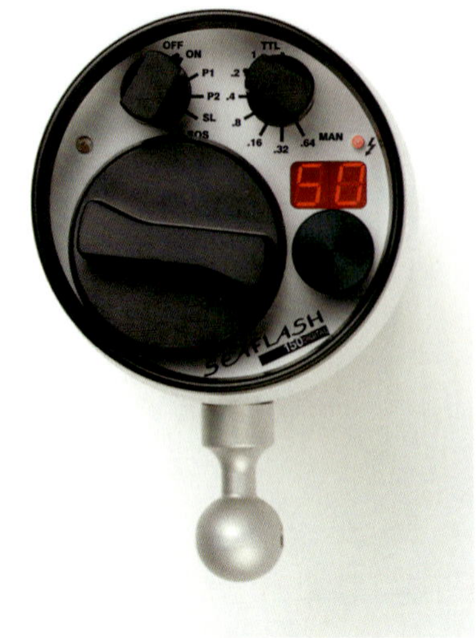

Flash units should have manual settings so you can control the illumination as needed (Photo courtesy of SEACAM)

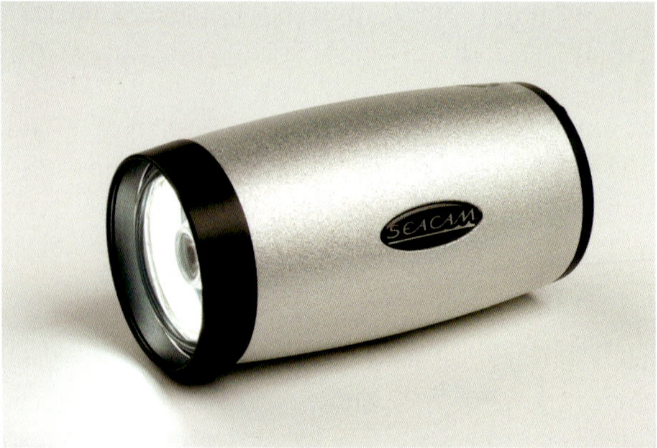

Flash units are indispensable for recovering colors that are otherwise lost below the water (Photo courtesy of SEACAM)

Another factor to consider when you select a flash unit is color temperature. Whether a flash unit gives off warmer or cooler light has implications for the appearance of the foreground and background of an image. This effect is most noticeable when you use your camera's automatic white balance feature, which can produce an undesirable color cast in the foreground or background. You therefore need to consider the effects you want to produce before you buy your lighting equipment. In digital photography, the Kelvin scale is used to specify the color temperature of light, and is designated with a capital letter *K*. In general, the warmer the color temperature of the flash, the bluer the water in the background will appear. Temperatures of 4700 to 5000 K are generally warm, and temperatures from 5000 to 5500 K are cool. In the event that something goes awry with the white balance, you can adjust it when you edit the image, as long as you save your exposures in RAW format.

There are different types of cables and connection sockets you can use to control your flash units. N5 (Nikonos V), S6, Ikelite, and SEA&SEA are the most common manufacturers. Manufacturers also sell adapter cables that allow you to connect different brands of equipment; for example, you can connect an N5 cable on your housing to an Ikelite flash. If you plan to use two flash units, you can get a "Y" cord to split the single cable that connects to the housing into

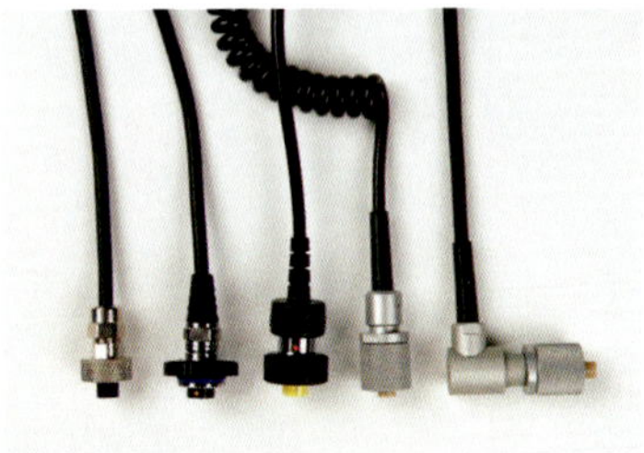

Different flash unit models have their own type of cable connections (Photo courtesy of SEACAM)

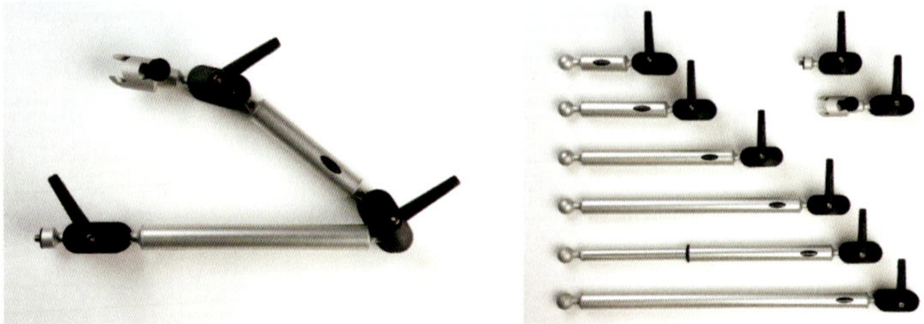

Use arms of various lengths to help you ideally position flash light for the subject (Photo courtesy of SEACAM)

two separate lines (one for each unit). Optical fibers can be used to connect a strobe as well, but they always need an internal, built-in camera flash to fire the external one.

Many lenses can be controlled either manually or automatically with through-the-lens (TTL) technology. With TTL metering, the camera measures the light that enters the lens and uses the reading to regulate the flash output. This feature is practical for many situations, but it can lead to problems in certain lighting situations (see section 2.7).

TTL technology requires that flash units either have integrated TTL capabilities or an external adapter attached to the housing or the flash unit cables.

Flash units can be powered by standard AA batteries or by battery systems that are specifically designed for certain flash units. AA batteries have several advantages: they are affordable, they can easily be replaced, and many rechargeable options are available. Specialized battery packs sometimes offer more power, and they are specifically designed for the flash unit.

Flash units are usually attached to the housing with arms that feature several joints. The length of the arms should correspond to the type of photography you are pursuing; you'll want longer arms for wide-angle images and shorter arms for macro images. Floats and weights allow you to retain a neutrally buoyant system under water. There are several strobe arm systems on the market. It is important to get one where the clamps tighten the arm pieces securely together, so that the arms will not come apart in a strong current. Clamps with long levers make it easy to do that.

SUMMARY:

- The most important consideration in choosing a flash unit is its maximum power output, which is expressed as a guide number.
- A good flash unit should have a guide number of 12 or higher.
- The color temperature of the flash determines whether an image will have a cool or a warm look and feel.
- Flash units can be connected either by cables or with optical fiber.
- A TTL converter makes automatic metering possible, but it sometimes results in false values when you shoot wide-angle photos.
- Flash units can be powered by standard AA batteries or by specialized battery systems.
- Flash arms are used to position flash units around the camera housing.

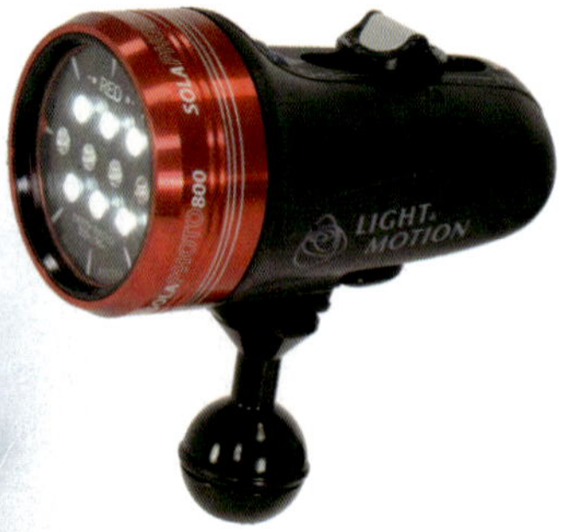

With the help of accessory focus lamps, your camera autofocus will be able to zero in on subjects that are otherwise shrouded in shadows (Photo courtesy of Light & Motion)

1.4 Focus Lights

Many underwater situations pose a challenge for autofocus (AF) systems because there isn't enough ambient light for it to function properly. To get around this problem, you can attach a focus light to provide enough illumination for the AF system. It can be attached either to the housing itself or to a flash arm. Many flash units are equipped with a built-in pilot light that can be used as an auxiliary AF lamp. Pilot lights are relatively weak, though, and they are a drag on the power supply for your flash units. Additionally, a pilot light is often a spotlight that is located in the center of the flash. The disadvantage of this arrangement is that you must point the flash directly at the subject, which limits your ability to compose your shot and take the picture. A weak pilot light offers no real benefit and is generally not worth the extra cost.

Some compact focus-assist lamps can be charged from the outside without the need to open the light—Light & Motion is one brand that offers units like this.

A red light is also a practical tool for taking pictures of animals that shy away from light.

The light emitted from a focus lamp won't affect the appearance of your photo because the illumination provided by the regular flash unit will overpower it. The focus lamp will be visible only if you have a particularly fast setup on your camera (high ISO, slow shutter speed, and open aperture). Flashes with a built-in photocell can handle this problem because you can set the lamp to go out as soon as the main flash is detected.

SUMMARY:

- In situations with insufficient lighting, AF systems can have trouble making your subject appear sharp.
- Focus lamp accessories can help AF systems focus on objects in low lighting.
- Integrated pilot lights, which are built in at a fixed position in some flash units, tend to be weak.
- A focus lamp with a red light can be helpful when you photograph animals that don't like light.
- Focus lamps that are too weak are not useful and are a waste of money.
- The light from a focus lamp won't appear in the final image because it is overpowered by the regular flash.
- An integrated photocell can turn the focus lamp off as soon as the main flash is detected.

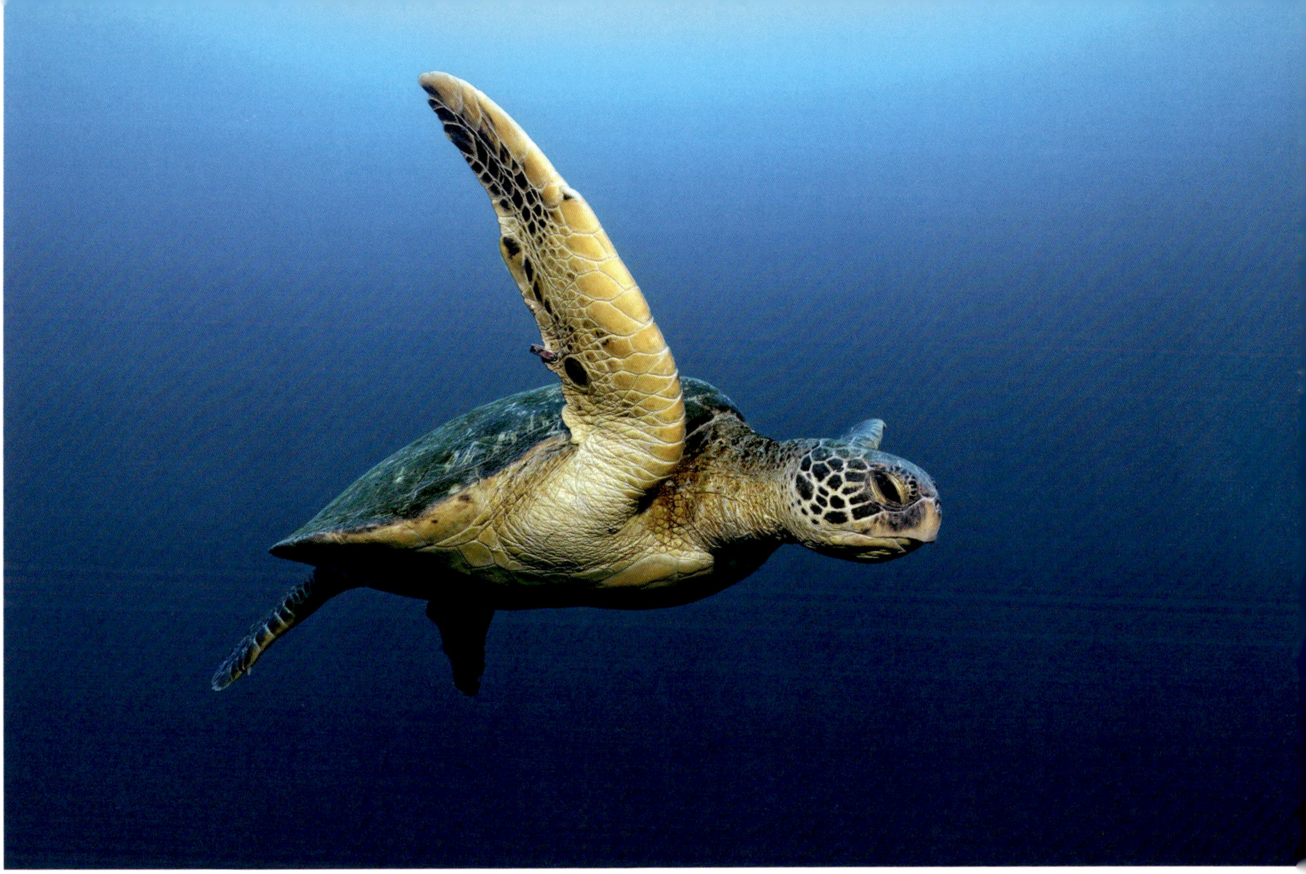

Sea turtles and other large animals look best when they are set against a blue background with no distracting elements

Canon EOS 5D Mark II • Canon 16–35mm wide-angle lens • 1/50 s • f/8 • ISO 400

1.5 Compact Cameras

For many photographers, compact cameras are often a first step in the world of underwater photography. Even though the information in this book is intended for use with a DSLR, many of the techniques and advice also apply to using a compact camera and can improve your results.

The biggest advantage of compact cameras is price, which often starts well below $1,500. Systems that include a camera, a housing, an external flash, and wide-angle or macro lens adapters are readily available.

When it comes to macro photography, high-end compact cameras can often hold their own in comparison to DSLRs, but wide-angle and fisheye applications really set DSLRs apart. The inferior quality of the lens and sensor in most compact cameras results in weak color gradients—particularly saturated blues, which are so important for underwater photography.

Compact cameras have a relatively limited range of focal lengths that are designed to operate above water. Because underwater photography depends on wide-angle and macro perspectives, this inherent weakness of compacts needs to be remedied with lens adapters. These tools can either enlarge the angle of view or, in the macro range, operate much like a magnifying glass. Accordingly, when you select a housing for a compact camera, you should make sure you can attach adapter lenses.

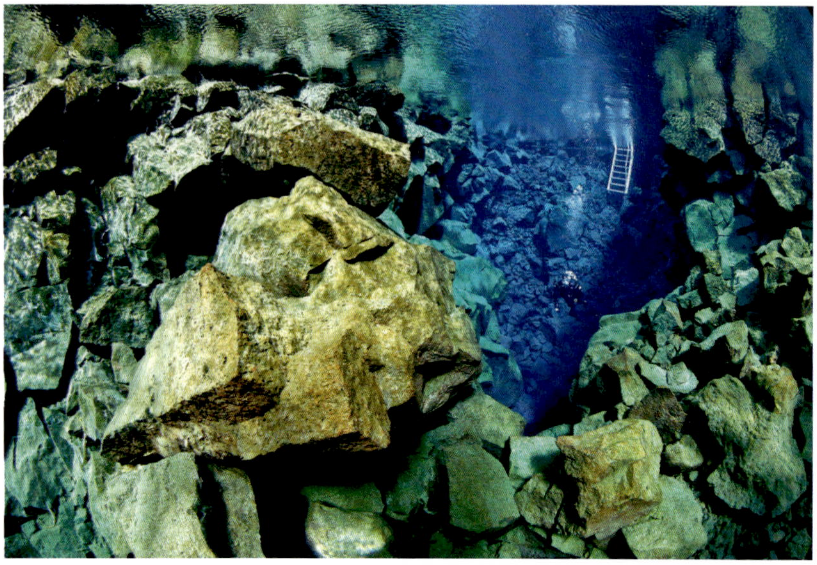

Including both a foreground and a background is a good way to depict a sense of depth in your pictures

Canon EOS 5D Mark II • Canon 8–15mm fisheye lens • 1/200 s • f/9 • ISO 800

An external flash unit should always be used with a compact camera. You might assume the reason is that the integrated flash is too weak, but that's not the whole story. The main problem is the built-in flash is usually located close to the lens, which causes *backscatter*—floating particles in the water that reflect the flash light and show up in your picture. External flash units can avoid this problem while also providing a stronger flash output.

Most compact cameras are equipped with an automatic metering option (TTL) to control flash units, and they generally produce passable results. With that said, you should look for a compact camera that offers manual controls because you need to correct over- and underexposure. In a best-case scenario, a compact camera should include controls similar to those on a DSLR so you can manually and easily adjust the aperture, shutter speed, and ISO.

Working with a compact camera is an ideal and cost-effective way to develop a feel for finding subjects and learning to have fun with photography under water. Many of the following chapters apply to taking pictures with either compact cameras or DSLRs.

SUMMARY:

- A compact camera can function as an affordable introduction to underwater photography.
- Many methods and techniques for DSLRs apply to compact cameras.
- You will need to compensate for the limited range in focal lengths of most compact cameras by using wide-angle and macro lens adapters.
- External flash units are indispensable—both with DSLRs and compact cameras.
- TTL metering is simple, but you should manually override it as circumstances warrant.
- When you select a compact camera, look for one that includes exposure compensation and setting options comparable to those on DSLRs.

1.6 Preparing Your Equipment

When it comes to underwater photography, it's critical to meticulously prepare your camera equipment. If you discover that you're missing something when you arrive at your destination, it's usually too late to find a replacement. Gather your equipment before you travel and test everything to make sure it's all functioning properly. For example, make sure your flash units and dials and knobs work, and check for cracks in your O-rings. If anything is amiss, this is the time to get a replacement.

After you arrive at your destination, don't immediately assemble your camera system. Wait for a quiet and relaxed moment when you can concentrate. When you head out for a dive, assemble your gear either at the port or at the location of your dive, rather than while you're traveling on the water, especially during a rough crossing. Large waves not only pose a threat to the safety of your equipment, they also threaten your well-being because you're more likely to get seasick.

Even if you recently inspected and cleaned your O-rings, recheck them at your destination. Look for any imperfections and, ideally, clean all your seals. Again, test all your knobs and dials to confirm that they perform their intended functions.

Napoleon fish, such as this one found off Egypt, make great subjects because they aren't afraid of divers

Canon EOS 5D Mark II • Tokina 10–17mm fisheye lens • 1/60 s • f/5.6 • ISO 200

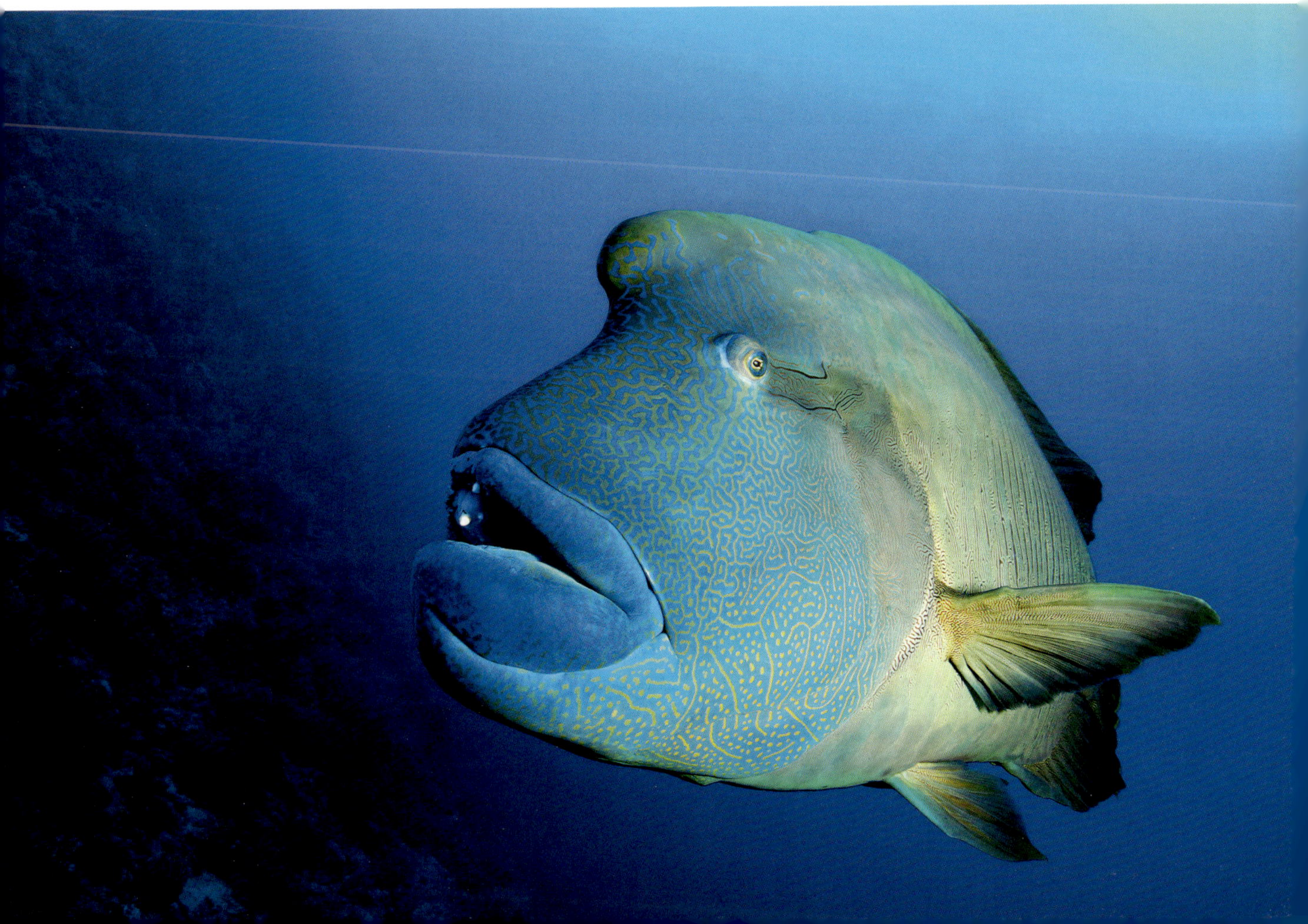

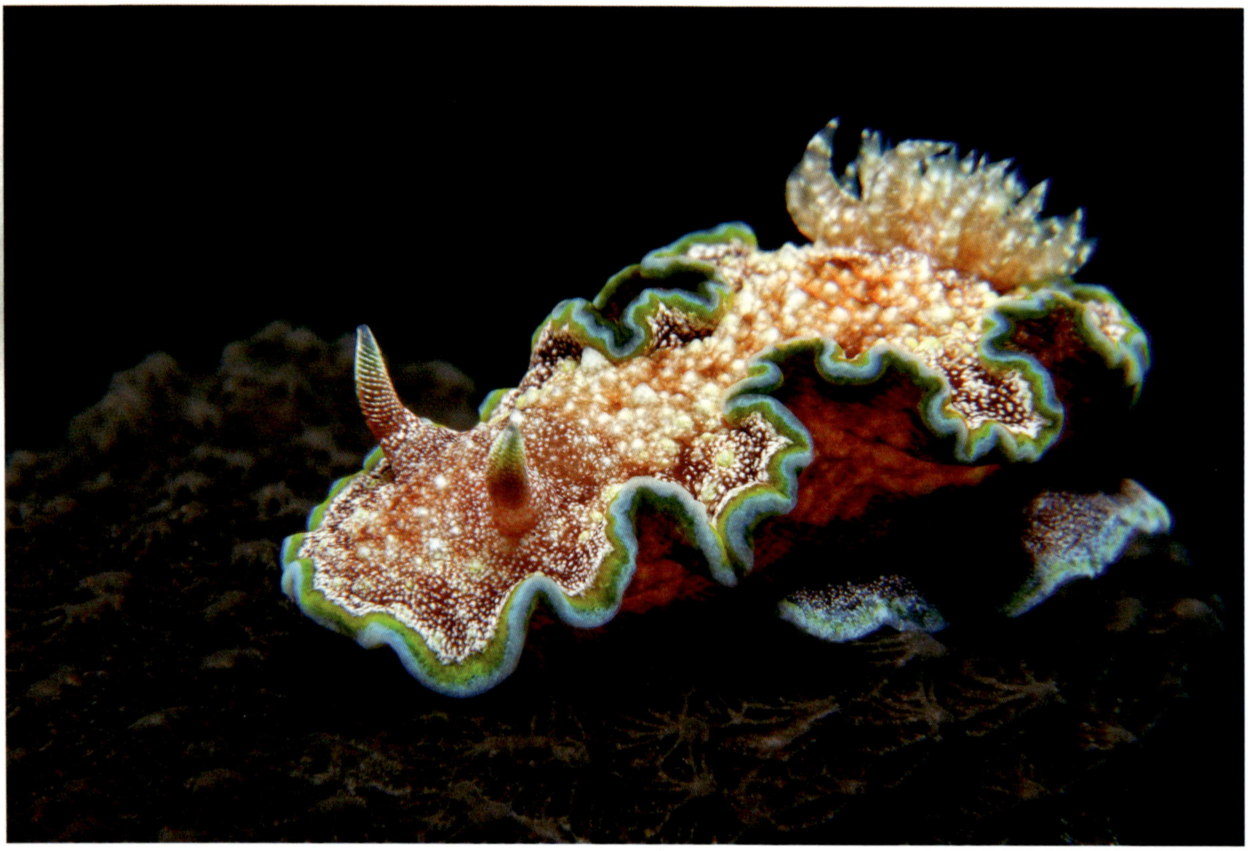

A low camera position can produce interesting photos of small subjects like this nudibranch

Canon EOS 5D Mark II • Canon 100mm macro lens • 1/125 s • f/32 • ISO 400

Make sure the cable that connects your camera to the flash socket is not crimped or kinked, otherwise the cable may break. It can also get caught when you close the housing, which is another common source of damage. If you ever detect difficulty or resistance when you close your housing, never force it; instead, check all your seals and look for obstructions. It's possible that an O-ring hasn't engaged properly. You should always have a backup connection cable and replacement O-rings on hand.

Before you insert your camera into an underwater casing, remove all attachments, like the strap and eyecup, because they can get caught or prevent the housing from closing all the way.

When you attach the sync cord to its port, insert the plug as far as it will go, then turn it to engage the threads, ensuring that you establish a good electrical connection. Sync cords tend to break easily, which is one reason you should always handle them with care and never store them with stress on the cable. Leave your sync cords attached to your camera as long as possible; don't disconnect and reconnect them frequently. This protects the cables and minimizes the chance that water drops will land in the port.

After your equipment is prepped and ready, take a test picture to check your system. Did the flash fire? Is the autofocus working properly? Is the memory card in place? Is the lens cap removed? Are all the settings operational? Do a final visual inspection of the connections and seals. At the end of this book you will find is a comprehensive checklist for preparing your equipment.

Finally, make sure the batteries in your camera, flash units, and lamps are fully charged; make sure the internal date and time in your camera are correct; and make sure your memory card is formatted. If you're using a polycarbonate (plastic) housing, remember to include a silica gel packet to prevent your housing from fogging up.

To test if your housing is tightly sealed, you can place your underwater housing in a tub used to clean your equipment. It's normal for small bubbles to appear on the outside of your housing, but you should be able to wash them away easily and new bubbles should not reappear. After a successful immersion test, store your camera in a secure location, not in direct sunlight, until it's time for your dive.

If you're in a rubber dinghy, try to find a safe spot for your equipment. Your lap might be the safest place. After you get into the dinghy, you shouldn't open your camera again, but if you must, wait until the other divers are in the water and then con-

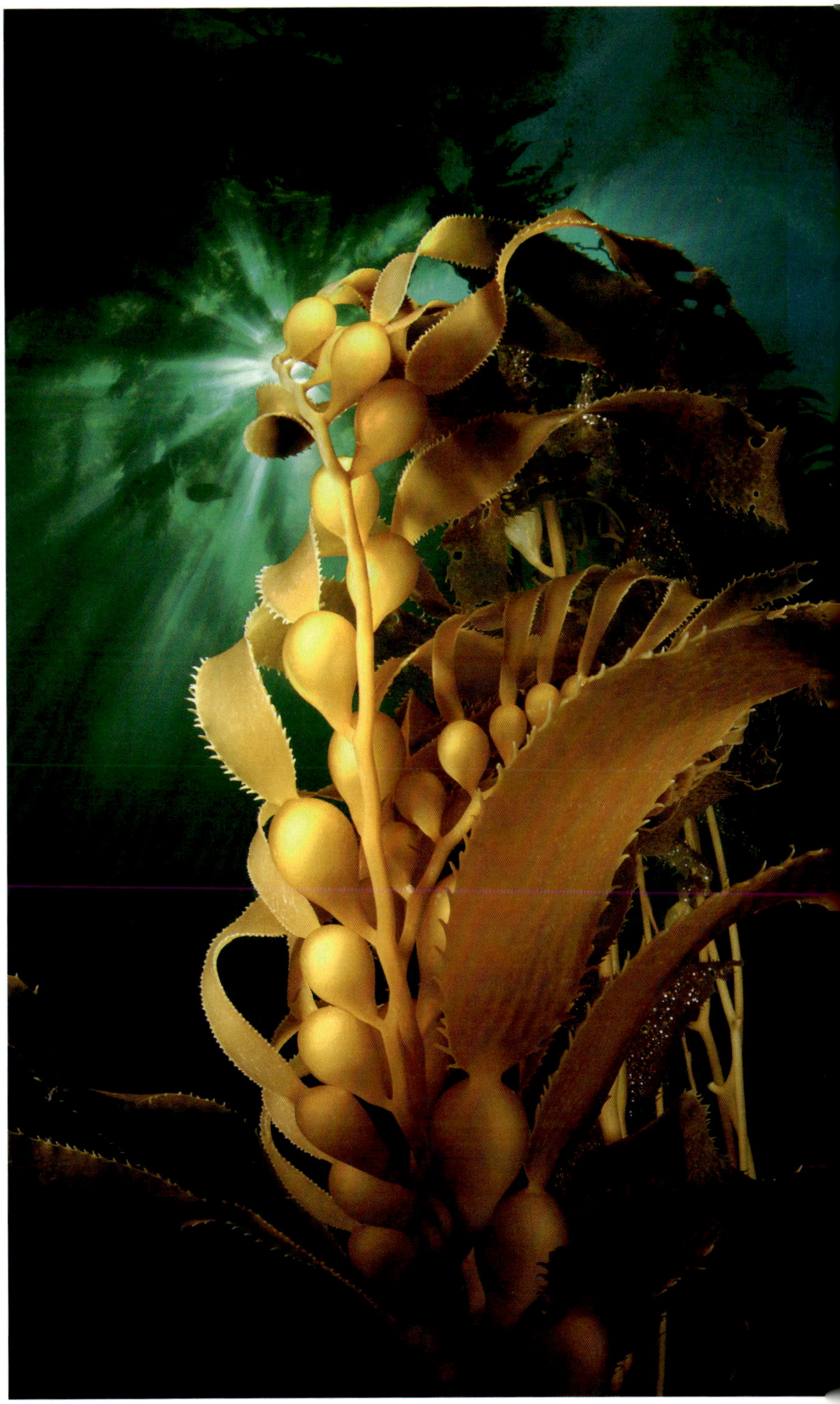

If the midday sun is too bright, you can compose a photo so the subject blocks it and still includes the rays of light

Canon EOS 5D Mark II • Canon 8–15mm fisheye lens • 1/100 s • f/22 • ISO 400

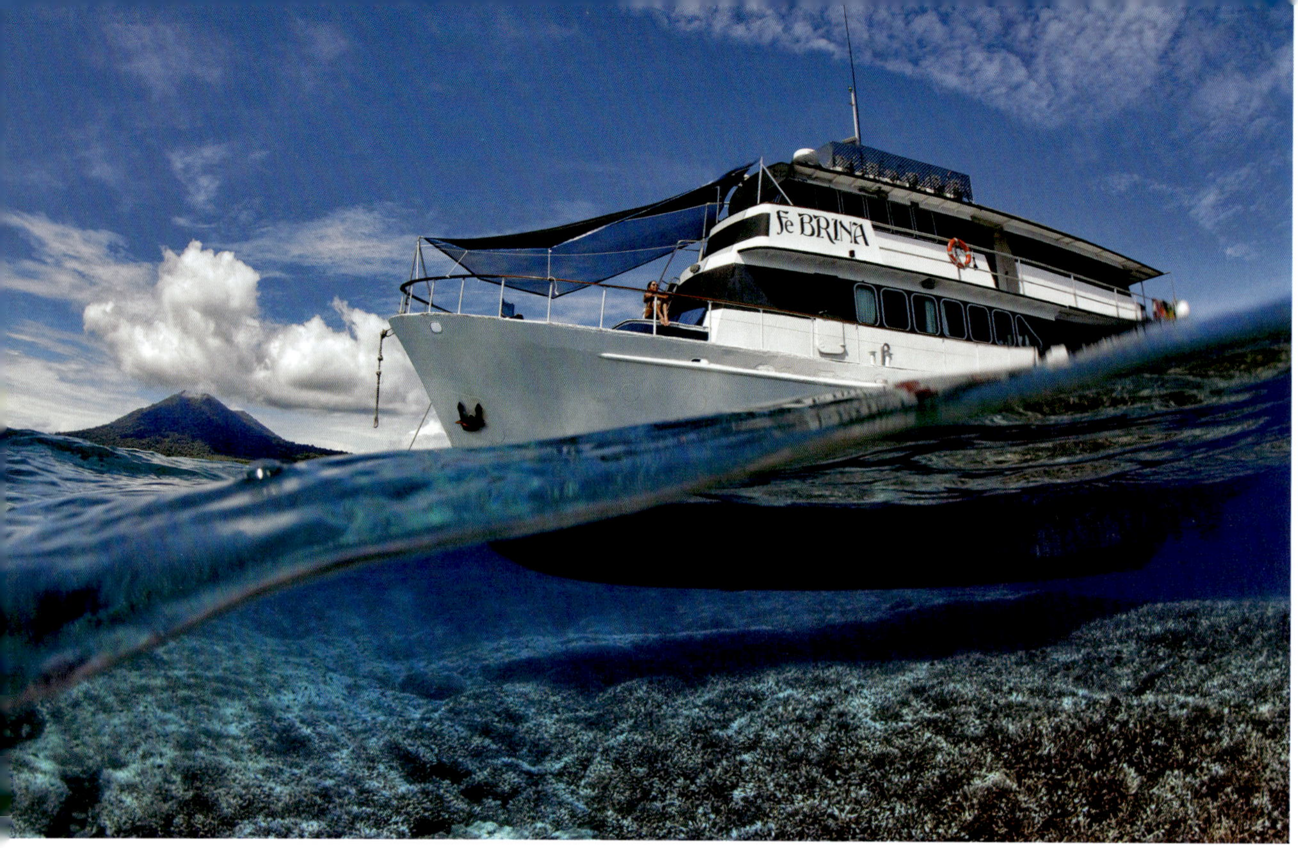

Shallow waters lend themselves to split waterline photos because natural sunlight often eliminates the need for flash

Canon EOS 5D Mark II • Tokina 10–17mm fisheye lens • 1/160 s • f/16 • ISO 200

centrate on your equipment when you have some peace and quiet. If your neoprene suit is already wet, be careful that water drops from your body don't land in the housing.

Don't open your camera at all after it contacts the water because the tiniest grain of sand can compromise a seal.

When all else fails, it's better to skip taking pictures on a dive and simply enjoy the underwater world rather than risking—and worrying about—a flooded housing.

SUMMARY:

- Assemble your equipment before your trip and test everything thoroughly and buy any needed replacement parts.
- When you arrive at your destination, assemble your gear in a relaxed and quiet environment—avoid attempting to do this during a rough crossing.
- Clean and lubricate all seals and O-rings.
- Remove all accessories from your camera, such as the strap and eyecup.
- Take special care with internal and external flash sync cords because they have a tendency to break.
- Take test pictures to verify the functionality of the flash, autofocus, and memory card. Make sure you can control the camera settings. Is the lens cap off?

- Load all the batteries and format the memory card.
- Shortly before your dive, take another test picture and check for leaks in a cleaning tub.
- Store your equipment safely, out of the sun, until it's time for your dive.
- Keep your camera safe during outings in a rubber dinghy.
- After you're in the rubber dinghy, open your housing only in emergencies.
- It's better to dive without your camera than to risk a flooded housing.

1.7 Protecting Your Equipment

The proper care of your equipment is critical to ensure its durability and to prevent water leaks. When other divers disappear to soak up some sun, we photographers still have work to do because our gear requires careful and thorough maintenance so it continues to operate at high underwater pressures.

Any time you open the housing or a port, or when you change the battery in a flash unit, the corresponding O-rings must be cleaned and lubricated again. Even if an O-ring looks clean and you didn't dive anywhere near the sandy floor, you should clean it again to prevent any mishaps. The best way to clean an O-ring is under running water or with a lint-free towel. A paper towel will usually do the job, but make sure no remnants of the paper towel are left behind. Check carefully for grains of sand. If you find any, clean the O-ring again and then lubricate it to keep it smooth and to prevent it from cracking. Applying more lubricant does not guarantee a better seal; in fact, too much lubricant can have the opposite effect and can actually cause water leaks. For an O-ring with a diameter of 8 inches (20 cm), a drop of lubricant the size of a grain of rice is adequate.

The surface on the backside of the seal, such as where it sits against the housing, also needs to be inspected and cleaned. You can clean an O-ring groove with a paper towel or a cotton swab, but make sure no fibers are left behind. Even if you don't open any of your housing's seals, they still need to be cleaned. One cleaning per day is a good rule of thumb.

Dome and flat ports also need to be cleaned, but use extreme caution and apply minimal pressure to prevent scratches. If the lens of a dome port is dirty—salt deposits are a common culprit—use a damp cloth to carefully wipe away the debris. Products designed to clean eyeglasses are perfect for this and will leave the lens free of residue. Don't use a microfiber cloth to clean an acrylic dome port. Acrylic ports are made of plastic, so a slight electrical charge might be produced that will attract dust particles.

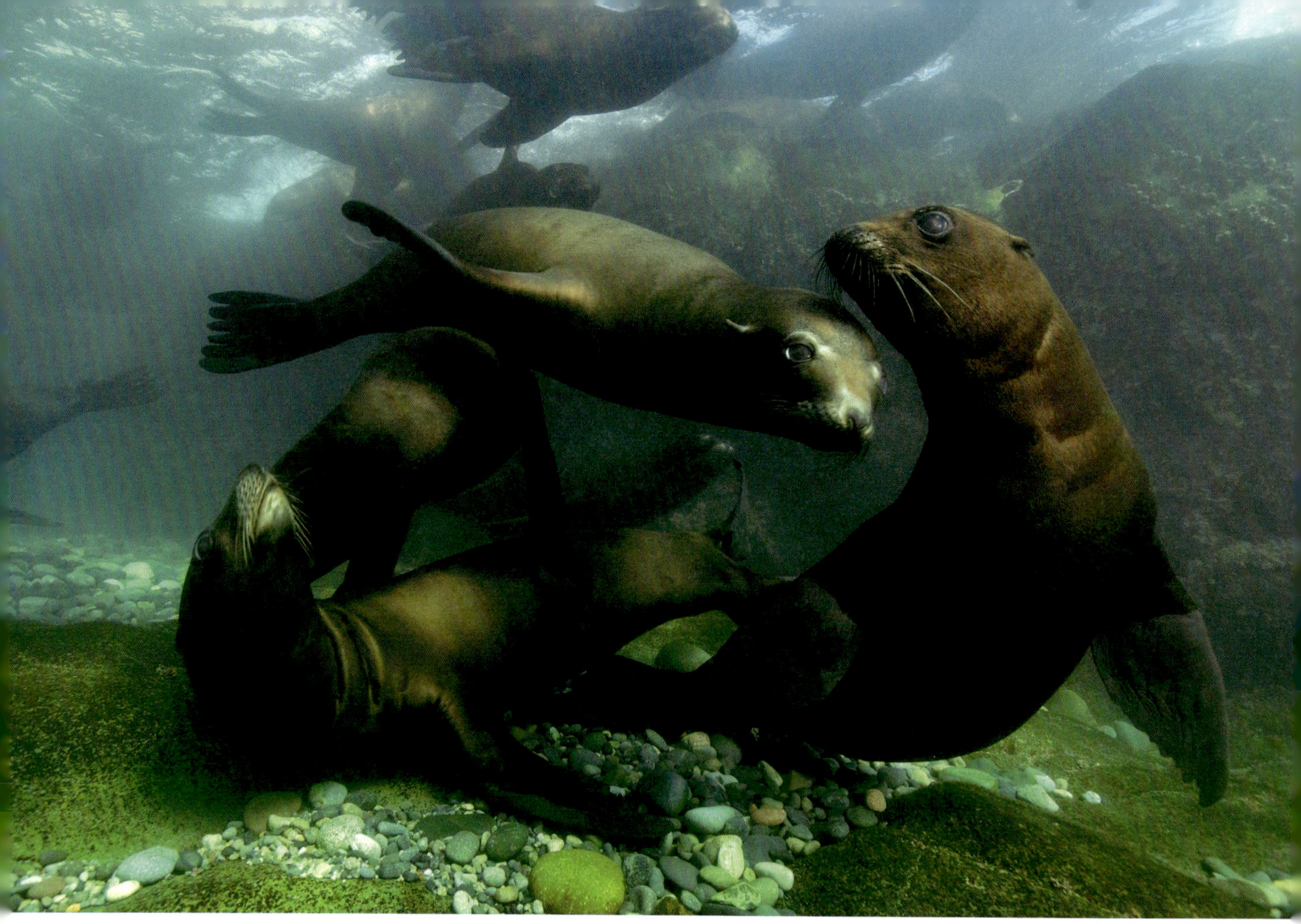

High-quality, powerful flash units are required to photograph sea lions because their dark coats absorb so much light

Canon EOS 5D Mark II • Canon 17–40mm wide-angle lens • 1/200 s • f/9 • ISO 400

After your dive, wash your housing and all its attachments in fresh water or a bath specifically designed for the purpose. Containers used to wash diving equipment are not suitable for washing your delicate camera gear because the water is often not changed often enough and can therefore have a high salt content. If you can't wash your gear thoroughly right after your dive, wrap it with a damp cloth to prevent salt deposits from forming. You can clean your equipment thoroughly later.

Use a lint-free cloth to completely dry the housing before you remove your camera from its casing. Don't use that towel for anything else because other substances, like salt, oil, and sunscreen, can contaminate your equipment.

When your travels are over, the care of your equipment is not. To remove all the salt crystals, especially those that may be deposited in the buttons and knobs, soak your fully assembled and watertight casing for 12 to 24 hours in distilled water. Any remaining salt deposits will dissolve in the bath. For good measure, use a toothbrush to eliminate all residue. Don't use normal tap water or you'll end up with lime scale. Dry your equipment thoroughly and let it sit so any remaining moisture evaporates completely before you put it away.

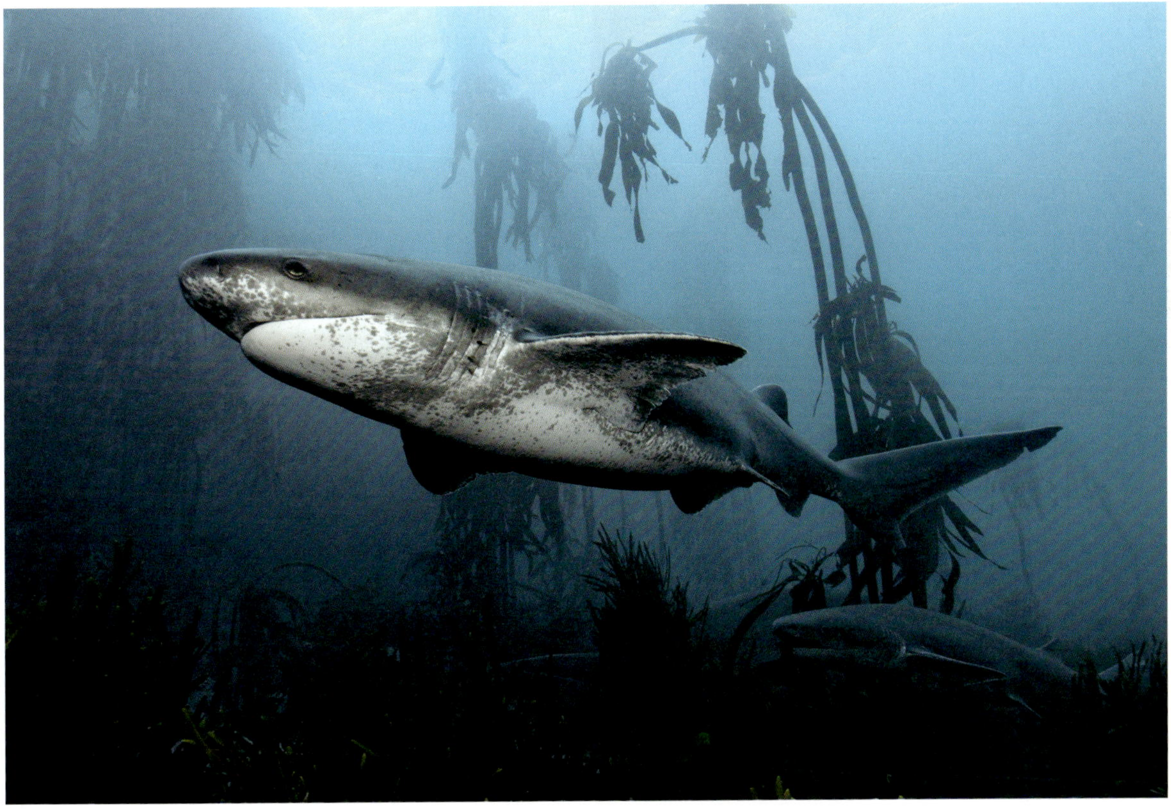

The atmosphere of a photo is often determined by its background

Canon EOS 5D Mark II • Canon 17–40mm wide-angle lens • 1/80 s • f/8 • ISO 400

Store your equipment in a dark area that is protected from direct sunlight. Your housing may look cool in a display cabinet, but prolonged exposure to temperatures above 120°F can cause the O-rings to age quickly and cause damage.

SUMMARY:

- Correct and disciplined care is the best way to ensure your equipment stays fully functional for as long as possible.
- The towel you use for cleaning your camera should not be used for anything else.
- If your housing has already been in the water and you have to open a seal, clean and lubricate the seal again.
- A small quantity of lubricant is sufficient for an O-ring.
- The O-ring groove, the O-ring, and the backside of the seal must be meticulously inspected for cleanliness.
- All seals should be checked and cleaned at least once per day.

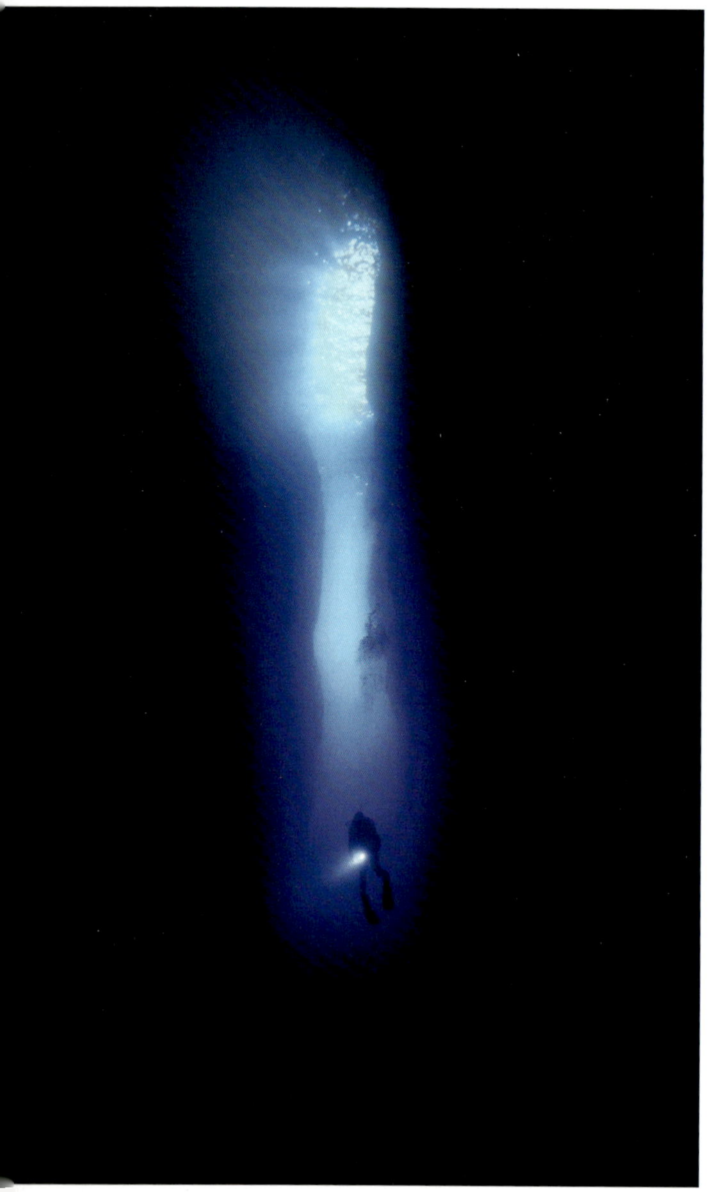

A minimalistic composition can often say more than a composition with too many elements

Canon EOS 5D Mark II • Canon 17–40mm wide-angle lens • 1/20 s • f/4 • ISO 1600

- Use extreme caution and minimal pressure to clean the glass lens of a dome or plan port.
- Use freshwater to rinse your equipment after every dive, or wrap it with a damp cloth and then wash it at the earliest opportunity.
- After your travels have ended, soak your casing for 12 to 24 hours to dissolve any remaining salt deposits.
- Protect your housing from direct sunlight.

1.8 Transporting Your Equipment

Transporting equipment is problematic, especially when airplane travel is involved. It seems there is never a perfect solution. A collection of photography equipment, including a DSLR, an underwater housing, flash units, and accessories, can weigh between 44 and 66 pounds, and this is in addition to diving equipment and clothing. A sturdy box or case will work for a car trip, but with airline luggage regulations, every pound of extra weight can be expensive.

What will you actually need for your trip? One way to figure it out is to create a backward checklist shortly after you return from an excursion. Make a list of all of the gear you took and note if you actually used it. Aside from redundant pieces you intentionally brought as backups, any items you didn't use can be left home next time.

The safest protection for transporting your gear is a sturdy plastic case—a Peli case is one example. A good case protects your equipment from external impacts and the interior is padded with foam. Unfortunately, cases like this weigh a lot—up to 22 pounds—which is counterproductive when you try to trim the weight of your luggage. Excessive weight is less of a problem if your airline has lenient baggage restrictions, but because overweight baggage rules are becoming more strict, these cases aren't always a viable option.

A lighter option is to pack your photo equipment in a smaller plastic box and put it in a duffel bag. You can add foam padding, but it won't make your equipment as safe as it would be in a Peli case. Nevertheless, it can be effective if the weight of your luggage is strictly limited. One benefit using a common duffel bag is that it is not as conspicuous as a Peli case, which helps deter thieves.

Keep your expensive lenses and camera body in your carry-on luggage—either in a photography backpack or a rolling suitcase. Combining a rolling suitcase with a laptop case will attract less attention at the ticket counter because so many businesspeople travel like this. If your carry-on luggage needs to be weighed, it can help to wear your camera or pass it off to someone who's traveling with you.

Many photographers use a photo vest with several large pockets that can hold a surprising amount of gear. Anything clothing you wear doesn't count as carry-on luggage!

Before you pack your housing for a flight, remove the seals because the pressure changes can sometimes produce a vacuum. If this happens with a sealed housing, it can be difficult to open. Just remember, of course, to replace all the seals before your first dive!

The areas around the Galápagos Islands, Cocos Island, and Malpelo Island are popular for capturing photos of hammerheads

Canon EOS 5D Mark II • Canon 17–40mm wide-angle lens • 1/100 s • f/8 • ISO 400

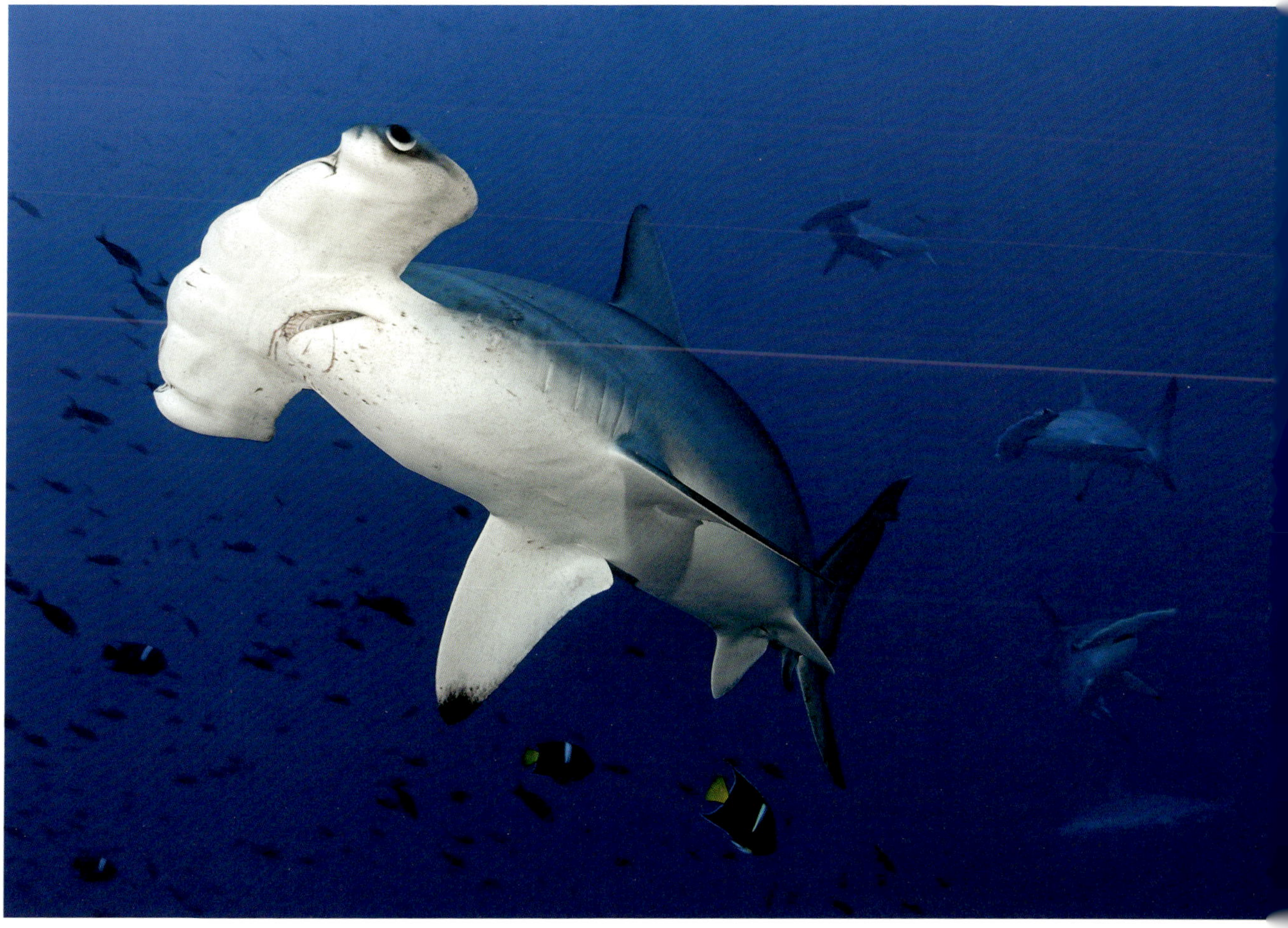

All the equipment you'll need for underwater photography can easily surpass $15,000, which makes purchasing insurance to cover theft highly advisable. Insurance policies commonly offer riders for accidents, negligence, and flooding. This extra coverage will make the premiums higher, but a water leak repair can easily cost a couple thousand dollars. You should look for an insurance policy that covers your equipment while it's in the care of an airline because the liability rules for airlines are highly restrictive.

SUMMARY:

- A sturdy plastic case (such as a Peli case) is the most secure way to transport camera equipment, but it may be too heavy.
- Storing equipment in smaller plastic boxes that are placed inside lightweight bags or rolling suitcases is a lighter option.
- A rolling suitcase and a laptop case will attract less attention at the airline counter.
- Always transport expensive lenses and cameras in your carry-on luggage; never check them with your airline.
- Open your housing's O-rings and seals before the flight to prevent a vacuum from forming.
- Insurance that covers theft as well as water leaks and lost luggage is highly advisable.

Patience is key for capturing photographs that depict animals in uncommon ways

Canon EOS 5D Mark II • Canon 100mm macro lens • 1/30 s • f/10 • ISO 800

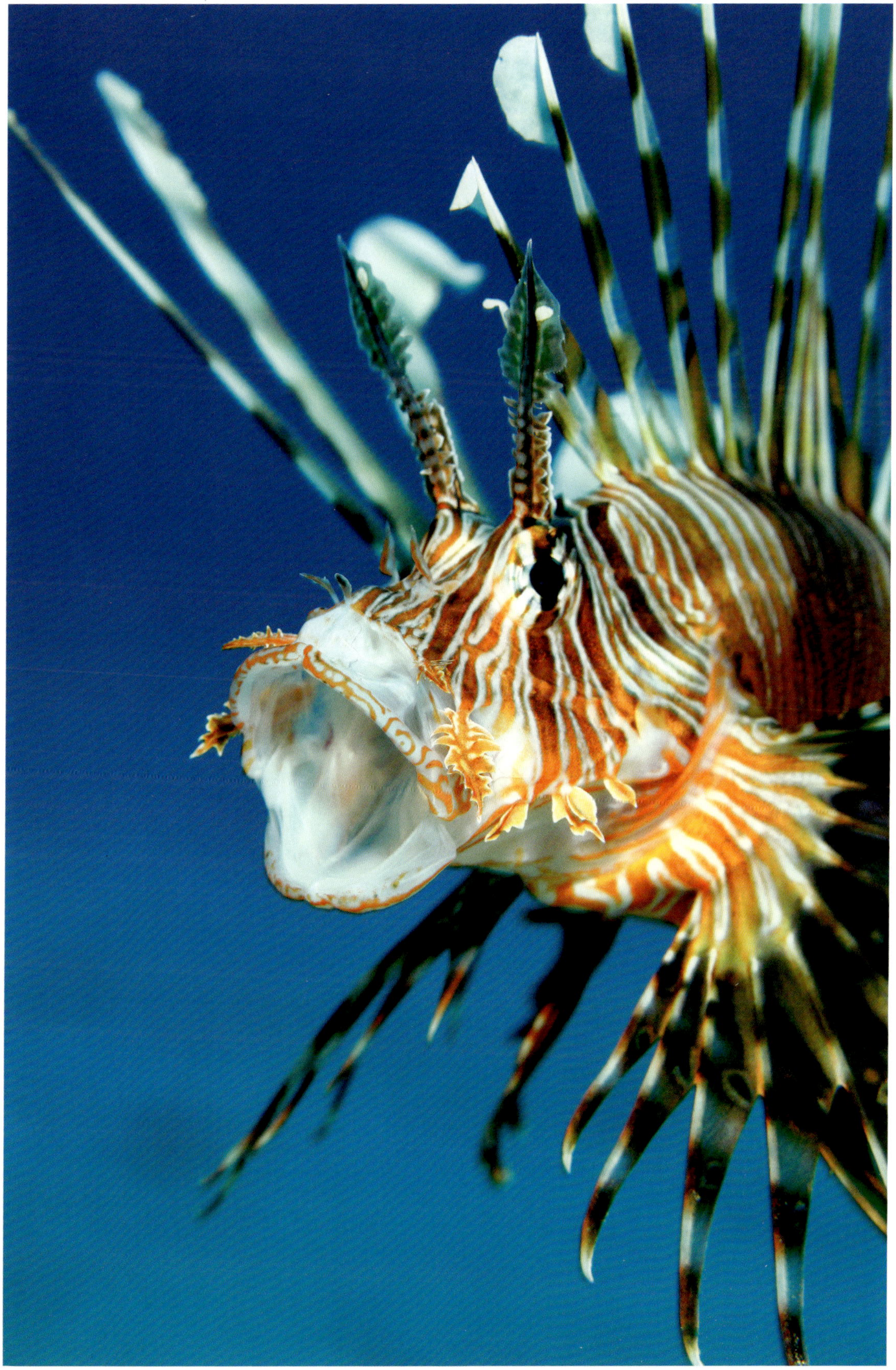

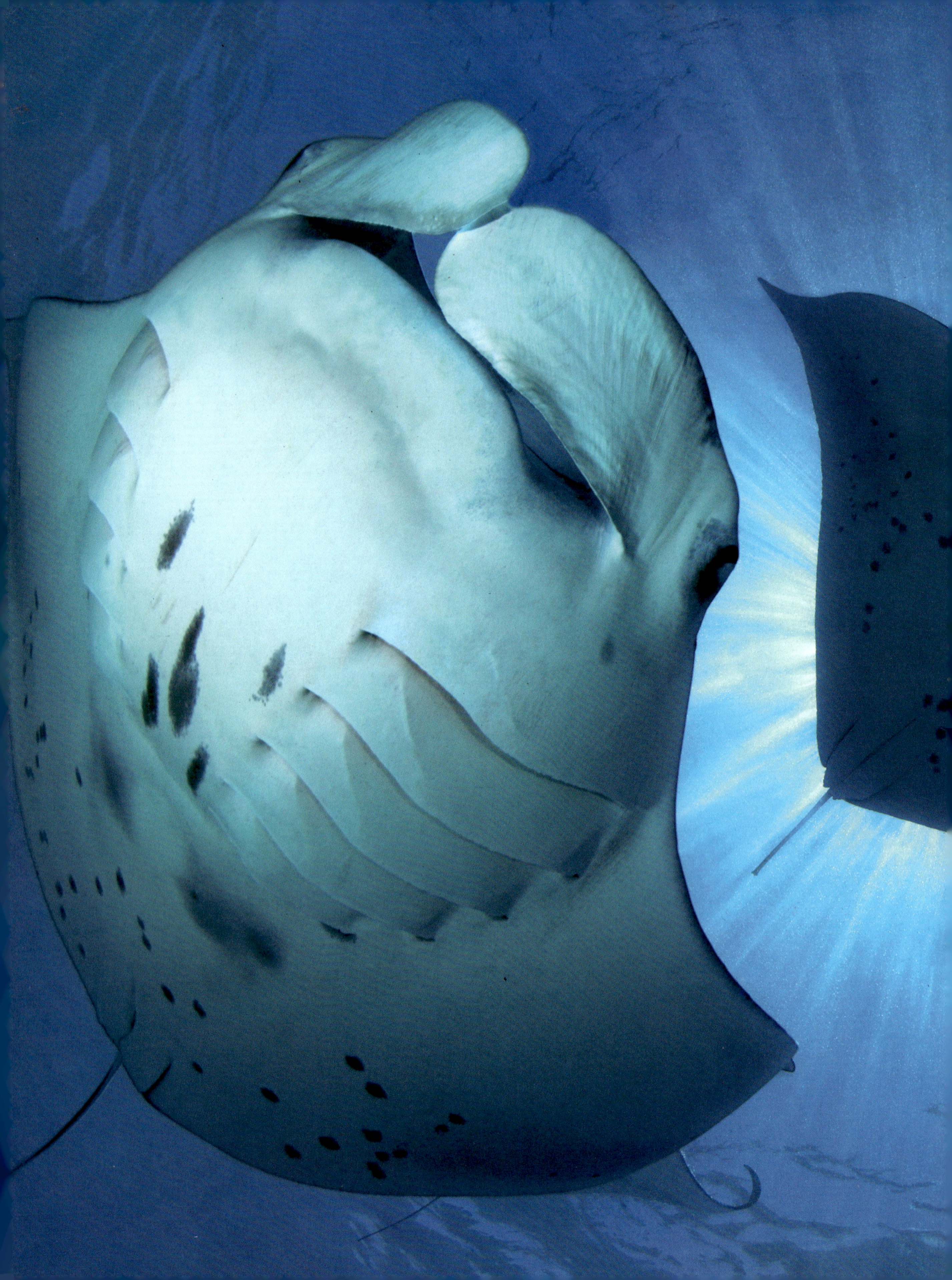

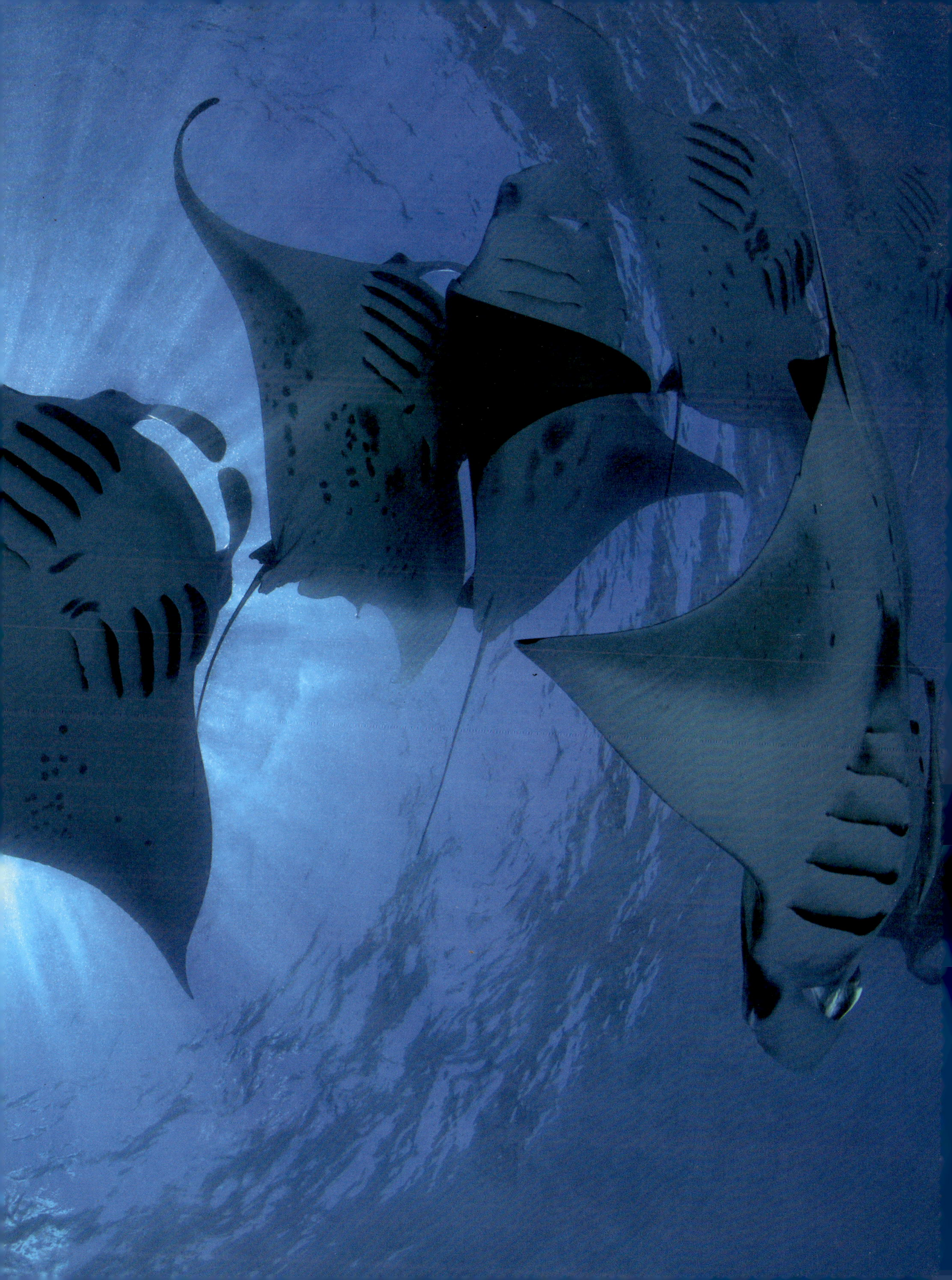

Case Study 2: Space Gliders

Luck is a by-product of effort, which explains how I ended up with this picture of so many manta rays. Luck played a role for sure, but extensive planning and preparations were just as critical.

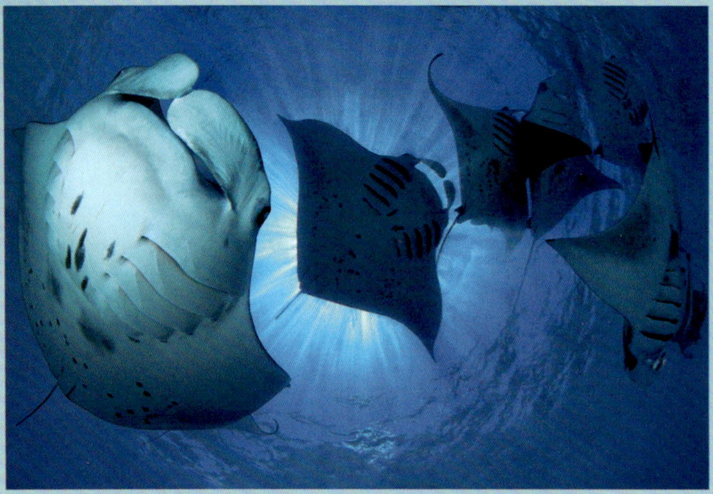

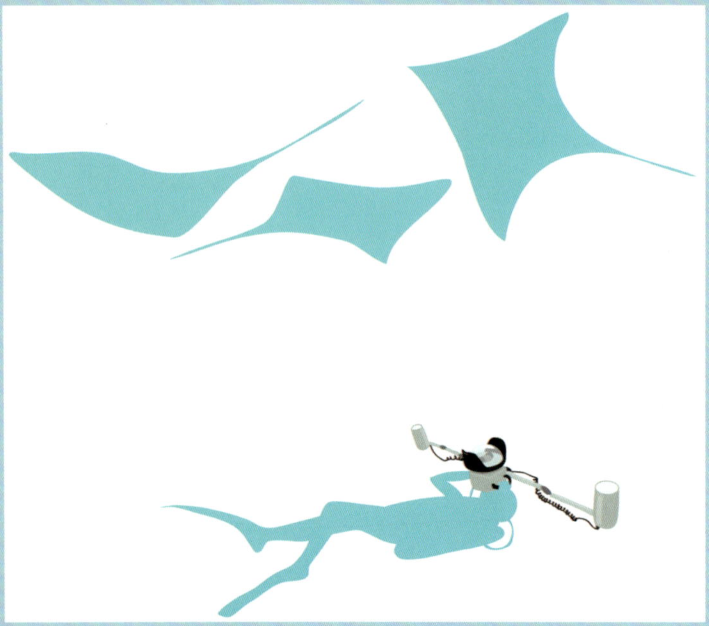

Canon EOS 5D Mark II • Canon 8–15mm fisheye lens • two Ikelite DS125 strobes • 1/320 s • f/9 • ISO 50 • flash at full power

Every year a few dozen of these rays visit a small bay in the Maldives, where they feed in waters that are particularly rich with plankton. National Geographic first reported on this phenomenon in 2008, and since then the area has become a tourist magnet where hundreds of divers and snorkelers try to find and swim with these majestic animals. But no one can say exactly when the manta rays will be in the area—sometime between August and October is the general consensus.

When I booked my trip, I made sure it fell between these dates. I picked a week when I knew the moon would be full. I don't know for a fact that the lunar cycle has anything to do with the habits of manta rays, but I can say for certain that the rays appeared the day after the full moon.

When so many rays populate these waters, the number of divers and snorkelers in the bay roughly doubles, which makes for difficult shooting conditions. It's almost impossible to capture a photo that isn't significantly marred by excessive floating matter (including humans). One way of dealing with this challenge is to move in the opposite direction of other people. You also have to pay attention to the patterns of the rays' movements so you can anticipate where they might swim next. Manta rays tend to follow a specific path that leads to areas that are particularly rich with food. If they swim in a particular direction—followed by dozens of divers—you can wait at their starting point and catch them on their return trip. I've learned that fact by simply watching the rays' behavior while I was in the water.

My goal for this particular outing was to photograph several rays in dramatic backlighting. To realize this goal in the midday sun without having parts of my photo overexposed, however, I had to have one of the rays blocking the sun to minimize its brightness.

I needed a fisheye lens to handle the expansive span of these creatures' fins. I also needed to be relatively close to the animals so my flash would still be effective. I positioned the flash heads as far from the camera as possible and set them to their maximum output. I used aperture-priority exposure mode to handle the highly variable lighting conditions. To prevent the shutter speed from being too fast to sync with the flash, I set the ISO value as low as possible. I could have achieved the same result by using a smaller aperture, but I reduced the ISO instead to ensure the best possible image quality.

To execute the picture as I envisioned, I had to swim on my back and hold my breath for as long as possible to prevent bubbles from appearing. This also meant I had to watch my diving depth meticulously to make sure I stayed at the same vertical position. Then all I had to do was wait for the animals to glide by, backlit by the sun. That eight or nine rays ended up in my image was a matter of luck indeed.

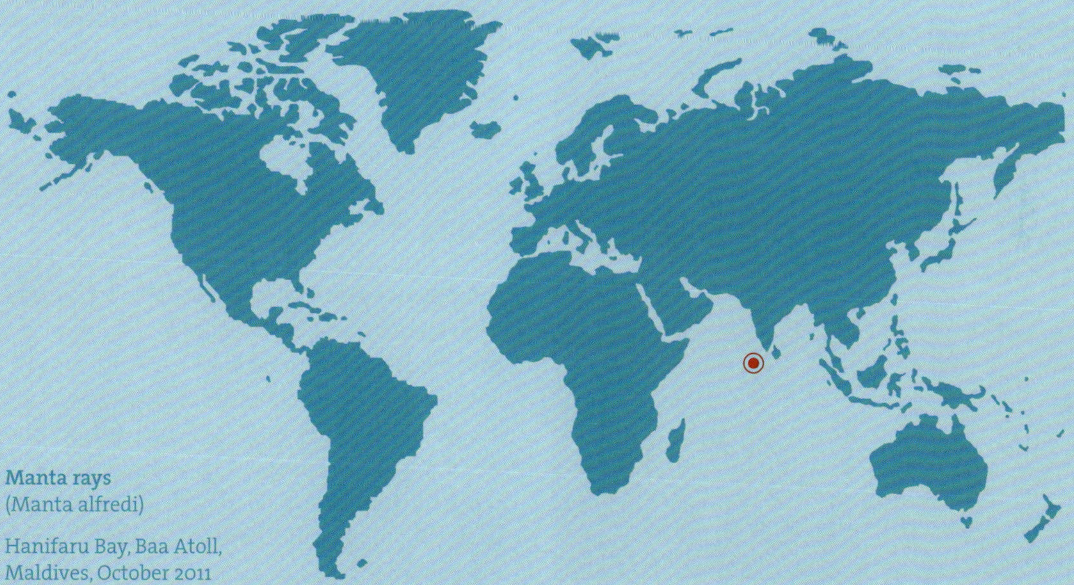

Manta rays
(Manta alfredi)

Hanifaru Bay, Baa Atoll,
Maldives, October 2011

2

The Basics

2.1 Diving and Taking Pictures

As soon as a camera is involved, the nature of a dive changes. To what degree this changes depends on the photographer's motivations and photography goals. Passionate photographers consider a dive successful only when they get a good image. Others approach a dive with a more relaxed attitude and may be satisfied even if the memory card is still empty when it's over. Divers have to decide for themselves how important photography will be during a dive.

The more time you spend under water with your camera, and the more discipline you exercise in searching for new subjects, the more your photographic results will improve.

Sunrise and sunset produce particularly attractive lighting in photos; both on land and under water. Twilight produces a world of magic below the surface because the shadowy light looks much different than the harsh light of midday. Anyone who is not willing to miss dinner or head out before breakfast will never experience these conditions. There's really no excuse for going on a dive without your camera because you will always find something worth photographing.

In the same way that you might anticipate the type of lens you'll want to use before you get in the water, you should also anticipate what opportunities might develop while you work. For example, after you finish shooting a backlit image, immediately reset your camera settings for a standard exposure so you'll be ready for whatever's next. It's better to reset your camera too often than to miss a great shot because you didn't have time to change the aperture, shutter speed, ISO, and flash in the heat of the moment.

Making a plan for what you intend to shoot before you go on a dive can be an effective way to focus on specific subjects. If making plans isn't feasible, then it's important to continually distinguish worthwhile subjects from others with less merit while you're under water. A change of perspective can work wonders, which is why it's critical to have a sense of how subjects will look in the final image. Evaluating subjects this way makes it much easier to

A basic and highly functional setup: one strong strobe positioned above and to the right of the camera brightens up the desired parts of the image.

Canon EOS 5D Mark II • Tokina 10–17mm fisheye lens • 1/100 s • f/8 • ISO 100

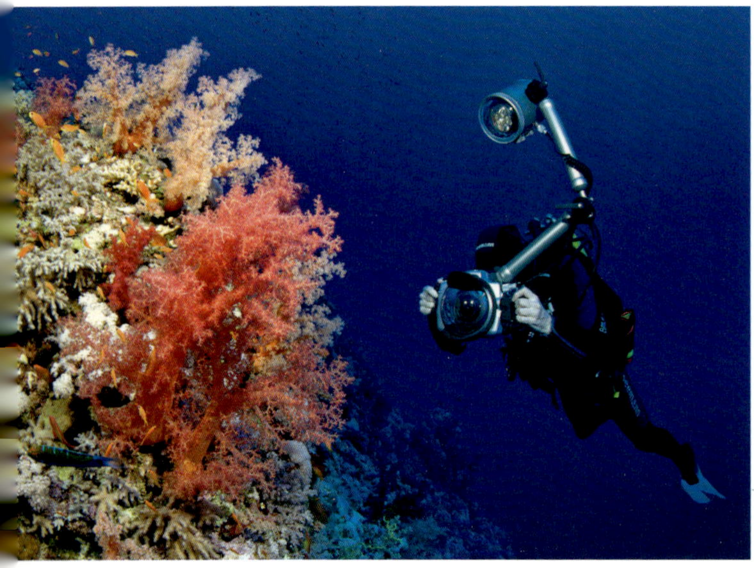

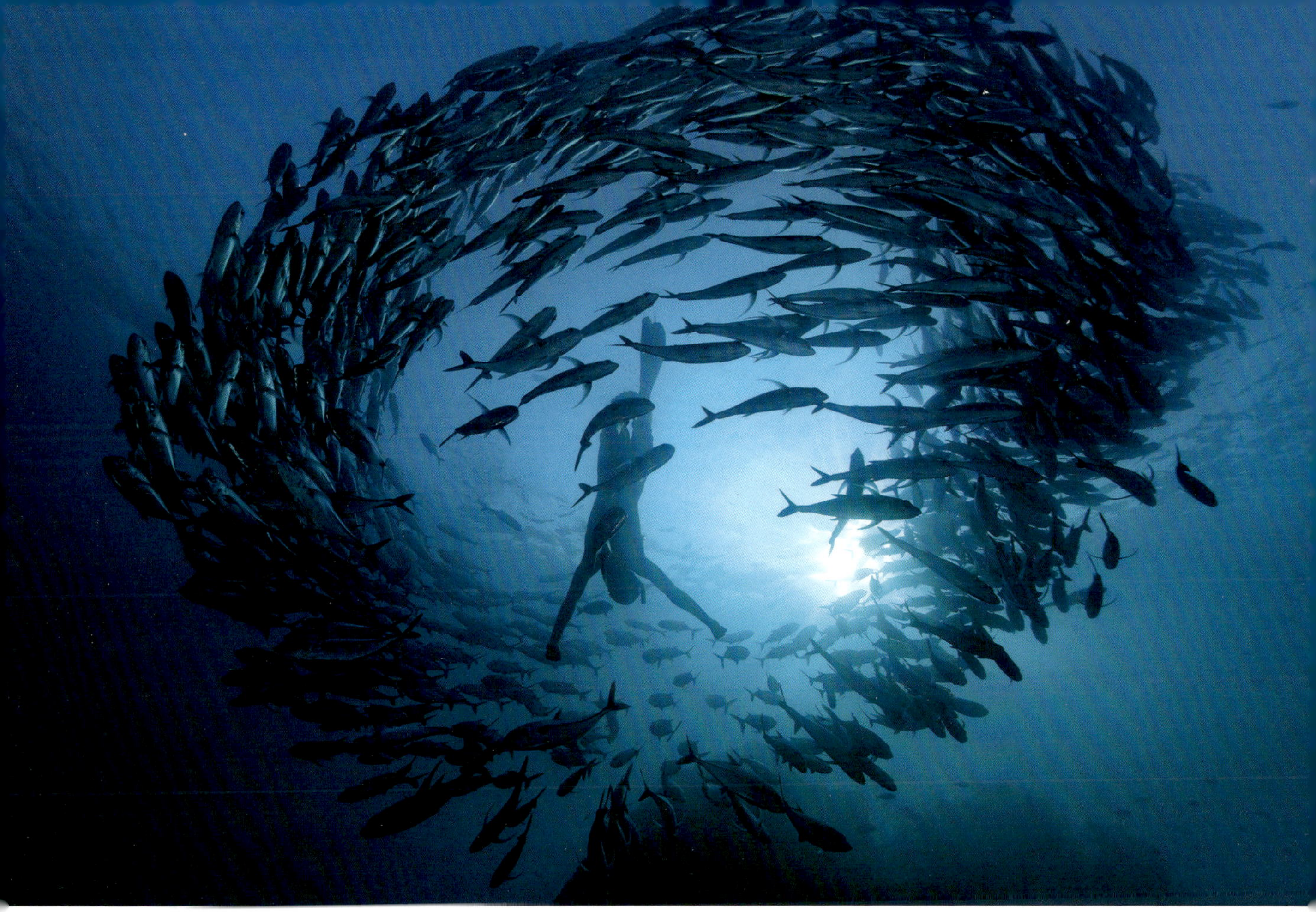

decide what to photograph. For example, you might debate which situation will produce the image you want: diving down 130 ft to photograph coral with a very dark background, or swimming a bit farther in search of another specimen that's in shallower water and brighter light.

Don't get too set on capturing a particular subject if it's not likely that your image will be successful. A particular shot may not pan out for lots of reasons. It may be the perspective or the flash settings, or it could simply be that the subject has disappeared. In situations like this, it's best to forgo the opportunity and swim on in search of a subject with more potential.

You need a lot of patience when you approach a shy animal, such as a blenny. You may need 30 to 45 minutes to get the shot you want, which requires a lot of perseverance from you and your safety partner. But this approach is exactly what's called for when you want an exceptional photo rather than just a passable one.

Take only as many pictures as you absolutely need because a lot of animals are highly sensitive to light. Spending time with an animal and waiting for just the right moment is significantly more gentle for both the wildlife and your memory card.

Sometimes it just takes a relatively simple subject to evoke passion for the underwater world with a picture

Canon EOS 5D, Mark II • Canon 17–40mm wide-angle lens • 1/200 s • f/10 • ISO 200

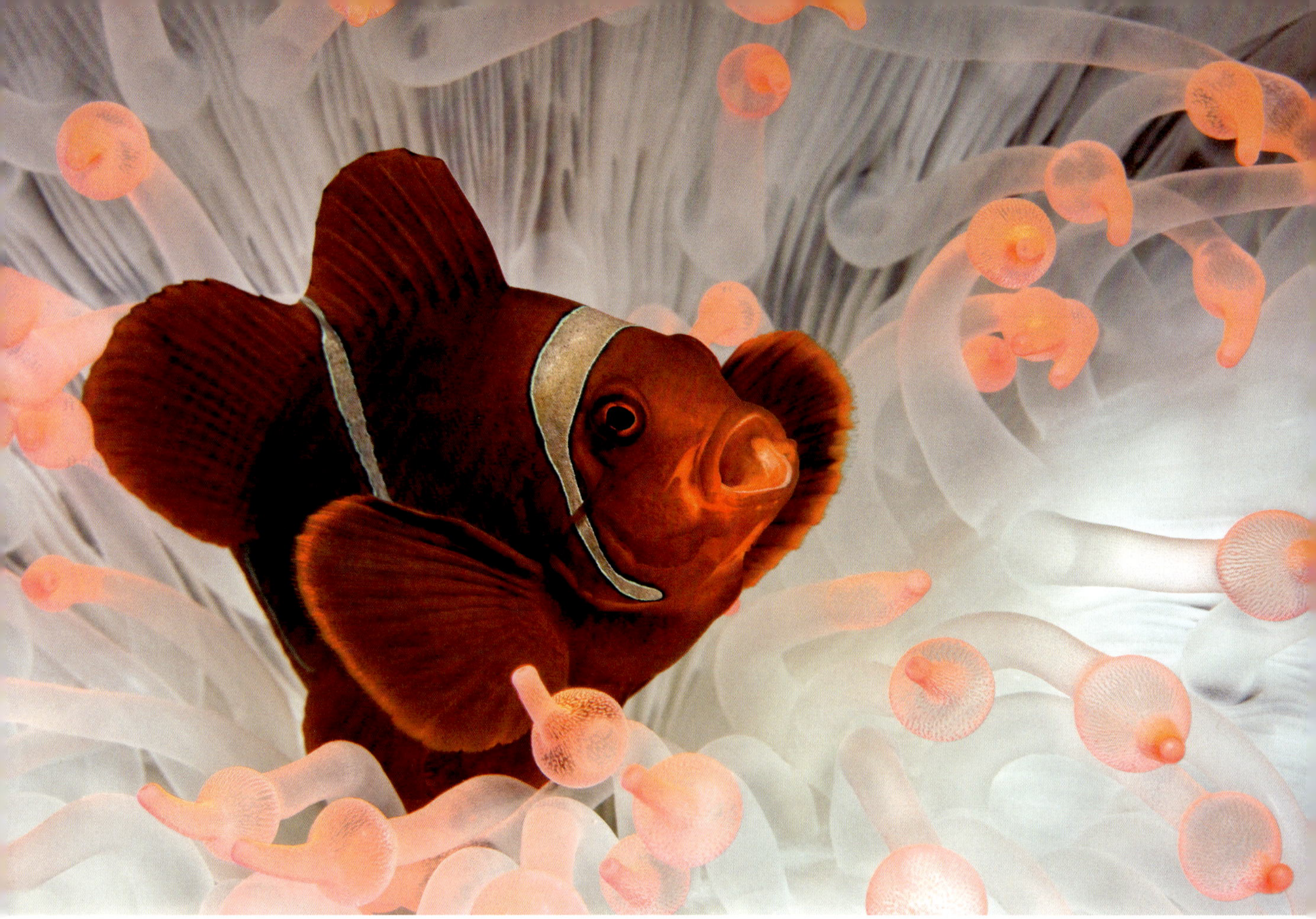

This anemonefish (commonly called a clown fish), enveloped by an anemone, would have been a good picture on its own, but capturing the scene just as the fish opened its mouth changed the image from good to great.

Canon EOS 5D Mark II • Canon 100mm macro lens • 1/160 s • f/20 • ISO 400

When you add accessories to your underwater housing, make sure you can still evaluate the image area on your camera's LCD monitor. Otherwise you'll miss out on subjects that disappear before you can properly sight them in the viewfinder.

As a rule, it is critical to honor the environment when you are in the water. No photo is worth breaking off a piece of coral, even if it can eventually grow back. Don't get lost in the photo—pay attention to what's around you. Divers should be perfectly balanced so they can avoid causing damage to the undersea environment.

Mastering an effective fin technique is key for preventing debris and other floating particles from clouding the waters around you. What good is it to have the chance to photograph a fascinating control panel at a shipwreck site only to end up with a murky fog? Respecting the environment will help you produce quality images.

Don't stress yourself. Bringing back one or two good pictures from a dive is totally enough and is better than having 20 images saved on the memory card that are only average.

2.2 The Behavior of Light Under Water

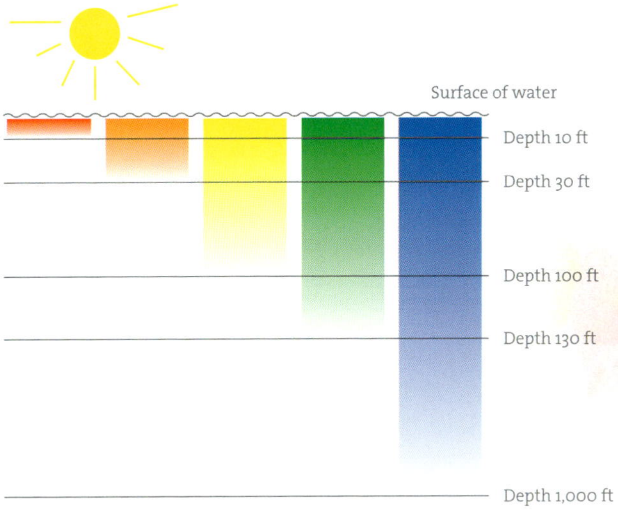

When we are under water, our eyes perceive our surroundings as colorful and vivid, yet underwater photos seem rather bluish and dull. Why is that? The human mind interprets missing colors so well that it subconsciously fills in colors for us. This is why the colors in a photo don't always live up to the colors we see during a dive. Artificial lighting, in the form of strobes and lamps, is critical for achieving brilliant, natural-looking colors in your images.

Just a few feet below the surface of water the color spectrum starts to diminish. At 10 ft in depth, red wavelengths of light are filtered out, orange is lost at 30 ft, yellow at 100 ft, and green at 130 ft. Only blue wavelengths penetrate to 500 ft, and at 1,000 ft no color is visible. Because red wavelengths penetrate only 10 ft under water, you need to be within 5 ft of your subject; light first travels from the light source to the subject, and then from the subject to your camera. At greater distances red wavelengths fall away steeply until there is no red at all.

The intensity of sunlight is dramatically reduced when it hits the surface of water—at 30 ft it's already decreased by 80 percent. If the water is cloudy, the loss of color brilliance and light intensity is even more dramatic. To counteract this problem, increase your ISO so you can keep your shutter speed fast enough to avoid blurry images.

Refraction is another property of light that affects underwater photography. It causes rays of light to change angle after they penetrate the surface of water. If you see a stick in the water, it looks like it's at a different angle under water, and the submerged portion looks bigger. The human eye experiences an optical shortening when you look through water, and everything seems about a third closer than it actually is. This phenomenon has a significant impact on how far you should position your flash from an underwater subject. Strobes that are too close to the subject can overexpose the scene. If they are too far, the image probably won't come out as good it could be.

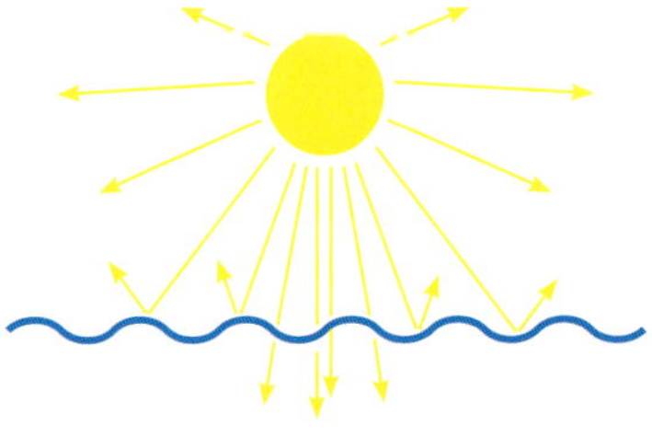

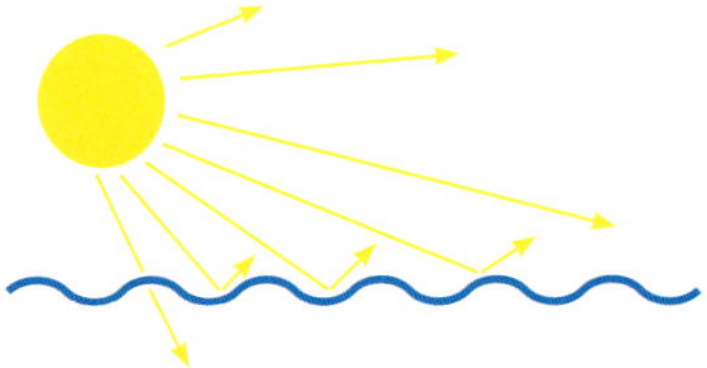

During morning and evening hours, a majority of sunlight reflects off the water's surface

SUMMARY:

- Water filters the color spectrum of sunlight; at about 130 ft, blue light is all that's left.
- Artificial lighting, such as lamps and flash units, can compensate for the absence of sunlight and bring the full spectrum of color back into your photos.

- Red wavelengths of light can travel only 10 to 15 ft below the surface of water.
- At 30 ft deep, the intensity of sunlight is reduced by approximately 80 percent.
- After light passes below the surface of water, its angle changes and causes objects to look about a third larger than they actually are.

2.3 Aperture, Shutter Speed, and ISO

Snapshots serve their purpose, but if you want consistently good results you need to thoroughly understand the interplay of aperture, shutter speed and light sensitivity (ISO). Automatic exposure modes are counterproductive under water because they often result in poor exposures. Because the aquatic world is relatively dark, automatic modes overcompensate and frequently produce images that are too bright. Serious photographers should use the manual (M) exposure setting to maintain full control over the aperture, shutter speed, and ISO. This is a fantastic way to accelerate your learning curve and understand how aperture, shutter speed, and ISO interact.

The aperture is like a floodgate that can be widened or narrowed to control how much light enters the camera at a given time. Aperture also influences depth of field. If the aperture is open wide (e.g., f/2.8 or f/4.0), lots of light will enter the camera, and the image will have a shallow depth of field. Smaller aperture openings permit less light and produce images with a greater depth of field.

The shutter speed defines the period of time that light is permitted to strike the sensor. While shooting under water you generally don't want the exposure to be any longer than 1/30 second, otherwise you'll run the risk of having your images blurred by camera shake. When you use flash, you'll also need to make sure the shutter speed doesn't exceed the *sync speed*, which is how long it takes the camera to tell the flash unit to fire after

Don't get mixed up:
The larger the aperture, or f-number, the smaller the opening

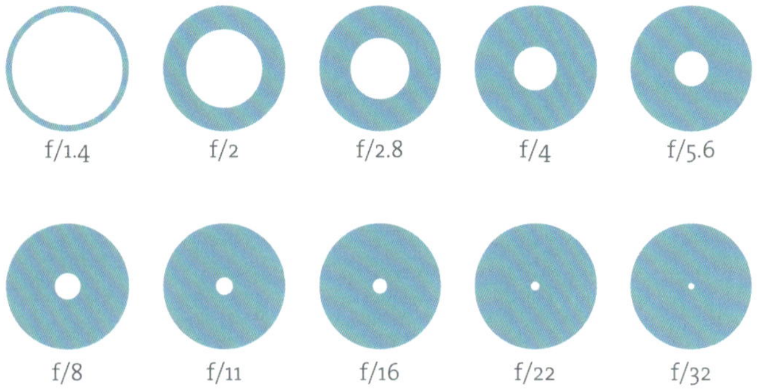

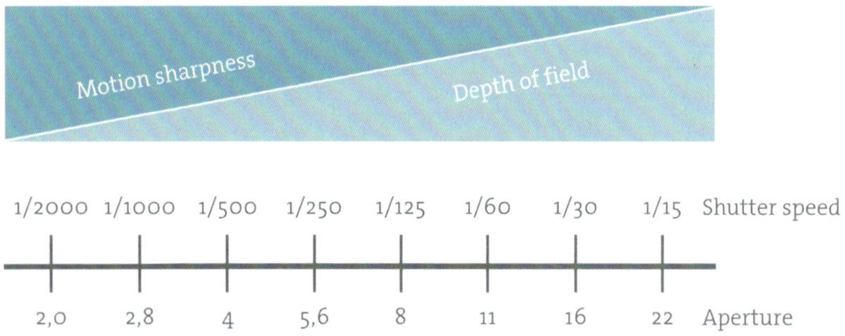

A large aperture produces better sharpness of a moving subject (i.e., freezes motion) and a small aperture produces a greater depth of field

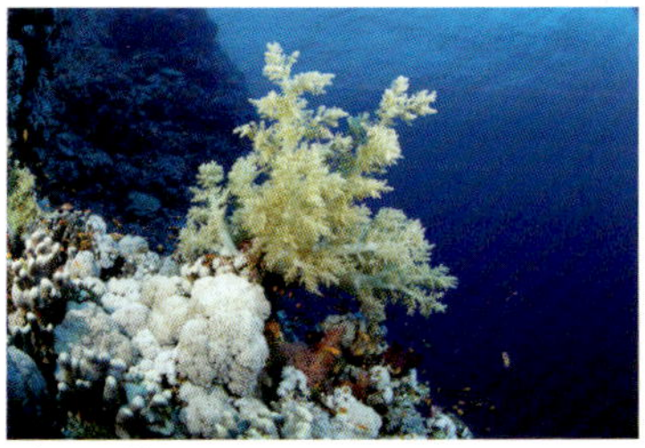
1/60 s, f/8, ISO 200

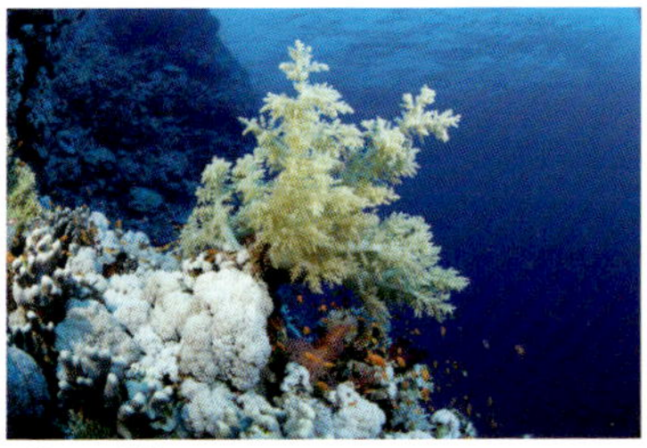
1/80 s, f/8, ISO 200

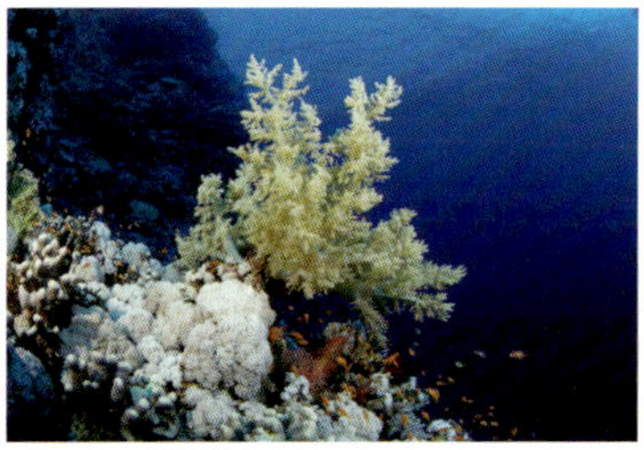
1/100 s, f/8, ISO 200

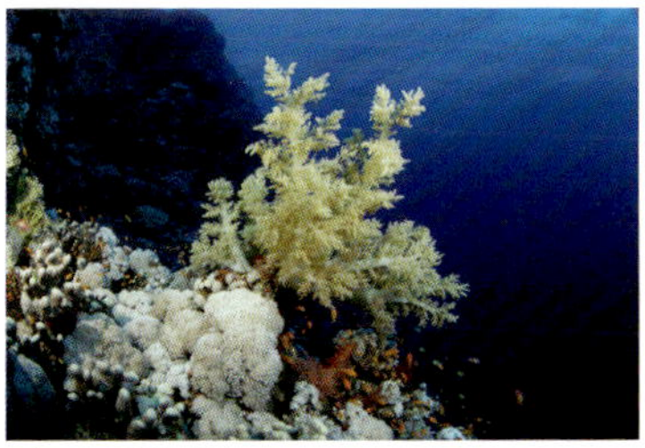
1/125 s, f/8, ISO 200

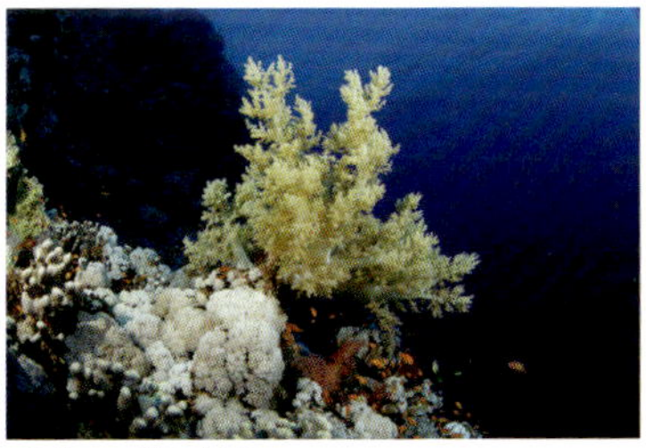
1/160 s, f/8, ISO 200

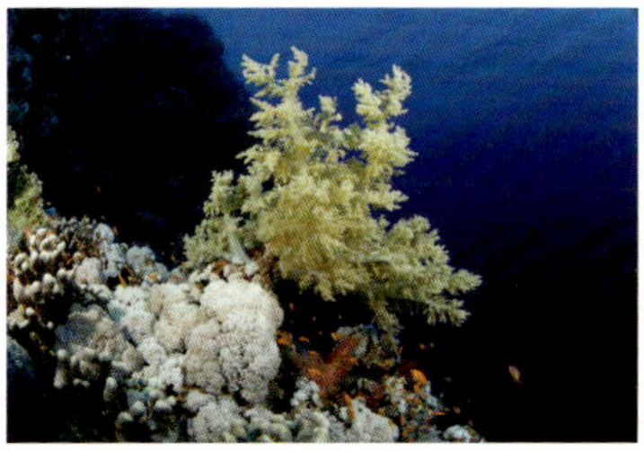
1/200 s, f/8, ISO 200

Decreasing the shutter speed results in a darker background. Providing the aperture and flash output remain constant, the foreground doesn't change in appearance.

the shutter opens. If the shutter speed is too fast, the flash light may never reach the sensor. Most DSLRs have sync speeds between 1/200 second and 1/250 second.

The ISO value defines the sensor's light sensitivity. Low ISO values (e.g., 100 or 200) produce the best image quality; higher ISO values may result in digital image noise similar to graininess you might see in film images. Modern DSLRs tend to have excellent ISO performance and produce great results at ISOs as high as 800. Even when you shoot at ISO 3200, the image is often acceptable for online use. It's better to use a high ISO than to entirely miss a shot.

Test your camera's performance by taking a series of images with increasingly higher ISO settings. Take the series of images in the dark, then view the results at 100 percent magnification and look for image noise. After you perform this exercise, you'll have a good idea of your camera's maximum acceptable ISO speed.

It's important to understand that a proper combination of aperture, shutter speed, and ISO is what establishes a correct exposure. Imagine three test tubes with liquid in them. The total volume can't change, so if fluid is taken from one tube, it must be placed in another so the sum stays constant. In photographic terms, it works like this: If the aperture number is increased one stop from f/8 to f/11, the duration of the exposure must also increase by one stop, from 1/125 second to 1/60 second. Alternatively, the ISO value could be raised from 100 to 200. Many combinations are possible to allow the sensor to receive the same quantity of light.

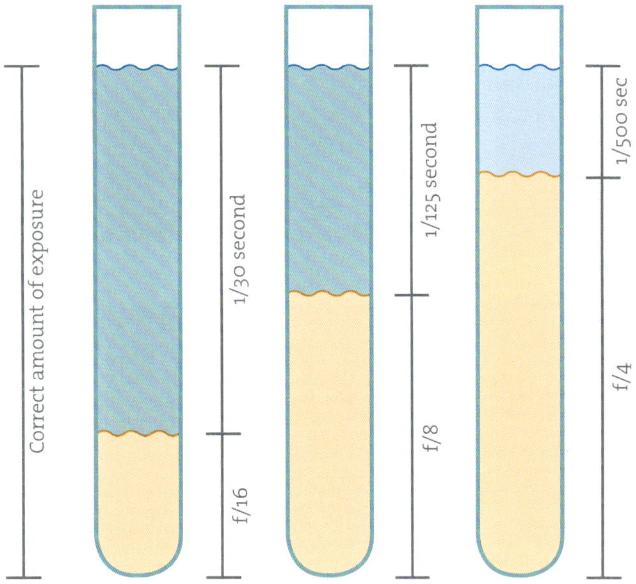

Various combinations of aperture settings and shutter speeds will produce your desired exposure

Another thing to be aware of when photographing under water is the background. When the background of an image is blue water, the intensity of the blue can be controlled with the shutter speed, which allows more or less ambient light into the image. For example, if your setup is f/8, with ISO 200, and strobes at half power, the intensity of the background will increase or decrease if you change the shutter speed. Take a look at the example pictures on the previous page.

When you internalize this fundamental principle, you'll be able to correctly and intuitively expose your images.

SUMMARY:

- You must understand the interplay of aperture, shutter speed and ISO to reliably create quality images.
- Shooting in the manual (M) exposure mode is highly advisable.
- A wide aperture allows more light to reach the sensor and produces a shallow depth of field; a narrow aperture permits less light and creates a larger depth of field.
- When you shoot under water, the exposure time should fall between 1/30 second and 1/200 second.
- The ISO value defines the sensor's light sensitivity.
- There are many combinations of aperture, shutter speed and ISO that can produce a properly exposed image.
- If you reduce the size of the aperture, you need to increase either the ISO or the shutter speed. You need to have a solid understanding of this concept.
- The shutter speed controls the intensity of the background, if no other camera settings are changed.

2.4 JPEG or RAW

Most DSLRs, and even some compact cameras, allow you to select either JPEG or RAW file format for your images. You may think RAW images look dull and JPEGs have more intense colors. But RAW images are analogous to film negatives—they need to be developed in image editing software, which takes a bit of effort (see chapter 6). JPEG images look finished right out of the camera, and you can still edit them later, up to a point. They take up less space on your memory card, but they also give you fewer post-processing options.

Images that are saved in RAW format do not suffer a reduction of quality, but the file sizes are a lot larger because they store so much information about the image. You can post-process RAW files to a much greater degree than is possible with JPEG files. With a RAW file, you can increase or decrease the exposure by up to two stops and recalibrate the white balance after the fact.

Cameras often have settings for variables like saturation, contrast, and sharpness that you can change before you take a picture. The effects of these changes are visible in a JPEG, but they don't affect a RAW file because the camera saves the complete, unaltered image data for a RAW file when it is written to the memory card.

The right crop can emphasize certain characteristics of an animal

Canon EOS 5D Mark II • Canon 17–40mm wide-angle lens • 1/160 s • f/9 • ISO 200

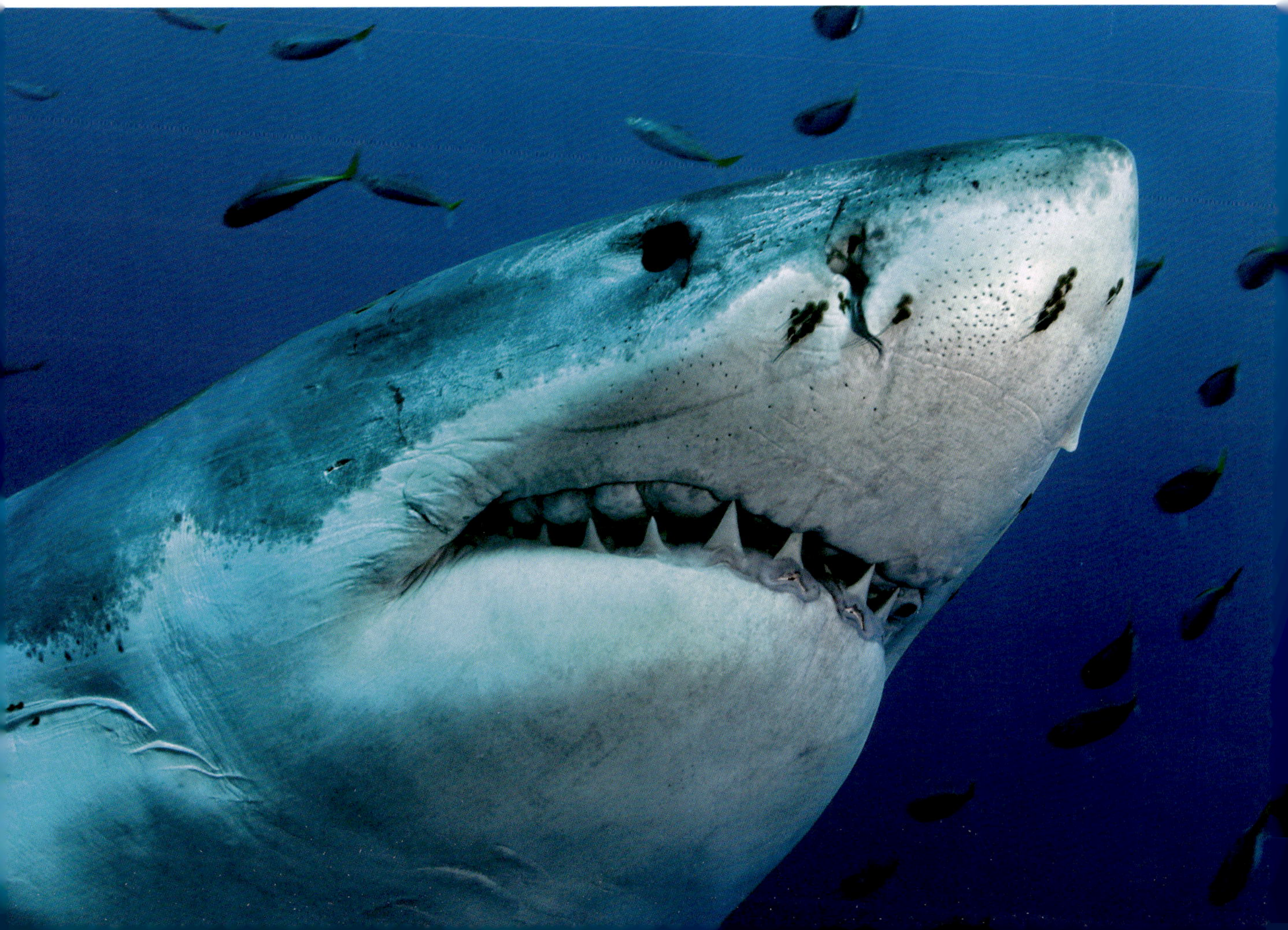

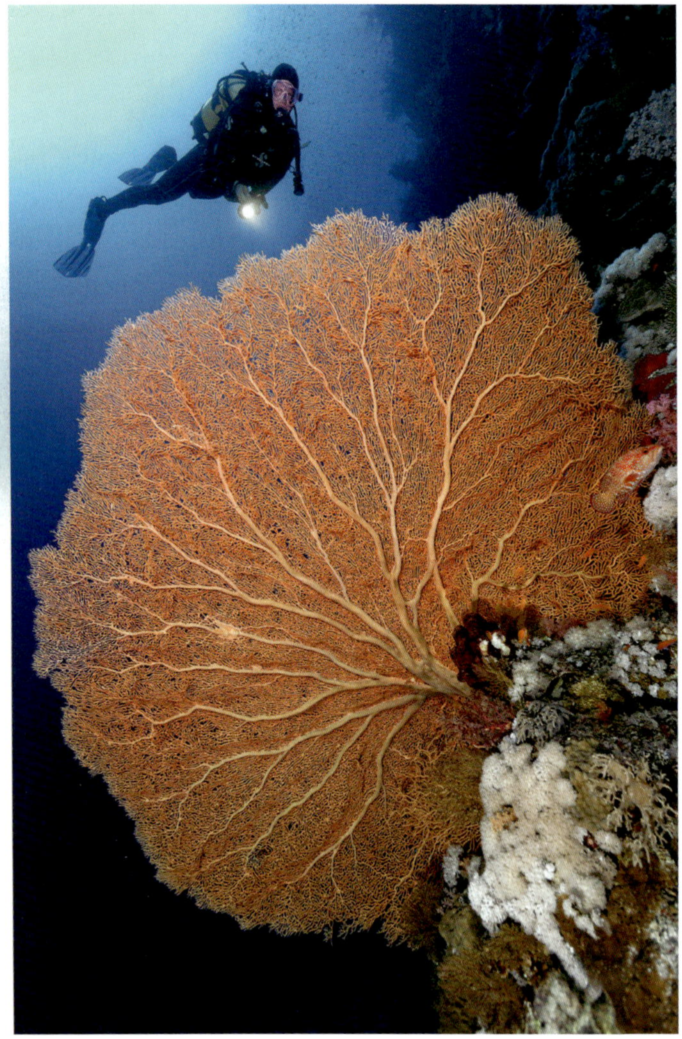

The lighting challenges under water make RAW format preferable because it gives you the most freedom to correct the exposure later.

If you're not sure which format to use, see if your camera allows you to save both JPEG and RAW files simultaneously. Obviously, this uses even more space on your memory card, but it allows you to wait until later to decide which file to use.

The decision of whether to use a RAW file or a JPEG file depends largely on the level of quality you want for your images and to what degree you want to engage with the image editing process. On one hand, RAW files always have superior quality—they are the only choice for professional photographers. On the other hand, if you need or want a picture quickly and maximum quality isn't necessarily a concern, then JPEGs may be the way to go.

Whatever file format you end up using, you'll want to choose Adobe RGB as your color profile because this color space reproduces the most colors. The advantages of Adobe RGB are most apparent in the exquisite color transitions and blues found in the submarine world. Though the color profile can be changed in a RAW converter, it's recommended to have it set to Adobe RGB, just in case you'll switch the camera setup to JPEG and forget to change the profile as well.

A diver in the image serves as a point of reference for viewers to determine the size of the coral

Canon EOS 5D Mark II • Canon 17–40mm wide-angle lens • 1/100 s • f/8 • ISO 200

SUMMARY:

- JPEGs take up less space, but they are lower quality.
- RAW files require more space, but they offer the best quality.
- RAW images tend to look dull at first because they need to be developed in post-processing.
- Camera settings that apply effects to an image are visible in JPEG files; they do not affect RAW files.
- In some cameras, images can be saved as both RAW files and JPEG files simultaneously.
- RAW files require post-processing; JPEGs are finished right out of the camera.
- Use the Adobe RGB color space for all exposures.

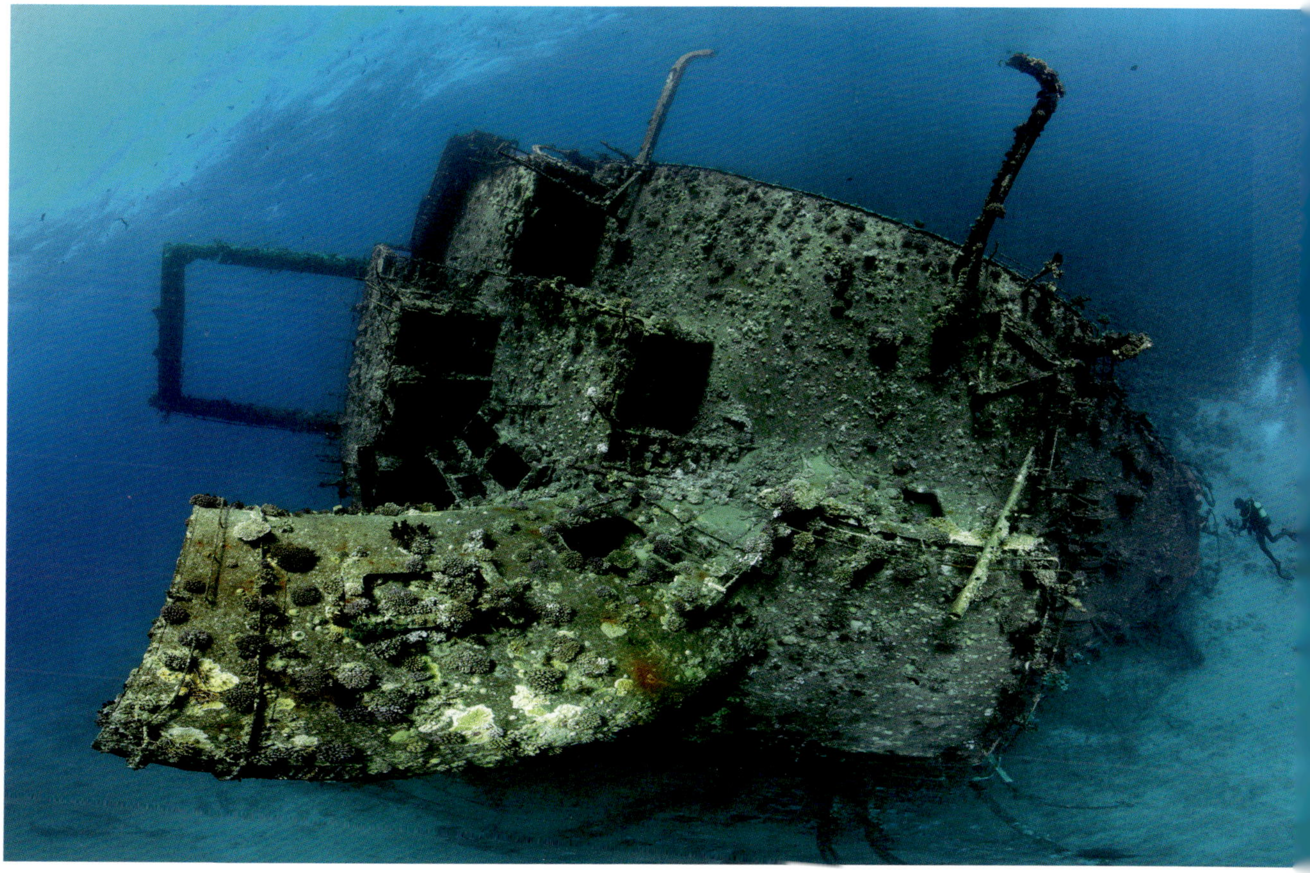

A panoramic shot of the Giannis D shipwreck in Egypt, taken with a red filter

Canon EOS 5D Mark II • Canon 8–15mm fisheye lens • 1/125 s • f/8 • ISO 400

2.5 White Balance

A good white balance reading is essential for accurate colors. It is given as a color temperature, which is measured on the Kelvin (K) scale. An inaccurate white balance reading can result in images that look too cold (blue) or too warm (red or sometimes green). When you choose the automatic white balance (AWB) option, the camera attempts to gauge the color temperature on its own.

Most DSLRs feature various preset white balance options that correspond to specific shooting circumstances. These presets help you choose an accurate color temperature in certain circumstances, such as when you shoot under florescent lights.

Unfortunately, there is no preset white balance option for shooting under water, which leaves you with three choices: using AWB, setting your camera to a specific color temperature, or taking a white balance reading.

To take a white balance reading, you need either a white or a neutral light gray surface so your camera can measure the temperature of the ambient light in the scene. You can use a white or gray card, the back of your hand, a compressed air cylinder, or a light spot of sand. Check your camera user's manual for how to manually set the white balance; the process varies from model to model. You need to take a new reading every time you dive to a new depth because moving up or down will result in a change of the ambient color temperature. Any artificial strobes or lamps that you'll use for your shot should be turned off; if they fire, the light they emit will interfere with the white balance reading. Manually setting the white balance can be time consuming, ideally done while shooting a stationary object, like a shipwreck.

Setting a specific color temperature is practical in situations that aren't predictable and for quickly moving subjects. It's often useful to choose a color temperature of 5200 K when you shoot with strobes that produce warm light at 4800 K. This combination results in a warm foreground and allows the water in the background to retain an attractive blue hue. The best way to figure out the ideal temperature for your particular camera–flash combination is to conduct a bracketing test at every multiple of 100 between 4500 and 5500 K. Then examine the results and decide which setting looks best.

If you shoot in RAW format, both the white balance and the color temperature can be adjusted later in an image-editing program. But it should be every photographer's goal to capture a picture as ideally as possible in-camera to minimize the number of corrections that will be required later.

SUMMARY:

- White balance determines how colors are reproduced in a picture.
- An inaccurate white balance can result in a blue, red, or green cast.
- The camera attempts to determine the white balance automatically when you use AWB.
- AWB presets don't usually produce good results when you shoot under water.
- Setting the white balance manually requires a white or light gray surface.
- After you manually set the white balance, keep your diving depth constant.
- Entering a specific color temperature can result in good color reproduction.
- You can adjust the color temperature of a RAW file retroactively during post-processing.

2.6 Flash Techniques

Using artificial light while diving is the only way to capture the brilliant colors that can be found in the natural world beneath the sea. A garden of coral shot at a depth of 80 ft without a flash will appear lifeless and blue, but if you take the same photo with flash, the coral will shine in all its colorful glory.

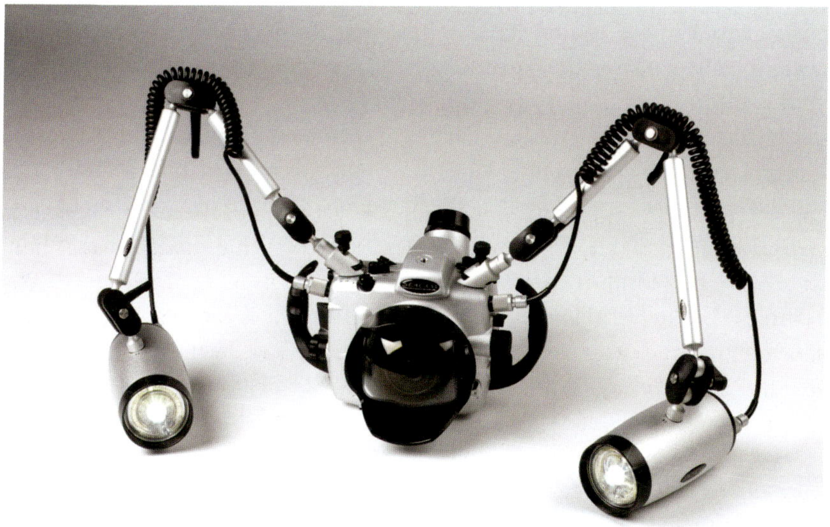

A complete underwater setup ready for a dive (Photo courtesy of SEACAM)

Most underwater photographers wonder if they need one flash unit or two. There is no definitive answer. Almost every picture can be taken with different lighting setups that involve one or several flash units. One exception is when a shot with a fisheye lens requires illumination for a very broad angle of view, such as in a cave or inside a shipwreck. In a situation like this, you'll need two flash units because one is not sufficient to illuminate the entire area.

There is no right or wrong way to use flash, just optimal and less optimal strategies, depending on the situation. For example, compare two shots of a fish: one with two flash units positioned on either side of the camera, and one with a single flash unit above the camera. Both approaches can be successful, but they produce different results in terms of how the light and shadows look.

There are a few basic flash techniques you can use regardless of the subject. For a quick solution, you can position one strobe above the camera, which will result in homogenous lighting with distinct shadows. The light

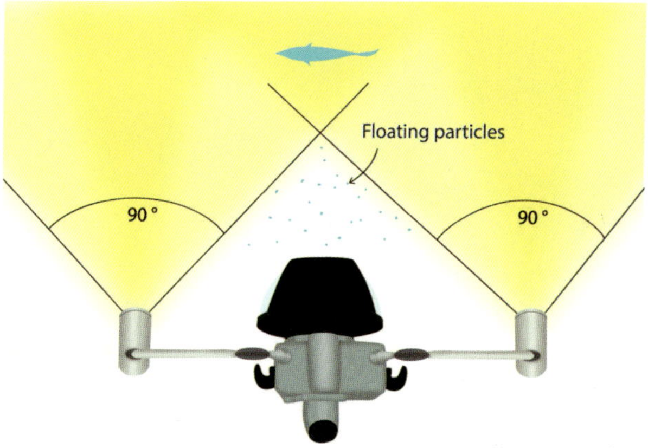

Using effective lighting techniques can help you avoid illuminating the floating particles directly in front of your camera

source needs to be positioned very precisely, though, because if it's misdirected at all, the subject may not be sufficiently lit.

Using two flash units makes it easier to get the proper exposure and gives you more flexibility when you compose your picture. The light is emitted evenly along a lateral, horizontal axis in front of you. The drawback is that two flash units require more time and attention to set up.

If a flash unit is positioned too close to a subject, it's easy to end up with parts of your image having stark contrast, excessive brightness, and possible overexposure. To avoid this, keep some distance between your light source and your subject.

Artificial light from a flash unit looks best when it is softened a little before it reaches the subject; soft light looks more natural than harsh, direct light. You can use a diffuser to achieve this effect, but you'll lose about one stop of light from your flash. Nevertheless, in most cases diffusers are still the best way to prevent unattractive, harsh lighting.

You can read more about specific flash techniques in chapters 4 and 5.

Discovering unusual situations is a matter of luck—they should be met with a quick hand and a level head

Canon EOS 5D Mark II • Canon 8–15mm fisheye lens • 1/60 s • f/8 • ISO 800

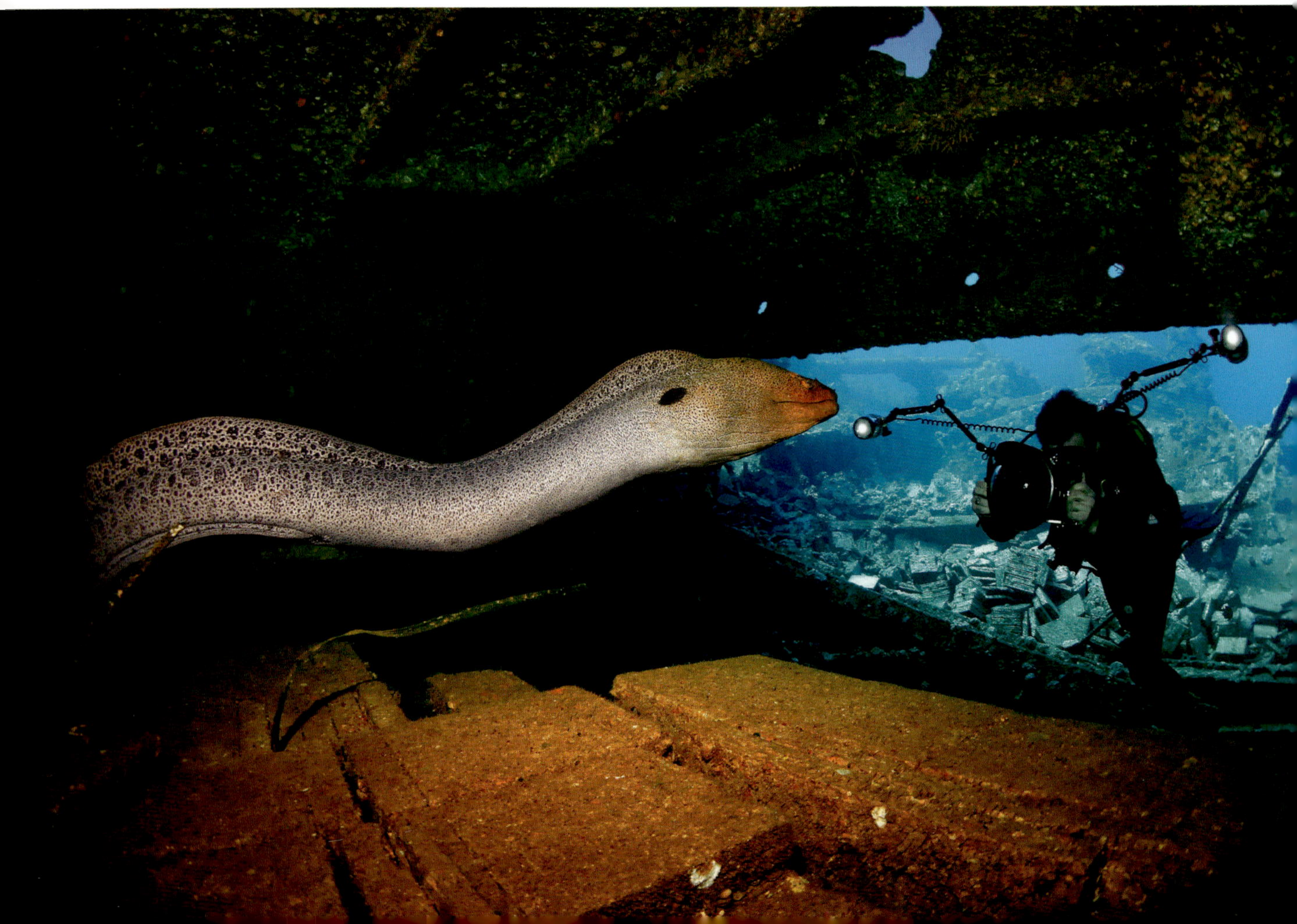

SUMMARY:

- Flash light brings underwater colors to life.
- The exact positioning of your flash units will have a significant impact on the look of your image.
- It's easy to use only one flash unit, but it requires very precise positioning.
- It takes longer to set up two flash units, but it's easier to illuminate a subject.
- The farther away your flash units are from your subject, the softer the light will look and the less likely you will end up with overexposed areas and harsh contrasts.
- Using a diffuser softens the light from a flash unit, but it reduces the light intensity by about one stop.

2.7 TTL or Manual

You can control how much light a flash unit emits in one of two ways: manually program the flash, or let your camera automatically control it with TTL technology.

When you use TTL metering to control the flash output, the camera discharges a preflash immediately before it takes a picture. The preflash pulse is not perceptible to the human eye. From the preflash, the camera evaluates how much light—both intensity and duration—the flash unit needs to emit. TTL metering is highly reliable for macro images, but keep an eye on it when you shoot wide-angle images because the ambient darkness under water often distorts the metering process and results in too much artificial light.

If you want to play it safe, control your flash output manually. Underwater strobes usually give you very precise control of power output, often in full-, half-, quarter-, and eighth-stop increments.

The more often you meter manually, the better you will understand it, and you'll get a good sense for how much light is needed to illuminate certain subjects in specific circumstances. It's always useful to do an exposure bracketing test with a simple subject. Keep all your camera settings constant and alter only the intensity of the flash output, then compare the resulting images.

Manually controlling your flash output takes a bit of time because you need to reevaluate your lighting for every situation. When you are shooting in conditions that require constant adjustments to the flash settings, TTL metering is often the way to go.

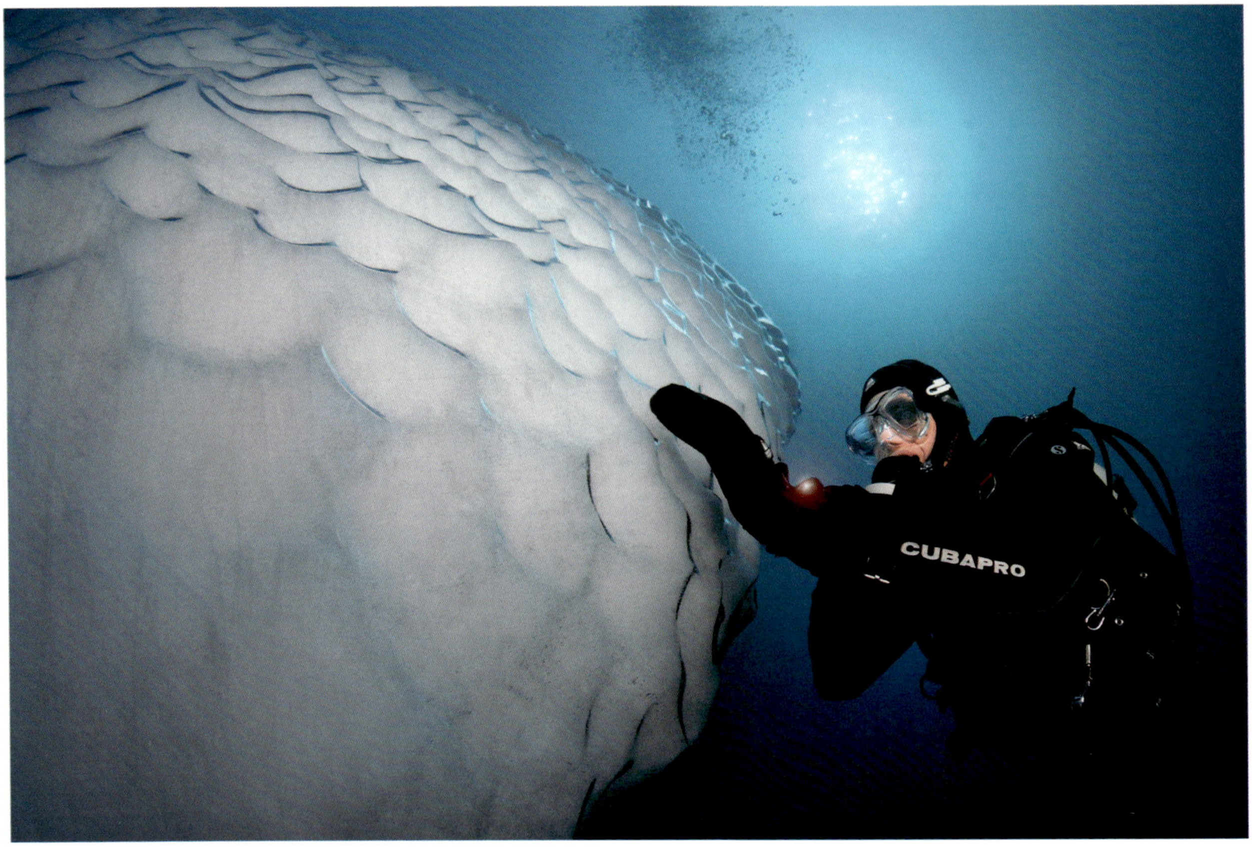

Including a diver endows a picture with an additional dimension because they portray an interaction between a person and his or her surroundings

Canon EOS 5D Mark II • Canon 8–15mm fisheye lens • 1/200 s • f/9 • ISO 100

Murky waters pose challenges to TTL metering—the lighting is often too intense. It's usually better to use manual metering in these situations.

Flash systems that are produced by camera manufacturers offer a proprietary TTL technology. Nikon calls its metering system i-TTL and Canon calls its system E-TTL. These metering systems produce exceptionally reliable results. But when it comes to underwater photography, such flash systems are not ideal because the maximum width of the beam is not very wide. For macro photography, though, they still have their right for existence.

Therefore, third-party flash units are the best choice when you shoot under water. And since flash units need to be compatible with different camera brands, a TTL converter is needed to communicate the signal from the camera to the flash unit. The converter can be located in the underwater housing, in the flash itself or as an adapter on the flash cable.

If you plan to use TTL metering, discuss equipment compatibility with a retailer before you purchase any flash units.

SUMMARY:

- You can control flash output manually or with automatic TTL technology.
- When you use TTL metering, the camera emits a preflash that it uses to analyze how much light the flash unit should emit.
- TTL metering generally produces good results for macro photography, but it's less successful for wide-angle shots.
- When you manually control your flash units, you can be very precise by using incremental output settings.
- Manual metering takes more time than TTL metering.
- It's often best to use TTL metering in situations with quickly changing lighting conditions.
- When visibility isn't great, skip TTL metering and control your flash units manually.
- TTL signals are transmitted between the camera and the flash unit by a converter, which can be located in the flash unit, in the underwater housing, or on the flash unit cable.

2.8 Histogram

A histogram is a graph that displays the distribution of tonal values for an image. After you take a picture, you can examine its histogram on your camera or on a computer. Additionally, while viewing the histogram, you can switch on the overexposure warning on your camera and it will show you which parts of the image are overexposed.

You can get a quick sense of whether a photograph is correctly exposed by looking at its histogram. If the tonal values in a histogram are mostly gathered on the left side of the graph, the photo has lots of dark areas and, in a purely technical sense, it is underexposed. If the tonal values are mostly gathered on the right side of the graph, the photo may be overexposed. Ideally, the distribution of values should look like a mountain on the histogram, with most values falling near the middle. Such a histogram indicates that a photo is properly exposed—again, in a purely technical sense.

If you are using exposure to create effects, you might intentionally overexpose or underexpose all or portions of an

Histogram examples

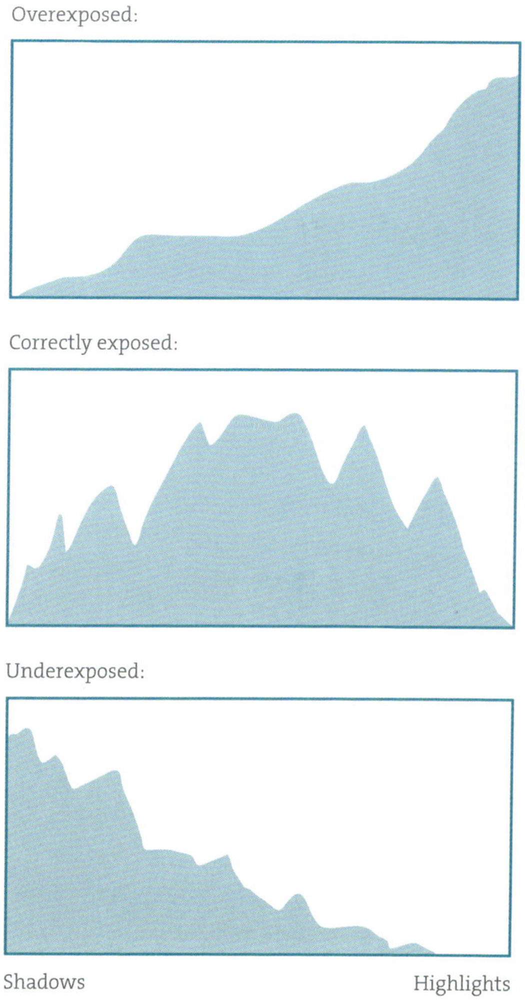

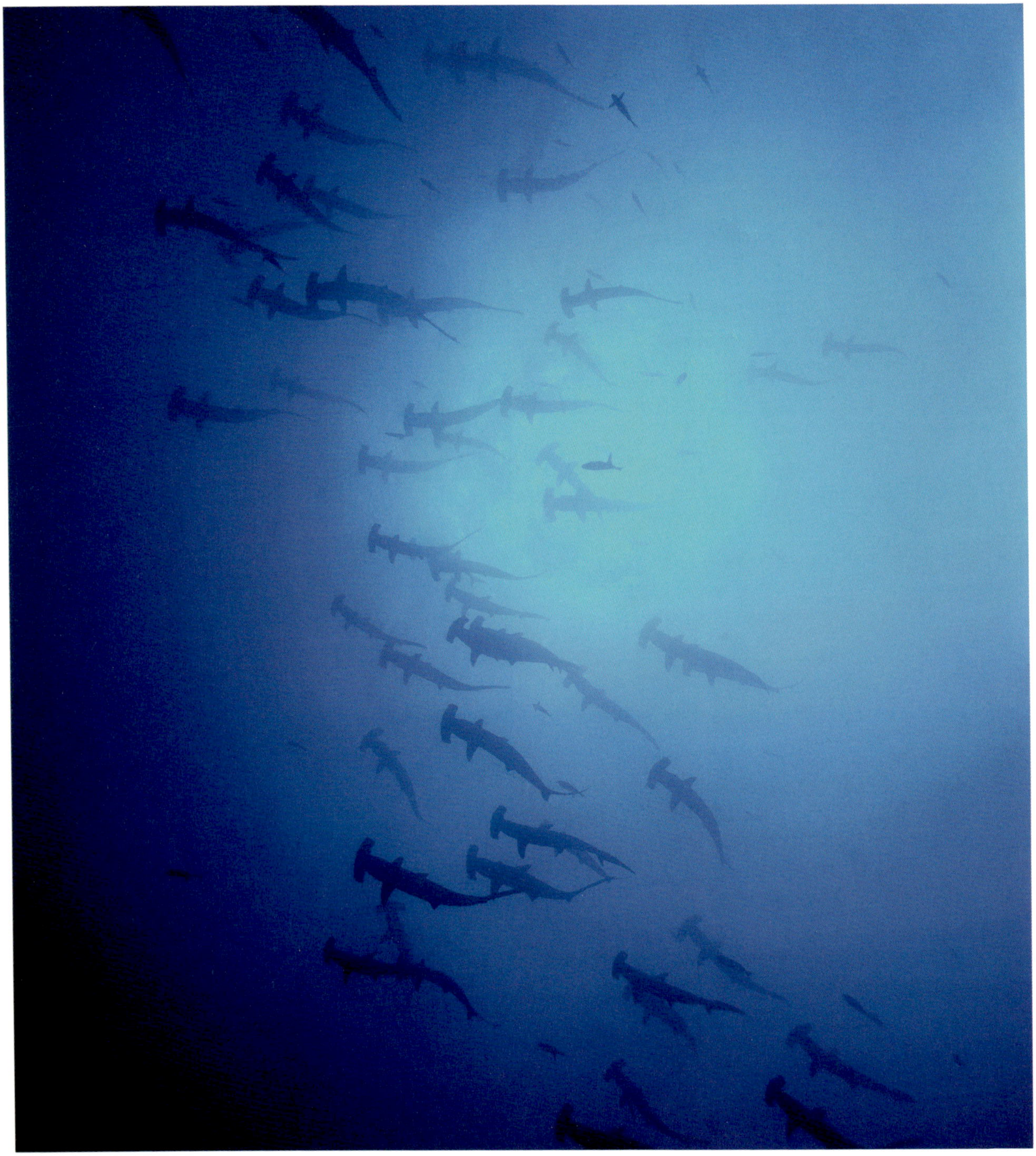

In a correctly exposed image there are no areas that are too bright or too dark

Canon EOS 5D Mark II • Canon 17–40mm wide-angle lens • 1/3200 s • f/4 • ISO 200

image. Photos like this are often referred to as *high key* or *low key*. The histogram is not useful in cases like this because it won't help you produce the exposure you want.

The histogram is particularly useful to underwater photographers. It can be one more way of gathering information about the exposure, which is helpful because underwater reflections often make it difficult to get a clear look at the LCD monitor on your camera. You probably don't want to inspect the histogram for every shot, but it's helpful to examine it when you test your exposure settings.

Over time you'll develop a sense for what a good histogram looks like, and you'll figure out how to use the information in the graph to alter your shots. But always remember that the histogram doesn't say anything about whether your photo is good or bad—it's a purely technical analysis of visual data.

SUMMARY:

- A histogram is a graph that displays the tonal values of a photo. You can use it to see if a picture is overexposed or underexposed.
- Dark values are displayed at the left of the graph; bright values are at the right.
- A picture that's properly exposed, in a technical sense, will have more tonal values in the middle of the histogram.
- Low-key and high-key images are exceptions to the previous statement.
- Always use the histogram as a control mechanism when you shoot under water.
- The histogram does not convey information about whether an image is good or bad.

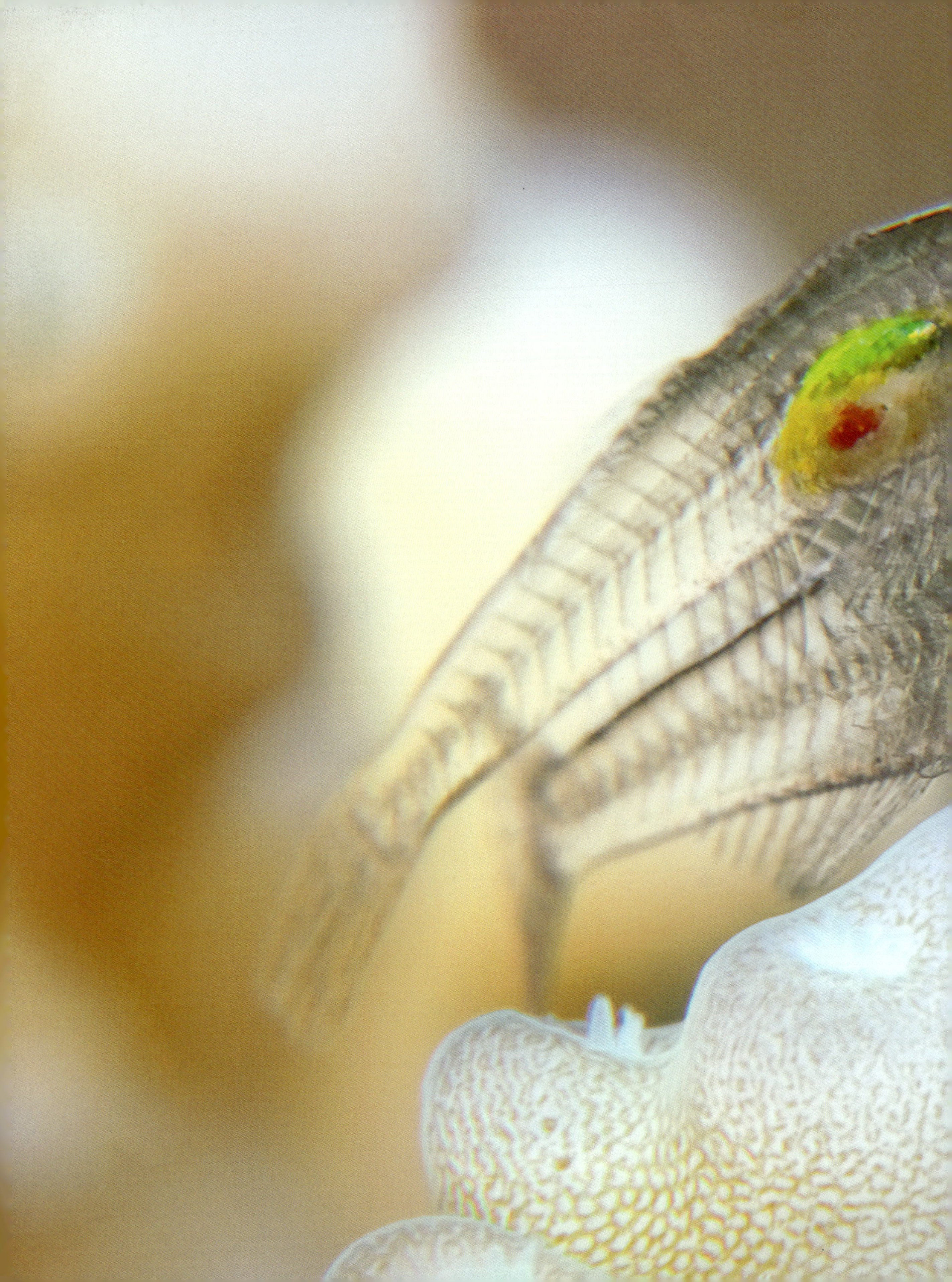

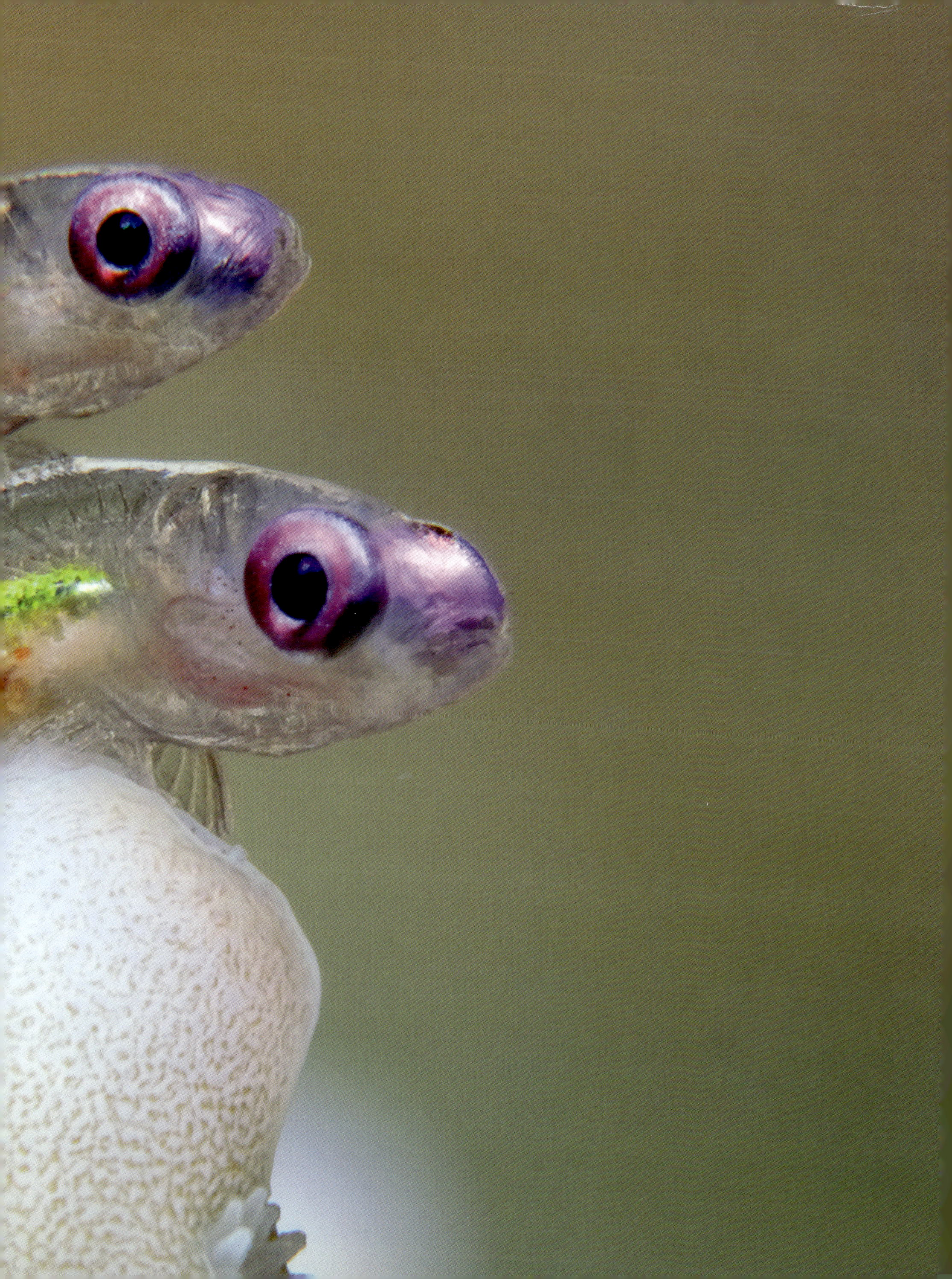

Case Study 3: Tea for Two

Canon EOS 5D Mark II • Canon 100mm macro lens • two Ikelite DS-125 strobes • Inon UCL-165 close-up lens • 1/125 s • f/22 • ISO 200 • flash: manual at half power

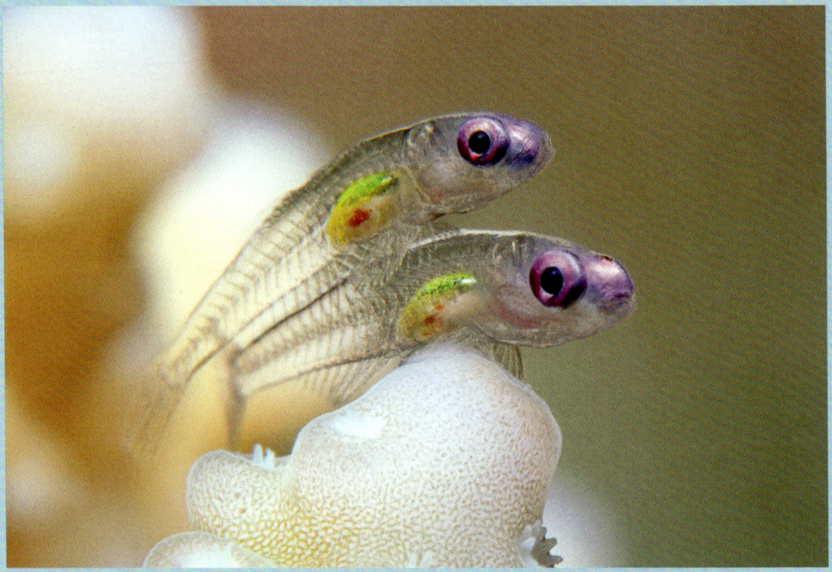

It isn't always about finding the most exotic dive spots in the world. You can get great photos on dives close to where you live—you just need a little extra patience.

On this particular dive, I couldn't find a more interesting subject, so I was trying to photograph a homely goby perched on a piece of hard coral. A second fish swam up and rested on the first fish. I wanted to make the most of the situation, so I quickly shot a few pictures before the gobies scurried off a few seconds later.

My goal for the exposure was to capture as much of the animals in focus as possible, which is why they are positioned sideways in front of the camera. If I had been looking at them head on, I wouldn't have been able to get their bodies in focus—only their heads and eyes would have been sharp. Because their transparent bodies are so distinctive, I chose to feature them in the photo.

The background is blurry, which directs the viewer's attention to the main subject. I also chose to position the fish in the center of the image area.

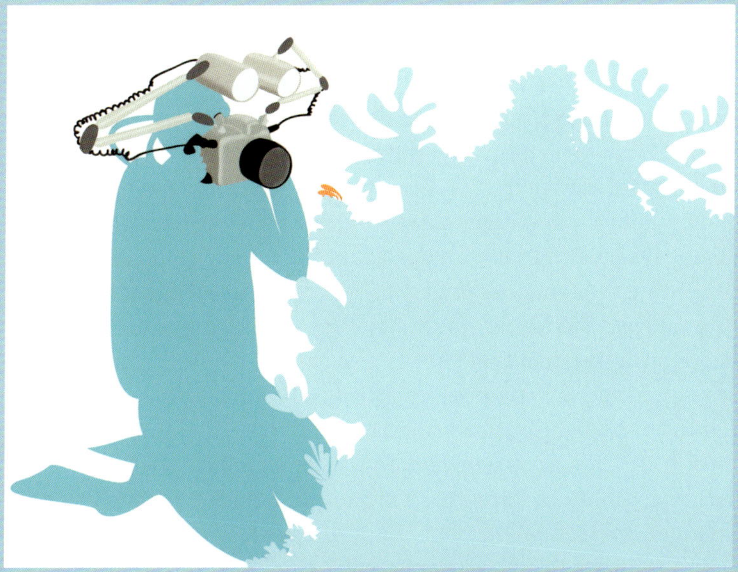

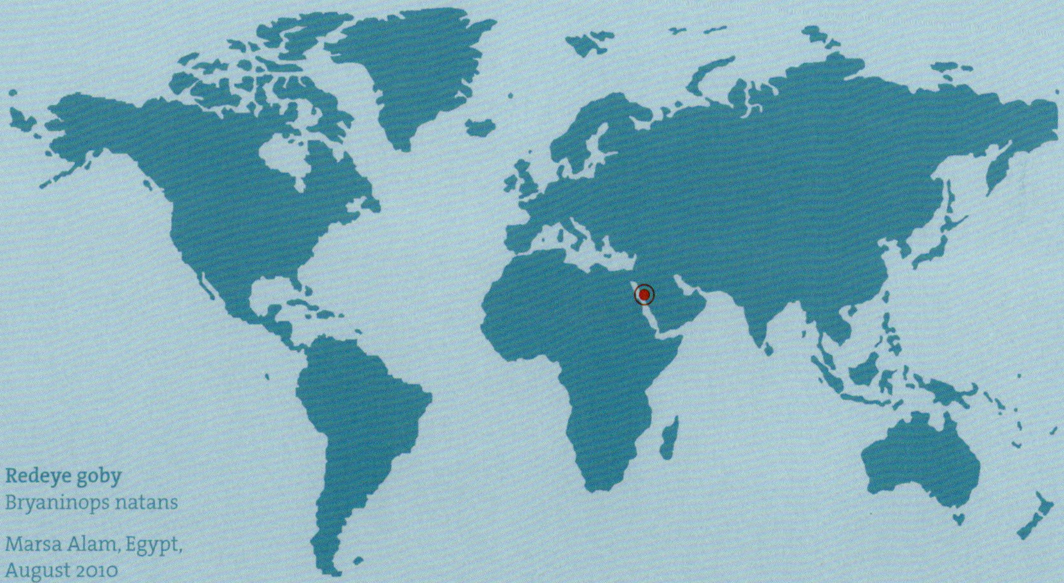

Redeye goby
Bryaninops natans

Marsa Alam, Egypt,
August 2010

3

Composition

After you've made your first foray into the world of underwater photography and you've figured out how to successfully expose your pictures, it's time to take the next step: create attractive compositions for your images. A truly successful picture requires much more than a proper exposure. Photos that have been skillfully composed will wake the emotions of viewers and convey a certain tone. What's the best way to compose pictures? It depends on the viewer—beauty is always in the eye of the beholder. Even jurists who pick winners in photography competitions disagree about which entrant should win. There will always be different opinions about the best way to compose images, but there are fundamental principles that most people agree contribute to attractive images. There is no way to measure how aesthetically pleasing a picture is, but certain elements of style appeal to most viewers.

Composing good aquatic photos is especially difficult because so many factors influence your work. Your buoyancy, the position of the subject, bubbles from your own breathing, your surroundings, and the subject itself simultaneously affect your ability to compose an attractive shot. Not only do you have to coordinate all these elements, but you also have to adjust your camera's settings and attempt to take the best picture possible.

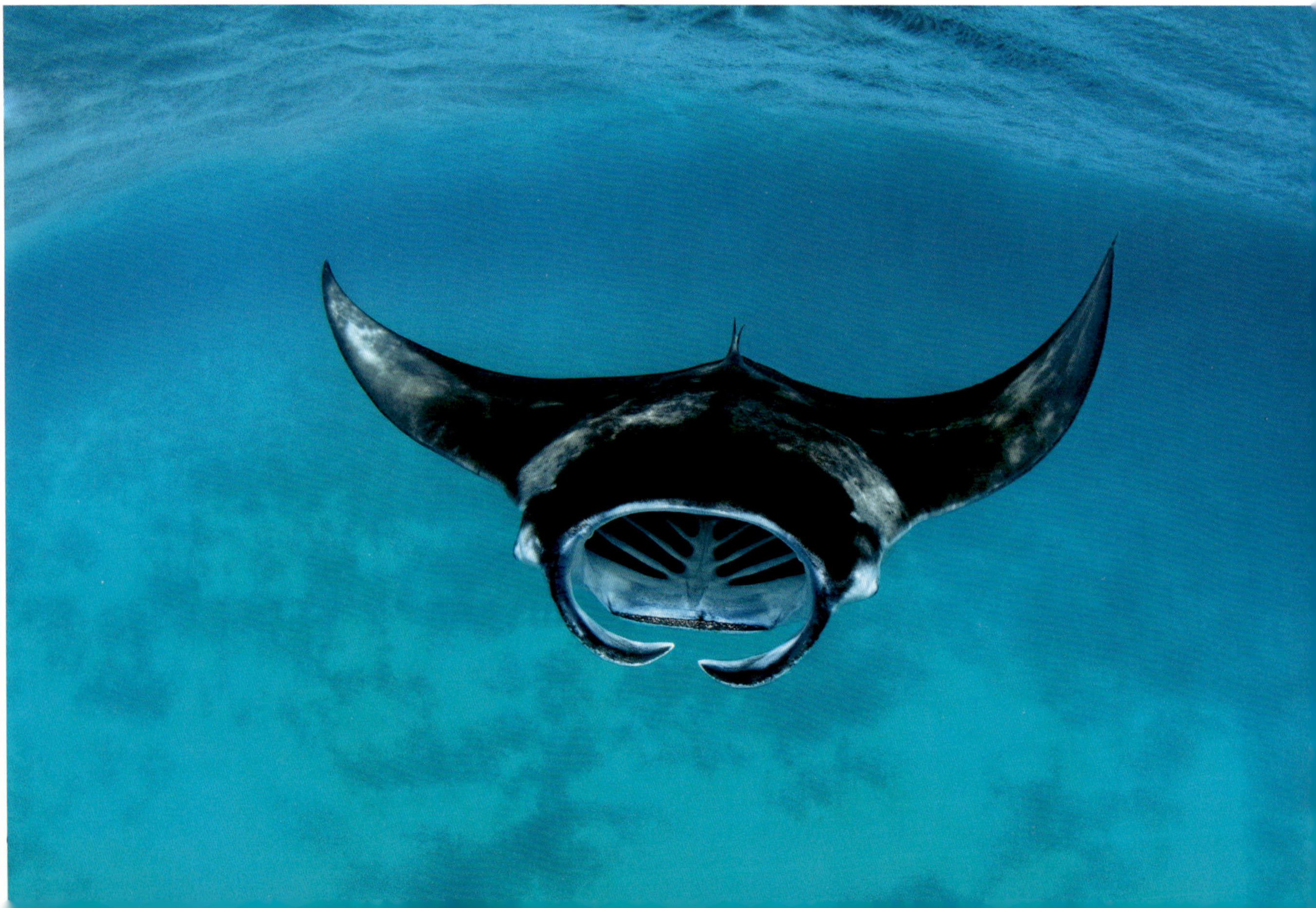

A simple composition, without distracting elements in the background, is generally a good recipe for a successful picture. Less is more.

Canon EOS 5D Mark II • Canon 8–15mm fisheye lens • 1/125 s • f/9 • ISO 50

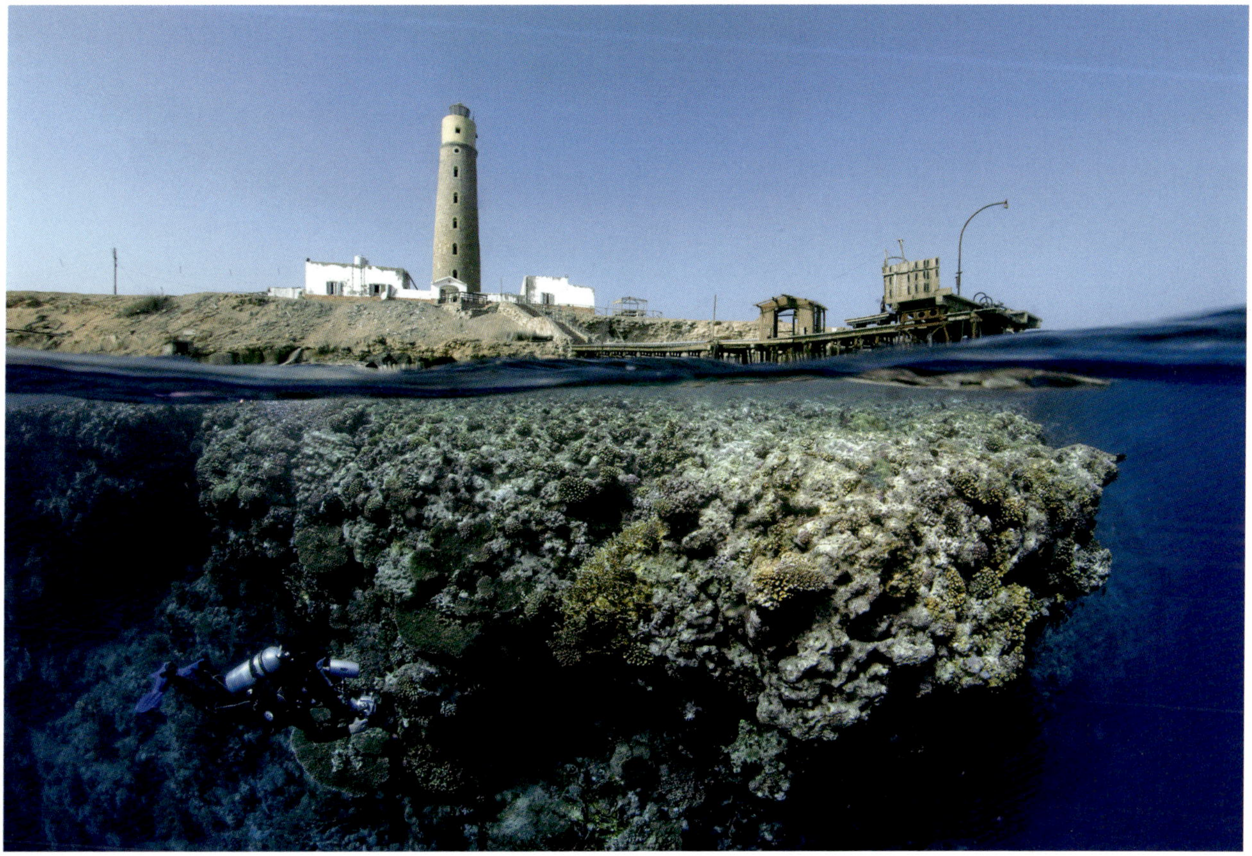

The best way to hone your composition skills is to test and practice your technique on easy dives, perhaps in nearby reefs or areas you know well. Trying to focus on composition while you're on a dive with a strong current is much more challenging—you'll learn more if you can concentrate on the design elements of your underwater images.

When you're getting started, find a simple subject and pay close attention to the elements in the foreground and background of your image. A picture of a nudibranch won't work well if the animal's backdrop is a bare, uninteresting section of reef. But if you can find a different perspective or use a different flash technique to isolate the nudibranch against a vivid blue background, then you're on to something.

What do the photos in your image library tend to look like? When you browse through your collection, do you find mostly blue backgrounds or poorly defined brown backgrounds? The answer will tell you a lot about whether you search for optimal backgrounds or if you have room for improvement. The background of a photo has a considerable influence on its overall effect.

It's also important to consider the proportions of the main subject in relation to the rest of the image. It's usually not a good sign if a viewer needs to search for your subject because the background is too busy or the subject itself is inconspicuous. Try to fill up the image area with the subject.

When shooting split waterline images, it's important to have interesting subjects both above and below the waterline

Canon EOS 5D Mark II • Canon 8–15mm fisheye lens • 1/200 s • f/22 • ISO 800

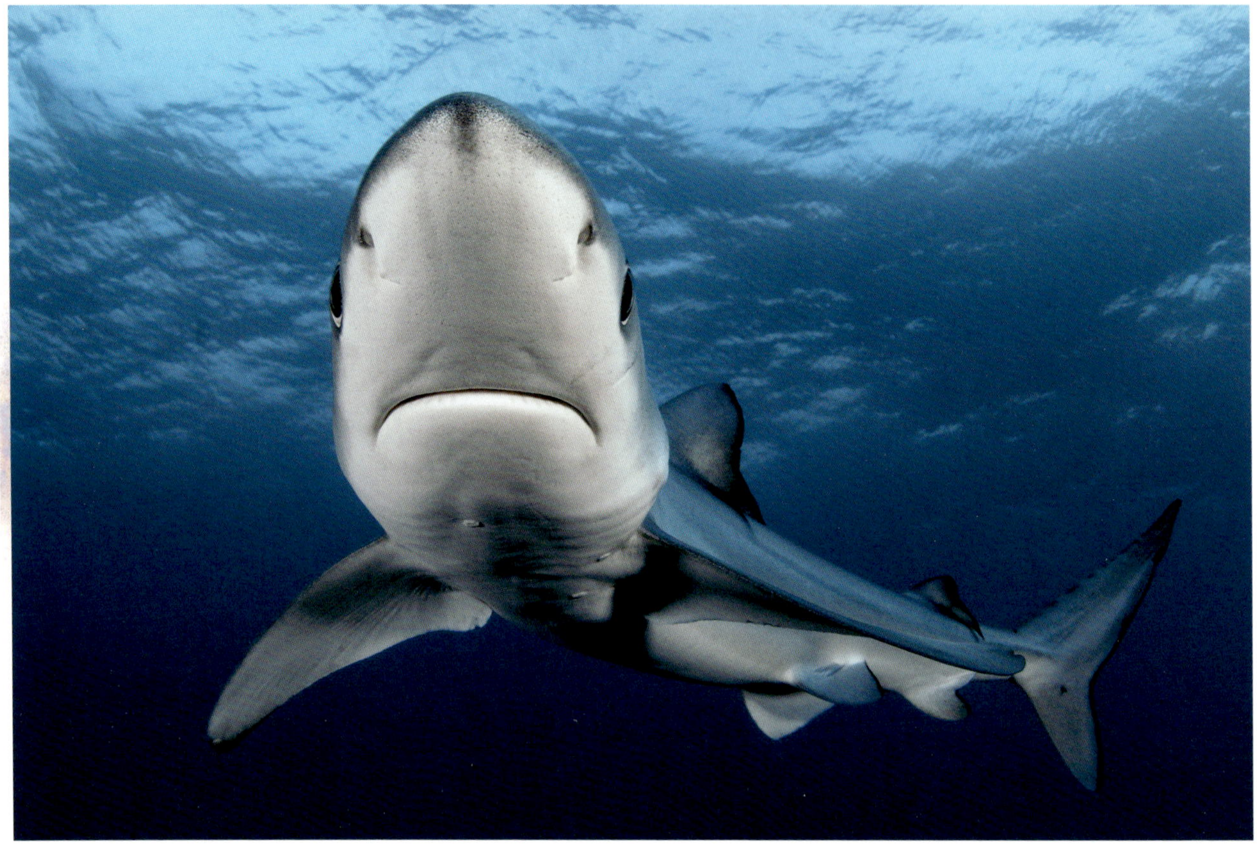

Placing the most important elements of an image in the golden ratio gives them even greater emphasis

Canon EOS 5D Mark II • Canon 8–15mm fisheye lens • 1/320 s • f/10 • ISO 400

If the subject is a relatively small element within a larger picture, it's important to guide the viewer's attention to it. There are various compositional ways of doing this, such as using the golden ratio or eliminating other elements from around the subject to eliminate distractions. You might want to create an image that works because of its simple elegance—less is more.

Check your composition by asking yourself some questions before you press the shutter release button: Do I really want to take this picture? What might bother the viewer? Are any elements in the picture distracting? If I'm photographing a fish, are its fins positioned in a pleasing way? Is it looking in the right direction? Determined photographers can always find a way to make a picture better.

Another thing to consider is where you want the edges of your picture to fall with respect to the subject. Pictures of sharks tend to work well when they take up the majority of the image area and all the animal's fins are within the frame. Accidentally lopping off an element can be distracting to viewers. Be aware of where the edges of your image are and work purposefully.

It's generally a good idea to leave a little space in front of an animal's head or nose, toward the direction of its movement. The extra space makes the animal look less constrained; if its head is too close to the edge of the image, it can seem imprisoned.

Showing animals in their natural surroundings is always a good idea—a clown fish in its anemone, a shark adrift in a sea of blue, or sardines in a school.

When animals are shown in their usual habitat you can be more deliberate when you compose your photo.

Another consideration is whether to shoot in portrait or landscape format, which is often dictated by the subject. If you're trying to depict the full length of a barracuda, landscape format is probably the right choice. If you're shooting a gorgonian on a steep face with the sun in the background, portrait format may be a better option.

Consider all these points, and those that follow, to improve your composition skills. But remember, they are not steadfast rules. The only thing that matters is if a picture pleases you and your viewers. Any rule can be broken as long as it serves this end.

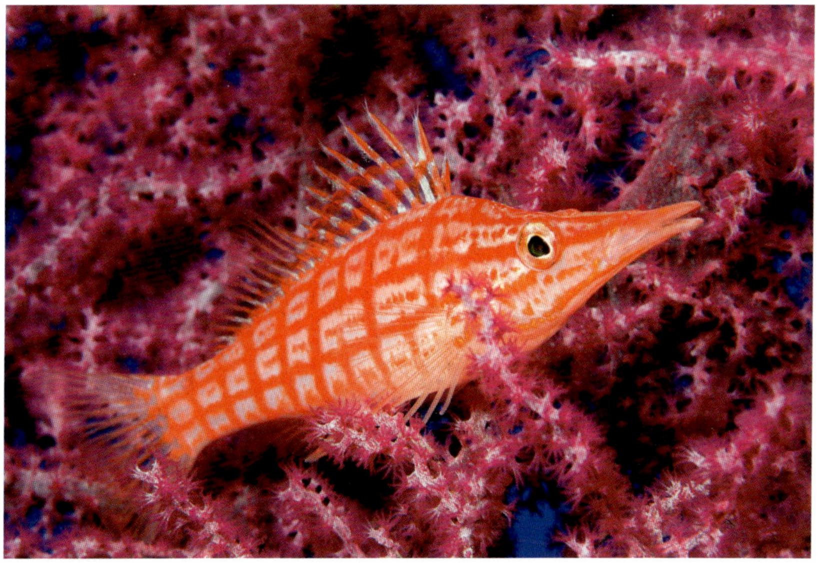

Photographing the side of this fish straight on allowed me to show its entire body in sharp focus

Canon EOS 5D Mark II • Canon 100mm macro lens • 1/30 s • f/16 • ISO 400

3.1 Perspective

Finding the best perspective is integral to a quality photo. Shifting your position or the position of your camera can make the difference between a decent picture and an excellent one—compare a subject surrounded by rich blue water and the same subject surrounded by an unsightly background. Being able to evaluate different perspectives under water is critical.

Stationary subjects, such as a piece of coral, are perfect for practicing perspective. Shoot the coral from all sides and compare the results later on your computer to decide which perspective works best. The more you practice this exercise, the better you will get at sensing which perspectives work.

Taking a picture while looking down on the subject is generally not desirable. It's nearly impossible to end up with anything other than a drab and lifeless background. In contrast, an eye-level perspective or one that looks slightly upward from just below the subject is ideal for many photos. This perspective makes it easy to isolate your subject in front of a blue background, which produces an elegant and beautiful juxtaposition.

Macro photos pose unique challenges for photographers in search of an ideal perspective. You're usually working close to the ground, which means you won't have much space to work with. Angle viewfinders can help solve the problem; they allow you to look through your viewfinder from above so you can work with a bit more distance between you and the ground.

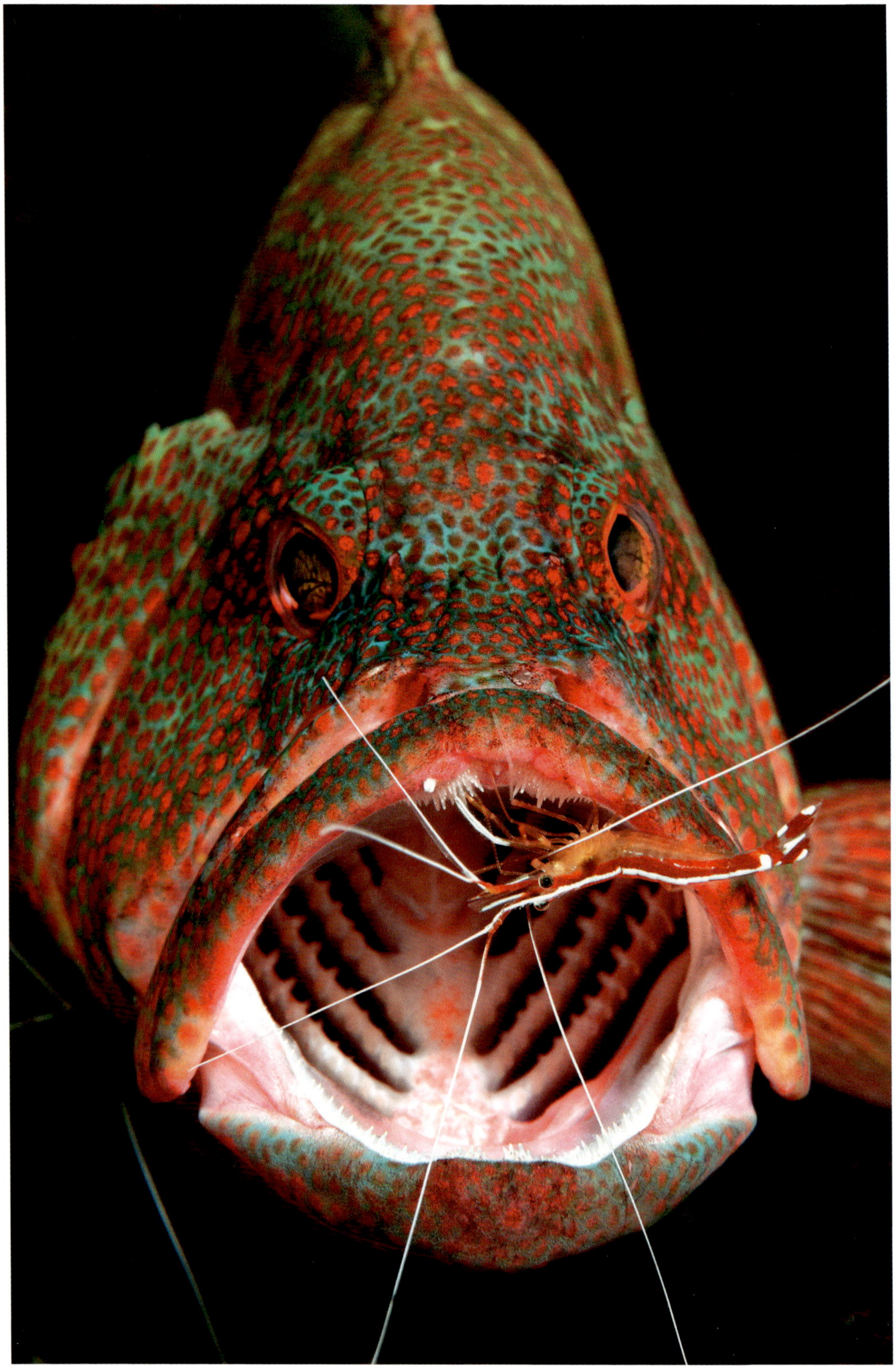

So called *cleaning stations* present great opportunities to capture well-composed photos while cleaner fish perform their service (although patience is required)

Canon EOS 5D Mark II • Canon 100mm macro lens • 1/125 s • f/18 • ISO 400

Head-on pictures of fish are almost always more interesting than those that show a tail fin. The latter inevitably makes it look like the fish is scurrying away, while the former allows the viewer to establish eye contact with the animal and identify it as a fish. This is easier said than done. Anyone who's ever tried to take a photo of a boxfish knows what I'm talking about. These bizarre animals have an uncanny knack for turning away from the camera at exactly the wrong moment. The best way to capture a fish head-on is to be patient and try to anticipate where it will swim next, and then position yourself accordingly. Never force an animal to swim in a particular direction!

SUMMARY:

- Perspective is a vital element of image composition.
- Isolating a subject against a background of blue water is better than depicting it in front of an unattractive backdrop.
- A perspective at eye level or slightly upward from below generally results in appealing photos.
- Shooting from above is generally not advisable because it often results in ineffective and distracting backgrounds.
- Photograph living animals head-on, rather than from behind.

3.2 The Golden Ratio

The golden ratio is a proportional relationship that the human eye finds naturally pleasing.

This ratio is often compared to the rule of thirds, which divides the image area into three equal vertical and three equal horizontal sections. The golden ratio is not located exactly where the grid lines fall, though; the ratio is more like 62 to 38 percent. This puts the golden ratio slightly closer to the center of the image than the rule of thirds. But what matters most is not exactly where to position your visual elements—it's being aware of this proportion and using it when it's most appealing.

The golden ratio is so pleasant to the human eye because it occurs so often in the natural world. Since our infancy we have seen it in leaves, blossoms, and the human body itself. Even Leonardo da Vinci made use of the golden ratio—the proportions in his *Vitruvian Man* are based on this proportional relationship.

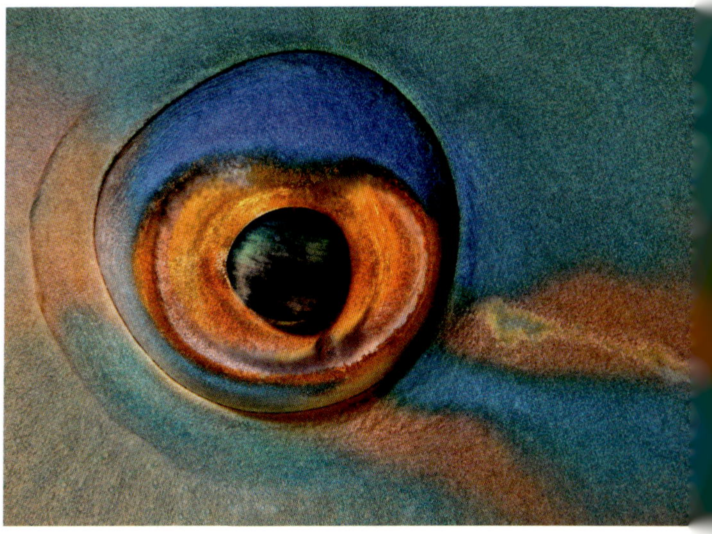

Fish eyes are best photographed using the longest focal length possible and they lend themselves particularly well to being positioned at the golden ratio

Canon EOS 5D Mark II • Canon 100mm macro lens • 1/125 s • f/18 • ISO 400

Placing the eye of a fish in the golden ratio is an effective way to give it more prominence. Positioning a diver or a small animal in front of a calm or monochrome background at this location can also produce attractive images.

The golden ratio is only one of many ways you can compose your images, and not every picture needs to follow it precisely. Combining various elements of design is much more exciting and can produce memorable results.

SUMMARY:

- The golden ratio is a proportion that is pleasant to human perception.
- The rule of thirds and the golden ratio are comparable; both move the subject away from the center of the image area.
- Examples of the golden ratio abound in nature, which is why it's a pleasing design strategy.
- Composing the eye of a fish in the golden ratio is an effective way to give it more emphasis.
- Make your photos more interesting by combining elements of design.

Prevailing lines and diagonals emphasize the photo's overall effect

Canon EOS 5D Mark II • Canon 17–40mm wide-angle lens • 1/60 s • f/8 • ISO 400

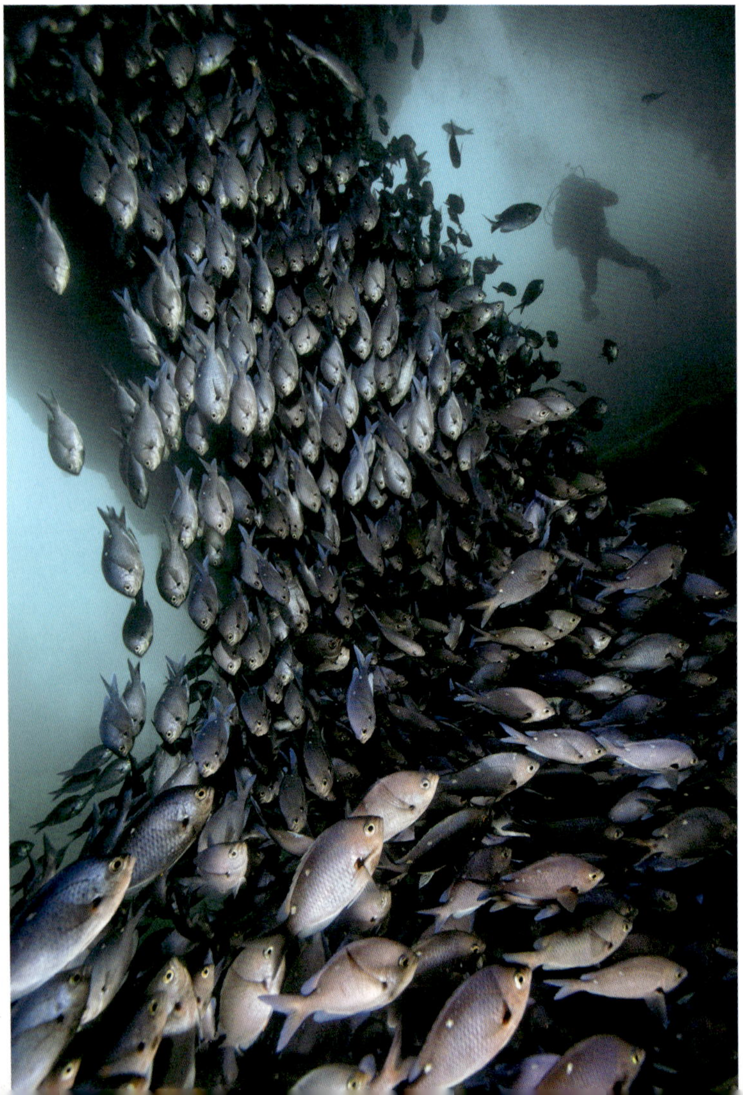

3.3 Lines and Diagonals

The lines in a photo can dramatically influence its overall character. Dominant lines aren't obvious in every picture, but water surfaces and stretches of sand seem very calm when they are horizontally positioned. Slightly uneven lines, by contrast, can have an unsettling effect on the viewer.

Carefully consider the lines in your picture and follow a design principle like the golden ratio. If a line like the edge of a sandy area passes directly through the center of an image, it can seem out of place. Shifting the line so it falls in the golden ratio or adheres to the rule of thirds will usually make a better impression.

When you take a picture with a particularly busy area along the bottom, such as a complex reef, you can introduce calmness by creating a stable line with the surface of water or the top of the reef.

At other times you may want to introduce tension into your picture. One way to do this is by holding your camera at a slight angle to create diagonal lines, which gives a dynamic look to the photo. Diagonal lines can make a scene look more lively and can emphasize the subject. When you include diagonal lines, don't make the slant too subtle or it could look like a mistake. Create a decisive slant of at least 20 or 30 degrees so viewers will know the effect was deliberate.

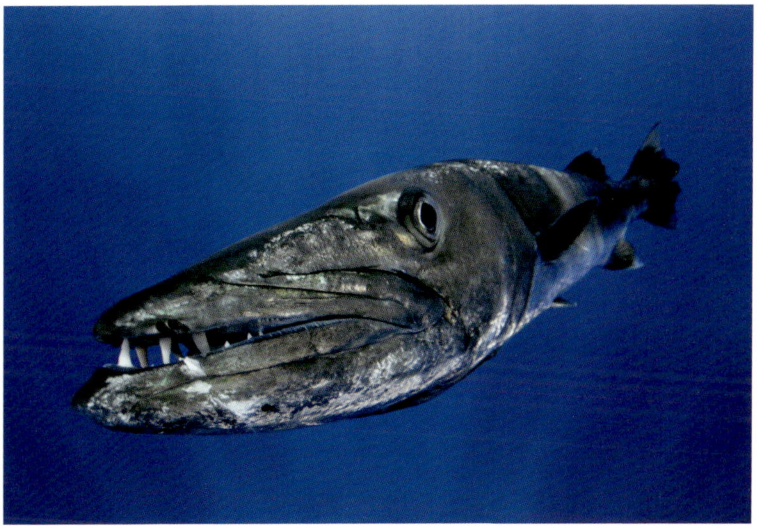

▲ Rather than holding the camera in a conventional horizontal position, an angled shot provides more excitement and adds tension in a picture

Canon EOS 5D Mark II • Tokina 10–17mm fisheye lens • 1/125 s • f/8 • ISO 200

The best way to practice creating diagonal lines is to find a relatively quiet spot with a diving partner. First capture the scene conventionally with level, balanced lines. Then repeat the shot, but tilt your camera to introduce diagonal lines. Which version do you prefer? Should you emphasize the calm aspects of the scene or document the exciting aspects of the dive?

Prominent slanted lines can be a good finishing touch for macro images. Rather than center a blenny within the image area, for example, you might set it diagonally.

▼ The central placement of the subject is further emphasized by prominent vertical and horizontal lines

Canon EOS 5D Mark II • Canon 17–40mm wide-angle lens • 1/200 s • f/10 • ISO 800

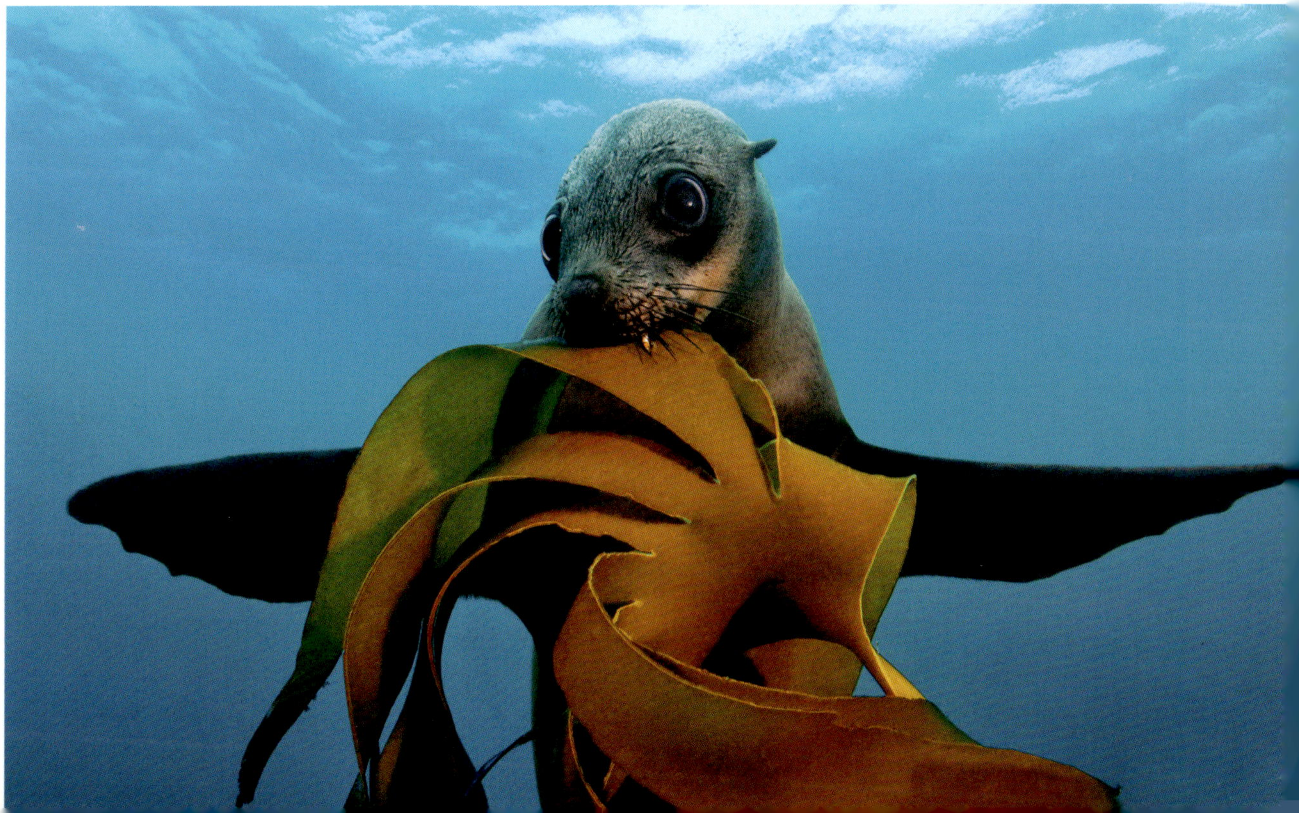

SUMMARY:

- The prevailing lines of an image are a critical element of composition.
- Horizontal lines establish calm and stasis.
- Diagonal lines invite tension and excitement into pictures.
- Positioning vertical or horizontal lines in the golden ratio can be an effective composition technique.
- The angle of slanted lines should be a minimum of 20 or 30 degrees.
- Work with your diving partner to try different ways of creating lines in an image.
- Introduce diagonal lines to put the final touch on an image.

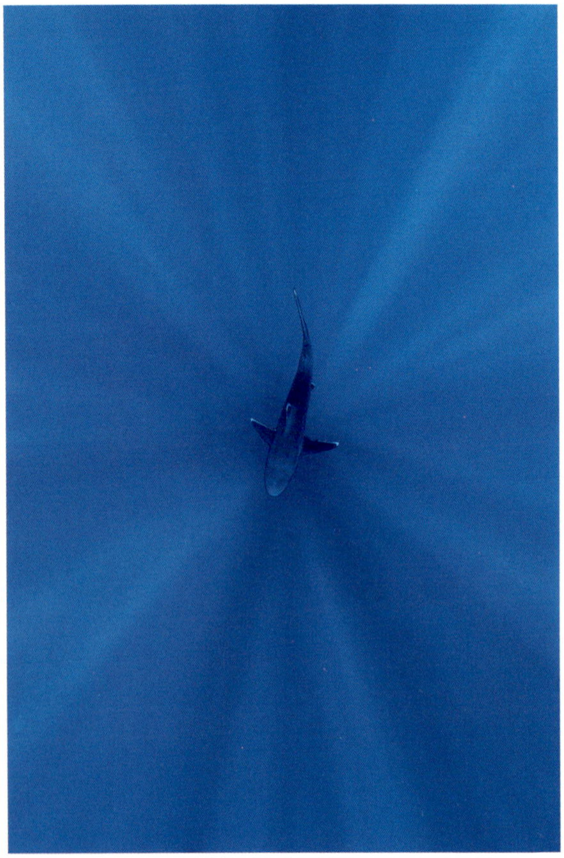

The streaks of sunlight guide the viewer's attention directly to the central subject and there are no secondary objects in the image that distract from its pull

Canon EOS 5D Mark II • Canon 17–40-mm wide-angle lens • 1/80 s • f/8 • ISO 200

3.4 Centering

The easiest way to compose an image is to position the main subject at the center of the image area. This is a tried and true method for beginning nature photographers who want to make sure they capture the subject. When it's used too frequently, however, this composition can hamper your photography.

Since the central autofocus point of your camera is at the center of the image area, photographers have a natural tendency to place the subject in the middle. You can manually change the position of your focus point so you don't allow it to limit your composition.

When you want to stress a particular visual element, positioning that element at the center of the image area is a good choice. Sunset shots above water often feature the sun in the center of the image because it gives the rays of light the most room and creates a pleasant overall effect. If you position a subject at the middle of the image area, be sure it's at the exact center so the effect looks intentional.

Placing key visual elements in the middle of a photo can be effective under the sea. Tube worms and disc anemones, for example, look good when they're placed in the middle of an image because their bodies radiate outward. Closeup pictures of fish eyes are also well suited to a central position.

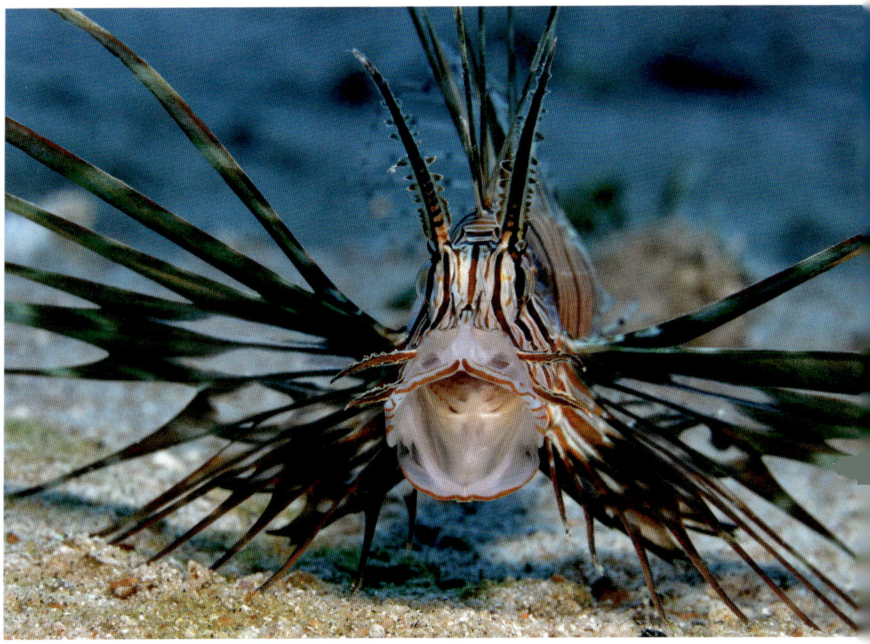

The animal's open mouth intensifies the effect of centrally positioning this lionfish within the image area

Canon EOS 5D Mark II • Canon 100mm macro lens • 1/100 s • f/16 • ISO 200

Compositions with the subject placed in the middle work best when there are no distracting secondary elements in the space around the middle of the image. Other objects can be unsettling, and zeroing in on one specific subject generally has the best payoff.

One particular situation that works well for this type of image design is frontal portraits of fish such as morays or blennies. You can take successful and memorable photos of these animals when they take up the majority of the image area and are centrally positioned.

When you use this compositional technique, however, don't forget that there are other ways to document the wonders of the sea. That blenny may look great when it fills up the middle of the frame, but it may look just as good if you include a bit of its surroundings and shift the animal to the golden ratio.

SUMMARY:

- Placing the subject at the center of an image is the most simple composition.
- Relying on central positioning is a safe way to ensure that you capture the intended subject.
- The central autofocus point gives photographers a tendency to rely on this style of composition, but you should use it only when the subject calls for it. Don't use it as a default.
- Some subjects—including tube worms, disc anemones, and fish eyes—naturally lend themselves to a central composition.
- Secondary objects in the image can be distracting in centrally focused compositions.
- It's usually effective to take fish portraits with a centered composition.
- Images that work well with a central composition may look just as good with a different design principle.

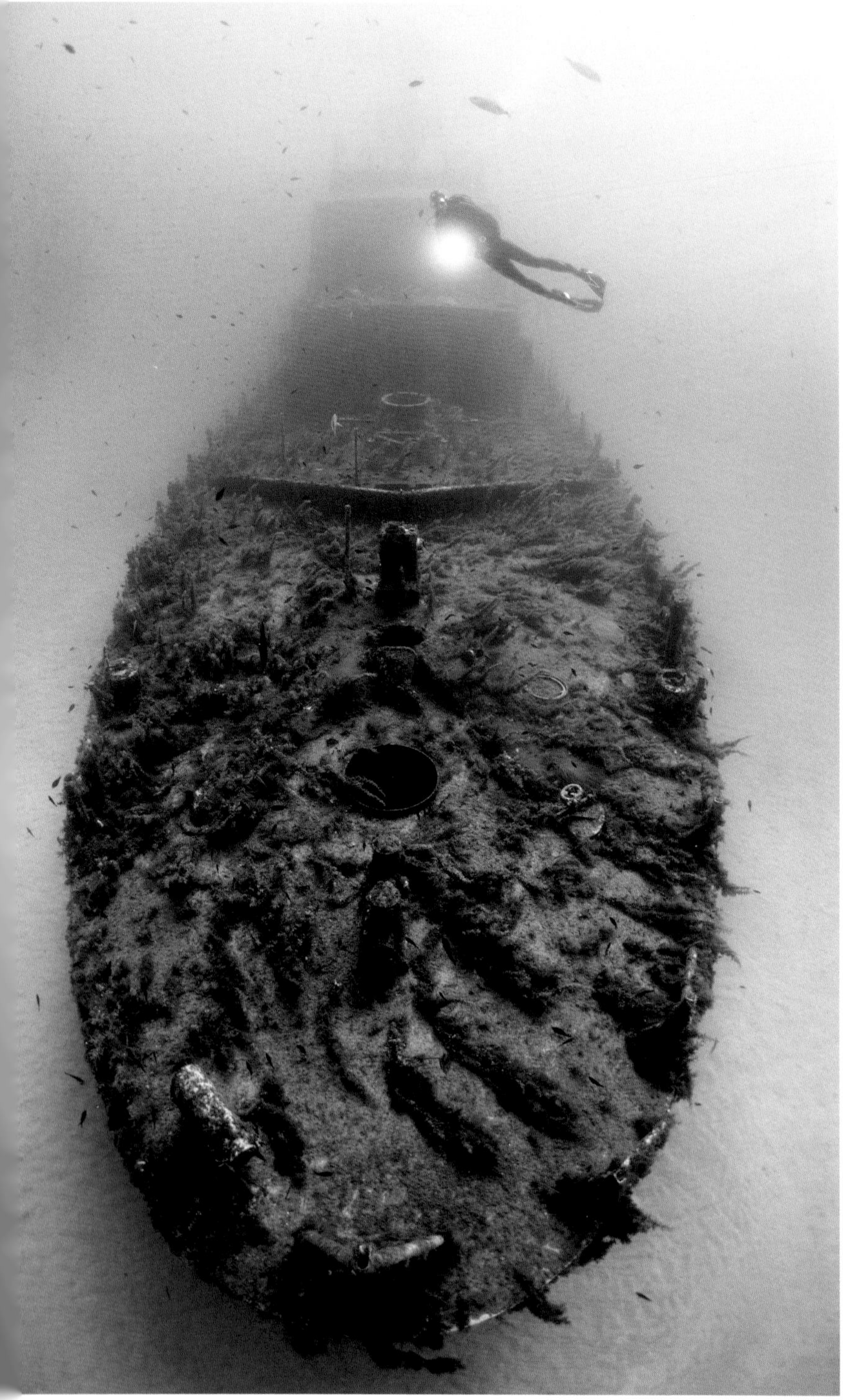

When wreckage is set against a light sandy area of the ocean floor, the resulting contrast increases the subject's prominence

Canon EOS 5D Mark II • Canon 17–40mm wide-angle lens • 1/25 s • f/8 • ISO 200

3.5 Contrast

Contrast between light and dark areas in an image may be used as a powerful compositional tool.

When you choose your subject and composition, always pay attention to contrast as it dramatically influences the look and feel of a photo. A light fish against a dark background draws viewers in, but a dark fish against a dark background may not be recognizable. The dark wreckage of a ship set against a light patch of seabed really jumps out and gives intensity to the scene.

This phenomenon is called *figure-ground contrast*. The figure (or subject) is more dominant if the background contrasts with it. The inclusion of marked contrast tends to intensify an image and makes it more attractive.

Photographers can use flash to intensify or soften contrast. Harsh, direct light intensifies contrast, often to an unnatural degree. To reverse this effect, you can use a diffuser to soften the light and diminish the contrast, or you can move your flash unit farther away from the subject. Frontal lighting isn't ideal for documenting the texture of coral, but sidelight causes shadows to form where light can't reach the furrows. It creates a fascinating contrast that emphasizes the coral's texture.

Cameras record a limited range of contrast that corresponds to the number of stops, or brightness values, that can be captured in a single image. An image with bright highlights and dark shadows can't be properly exposed throughout because the camera always tries to find a middle ground. In these situations it's usually best to expose either for the bright areas or the dark areas of the scene. Of course, this results in areas that are either too bright or too dark, so you have to decide which is more important. In general it's preferable to expose for the highlights rather than the shadows because excessively dark areas aren't as distracting as overly bright areas.

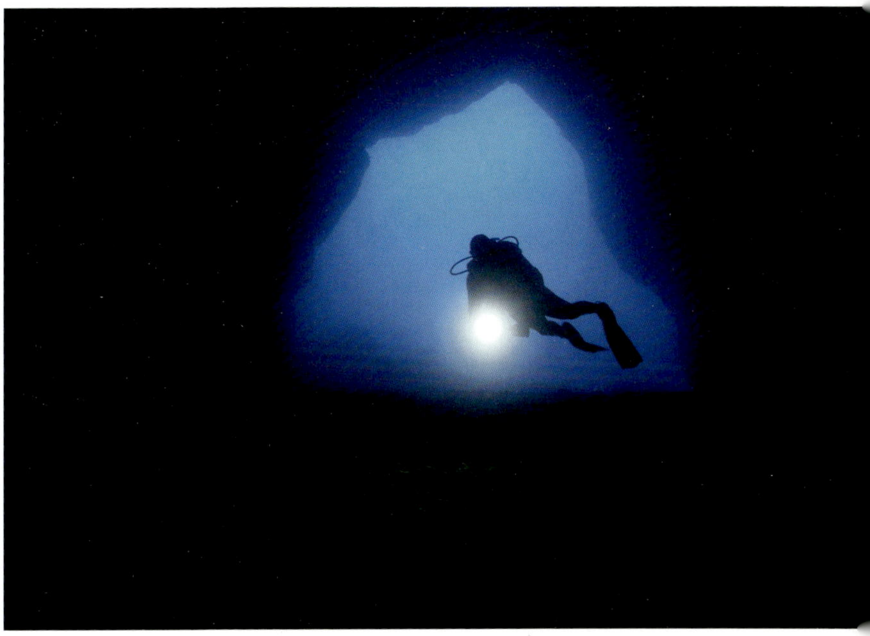

▲ There are two silhouettes at play in this picture's composition: the diver and the entrance to the cave

Canon EOS 5D Mark II • Canon 17–40mm wide-angle lens • 1/25 s • f/8 • ISO 800

You can exploit the limited dynamic range of a sensor for compositional purposes. For example, in a scene of a diver at the entrance to a cave, you can set the exposure values based on the highlights. This will cause the dark areas to lose most of their detail, and the stark contrast will draw the viewer's attention to the brighter areas of the picture.

Silhouettes of fish, especially sharks, make good high-contrast subjects. Turn off your flash units to further intensify the contrast.

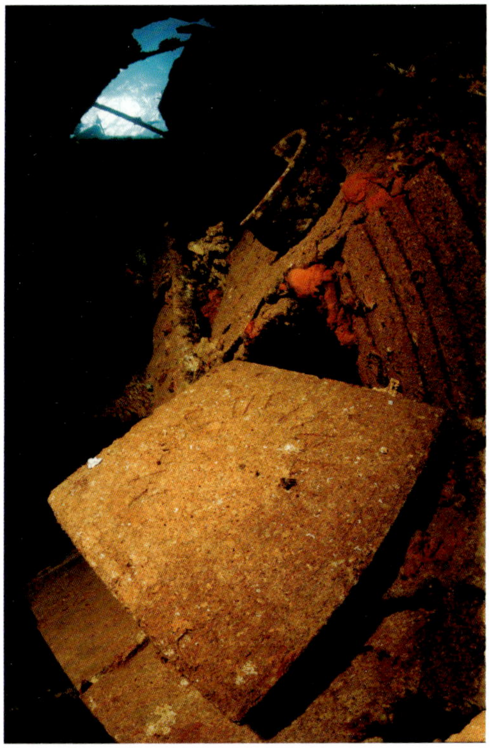

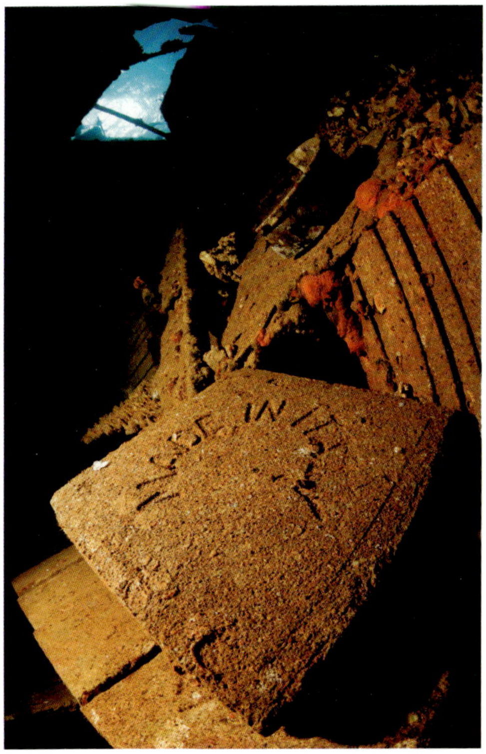

The photo on the far left was lit from above and the lettering on the tile is barely visible. The photo on the right was shot with the flash positioned to the side, and the lettering is prominent.

Canon EOS 5D Mark II • Canon 8–15mm fisheye lens • 1/200 s • f/16 • ISO 100

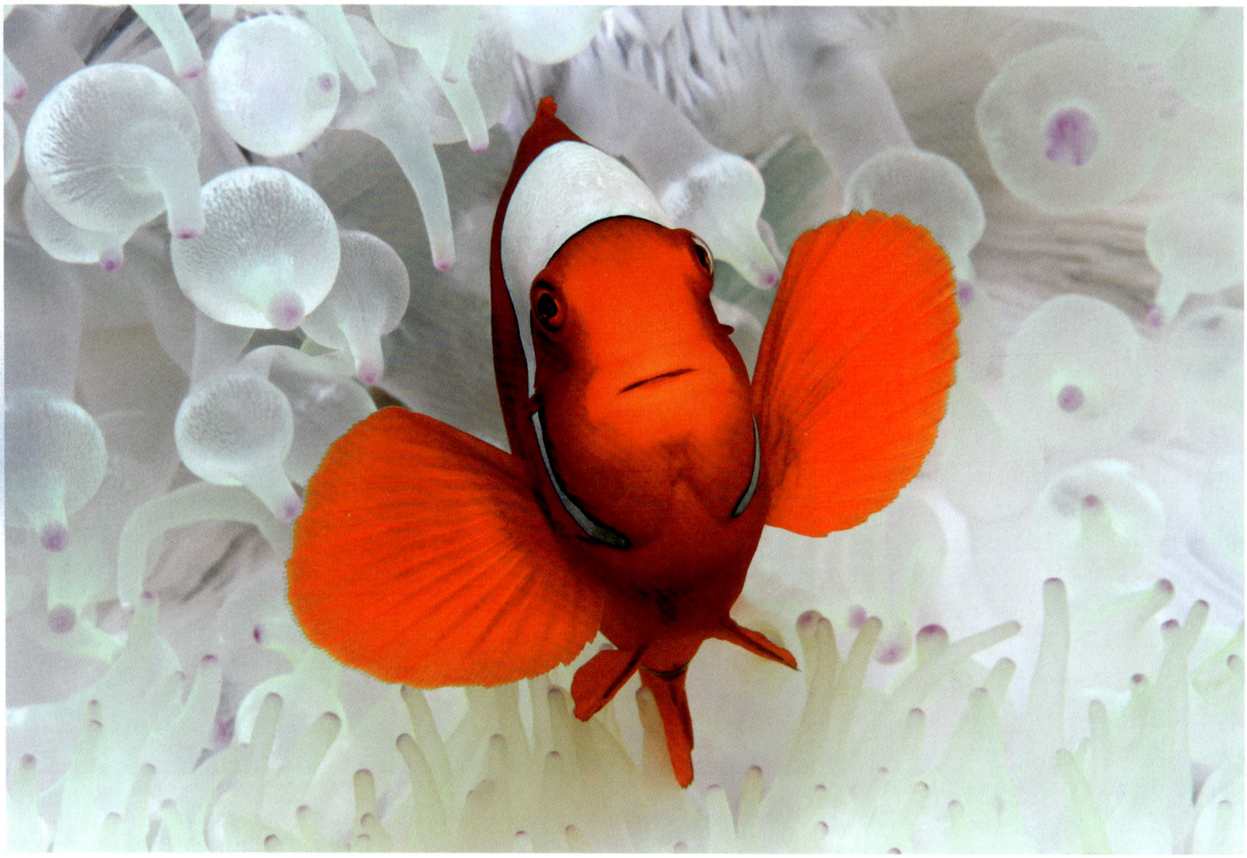

▲ Anemonefish are ideal subjects to practice taking pictures of fast-moving subjects.

Canon EOS 5D Mark II • Canon 100mm macro lens • 1/125 s • f/22 • ISO 200

SUMMARY:

- Contrast can emphasize subjects and intensify the overall effect of an image.
- Moving the flash farther away from the subject or using a diffuser can reduce the intensity of the contrast.
- Cameras can capture only a limited range of brightness values. Contrasty scenes often surpass this range.
- When a scene exceeds your camera's dynamic range, expose for either the bright areas or the dark areas.
- Animals and entrances to caves can be captured as silhouettes to further emphasize contrast. Disable the flash when you want to create this effect.

▶ The colors of these two gobies provide a vivid contrast against the blue background. The slight angle of the composition adds to the liveliness of the image.

Canon EOS 5D Mark II • Canon 100mm macro lens • 1/100 s • f/14 • ISO 400

3.6 Color

Color plays an integral role in the design of any image. Each color has unique psychological connotations even though they're mostly subconscious. You can enhance your photos by using color, therefore you should be aware of the

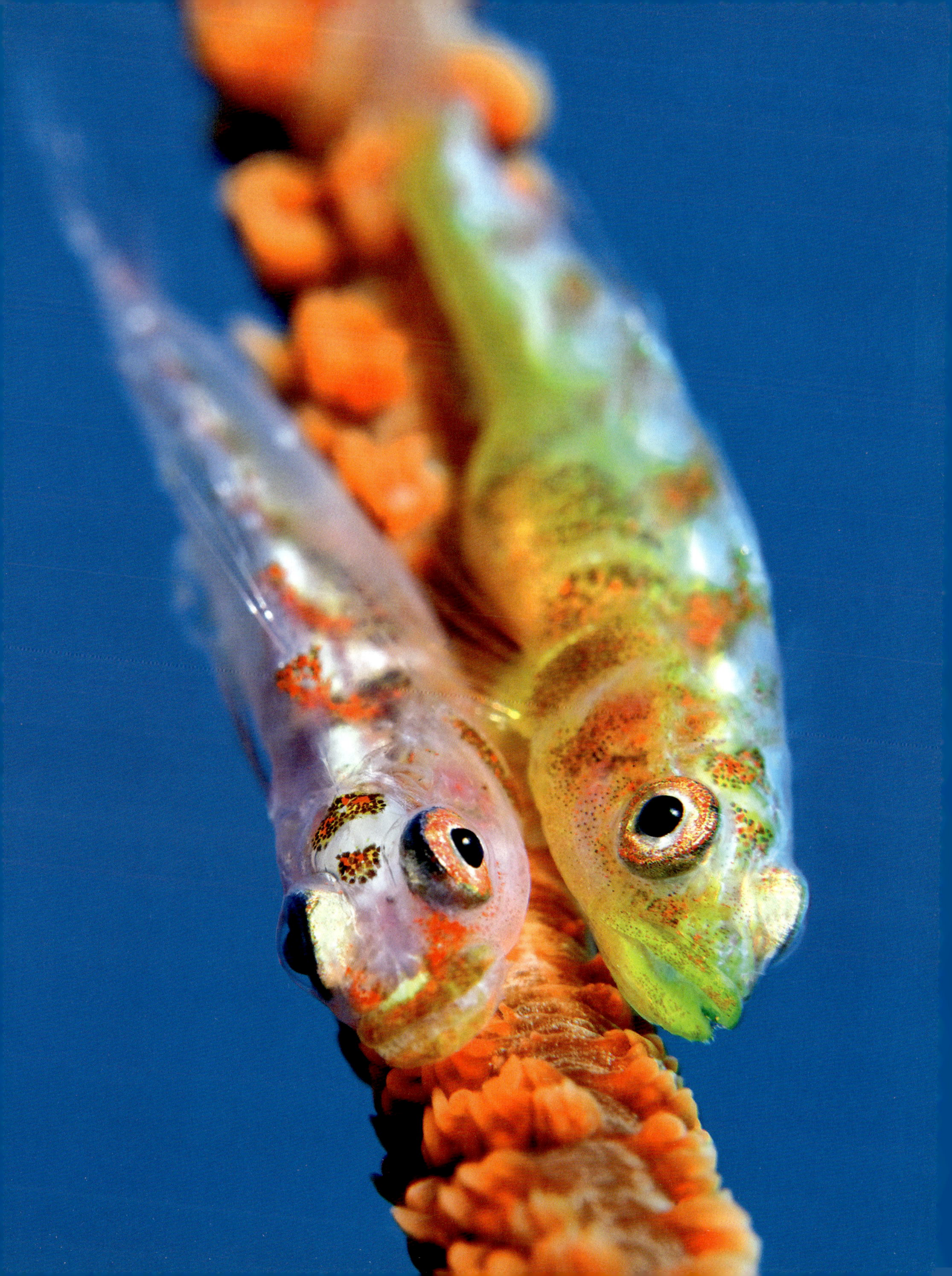

effects they produce. Red is a signal color that is often associated with heat, fire, and activity, but it can also serve as a warning. Orange has a positive, invigorating, and optimistic effect because it's a bright, warm color. Yellow often conjures feelings of ease, comfort, and weightlessness. Green conveys a sense of a new beginning and growth, and it produces feelings of harmony and stability. Blue often suggests calm, distance, or depth, and we often associate it with air or water. Divers in particular may associate blue with the ocean, which can stir feelings of happiness.

Combining colors is a powerful image design technique. It's important to recognize, however, that some colors pair better with others. Red, yellow, and blue are primary colors, and they always go together. Secondary colors are produced by mixing primary colors to yield orange, violet, and green, which also work well together. Complementary colors—red and green, orange and blue, yellow and violet—provide very high contrast in color and work well when you want something to really stand out.

The interplay of colors is particularly vivid beneath the sea, where a red soldierfish will stand out in front of a cyan background, a yellow butterfly fish will provide a stunning contrast with the deep blue sea around it, and the soft green of an anemone is accented by its magenta tentacles. During your next dive, evaluate the submarine colors you see, and think about which color combinations form attractive combinations.

An important disclaimer is needed here: You won't be able to see any of those colors unless you have the appropriate artificial lighting. Bring a lamp or a focus lamp on every dive—even in daylight. Or you can take test shots and look at them on your camera afterwards.

Monochrome images are also popular. In a monochrome image, there is a solid surface that is ideally free of shadows. The solid area may be a patch of sand, a background that's obscured in a blur, or a fish camouflaged on a piece of coral. Monochrome colors work as a backdrop for photographs, but they can also be the main feature of an image to create a restful mood.

SUMMARY:

- Color plays a big role in photographic composition.
- Red stands for danger, orange for optimism, green for a new beginning, and blue for distance or the ocean.
- Combining colors effectively is an important stylistic skill.
- Monochrome areas, or parts of an image that exhibit one color, have a stabilizing effect and can direct the viewer's attention to the primary subject.

3.7 Exceptions

All these design rules are only suggestions for how you might compose your images. It is ultimately up to you to decide if a particular design style will work for your photo. The guidelines in this chapter simply suggest how you *might* approach a situation rather than dictate what you *must* do. An effective mix of design elements depends on your personal experiences and abilities. When these standard design principles become second nature, you can start to think about how to break them intentionally. Taking this risk requires a good sense of how you might compose an image under particular circumstances. The design principles mentioned in this chapter are tried and true—breaking them won't usually produce a better or more creative photo.

You can develop your sense of when to try something else based on lots of trial and error. Why not take a picture of a wreck site from directly above? Why not experiment with positioning your light source behind the subject rather than in front of it, just to see what happens? Instead of setting up a traditional pose with your diving partner or model, try a different approach and see how it turns out. Be creative!

Most divers are apprehensive about botching a photo because the time they have under water is always limited. This fear tends to make photographers cautious so they can capture perfect images with ideal positioning; they often fail to let their creativity roam free. If you want to play it safe, take a traditional photo and then take some risks and dispense with the rules to see what happens. Subjects that are only moderately interesting or scenes that don't really excite you are ideal candidates for trying something more creative. Many

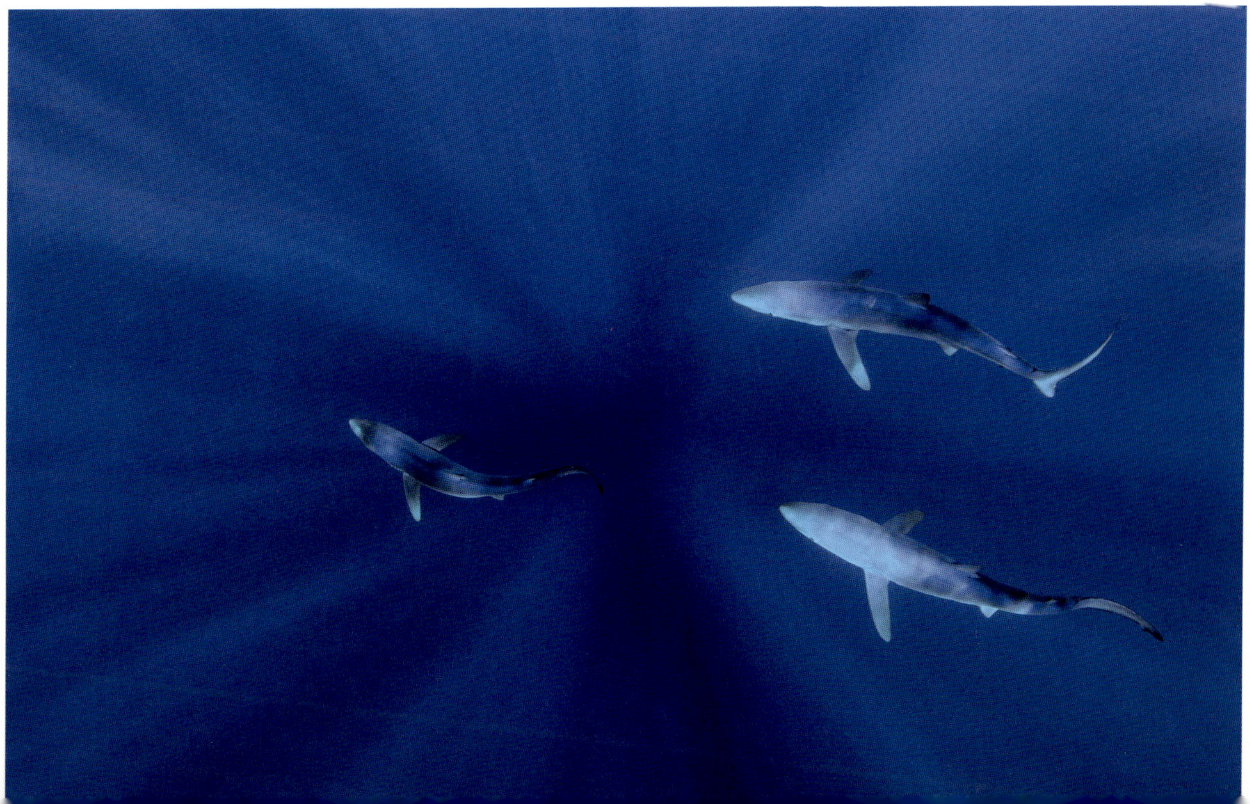

Though taking pictures with a downward perspective is generally not a great way to get an interesting photo, there are circumstances where it pans out. In this example, the streaks of sunlight and the camouflage of the sharks make for an interesting composition.

Canon EOS 5D Mark II • Canon 8–15mm fisheye lens • 1/100 s • f/10 • ISO 400

people never take risks because they're worried about adhering to accepted design conventions. Try to overcome this fear so you can find new ways of looking at things. If your experiment doesn't pan out, you can delete the image without ever showing it to anyone else. That's the worst that can happen.

When you get more experience, you'll be able to decide when and how to ignore the conventional rules of image composition in favor of a more creative approach.

SUMMARY:

- The rules of image design can be broken.
- Combining certain design techniques and ignoring others may result in better images—it's entirely up to you.
- A wealth of practice and experimentation will help you figure out when to disregard standard image design conventions.
- Learning to accept that some images will be failures makes it easier to let your creativity take charge.

3.8 Creativity

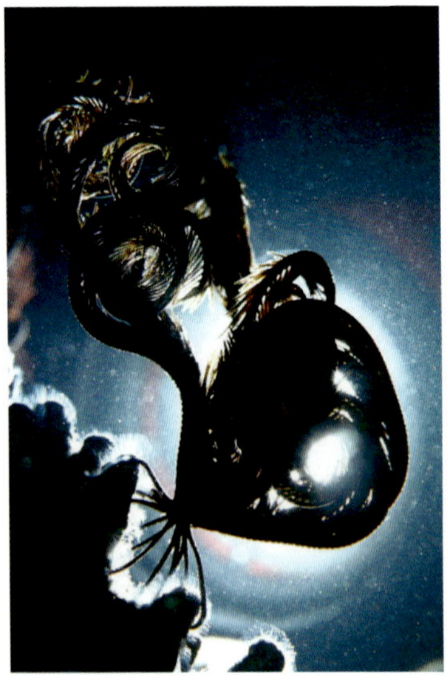

Familiar subjects can take on an unfamiliar appearance if you use creative exposure techniques such as positioning a flash behind your main subject

Canon EOS 5D Mark II • Canon 100mm macro lens • 1/60 s • f/16 • ISO 200

Practice, practice, and more practice! Not everyone lives near water nor do they have the chance to go diving every weekend. Knowing this, you should never go diving without your camera.

Areas that are not particularly known for diving attractions are ideal spots to mix things up and take some creative risks. It's all about making the best of what's on hand. It isn't easy, of course, but taking risks and trying unconventional techniques will result in outstanding rewards. Fortune favors the bold.

Consider how you might capture a feather star in an unconventional way. Maybe your diving partner can hold a slave flash behind the creature so when your main flash fires the slave will illuminate the feather star from behind. If your main flash is set to a modest output, this configuration will produce a stunning silhouette of the delicate creature. Examples like this abound. What's important is that you think critically about how to stage photographs in unconventional ways. Your creativity will flourish if you put aside the fear of making a mistake and try something new.

Light plays a key role in creative photography. Think about how you can use your strobes to create an unconventional shot. Different flash settings and positions are good places to start, but also experiment with light-shaping tools that can alter the appearance of light from your flash unit (see section 5.10).

Each year, a large photography competition takes place in Israel. Top photographers from around the world gather in a small area near Eilat—on the

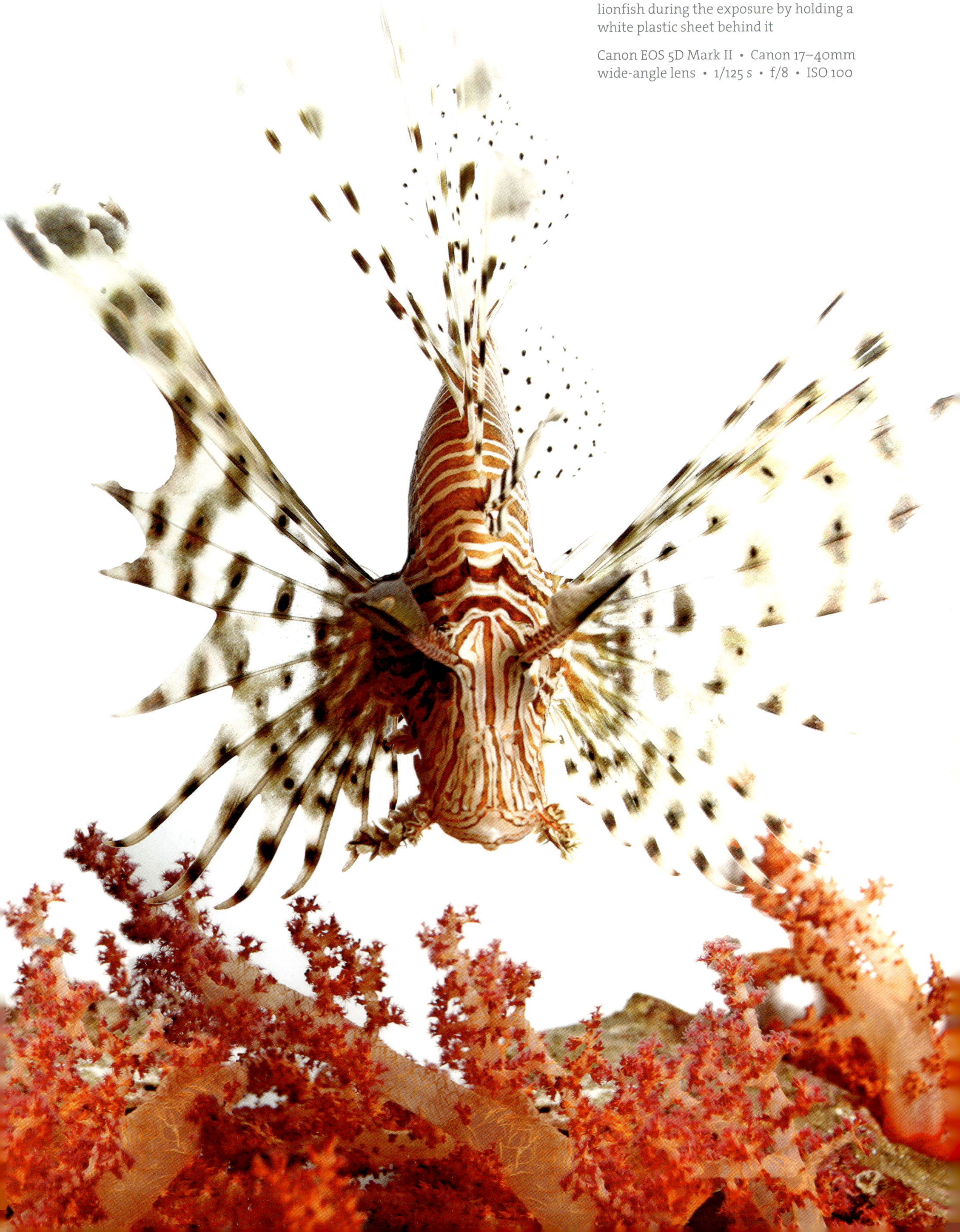

It was possible to isolate this common lionfish during the exposure by holding a white plastic sheet behind it

Canon EOS 5D Mark II • Canon 17–40mm wide-angle lens • 1/125 s • f/8 • ISO 100

When interesting photographic subjects don't materialize naturally, the task of finding something to photograph falls to your imagination

Canon EOS 5D Mark II • Canon 17–40mm wide-angle lens • 1/60 s • f/11 • ISO 200

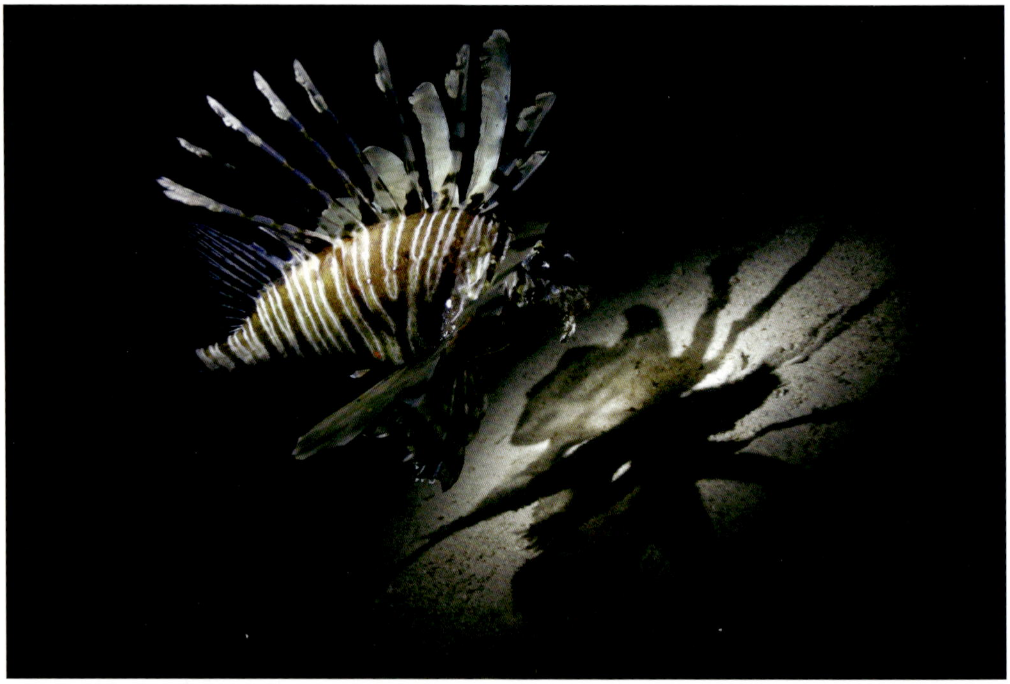

Try to recognize and quickly capture comical situations

Canon EOS 5D Mark II • Canon 17–40mm wide-angle lens • 1/125 s • f/16 • ISO 400

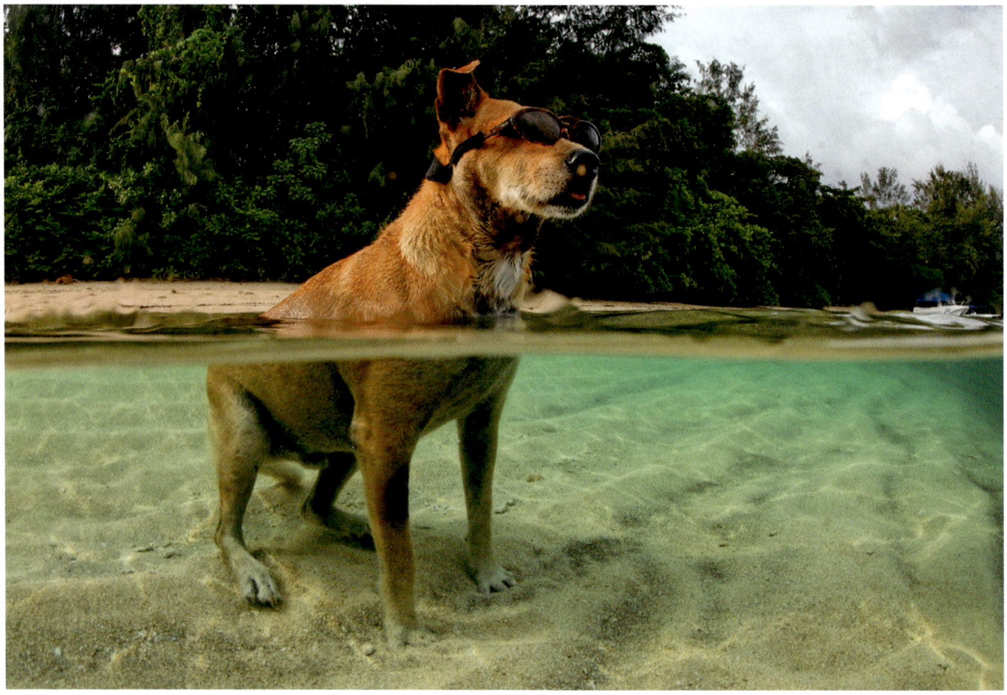

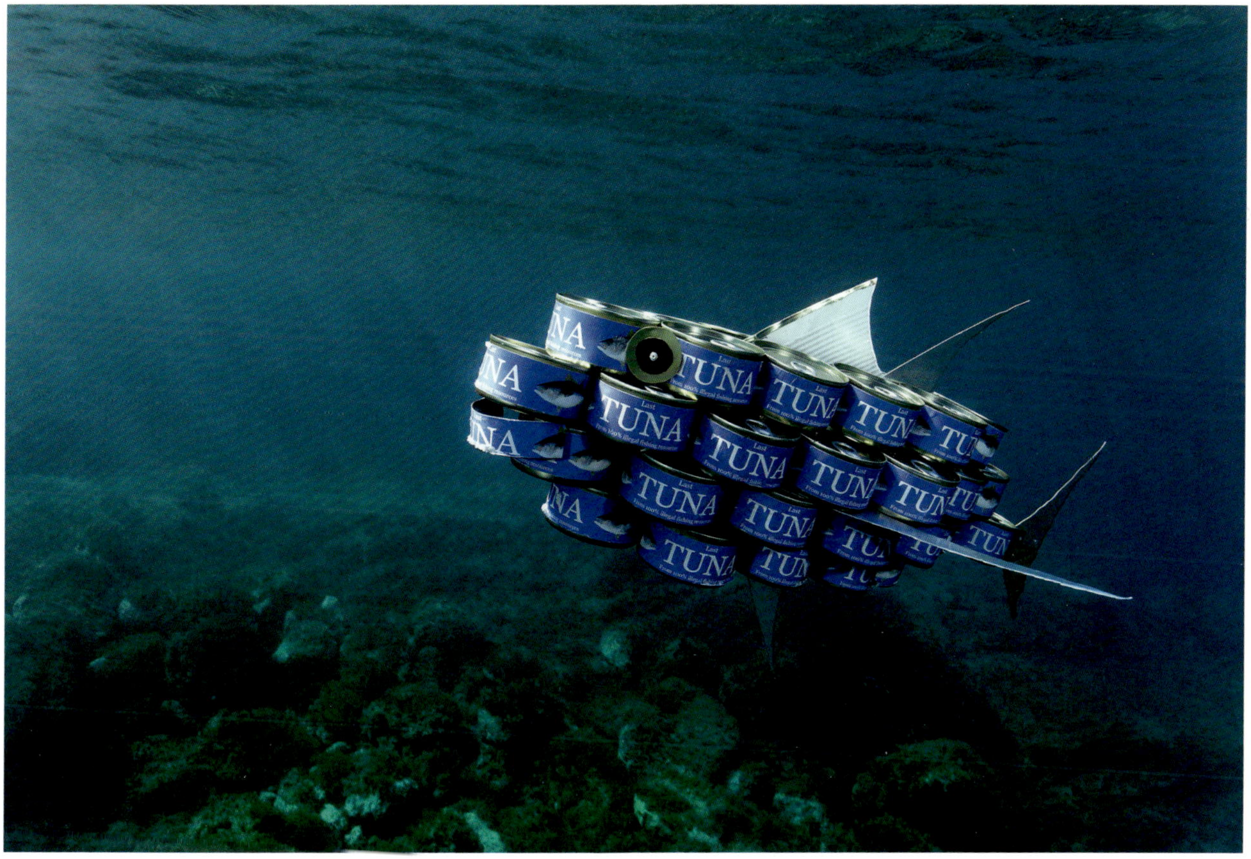

Red Sea—to see who can produce the most fascinating images during the three-day contest. The diving in the area is not bad, but it's not as captivating as what you can find in the reefs of Egypt. Nevertheless, the competition produces stunning photos each year as photographers strive to overcome the dearth of exciting subjects with creative ingenuity.

You can overcome poor shooting conditions with a combination of creativity, technical ability, and willingness to break traditional design conventions. Better photographs await those who are willing to try.

The only light used for this exposure came from the diving partner's lamp—a lighting setup deliberately employed to produce the fascinating shadows on the ocean floor

Canon EOS 5D Mark II • Canon 17–40mm wide-angle lens • 1/50 s • f/4 • ISO 3200

SUMMARY:

- Never go on a dive without your camera.
- Well-known or unspectacular dive sites foster creative photography.
- Don't be afraid of making mistakes and be open to trying new things.
- Altering the appearance of light is a huge part of creative photography.

- Different and unconventional perspectives produce fascinating results.
- Entering photography competitions can help you to improve your own photography.
- How quickly you develop your creativity and how much you master your craft depends on you and how motivated you are.

3.9 Learning to Compose

Composing and designing images is a skill that can be learned. Traveling frequently and photographing often is one way to accelerate this learning process. Your concentration while diving is just as critical as searching for new perspectives and subjects. Above all, continual reflection is required so you can learn from your mistakes and create better pictures next time.

One way to improve is to take a critical look at your photos and ask yourself if anything about a particular photo bothers you. If so, it's safe to assume that other viewers will also pick up on it. It's highly motivating to critically evaluate your work and strive for improvement.

One of the best ways to improve your eye is to analyze as many underwater photographs as possible. Scour diving magazines, the Internet, and underwater photography books. Which images are your favorites? For the ones you like, consider the following questions: How did the photographer expose the image? Where were the lights positioned? Did ambient light influence the picture? Were any standard design conventions, such as the golden ratio, used? What focal length did the photographer probably use? How far away was the camera from the subject? The more you analyze images with these critical questions in mind, the sharper your intuition will become for how to create your own successful pictures. This process isn't about imitating the work of others—it's about honing your sense of well-designed pictures and using this knowledge consciously and subconsciously.

Photography competitions are a good way to measure your ability against that of other photographers. Participate in competitions often to get a sense of where your images stand compared to the work of others.

If people make critical comments about your photos, don't take them as an insult—use them as motivation to create a better picture next time.

Many professional photographers offer workshops, either locally or on guided trips, in which they offer technical and practical tips. Lessons from experts make a great foundation for developing your own photography.

SUMMARY:

- Composition is a skill that can be learned, but the trajectory of progress depends on your motivation.
- Self-reflection is an integral step to improving your craft.
- Analyzing the photographs of others will help your photography improve.
- Entering your work in photography competitions is a good way to compare your work to that of others.
- Use criticism of your work as an incentive to improve.
- Workshops hosted by professionals offer a good foundation for advancing your vision and skills.

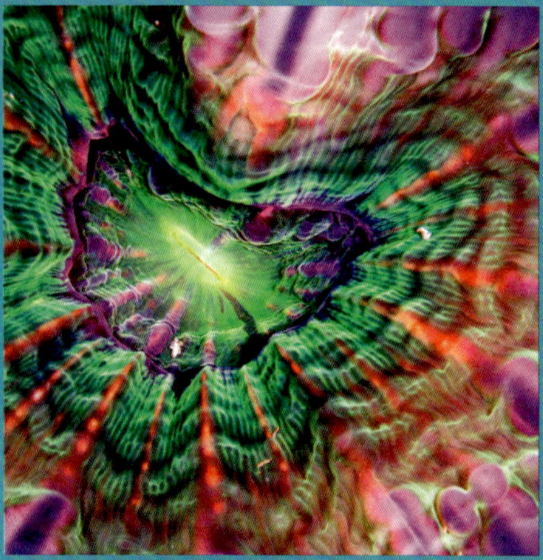
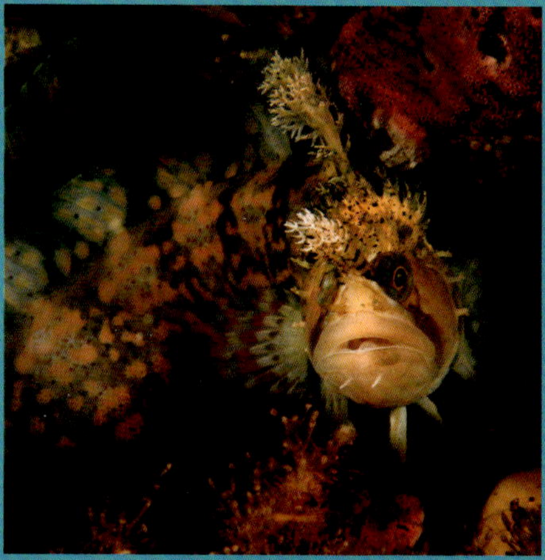
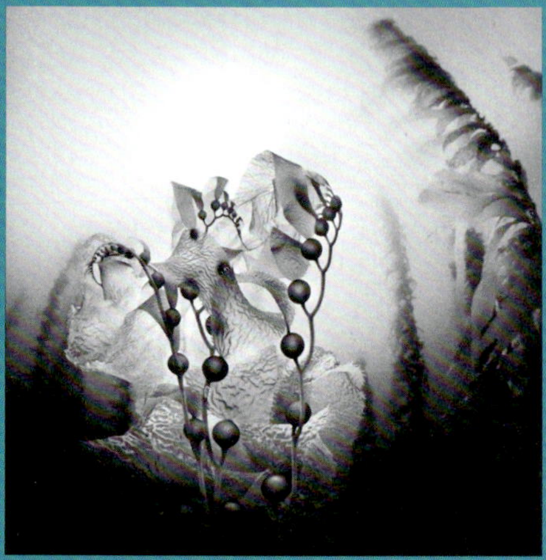
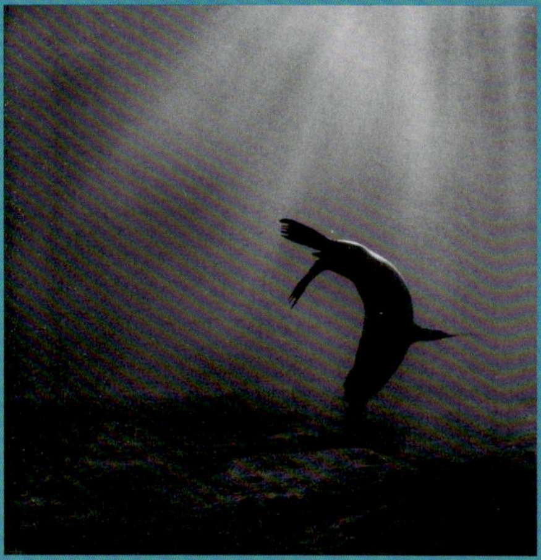
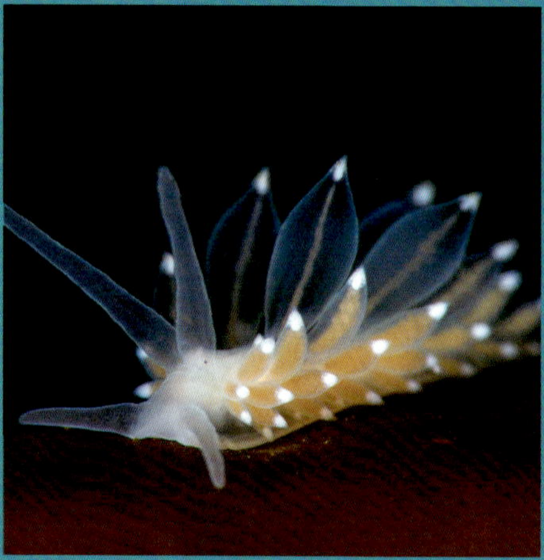
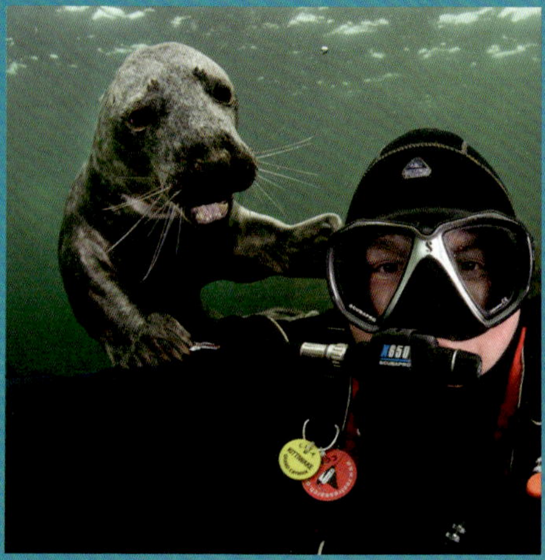
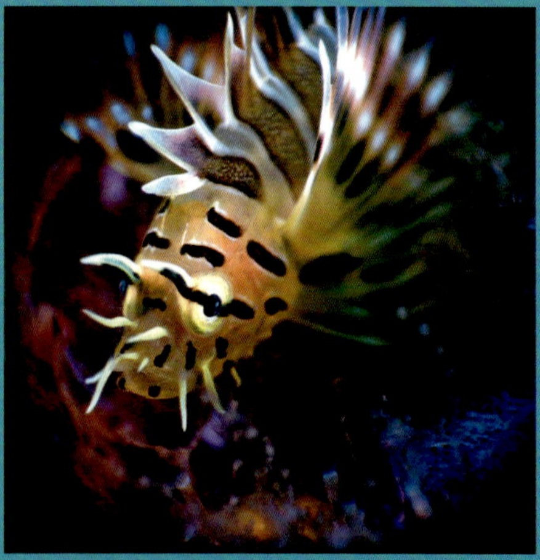
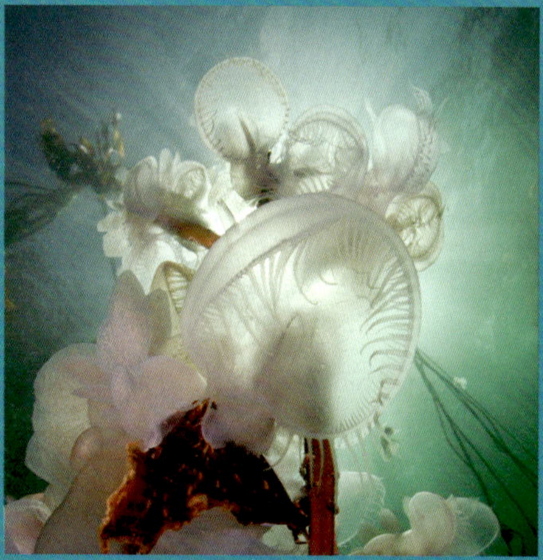
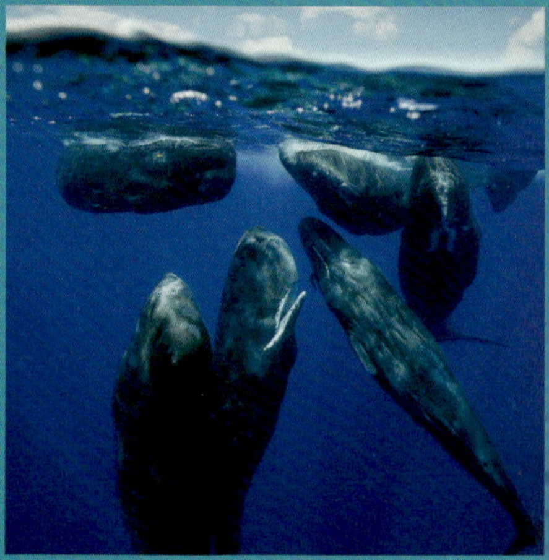

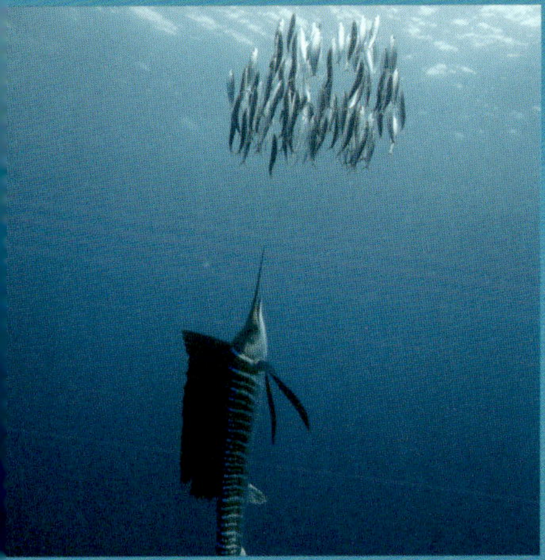

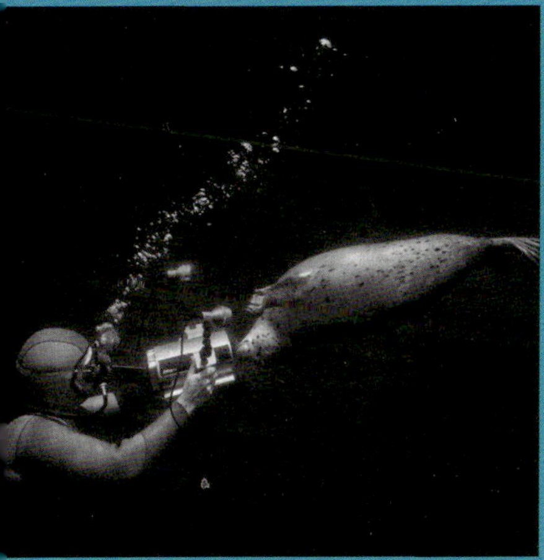

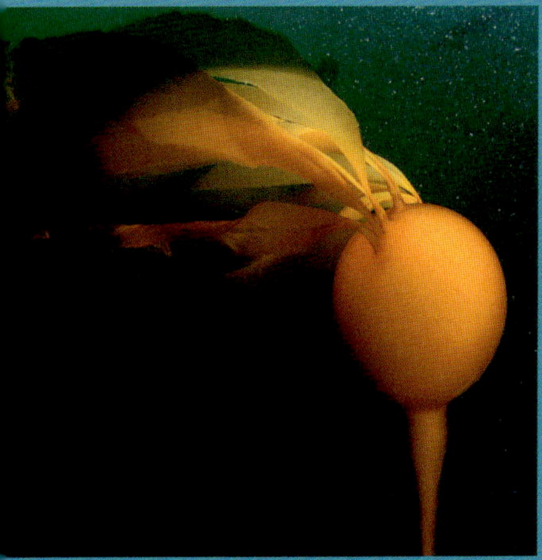

Guest Photographers Gallery

Richard Salas

Ernie Brooks

Alex Mustard

Imran Ahmad

Eric Cheng

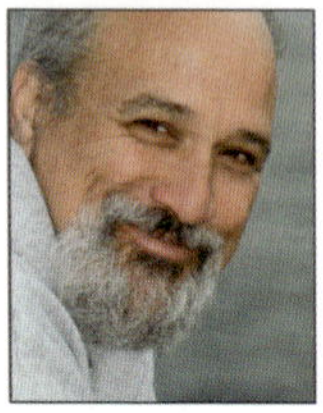

RICHARD SALAS

Richard Salas is a California native. He graduated from Brooks Institute of Photography in 1979, where he was first introduced to diving and underwater photography. During his last year and a half of school Richard was mentored by Ernest Brooks II.

Richard has been working professionally in digital media for over twenty-one years. He has authored two books, *Sea of Light* and *Blue Visions*, and is currently working on the third and final book of the trilogy, *Luminous Sea*. Richard makes his living as a photographer in Santa Barbara, California, where he lives with his wife Rebecca and youngest son Richard. Learn more about Richard at www.askphotoh2o.com.

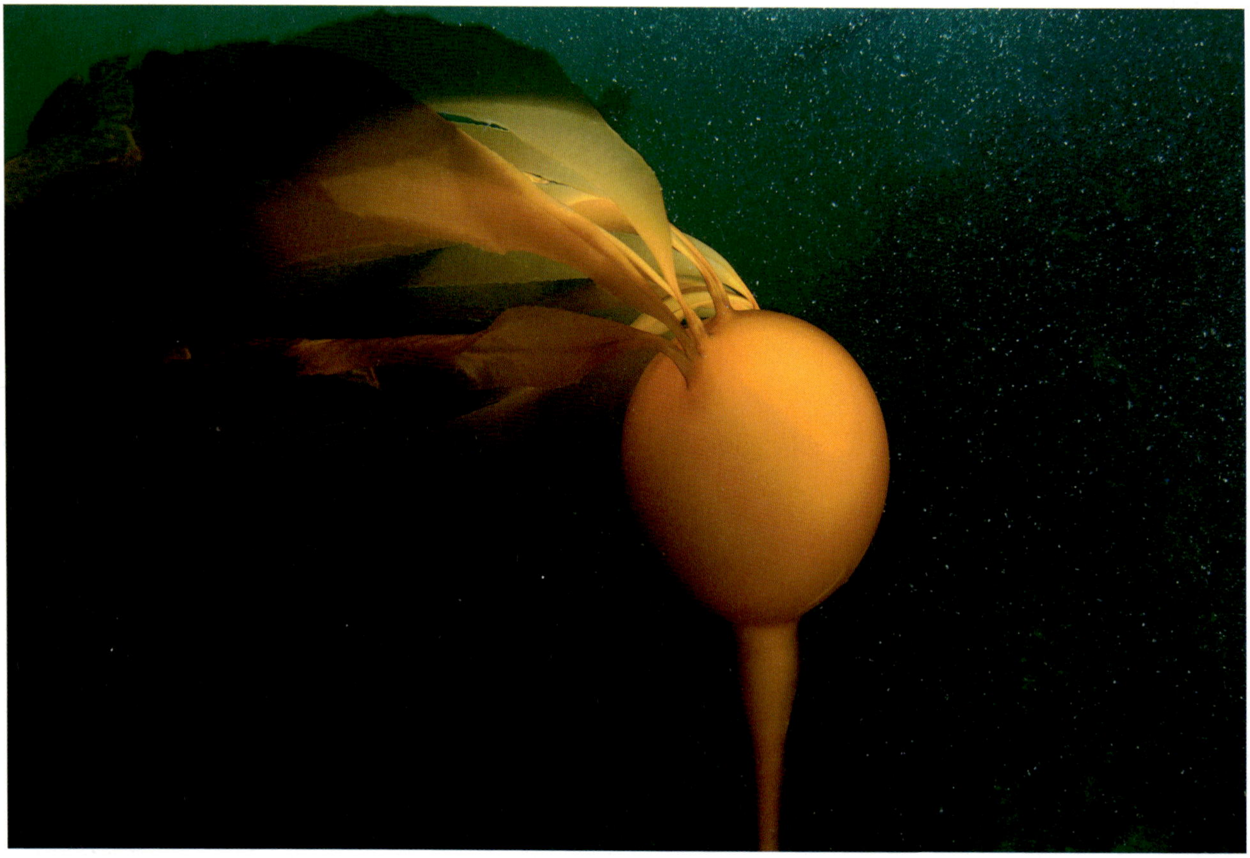

Bull Kelp, *Nereocystis luetkeana*
Husser Point, God's Pocket, BC, Canada, April 2013
Nikon 300s • Tokina 10–17mm wide-angle lens • 1/50 s • f13 • ISO 200

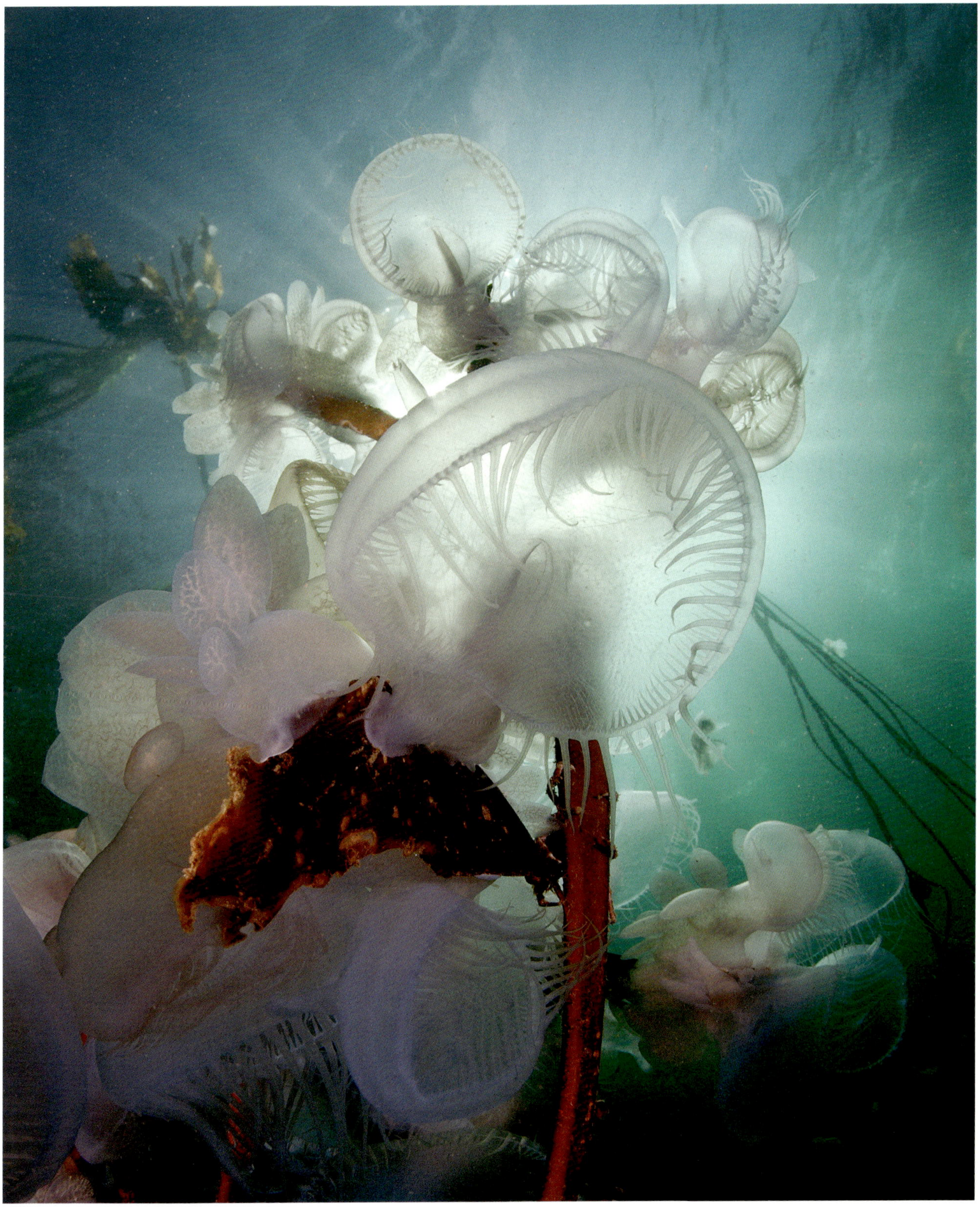

Hooded Nudibranchs, *Melibe leonine*
Hoodie Nudi Bay, God's Pocket, BC, Canada, April 2013

Nikon 300s • Tokina 10–17mm wide-angle lens • 1/250 s • f/11 • ISO 200

↓ Steller Sea Lion, *Eumetopias jubatus*
Hornby Island, Canada, January 2013
Nikon 300s • Tokina 10–17mm wide-angle lens • 1/200 • f/7.1 • ISO 200

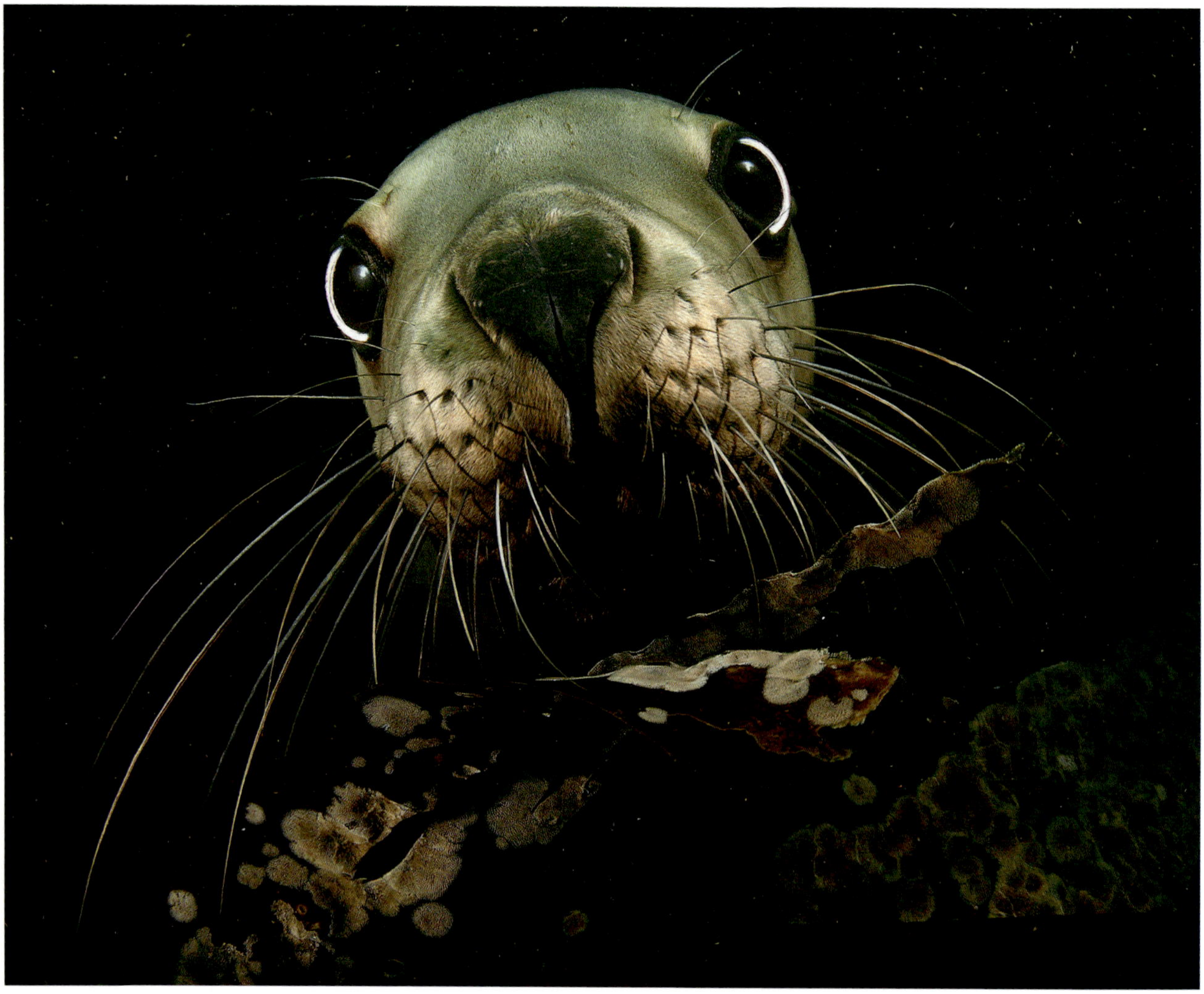

↗ Decorated Warbonnet, *Chirolophis decoratus*
Inian Island, Alaska, July 2013
Nikon 300s • 60mm micro Nikkor lens • 1/60 s • f/22 • ISO 200

→ Wolf Eel, *Anarrhichas ocellatus*
Fantasy Island, God's Pocket, BC Canada, October 2013
Nikon 300s • Tokina 10–17mm wide-angle lens • 1/60 s • F/18 • ISO 200

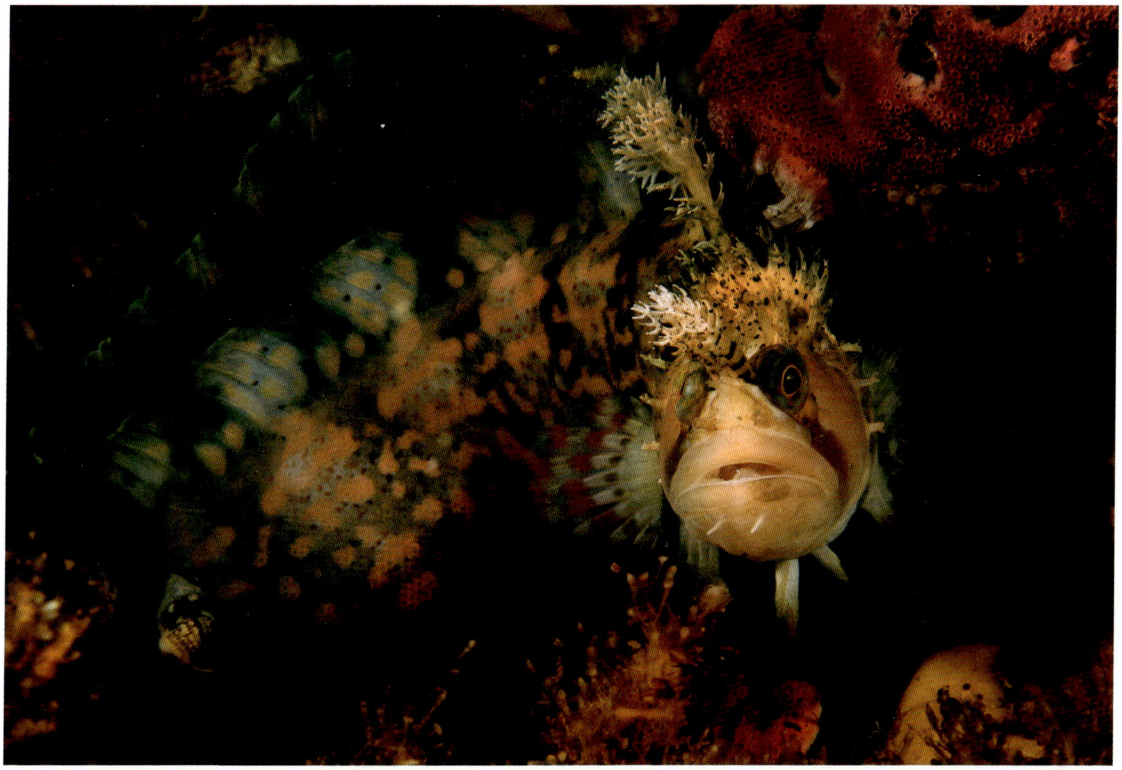

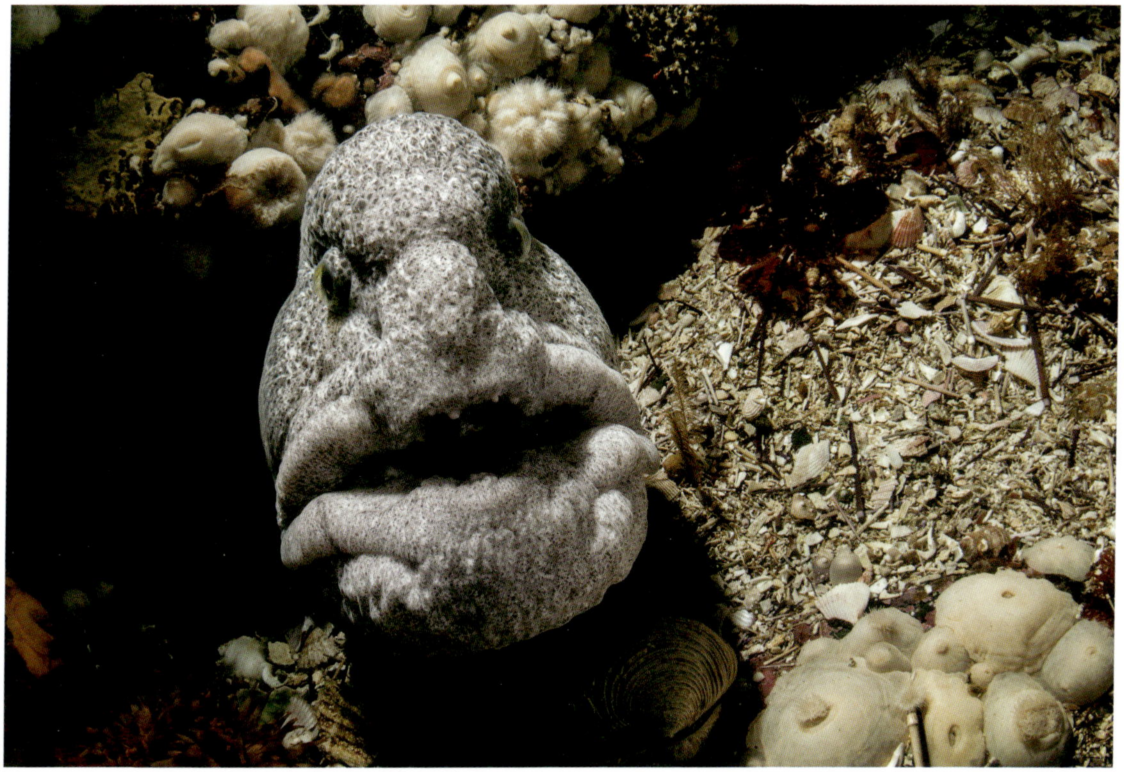

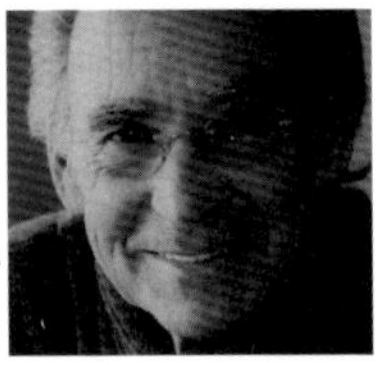

Photo by © Annie Crawley

ERNIE BROOKS

Ernest H. Brooks II (Ernie Brooks) was born to be a photographer, ambassador of the marine environment, educator, pilot, and legend of the sea. Born of Portuguese ancestry in 1935, he followed in the footsteps of his grandparents, father, and mother and mastered the fine arts of photography and seamanship. In honor of his forefathers, he founded the underwater photography program at Brooks Institute of Photography in Santa Barbara, California.

Ernie's images taken within the oceans of our Water Planet are exhibited in museums and galleries around the world. At the time of this writing, an exhibit called *Fragile Waters* is touring the United States, featuring Ernie's images alongside images from his mentor Ansel Adams.

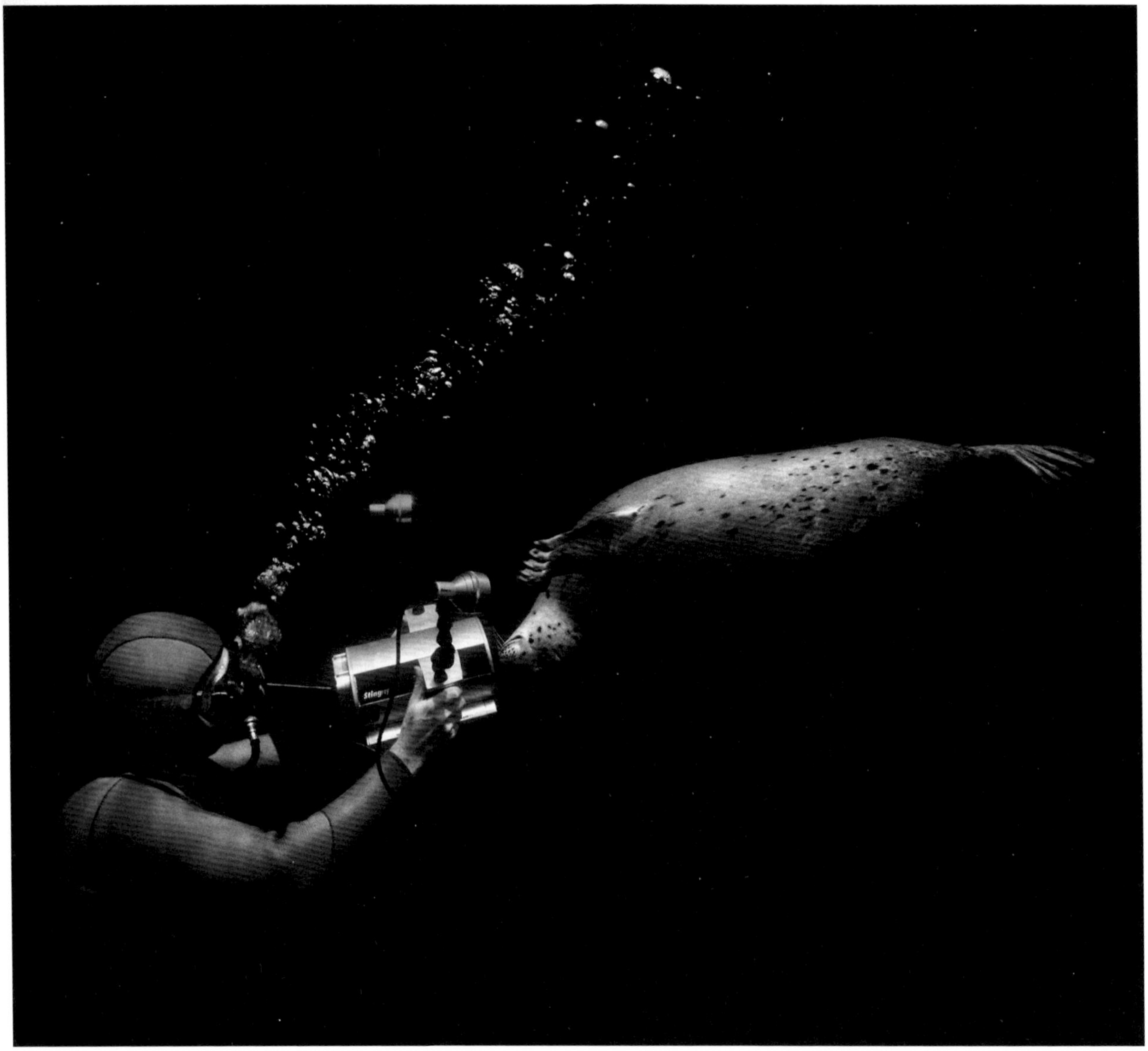

Michael Meets Spot: This image of the president of Light and Motion meeting "Spot" became the trademark of their global campaign.
Middle Anacapa Island, off the California coast, October 1994
Hasselblad SWC • 38mm lens • 70mm T-Max ISO 400 film • 1/125 s • f/8

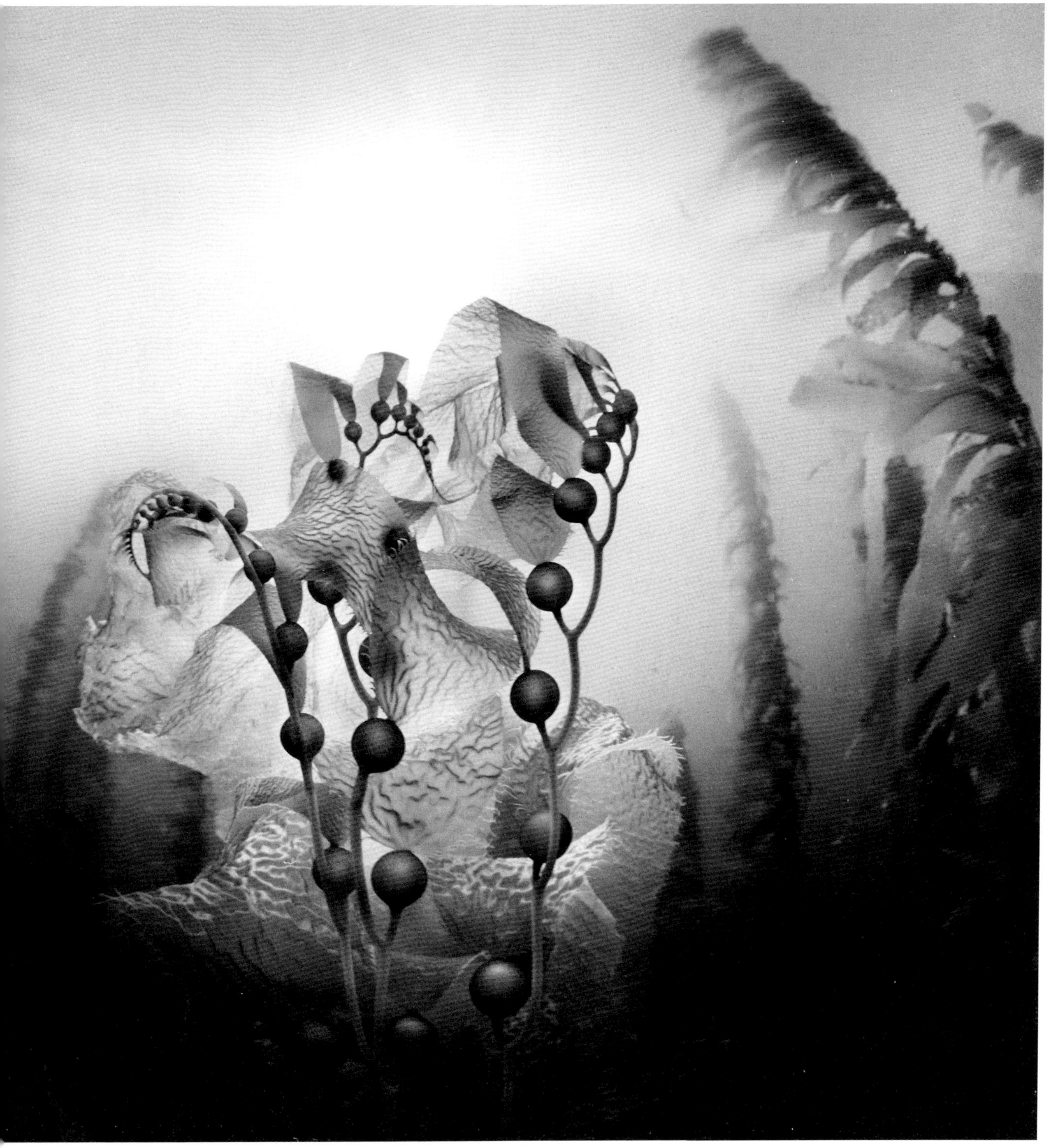

Sea Pearls I: Macrocystis, the towering redwoods of the sea, move in rhythm as one, their branches never touching.
Santa Cruz Island, Scorpion Anchorage, off the California coast, November 1998
Rolleiflex SLR • 50MM lens • T-Max ISO200 film • 1/125 s • f/8 • focus preset at 6″

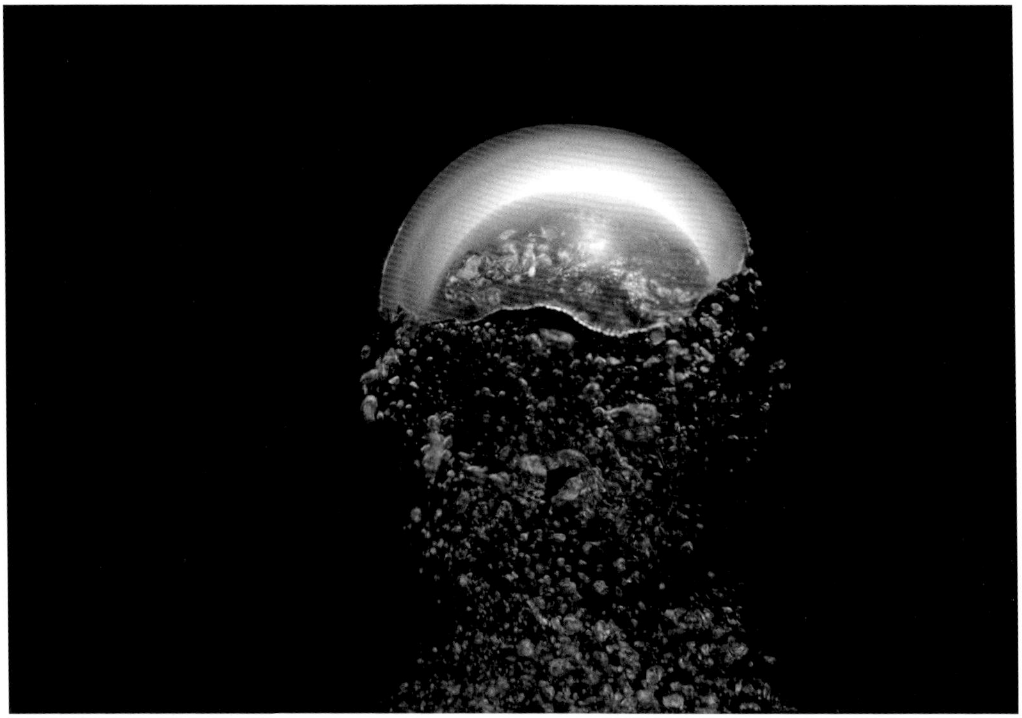

↑ *Evidence of Man:* Since my career began in 1956, I've continually searched for subjects that aesthetically bespeak man's presence underwater, like this diver's air bell rising to the surface.
Santa Cruz Island, Pelican Bay, off the California coast, November 1995

Hasselblad SWC • 38mm lens • 70mm T-Max ISO 400 film •1/125 s • f/3.5

→ *Freedom:* There are moments when all the elements fall into place: perfect early morning light, crystal clear water, a fabulous coral head, and my model—diver and photographer Lynn Funkhouser—who explores the coral setting.
North Tubbataha Island, Sulu Sea, Philippines, March 1996

Nikonos V • 20mm lens • 70mm T-Max ISO 400 film • 1/125 s • f/8

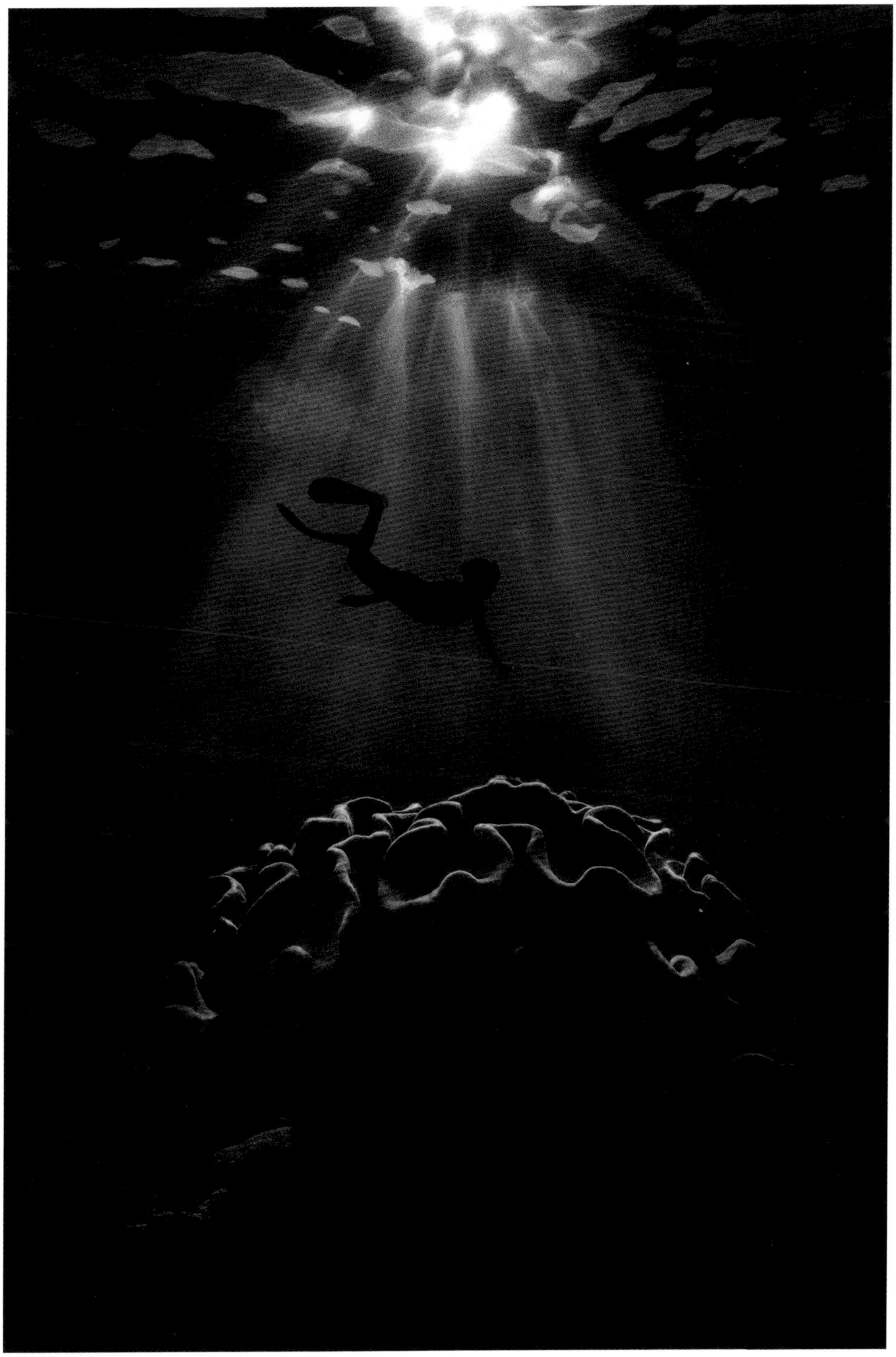

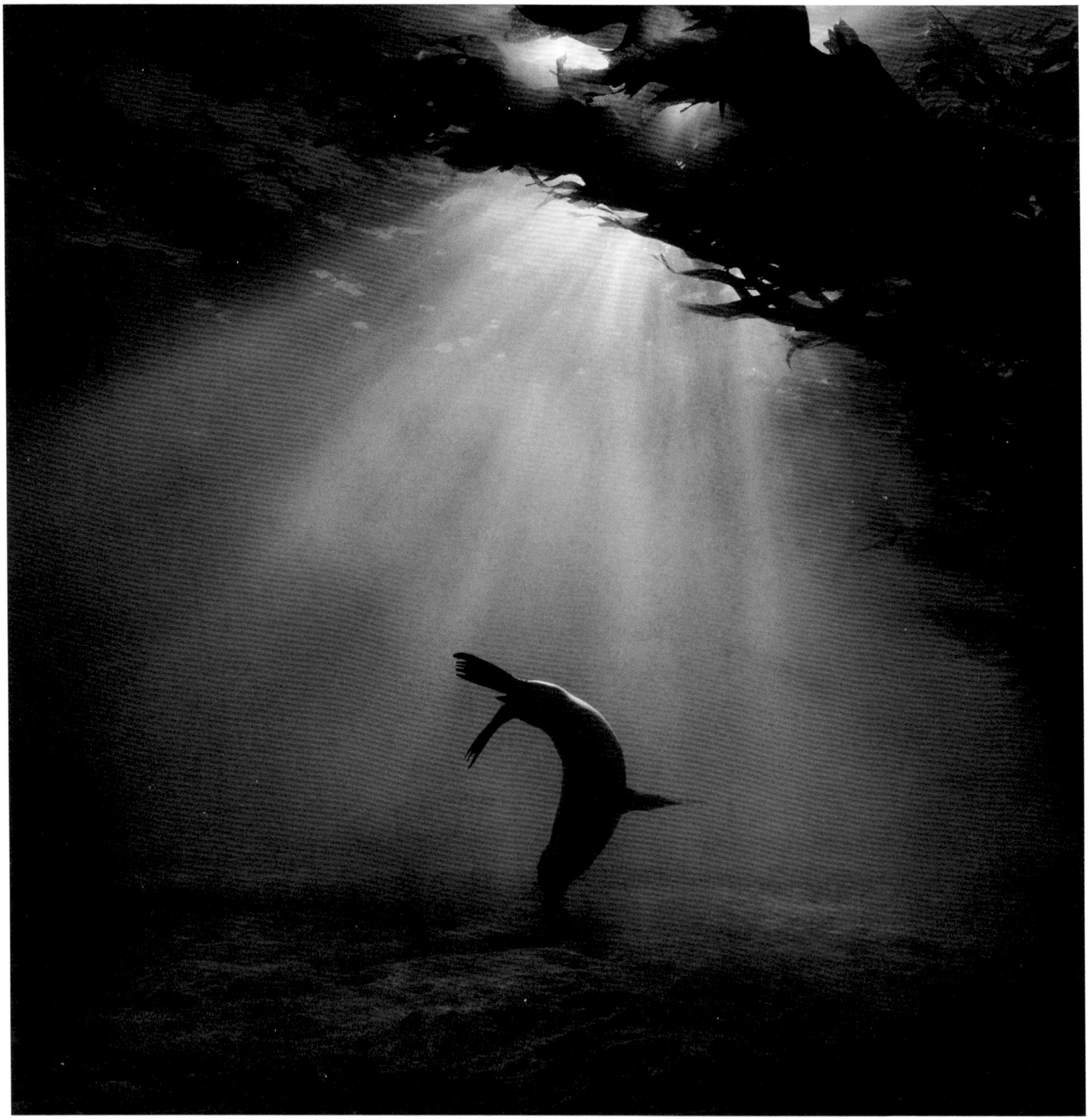

Pirouette: Light on center stage; she performs for me alone.
Santa Barbara Island, off the California coast, June 1993

Hasselblad SWC • 38mm lens • 70mm T-Max ISO 400 film •1/125 s • f/8

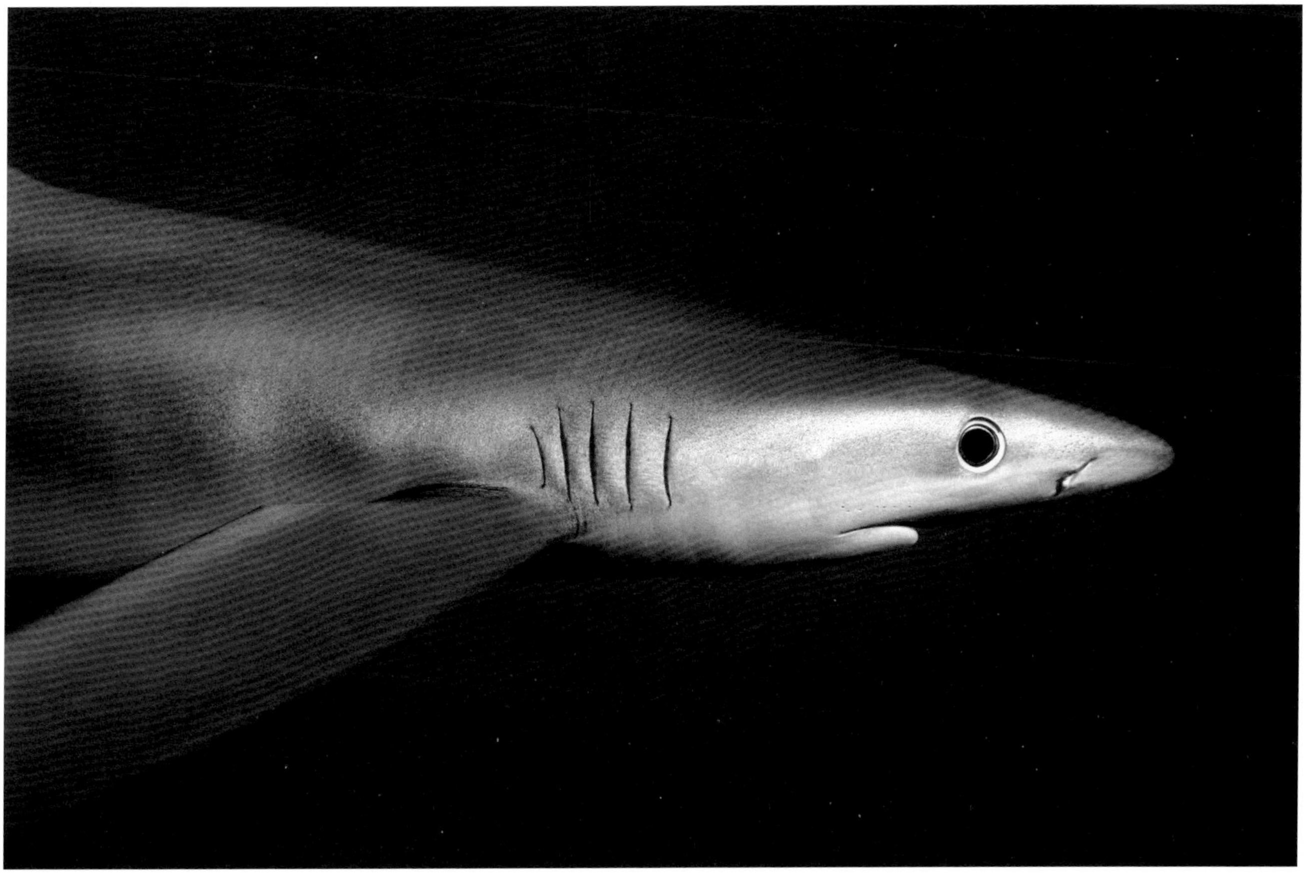

Blue in Profile: This ancient and quiet form glides past closely as I pan to match its speed. Big, sleek, and beautiful.
Anacapa Passage (between Anacapa and Santa Cruz Islands), off the California coast, September 1981
Hasselblad SWC • 38mm lens • 70mm Plus-X ISO 200 film • 1/125 s • f/8

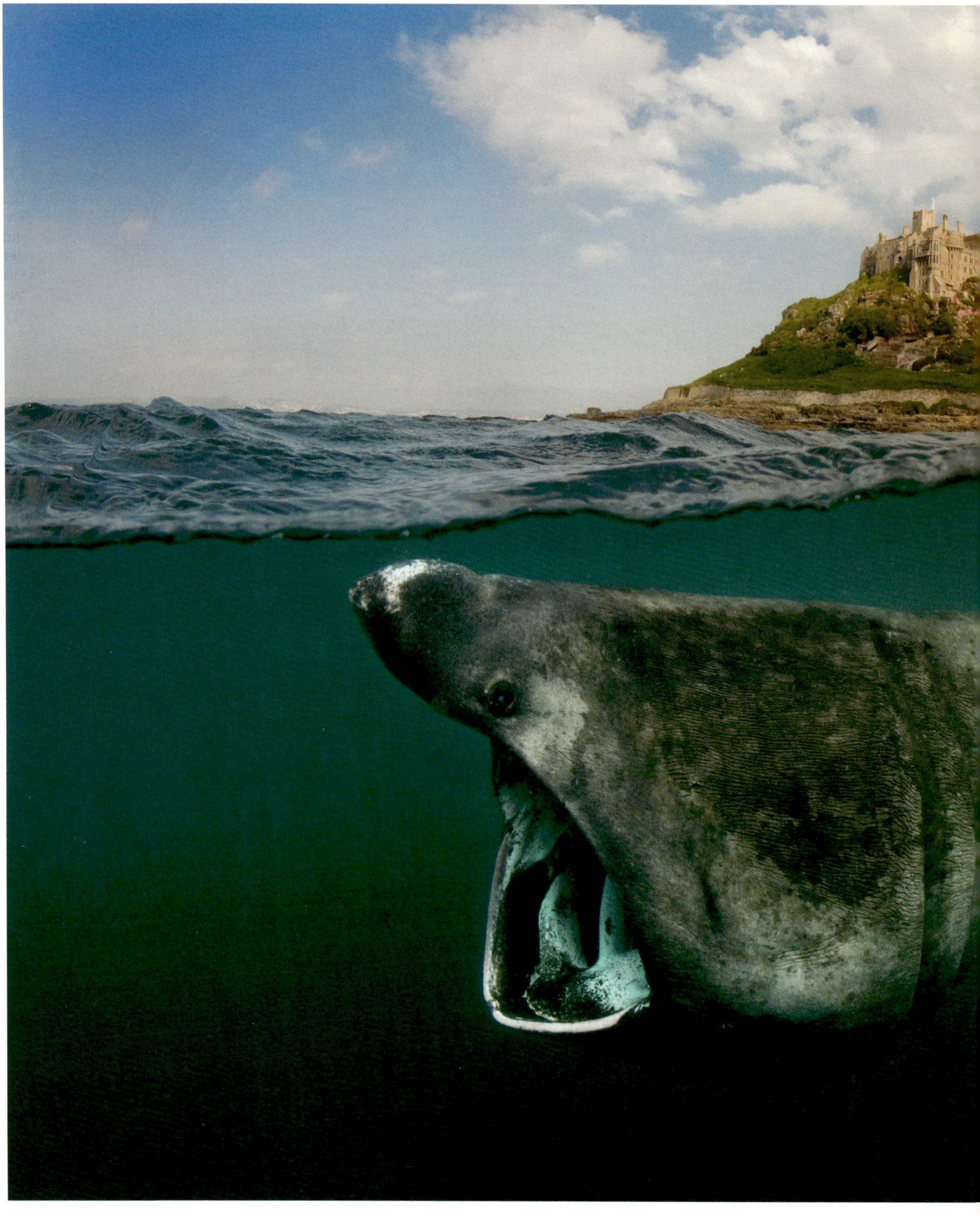

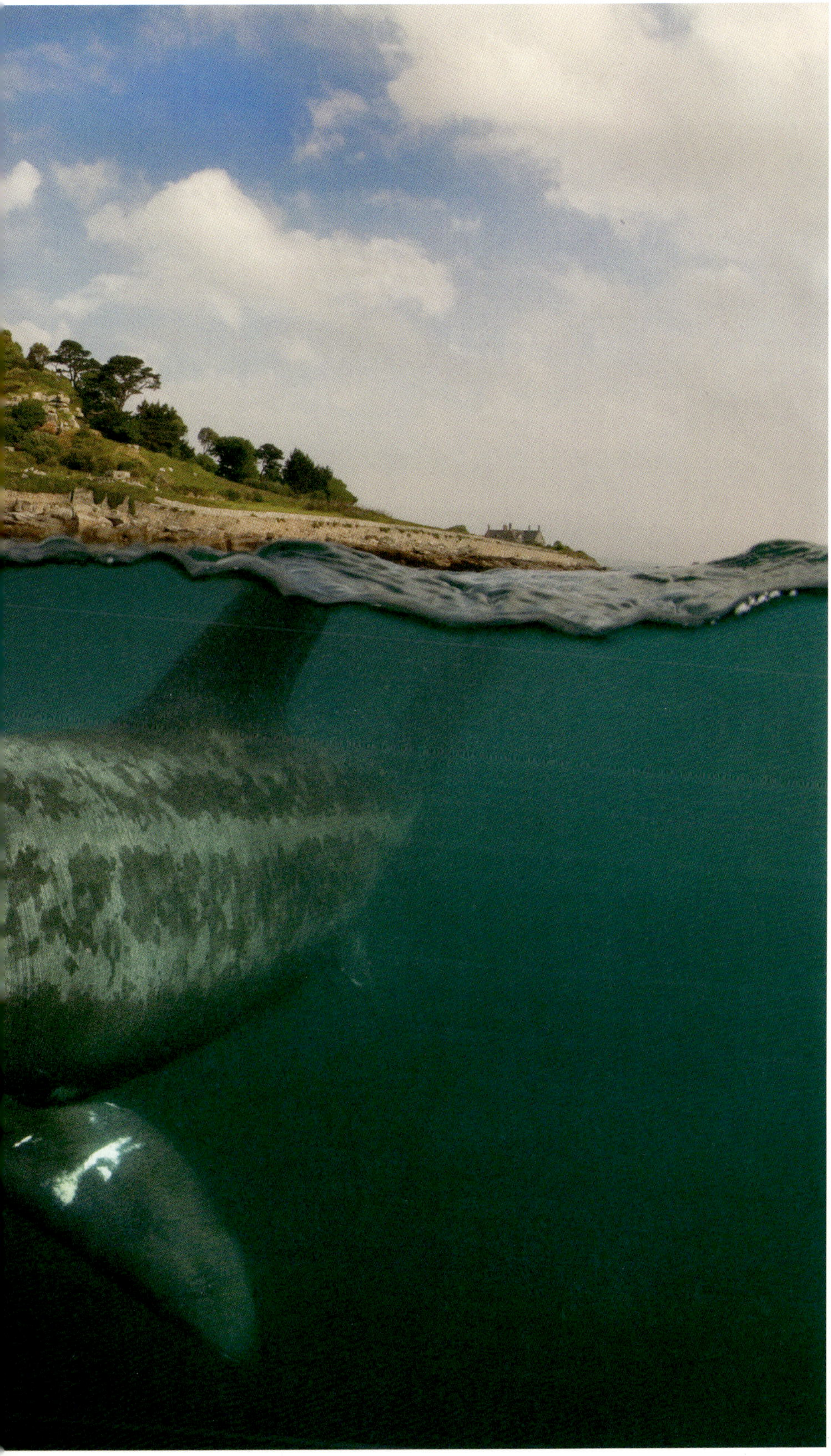

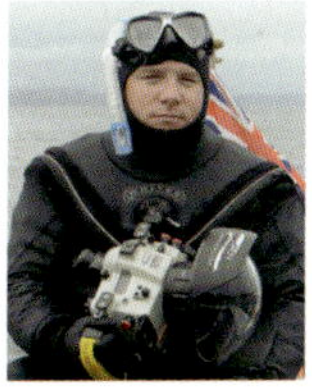

© Chris Gomersall/2020VISION

ALEX MUSTARD

Dr. Alexander Mustard, 39, from the United Kingdom, has been taking underwater photographs for 30 years and has worked as a full-time underwater photographer for the last ten years. His photographs have attracted numerous awards including being a category winner in the Wildlife Photographer of the Year, and in 2013 he was named European Wildlife Photographer of the Year as overall winner of the GDT contest. He was on the team for the 2020VISION conservation photography project in the U.K. He also leads highly popular underwater photography workshops at top diving destinations around the world. Visit Alex's website at www.amustard.com.

A digital composite showing a basking shark (*Ceterhinus maximus*) feeding on plankton around St. Michael's Mount, Cornwall, U.K., June 2010

Nikon D300S • 10–17mm lens • 1/160 s • f/3.4 • ISO 320

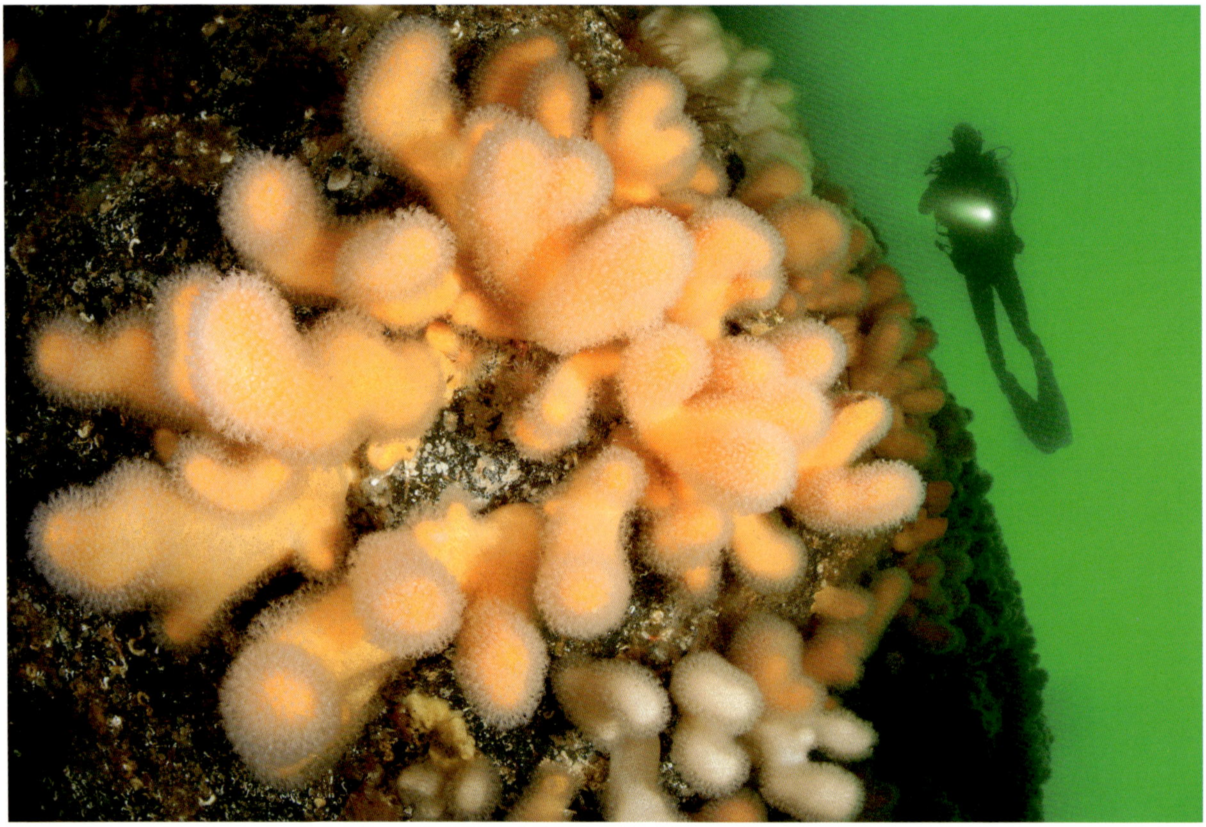

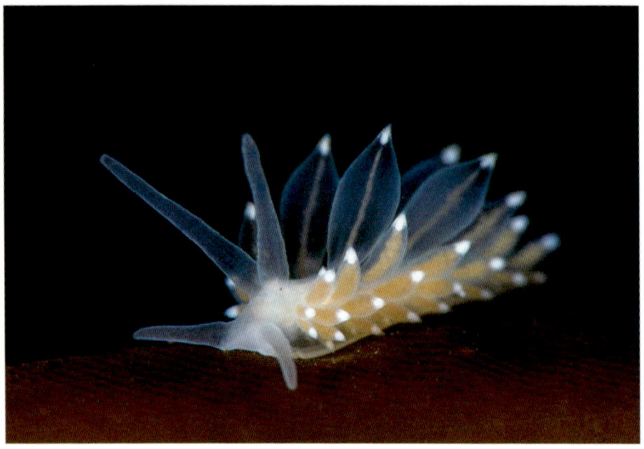

↑ Colorful deadman's fingers (Alcyonium digitatum, a type of soft coral) grow on a wall in Conservation Bay, Loch Carron, Scotland, Northeast Atlantic Ocean, April 2011

Nikon D700 • 15mm Lens • 1/100 s • f/2.8 • ISO 800

← A nudibranch (*Eubranchus farrani*) glides across a kelp leaf. Its basic eye is clearly visible at the base of the rhinophore. Shetland Islands, Scotland, British Isles, Northeast Atlantic Ocean, July 2013

Nikon D4 • 105mm lens • 1/320 s • f/4.7 • ISO 200

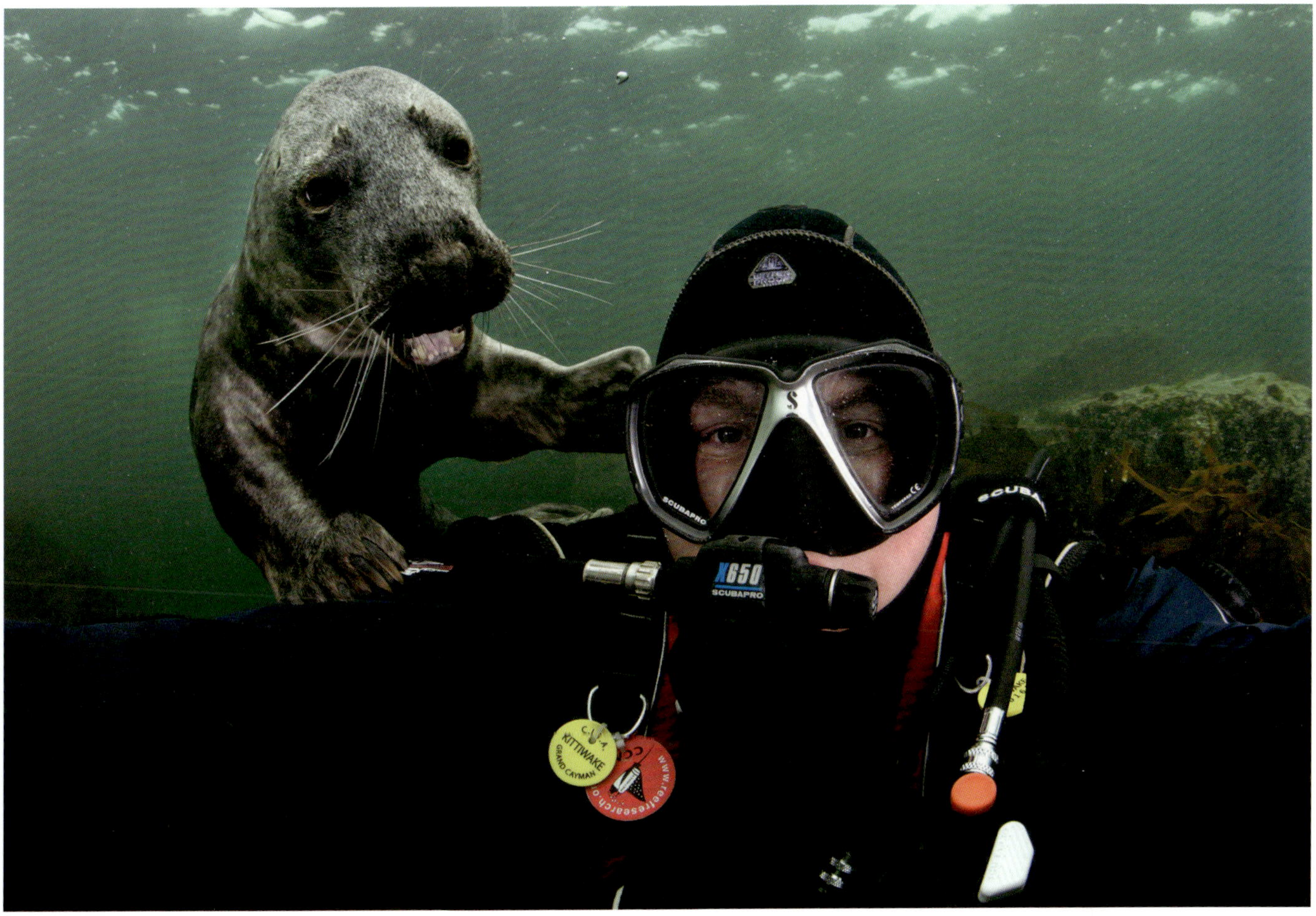

Underwater photographer Alex Mustard taking a self-portrait with a friendly, young grey seal (*Halichoerus grypus*). Farne Islands, Northumberland, England, British Isles, North Sea, July 2012

Nikon D4 • 15mm lens • 1/250 s • f/2.8 • ISO 800

IMRAN AHMAD

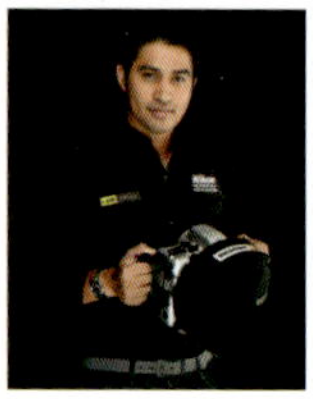

For more than 16 years, the award-winning underwater photography of Imran Ahmad has revealed the magnificence of life far below the water's surface. A celebrated and widely published Nikon Professional Photographer, Imran is committed to preserving and protecting the ocean's environment. His credo, "To always search and never destroy," has been his guiding light as he creates and shares his exquisite photographs in leading media worldwide including in the following publications; *Hidden Sanctuary, Ocean Tapestry, Edition Fifty Fathoms, The PURE Series,* and most recently, *Seychelles Unexpected Treasures*.

Imran is the founder of ESCAPEINC Dive & Photography where clients can find photographic solutions for corporate, commercial, wildlife, and underwater projects. Reaching beyond his homeland of Singapore, Imran's work is finding its way around the world with projects in Asia and beyond. Imran graduated from Middlesex University with a Bachelor of Arts in Film Making and is a member of the Ocean Artist Society. See more images by Imran at www.escapeinc.com.sg.

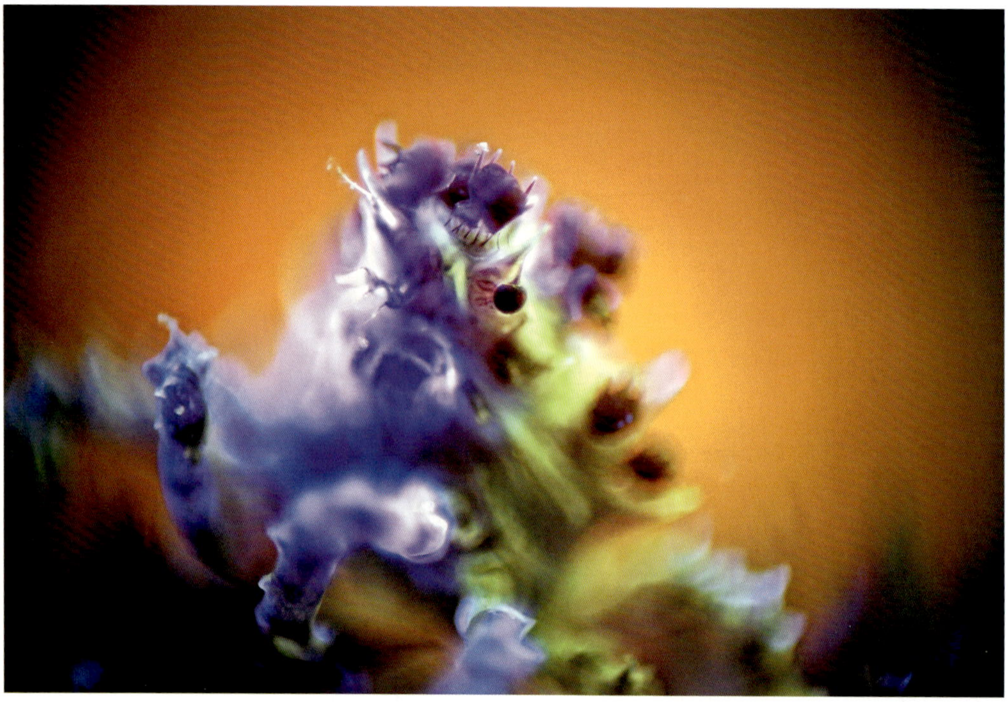

↑ *The Candy Store:* Candy Crab off Seraya, Bali, Indonisia

Nikon D3 • 105mm combo lens (reverse ring macro) • 1/320 s • f/2.8 • ISO 200 • Seacam with Ikelite 161

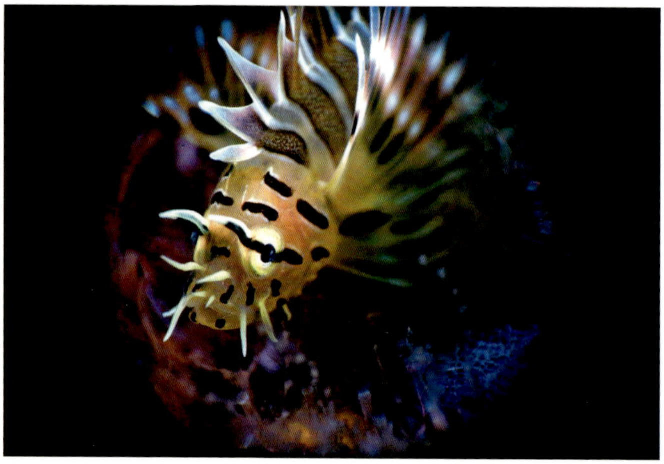

→ Flames: Juvenile lionfish off Seraya, Bali, Indonisia

Nikon D3 • 105mm combo lens (reverse ring macro) • 1/320 s • f/2.8 • ISO 200 • Seacam with Ikelite 161

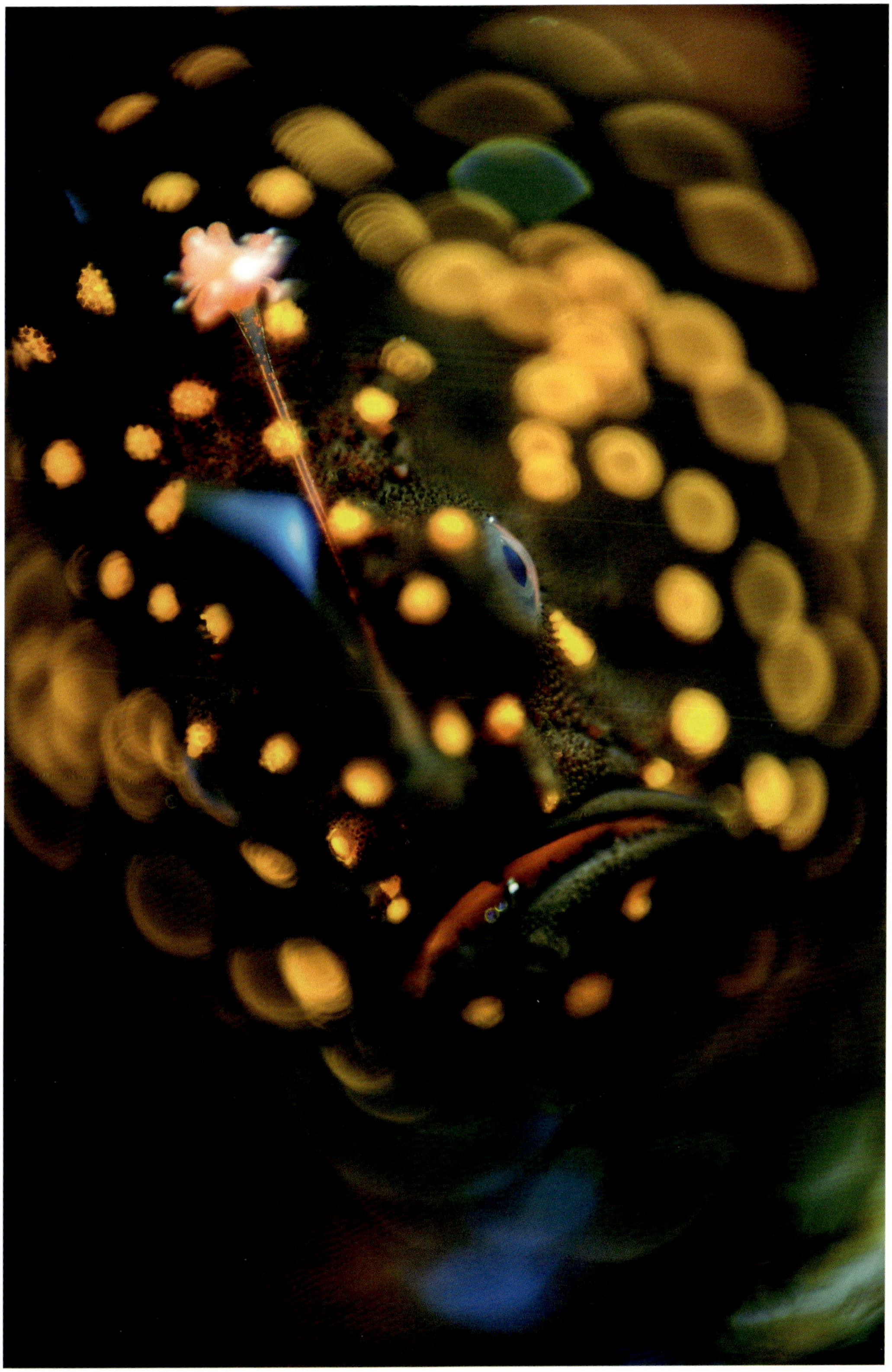

How do You Like Me Now! Frogfish at Mato Point, Anilao, Philippines

Nikon D4 • 105mm combo lens (reverse macro ring) • 1/250 s • f/2.8 • ISO 200 • Seacam • RGBlue light • Ikelite 161

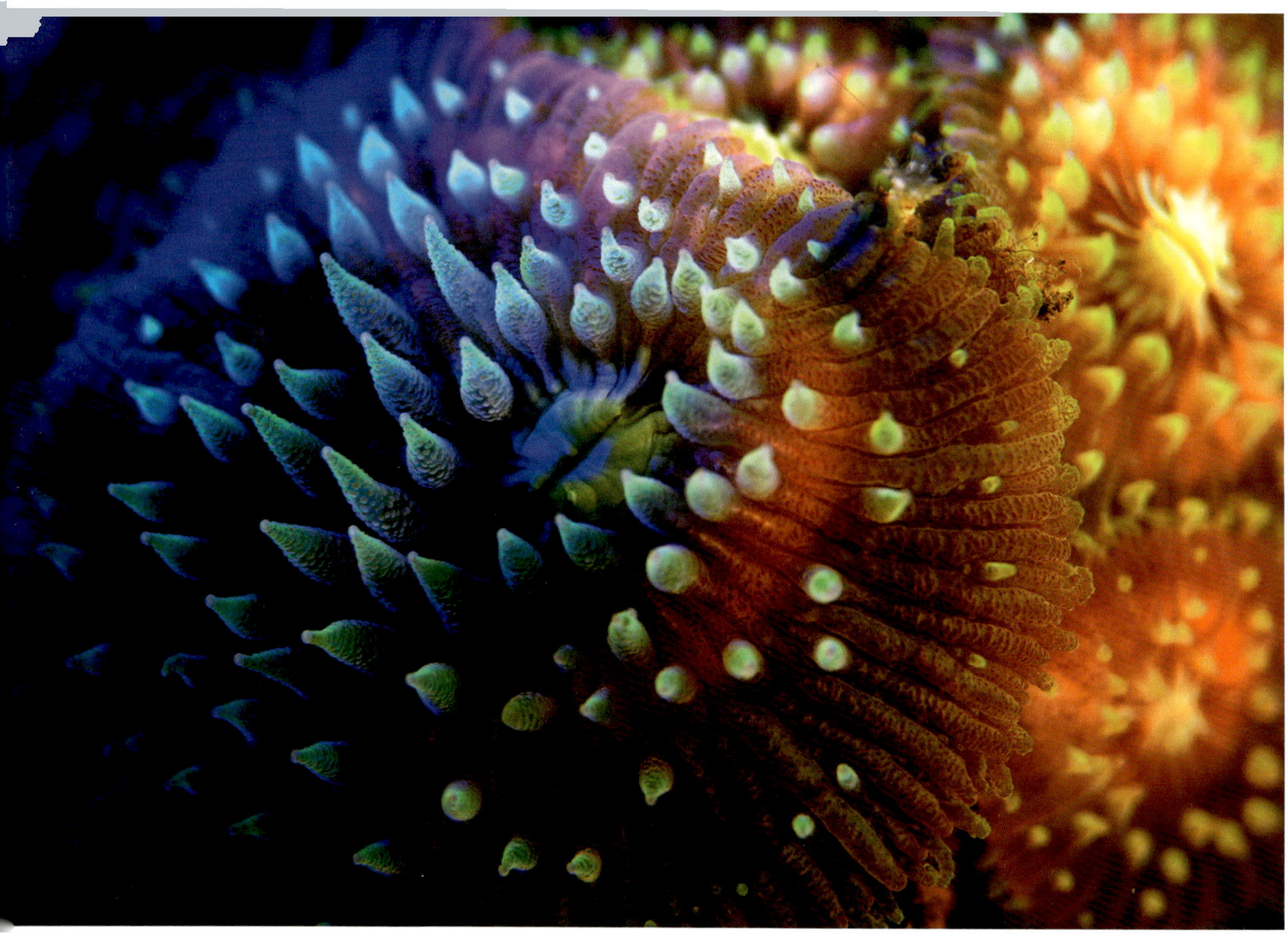

The Surreal: Hard corals off Seraya, Bali, Indonesia

Nikon D3 • 105mm combo lens (reverse ring macro) • 1/200 s • f/2.8 • ISO 200 • Seacam with Ikelite 161 • UV light • color filters

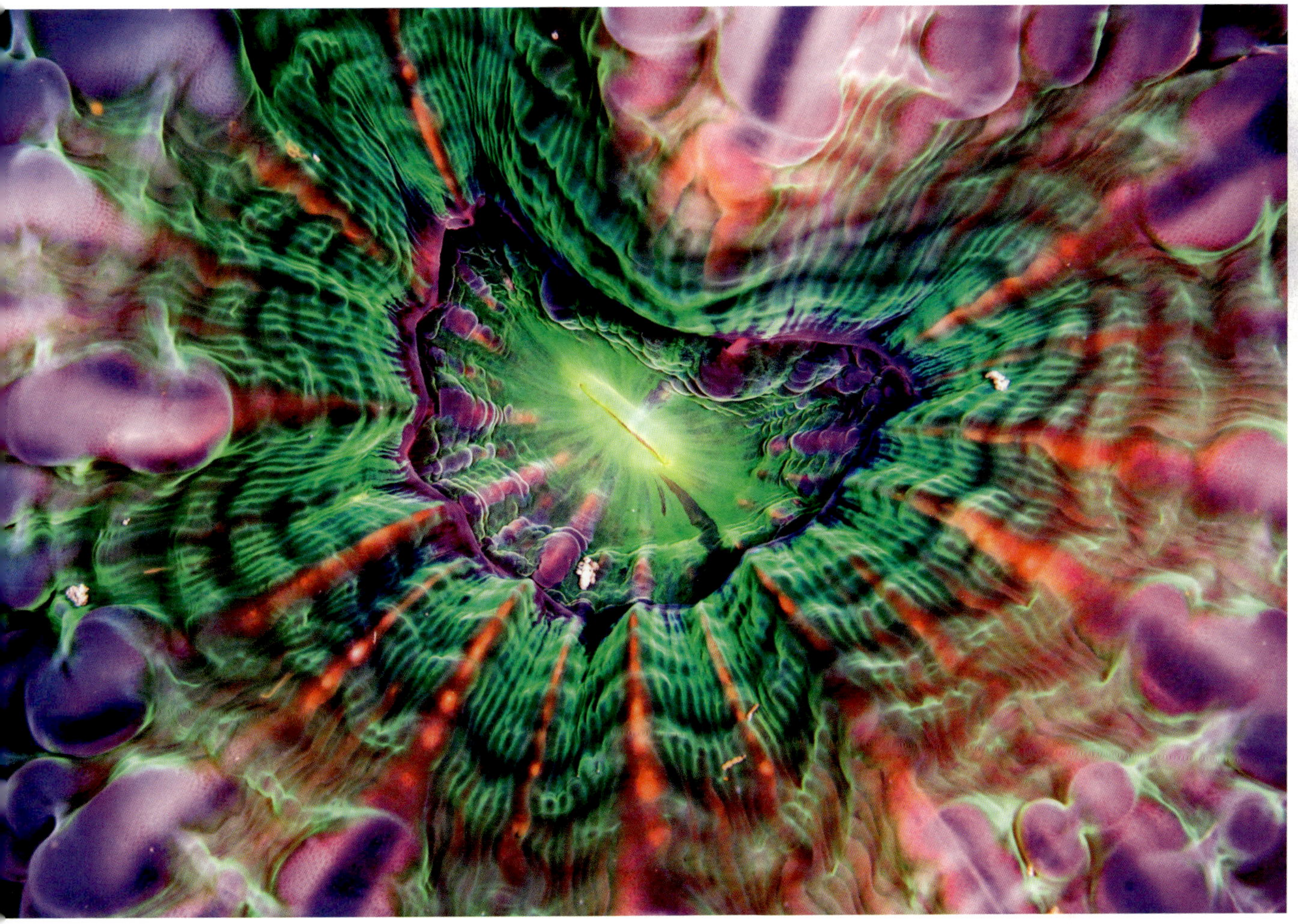

Fusion (Ocean Tapestry): Anemone in Brunei Darussalam (along the coast of northwestern Malaysia)

Nikon D7000 • 1/125 s • f/2.8 • ISO 400 • 60mm macro lens + 4 diopter • Seacam • Ikelite 161 • UV light and color filters

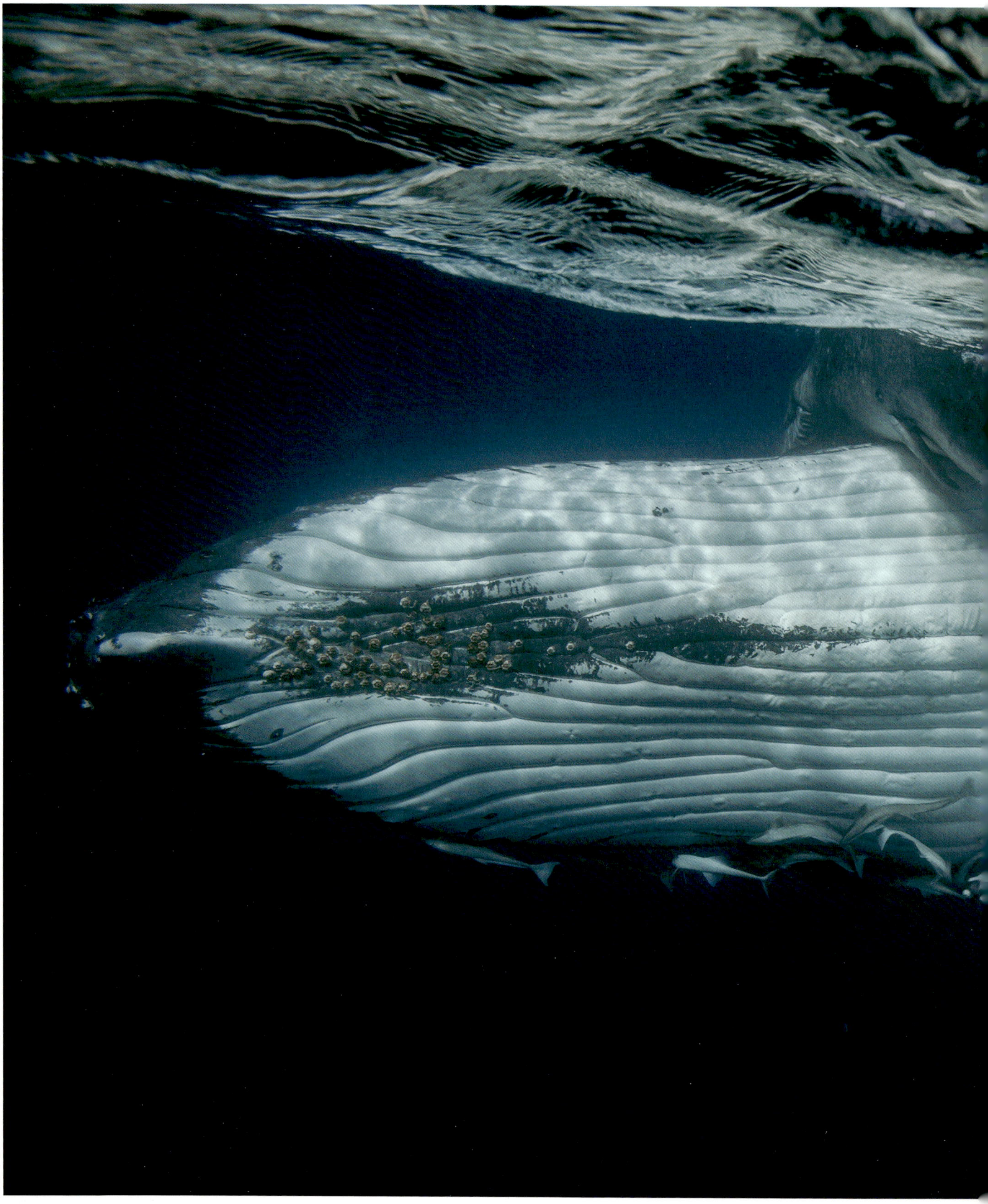

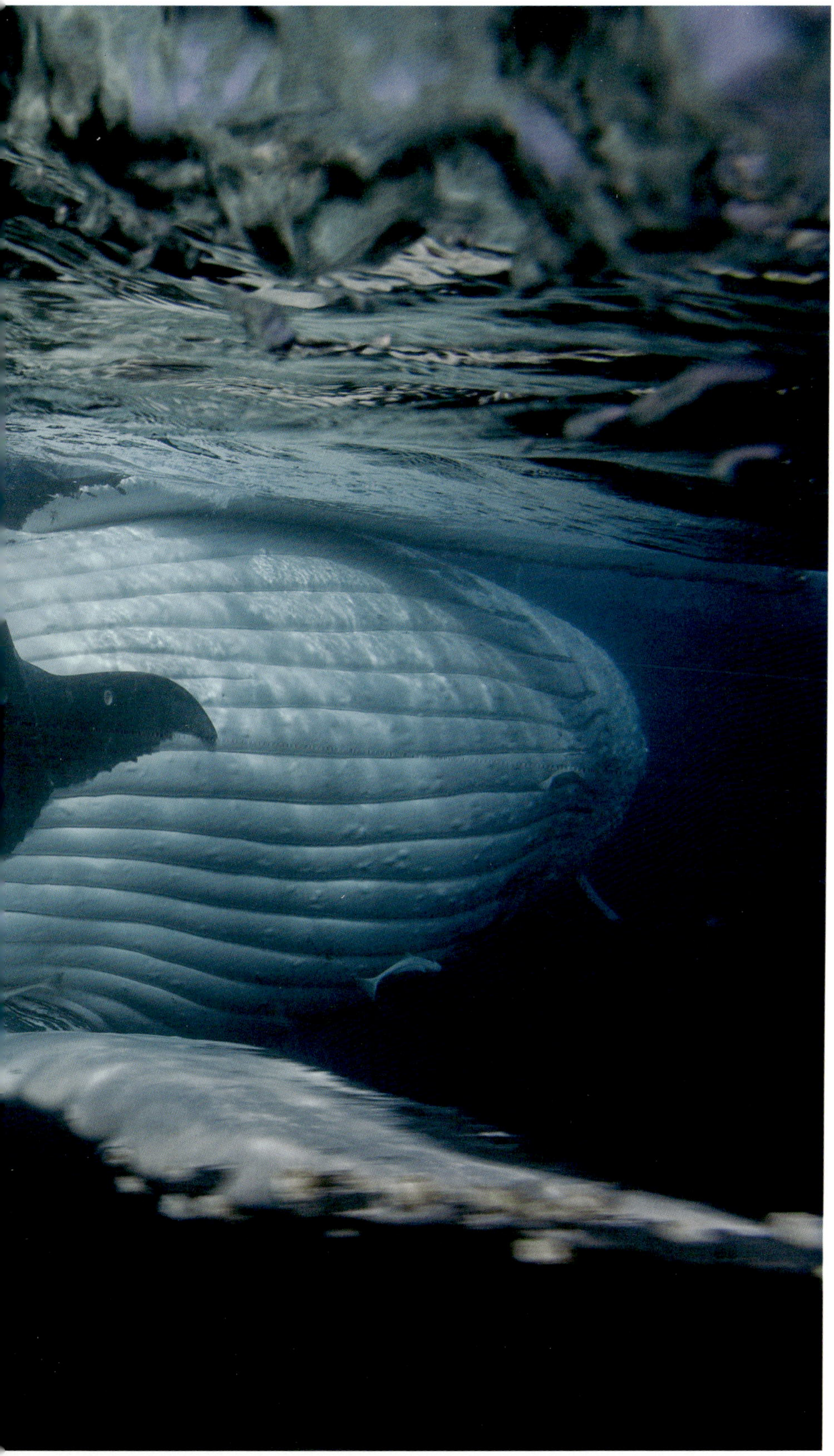

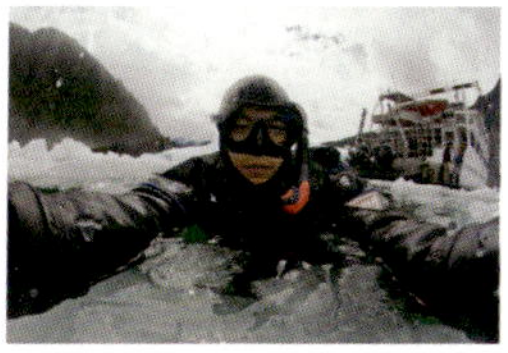

ERIC CHENG

Eric Cheng is an award-winning underwater photographer, aerial imager, publisher, and the Director of Aerial Imaging at DJI. His underwater images have won contests such as the prestigious Nature's Best Magazine photo competition, which has placed some of his work in the Smithsonian's Natural History Museum. Eric's photography has been seen in over a hundred magazines and books worldwide.

Eric is also the publisher of Wetpixel.com, the premiere online community for underwater photographers. Eric regularly leads photography expeditions and workshops around the world, and he has given seminars and lectures on an international stage.

A large mother humpback whale (Megaptera novaeangliae) holds up her young calf to help it breathe. Vava'u, Tonga, Pacific Ocean.

Canon EOS 1Ds Mark II • Tokina 17mm f/3.5 rectilinear lens (prime) • 1/125 s at f/18 • ISO 160

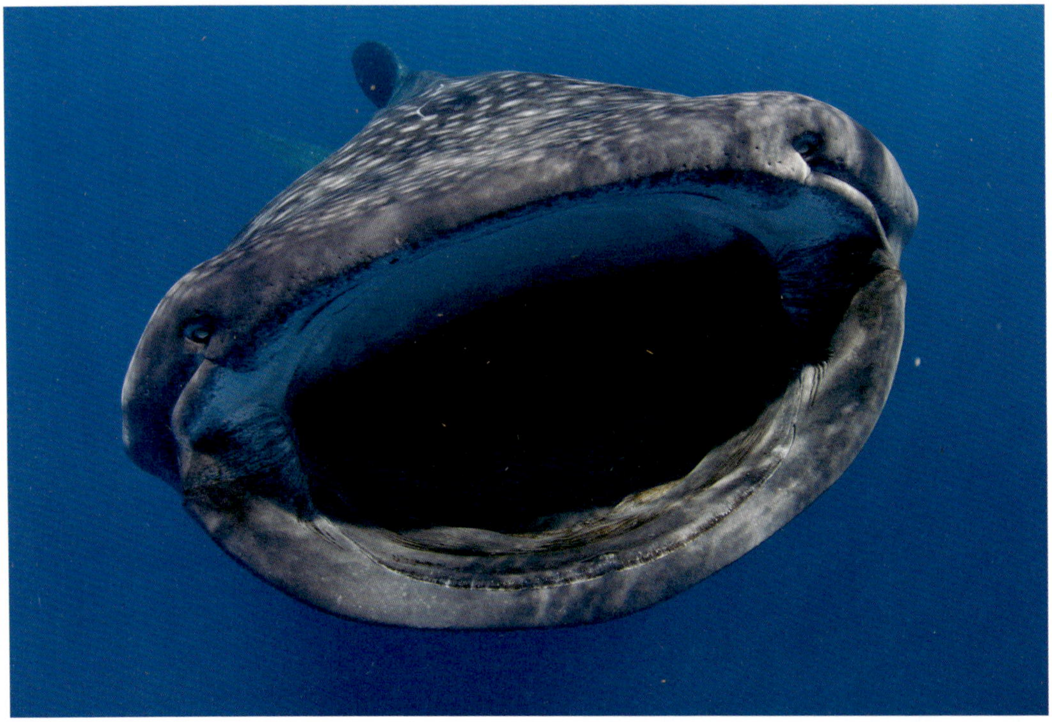

A whale shark (Rhincodon typus) with its mouth wide open as it feeds on tunny (bonito tuna) eggs. Isla Mujeres, Mexico.

Canon EOS 7D • Tokina 10–17 fisheye zoom at 12mm • 1/200 s at f/10 • ISO 320

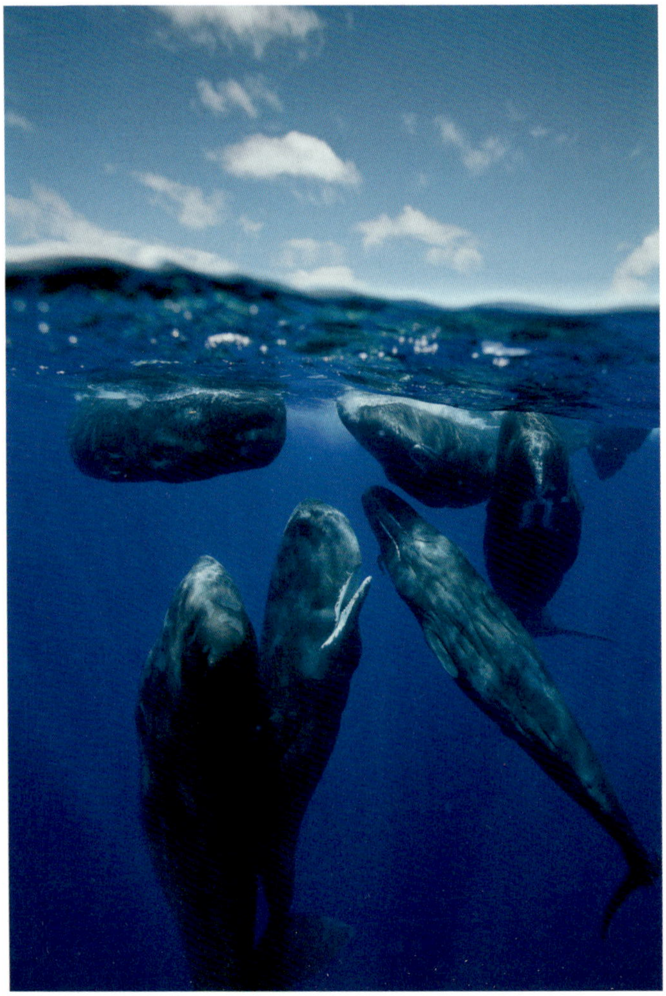

Split waterline image of a group of sperm whales (Physeter macrocephalus) rubbing up against each other while socializing.

Canon EOS 5D Mark II • Tokina 17mm f/3.5 rectilinear lens (prime) • 1/500s at f/8 • ISO 400

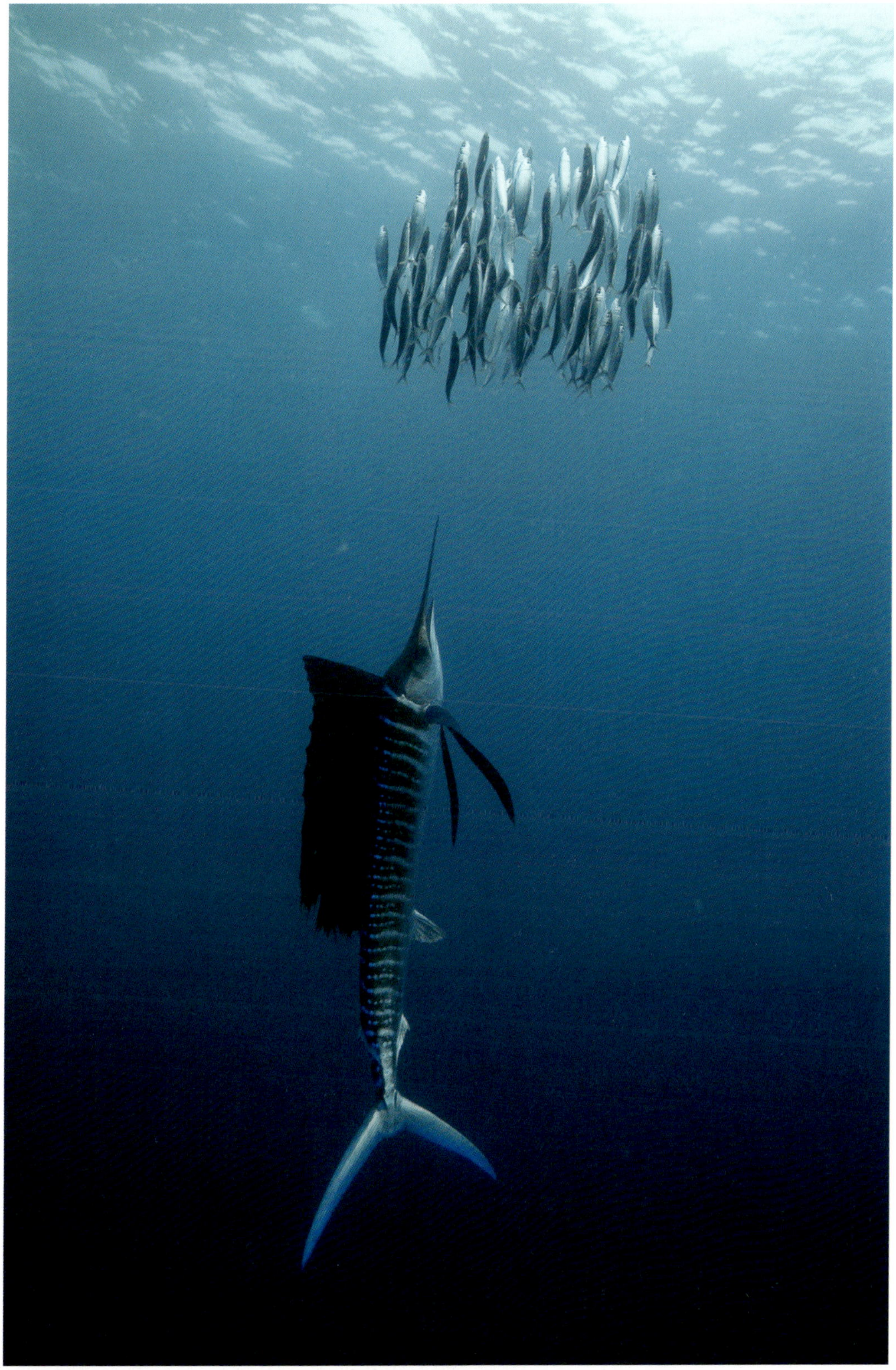

An Atlantic sailfish (Istiophorus albicans) drives a school of sardines up to the surface. Isla Mujeres, Mexico.
Canon EOS 5D Mark II • Canon EF16–35mm f/2.8L USM lens at 16mm • 1/250 s at f/7.1 • ISO 640

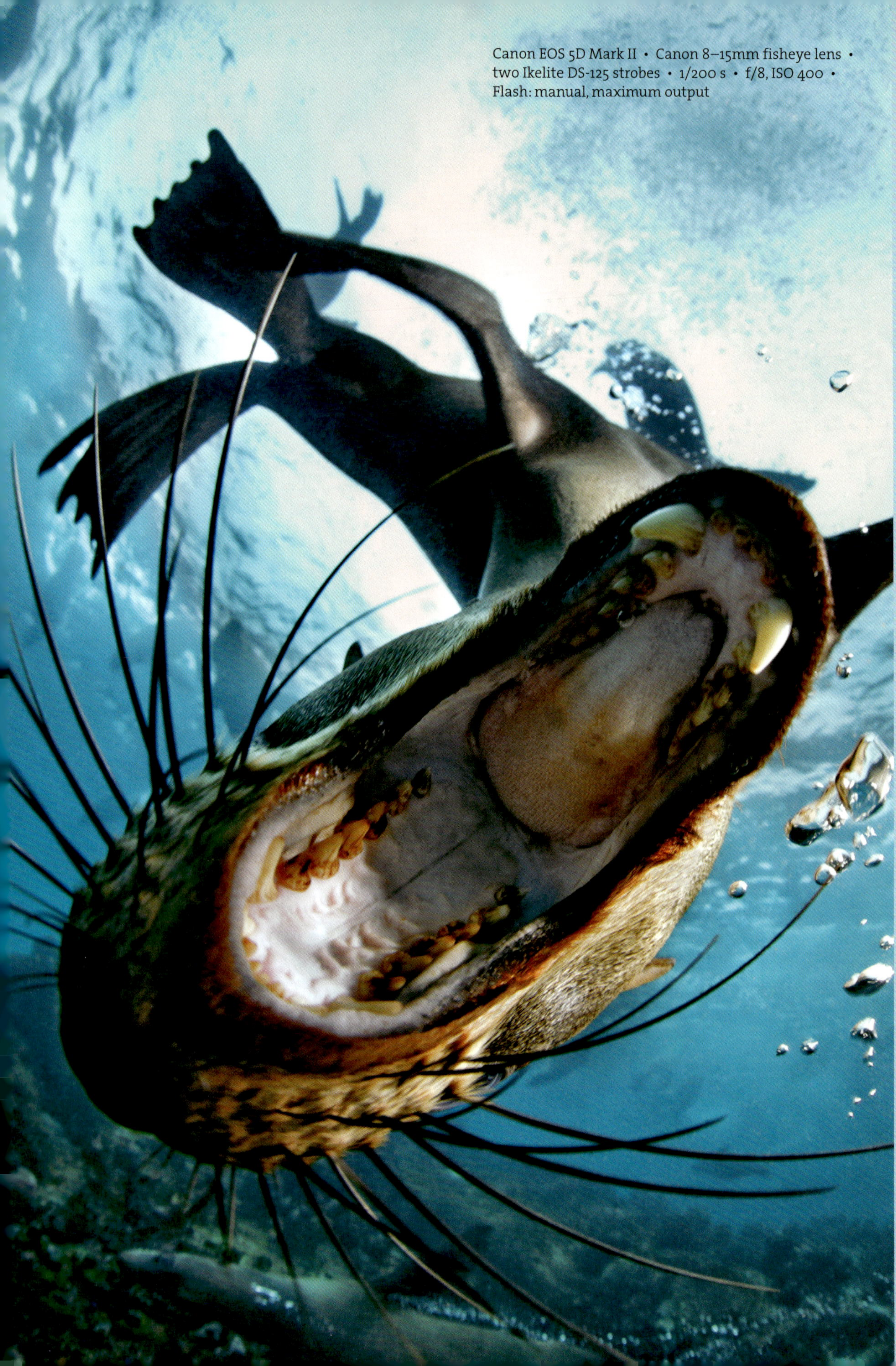

Canon EOS 5D Mark II • Canon 8–15mm fisheye lens • two Ikelite DS-125 strobes • 1/200 s • f/8, ISO 400 • Flash: manual, maximum output

Case Study 4: The Playmate

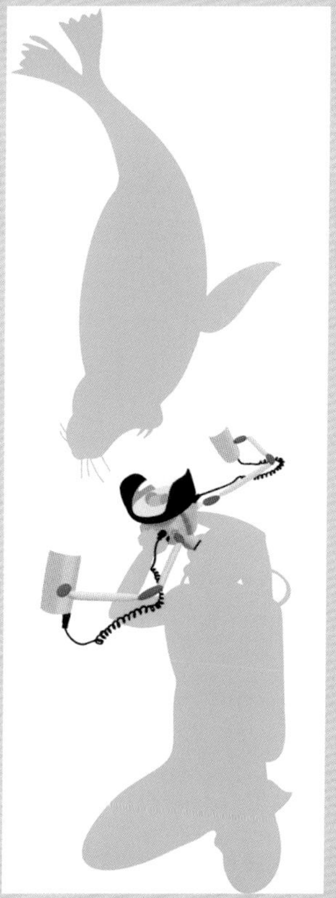

Taking pictures of seals is one of the most difficult challenges an underwater photographer can face. These agile creatures are incredibly fast, making it difficult to capture a successful image before they dart away. Another challenge is their exceptionally dense and dark fur, which makes it necessary to set your flash units to maximum if you want to capture detail on their bodies.

While diving off the coast of South Africa, I quickly learned it was futile to try to follow the animals. Instead, I knelt on the rocky ground and waited for one of them to approach me. In anticipation, I set the shutter speed to 1/200 second so I could freeze the seal's motion, and I bumped up the ISO value to compensate for the ambient light. I had metered my exposure by looking out horizontally at the level of the animals. But all of a sudden, this playful fellow approached me from directly above with its mouth wide open as it inspected its reflection in my dome port. I had no choice but to use the settings I had already set, even though they weren't ideal. I was able to capture only one image, and the background ended up being too bright as my camera was pointing toward the surface of the water. I used a RAW converter to correct it in post-processing, and I brightened up the dark areas. The format of the image is original to the photo as I captured it.

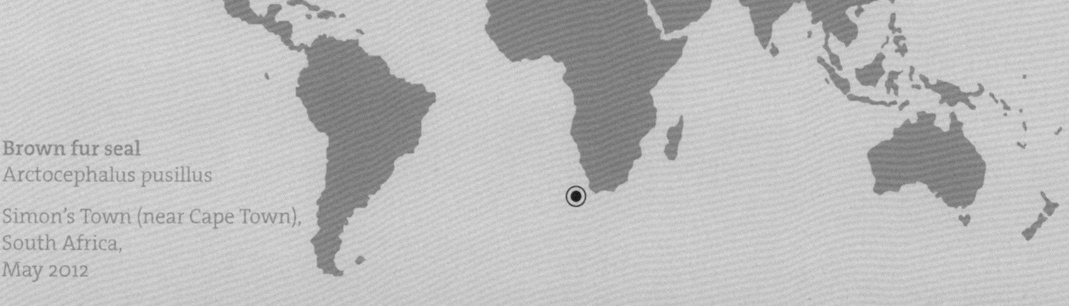

Brown fur seal
Arctocephalus pusillus

Simon's Town (near Cape Town), South Africa, May 2012

4

Wide-Angle Photography

Moods, emotions, and encounters under water are best conveyed in wide-angle photographs. When you first glance at a wide-angle photo, you can tell if it was taken at night or during the day, whether the water was clear, and maybe even the approximate depth at which the photo was taken.

The exceptionally broad angle of view that wide-angle lenses offer makes it a challenge to avoid including distracting elements, such as other divers, in the backgrounds of your pictures. It would be frustrating to see part of another diver's fin or an outcrop of unattractive coral in the background of your beautiful picture of a sea turtle from your trip to the Caribbean. These challenges make wide-angle shots the most difficult type of underwater photography.

You can usually avoid distractions if you include the surface of water in your composition. This gives the impression that you are shooting with an upward perspective, which generally produces pleasing results. It also gives viewers a visual anchor because the water's surface functions like the horizon in landscape photographs. It gives viewers a point of reference so they can interpret other elements in the photo.

When you see wide-angle photos that you particularly enjoy, pay attention to how many of them include the water's surface. You'll find some photos without it, of course, but many of them will include it. On your next dive, take some pictures with the water's surface visible and compare the results with your other photos that don't show it. You'll be surprised how effective this design technique can be.

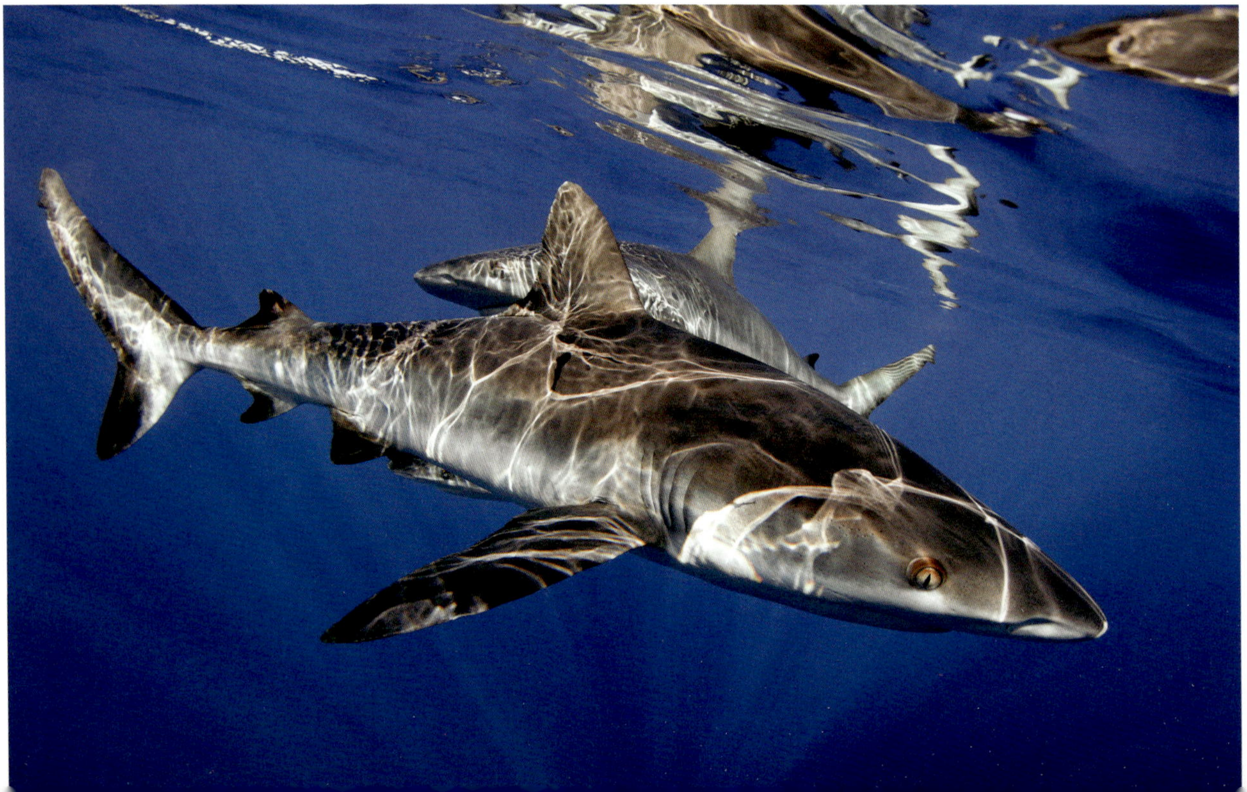

Including the surface of the water in a wide-angle image helps the viewer make sense of the photo

Canon EOS 5D Mark II • Canon 17–40mm wide-angle lens • 1/500 s • f/9 • ISO 800

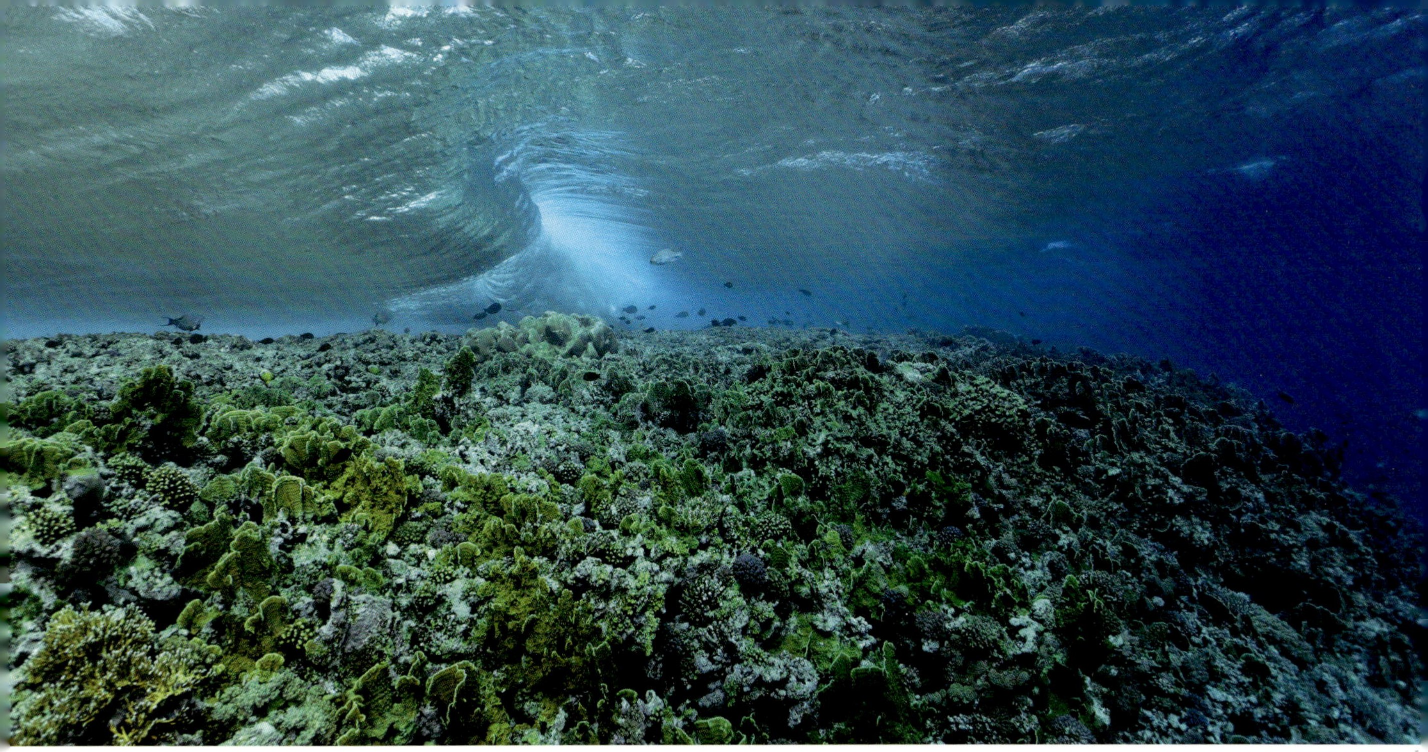

It's rare to find attractive reef landscapes as close to the surface of the water as I did here off the Brother Islands in Egypt

Canon EOS 5D Mark II • Canon 17–40mm wide-angle lens • 1/200 s • f/8 • ISO 100

4.1 Lenses

Wide-angle photography relies primarily on fisheye and super-wide-angle lenses because they allow you to get close to a subject and still depict it in its entirety.

Fisheye lenses can reach an angle of view up to 180 degrees, as measured across the image diagonal. The fisheye effect gives images some specific characteristics: lines that pass through the center of the image are straight; as you move away from the center of the image, the lines become increasingly curved. For example, in the interior of a shipwreck the proportions of the helm will be correct, but the ceiling and floor will be markedly curved. The closer you are to the subject, the more exaggerated the effect. This is why when using fisheye lenses for closeup pictures of people, it makes them look like they have gigantic noses or hands the size of frying pans. It's important to understand this effect so you can use it effectively in your compositions.

Fisheye lenses are also practical when there is poor visibility in the water. Shooting your subject at close proximity makes the background seem farther away than it really is, which improves the visibility in the photo.

Fisheye lenses are particularly effective for shots of shipwrecks, whales, schools of fish, and large manta rays.

Super-wide-angle lenses are available as zoom lenses, which offer a bit more flexibility than fisheye lenses. You can shoot a reef landscape one minute and capture a portrait of a reef dweller the next.

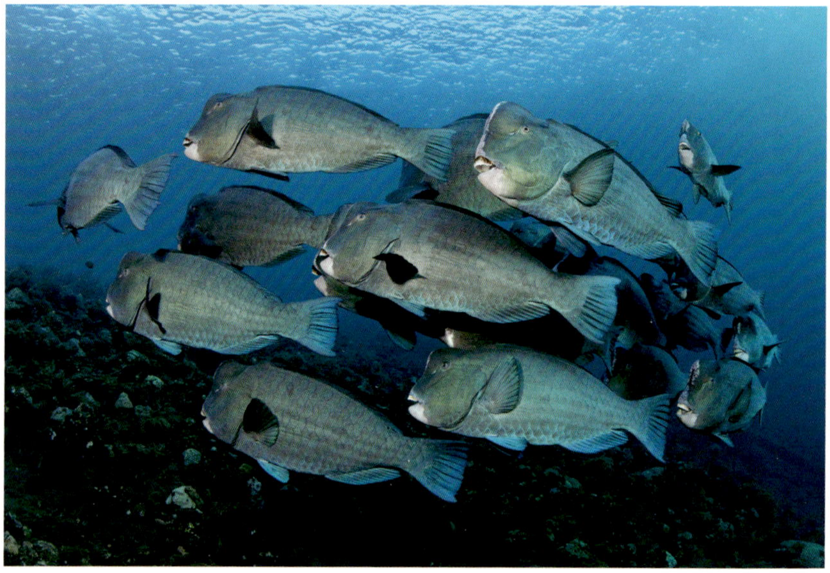

Getting in the water as early in the morning as possible can increase your chances of finding schools of fish still in their nightly resting places before they move apart and spread out over the reef

Canon EOS 5D Mark II • Canon 8–15mm fisheye lens • 1/80 s • f/8 • ISO 400

Wide-angle lenses distort the environment much less than fisheye lenses—they reproduce most lines without creating a curve. Subjects like sharks, medium-sized coral gardens, gorgonians, larger animals such as Napoleon fish, and small wrecks are ideal candidates for this type of lens.

All wide-angle and fisheye lenses have a large depth of field. If you are about 3 to 6 feet away from the subject, an aperture of f/8 will be sufficient to capture it and the background sharply. If your subject is closer—in the 10 to 20-inch range—the background can quickly start to lose sharpness. Increase the aperture to f/11 or f/16 to capture the background in focus. Generally speaking, use a larger angle of view for larger subjects.

SUMMARY:

- Fisheye lenses have exceptionally large angles of view.
- Fisheye lenses distort the outside area of an image by causing lines to curve. They can focus at very close distances.
- Fisheye lenses are particularly useful when visibility in the water is poor.
- It's often effective to capture large subjects with a fisheye lens.
- Wide-angle lenses offer more flexibility. They can be used to shoot sweeping reef landscapes and portraits.
- Wide-angle lenses reproduce straight lines.
- Both fisheye and wide-angle lenses have a large focus range.
- The larger the subject, the larger your angle of view should be.

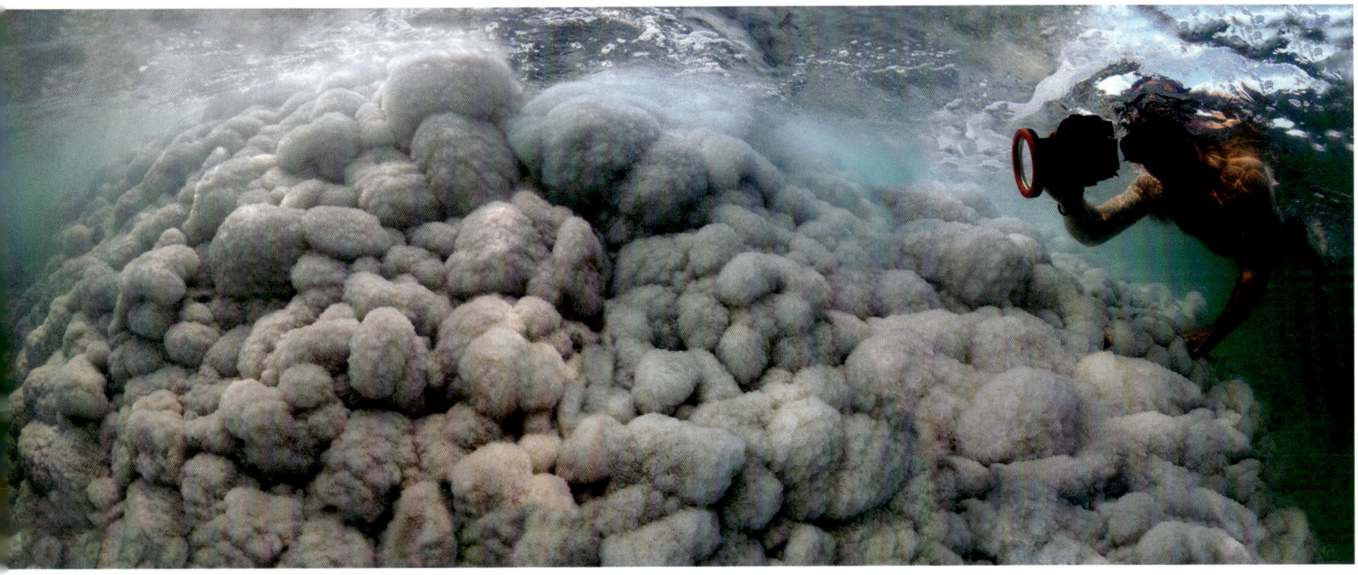

4.2 Exposure

Always keep your camera handy. This image was taken during a spur-of-the-moment swim in the Dead Sea, where these beautiful stones covered in salt deposits were unexpectedly discovered.

Canon EOS 5D Mark II • Canon 8–15mm fisheye lens • 1/160 s • f/22 • ISO 400

Before your dive, program your camera's exposure settings based on what you expect the underwater lighting conditions to be, then you'll have to make only small changes after you're in the water. Nothing is more frustrating than a missed opportunity because your camera wasn't set up for a shot. If you're relatively new to underwater photography, it can be difficult to anticipate the exposure settings you'll need, but your intuition will get sharper as you gain more experience.

The combination of settings you'll need depends on the weather and the visibility of the water. Programming your camera at f/8, 1/125 second, and ISO 200, and setting your flash units to half power, is often a good place to start. After you're in the water, you can easily fine-tune the settings to compensate for the actual conditions.

If your goal is to capture water that has a rich blue tone, first do the following: When you get to your dive depth point your camera toward the open water and keep it parallel to the surface (not tilted upward or downward). Don't include coral, reefs, or rocks in your image area—just water—and aim roughly in the direction you plan to shoot. Now your camera's exposure meter will gauge what the actual lighting conditions are. If the exposure meter is in the middle, the water's blue color will be too bright. To get a deep blue tone, adjust the exposure down by one stop. Alter the shutter speed instead of the aperture. For example, if your image is too dark, you might decrease the shutter speed to 1/100 second, 1/80 second, or even longer, but don't use a speed slower than 1/30 second because camera shake can ruin your picture. If you still don't

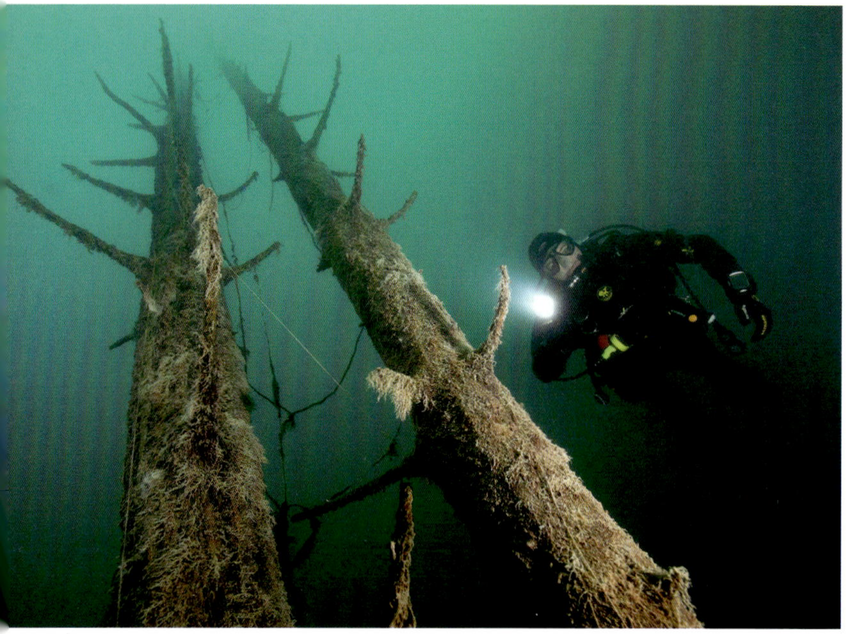

have enough light, you can bump up the ISO to increase the sensor's light sensitivity.

Naturally, you need to change your exposure settings as the lighting conditions change. This can happen, for example, if you increase or decrease your depth or if the ambient light changes. Don't meter your exposure based on bright sunlight or a reef landscape because you'll end up with wildly inaccurate exposure values.

If your strobes produce light that's too bright, you may need to use a higher f-stop—which decreases the size of the aperture—to permit less light to reach the sensor. When you make this adjustment, however, you also need to adjust the other exposure settings: shutter speed and ISO.

What at first may seem like an uninteresting subject can be vastly improved with an interesting perspective, a thoughtful composition, and the inclusion of a diver

Canon EOS 5D Mark II • Canon 17–40mm wide-angle lens • 1/160 s • f/8 • ISO 400

Taking a test shot and looking at it on your camera's LCD monitor is a practical way to examine your exposure settings.

If you are using flash units, you usually can't set your shutter speed faster than 1/200 second. Faster shutter speeds won't allow the flash light to affect your exposure because the shutter will open and close before the flash units will fire. This limit, called the flash sync speed, varies among camera models. Some have faster sync speeds of about 1/250 second, and the sync speeds for older models are often closer to 1/180 second. Check your camera's user manual to discover the sync speed for your camera.

A practical aperture for wide-angle photography is f/8 to f/11. Any setting in this range will produce a good depth of field and capture a sufficient amount of ambient light.

When you shoot rapidly moving animals, you often want your flash units to fire in quick succession. Increasing the ISO value and decreasing the power setting on your flash units is one way to make them cycle faster—the diminished output means they can recharge faster.

Areas in an image that are overexposed don't contain any visual information—blown-out highlights appear as solid white areas. Make use of your camera's overexposure warning to avoid this problem. Your camera will identify the overexposed areas and let you know that your picture may not be properly exposed. When you shoot wide-angle images, inspect your photos on your camera's LCD monitor and check the histogram for any potential problems (see section 2.8).

SUMMARY:

- Program your camera before you get into the water, based on what you expect the conditions to be.
- Try this combination of settings before you dive: f/8, 1/125 second, ISO 200, and the flash units set at half power.
- Adjust the exposure settings as you increase and decrease your depth.
- Keep the shutter speed between 1/200 second and 1/30 second.
- Keep the aperture between f/8 and f/11. Use different f-stops only for exceptions.
- Turn on your camera's overexposure warning.
- Use the histogram to evaluate your exposure settings.

4.3 Using Flash

The position and power of your flash units have a big impact on how your pictures turn out. Artificial light not only revitalizes the vivid colors beneath the sea, it can also define shapes and establish a certain atmosphere.

Most underwater subjects require only one flash unit, but the position of the unit is of utmost importance in order to achieve the lighting effect you want. Always know where your flash unit is pointed and what effect the angle of light will create. For the best results, realign your flash unit for every new subject. Using it in the same position from photo to photo will work only in rare circumstances. It's often effective to position your flash unit above your camera with a distance of about 20 to 31 inches from your housing. If you're not sure how the flash position will impact your image, you can always take a test photo and analyze it on your camera display to see if you need to reposition your strobe.

When you use two flash units, the basic approach is to have them on the same horizontal axis as the camera, on each side of it, and as far away from the camera as possible. Sharks, schools of fish, and reef landscapes benefit from this particular lighting setup. When you work with two strobes, you need to adjust them for each subject to produce purposeful lighting effects. For example, you need to reposition each strobe if you want a piece of coral on the left side of the image to receive only a small amount of light and the diver on the right side of the image to receive more light. Of course, it takes longer to adjust two flash units than just one.

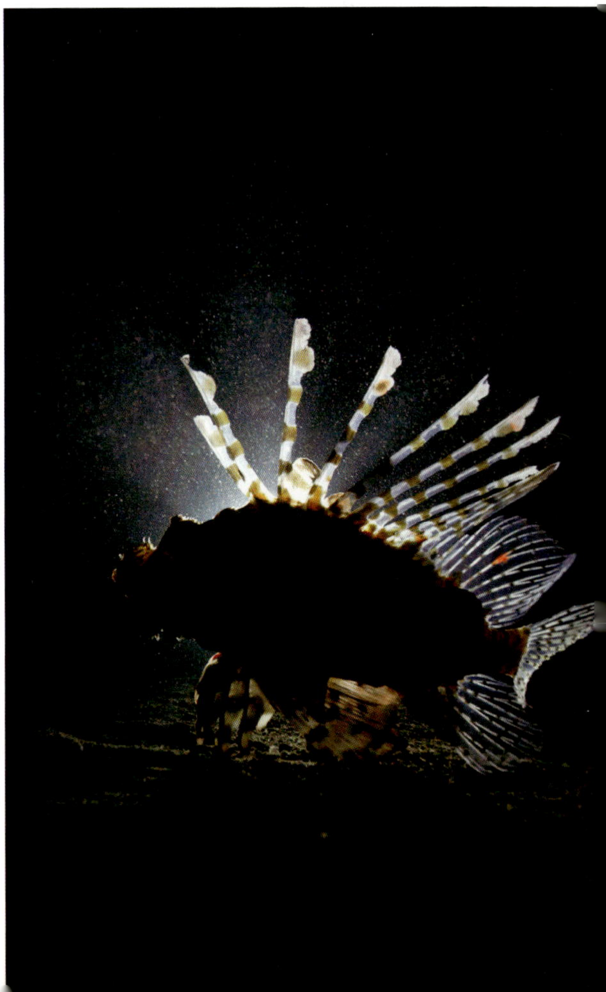

A single flash unit positioned directly behind an animal produces an entirely new and creative look

Canon EOS 5D Mark II • Canon 17–40mm wide-angle lens • 1/125 s • f/8 • ISO 3200

You can position your flash units in all kinds of configurations around your camera. What matters most is the subject and the effect you want to create. When you use two flash units, you can position them next to each other and directly above the camera housing to imitate the effect of a single flash. Avoid positioning the flash units too far forward when you shoot with a wide-angle lens because the broad angle may capture them in your photo, or the units may cast stray light into the front port.

Backscatter can be a problem when using strobes. If your units are positioned incorrectly, you'll end up illuminating countless tiny particles that will show up in your picture. The prevalence of these floating particles varies considerably. You can limit them in your photos by carefully positioning your light sources. If the particles are on the same level as your primary subject, you'll have to live with them until you can erase them from your image in post-processing.

What's the best way to minimize the appearance of floating particles? The strategy is simple: position your flash units as far away from your camera as possible. Such a configuration produces an empty space between your camera and the subject. This space receives very little artificial lighting, which prevents the particles from showing up in the first place. If your flash units are too close to your camera or if they are pointed toward the center too much, they will illuminate the space and the particles, making them visible in your photos.

The light from an underwater flash unit spreads out at an angle of about 70 to 80 degrees—think of it as a cone of light that extends outward from the bulb. You can use a diffuser to increase the angle to 90 or 100 degrees, but you'll also sacrifice about one stop of light intensity. As you imagine the cone of light emanating from your flash unit, you want its edge to illuminate the subject straight on. When you use two flash heads, allow the two cones of light to overlap a little at the position of the subject. With time you'll develop

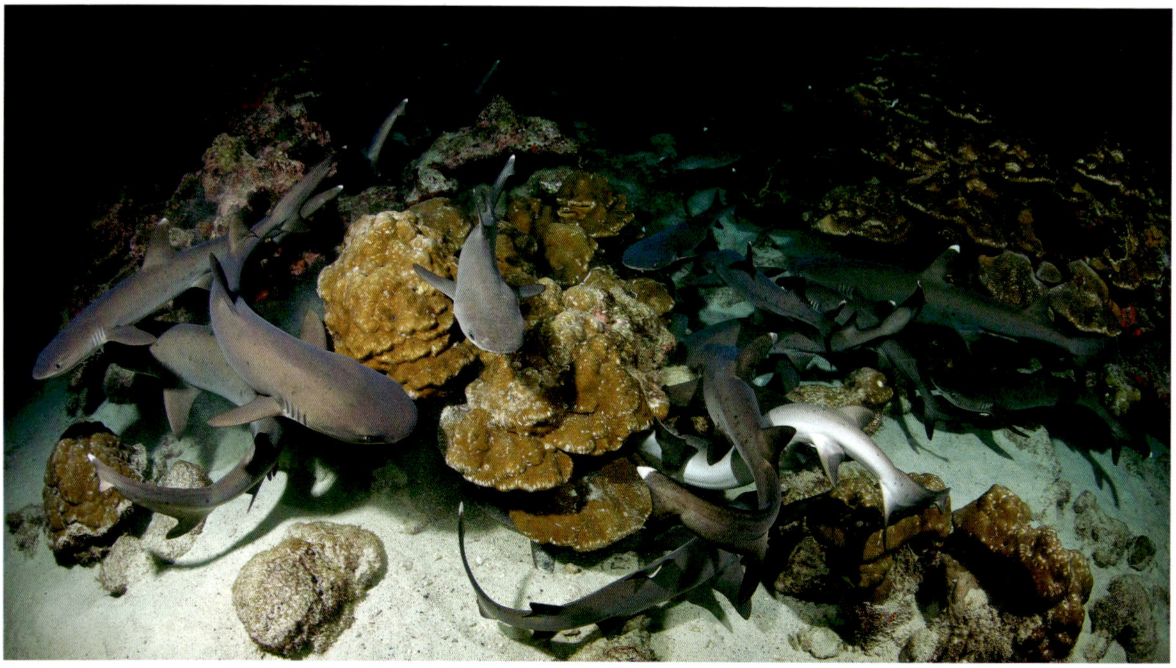

Flash units are indispensable for underwater photographers who want to capture subtle tones in their photos

Canon EOS 5D Mark II • Canon 8–15mm fisheye lens • 1/125 s • f/9 • ISO 800

a better sense of the area that your flash units illuminate.

There are, of course, exceptions to these general guidelines. Sometimes you'll need to position your flash units close to your camera housing, like when the subject is very close to you. Failing to get enough light to your subject is worse than too much light. It's better to get a few floating particles in a photo than to miss a great opportunity.

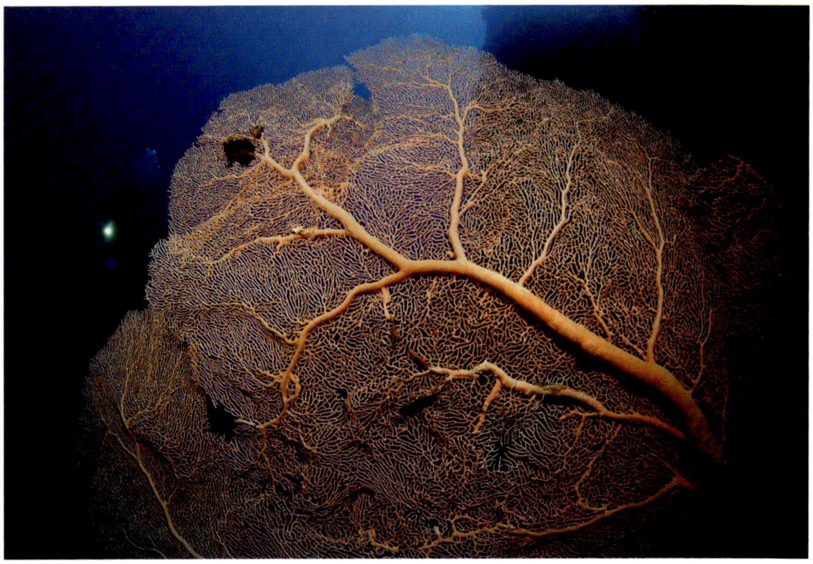

Without flash, this coral would look dull and bluish

Canon EOS 5D Mark II • Canon 8–15mm fisheye lens • 1/125 s • f/16 • ISO 200

A good exercise is to practice with your lighting equipment in a swimming pool. Place your flash unit approximately 7 ft from the wall of the pool, take a picture, and inspect the illumination pattern. Repeat the test with both one- and two-flash configurations, and with and without a diffuser. You might also practice with a diving partner. Who wouldn't be excited to volunteer in exchange for a few pictures from a budding professional photographer?

SUMMARY:

- Artificial light is required to give underwater photographs atmosphere and bright colors.
- One flash unit suffices for most subjects.
- When you use only one flash unit, you must take care to position it carefully.
- You can get a more even distribution of light by using two flash units, but they will require more time to set up and adjust.
- Adjust your flash for every subject to get the best possible results.
- You can position your flashes all around your camera, but be careful not to place them too far forward.
- Avoid floating particles by directing your flash units outward as much as possible.
- Only the edge of the light from your flash unit should illuminate the subject.
- For subjects that are close to you, point your flash units toward the middle.
- Practice with your flash units in a pool to give you more confidence in open water.

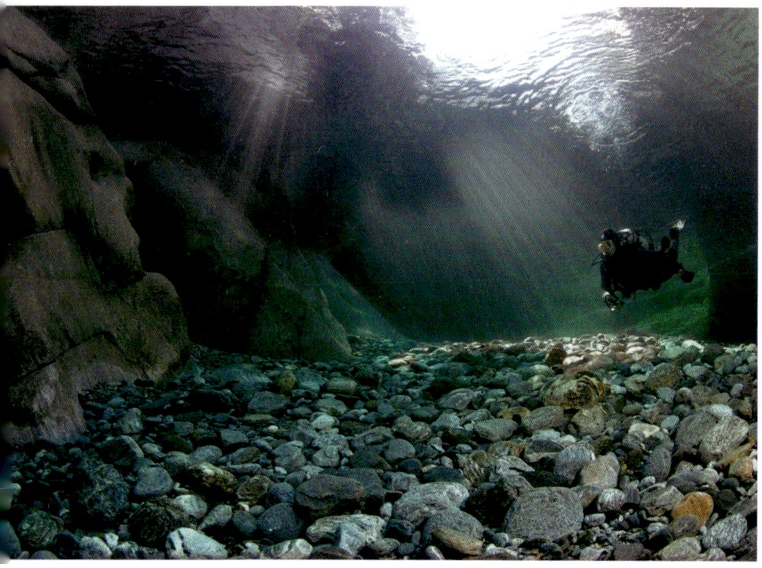

Capturing the play of natural light is just as much a part of wide-angle photography as managing artificial light sources

Canon EOS 300D • Tokina 10–17mm fisheye lens • 1/160 s • f/7.1 • ISO 400

4.4 Finding Subjects

Over time you'll learn how to recognize the types of subjects and perspectives that will result in interesting pictures. The more you practice, the better you'll get at anticipating what will appear in your viewfinder. Open eyes and concentration are absolute musts when you search for underwater subjects.

When you shoot wide-angle photos, you generally won't overlook obvious opportunities. Nevertheless, it's helpful to have a diving partner to point out that shark you somehow missed. It's always helpful when your diving partner knows what types of subjects you're looking for to help you locate them.

Ask yourself how a particular subject might look in a photo. How would this gorgonian look against deep blue water? Is this nudibranch resting on a photogenic background? Is there a way to alter my perspective or use flash to create a more interesting picture? If there's no way to rescue a shot, abort the effort and search for something else that will make a more interesting photograph.

When you find a worthy subject, take time to find the right perspective. Swimming around the subject one more time is a great way to evaluate the optimal angle of view. Look through your viewfinder frequently to see how the subject looks in relation to the other elements in the image area.

After you have decided on a subject that looks promising, ask yourself if there is anything distracting in the image. Is there another diver in the background? Is there something unsightly in the foreground? Is there some sort of distraction within the image area that you can eliminate by changing your camera settings or by reframing the shot? Doing away with unwanted elements will result in a better overall picture. Once you find the right position, invest some more time and wait until the subject does something interesting, such as opening it's mouth. Some professional photographers will spend an entire dive with the same subject, just to come back with one really good photo.

It's important to remember that not every picture will be a fantastic one—sometimes the circumstances make it impossible.

SUMMARY:

- Always concentrate when you're diving, and stay focused on your hunt for potential subjects.
- A diving partner can identify wildlife that you've overlooked.
- Imagine how something will look in your viewfinder to help you determine its worth as a subject.
- Can a potential subject be isolated against a blue background, or is it positioned over a photogenic background?
- It's better to look for other subjects if the circumstances prevent you from getting the shot you want.
- Try different angles to find the best perspective.
- Eliminate distracting elements by changing your perspective or adjusting your camera settings.
- Not every situation will yield a flawless image.

4.5 Shooting Distance

Getting close to your subject is one of the basic objectives of underwater photography. When you're too far away, it's impossible to produce a brilliant image because water is dense and it filters out colors. To counteract these problems, you need to get up close. This isn't a problem for stationary objects like corals, but moving subjects are a completely different matter. Sharks in particular are quite shy, making closeup pictures of them fairly rare. They will usually keep a safe distance from you and your camera. Don't be discouraged, though; persistence is key. (See the next section about tracking.)

Veteran underwater photographers are familiar with this scenario: A shark swims past you at a distance of 16 ft. The other divers assume you got a great shot because it was so close, but they'll often be disappointed because the animal was just too far away. Even if a shark seems extremely close, water can distort our sense of distance. You need the shark to be 3 to 7 ft away to get a successful picture.

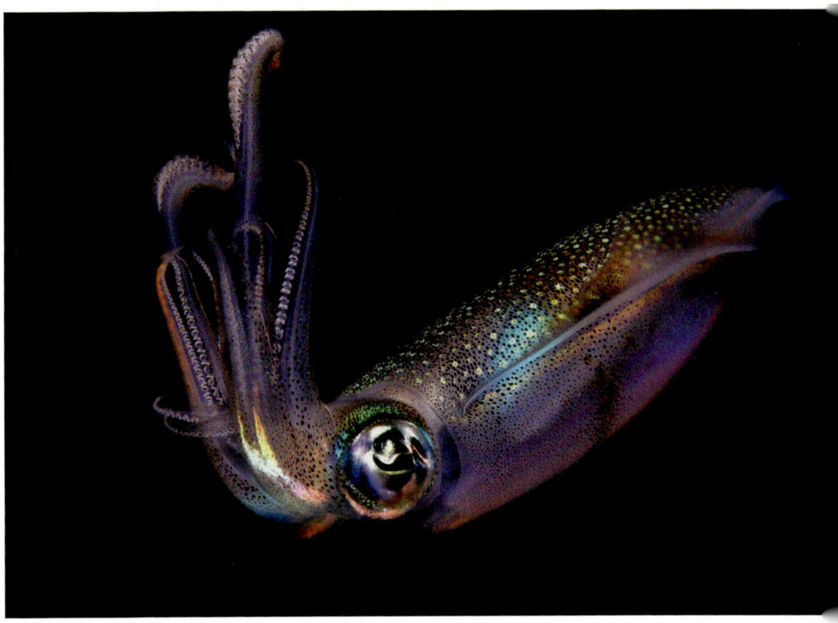

When you dive at night, keep an eye on the water's surface where stunning reef squids can sometimes be found

Canon EOS 5D Mark II • Canon 100mm macro lens • 1/125 s • f/20 • ISO 200

Patience and recognizing just the right moment are equally important when it comes to capturing a successful picture of a school of fish

Canon EOS 5D Mark II • Canon 8–15mm fisheye lens • 1/80 s • f/8 • ISO 200

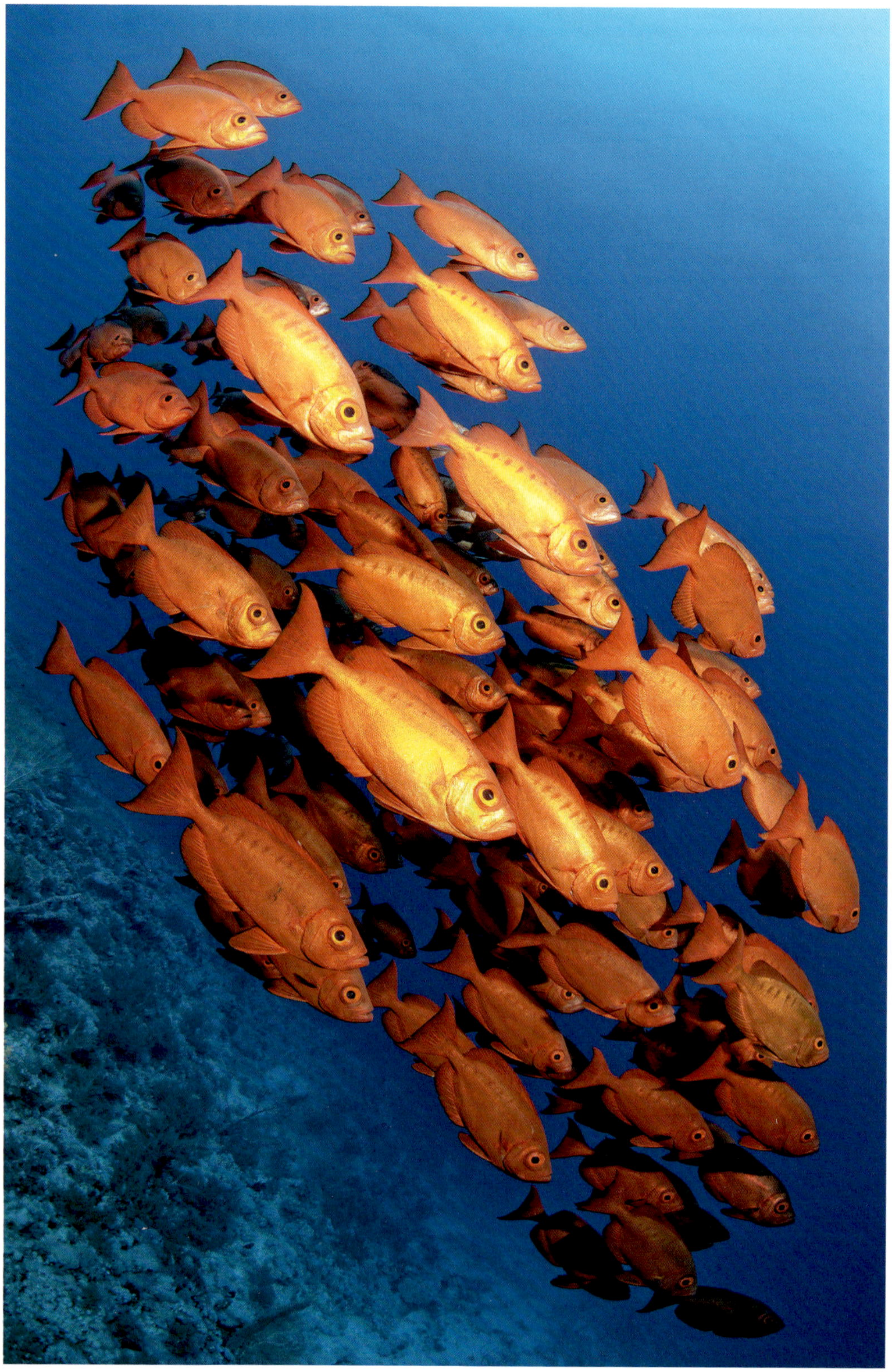

To help you evaluate your shooting distance, remember that you want the subject to take up most of the image area in your viewfinder. This means you need as little water as possible between your lens and the subject, and you need enough light from your flash unit to reach the subject so its natural colors will be captured in your photo.

As the size of the subject increases, this gets more difficult. You need lots of patience to shoot a school of fish, for example, because you need to wait for the school to be compact enough that you can get up close.

Wide-angle lenses, and fisheye lenses in particular, lend themselves well to this type of photography because they can focus on subjects that are very close and still allow the subject to take up the majority of the image area.

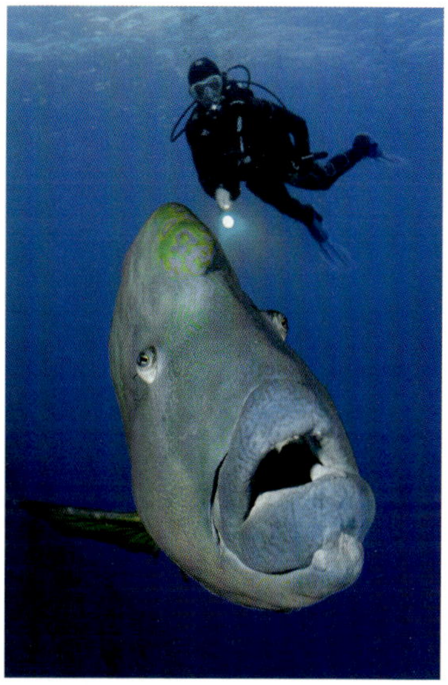

Exposing both the subject and a diver properly is one of many challenges

Canon EOS 5D Mark II • Canon 17–40mm wide-angle lens • 1/30 s • f/10 • ISO 200

SUMMARY:

- Being close to your subject is a fundamental principle of underwater photography.
- It's easy to get close to stationary subjects—moving subjects, not so much.
- Large fish often seem like they are close enough for a successful photo, but they need to be just 3 to 7 ft away.
- Compose your photo so the subject takes up most of the image area.
- Be patient when you try to get close to an animal or a school of fish.

4.6 Getting Close

How do you get close enough to an animal to shoot a winning picture? The answer is simple: you need experience. After you log lots of hours in the water you'll develop a sense of how certain animals behave, and you can use your understanding of their patterns to prepare for your shots. This will help you find the right position from which to capture the photo you want.

Learning about the animals you intend to photograph is a good way to develop the skills that will help you approach them. Reading books about their behavior patterns is a good place to start. Even more important, however, are your impressions while you're under water. Observing a creature for a while and picking up on its movement patterns is the best way to hone your tracking skills. If you recognize that a shark seems threatened, it's best to relent and give the animal some space.

There is never a situation that will turn out well when swimming fast toward an animal. A strange creature paddling around and breathing heavily will send even the calmest sea life fleeing. It's much wiser to use a slow, careful

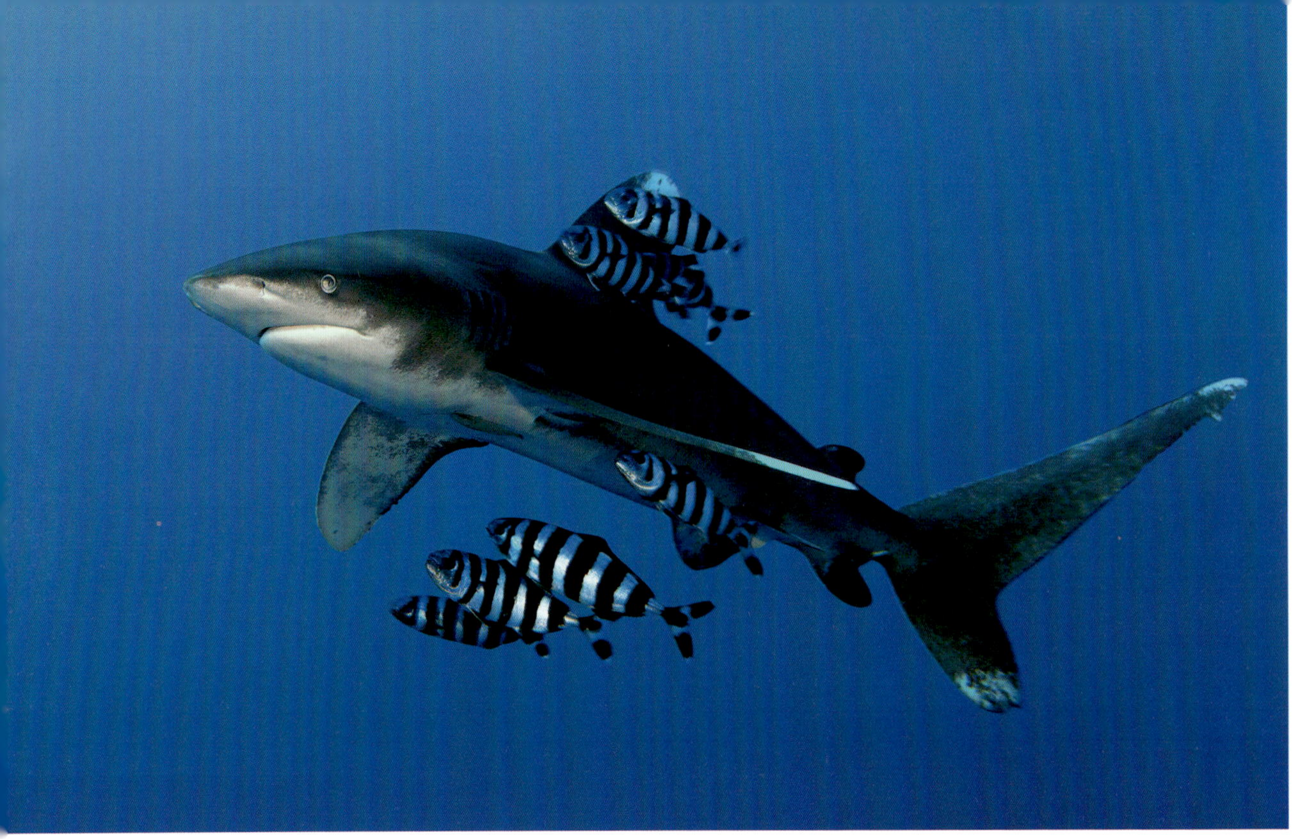

Sharks are usually afraid of unfamiliar movements and air bubbles. Oceanic whitetip sharks like the one pictured here, however, are very curious and often swim up close to divers.

Canon EOS 5D Mark II • Canon 17–40mm wide-angle lens • 1/30 s • f/8 • ISO 100

strategy. The best way to approach an animal is to incrementally move closer using careful movements and shallow, even breaths. The bubbles that form when divers exhale under water tend to frighten aquatic life.

The best way to get up close and personal with aquatic life is to use a closed-circuit rebreather. These costly systems require lots of maintenance, but they are the only way to get a bubble-free dive.

Rebreather systems are particularly useful when you take pictures of hammerheads because these shy animals scurry away to a safe distance at the first sight of air bubbles. A diver armed with a closed-circuit rebreather who hides behind a large boulder can watch the bizarre creatures swim by mere inches away.

SUMMARY:

- There is no substitute for experience when you want to get close to aquatic life.
- Diligently observing and studying animals can help you build experience.
- Always approach animals slowly.
- Avoid quick movements.
- Air bubbles frighten sea life more than anything else.
- Rebreather units are optimal for photographing large sea life.

4.7 Wrecks

The sights and discoveries to be found within rusty shipwrecks have always fascinated divers. The number of wrecks at the bottom of the sea tell a tragic story—none more so than the most famous wreck in the world: the *Titanic*. The world-famous colossus is rusting away at a depth of about 13,000 ft, which means it's well beyond the reach of most divers and their cameras. Nevertheless, there are countless other wrecks at manageable depths for you to explore and document. In addition to shipwrecks, you can find downed aircraft, old army tanks, and other long-lost vehicles.

Wrecks that are still standing upright in good condition are ideal candidates for producing fascinating pictures. The more destroyed a wreck is, the harder it is to depict it as a sunken relic.

It's worth spending an entire day at a wreck site to explore all the hidden treasures and observe when the lighting conditions are the best. If you don't have this luxury, ask at a local dive center to see if anyone knows what time the lighting conditions are best for shooting. Taking advantage of good natural light is critical because in most cases your flash units will not be powerful enough to illuminate the entire scene. You need sunlight for the best photographs. In general, wrecks at shallower depths are easier to photograph because more sunlight reaches them.

It's often ideal to shoot the bow and stern because they are very striking and make it easy for viewers to recognize the subject. Sideways perspectives are difficult to pull off because they require shooting alongside the hull, which is rarely attractive. You're usually better off concentrating on the structure

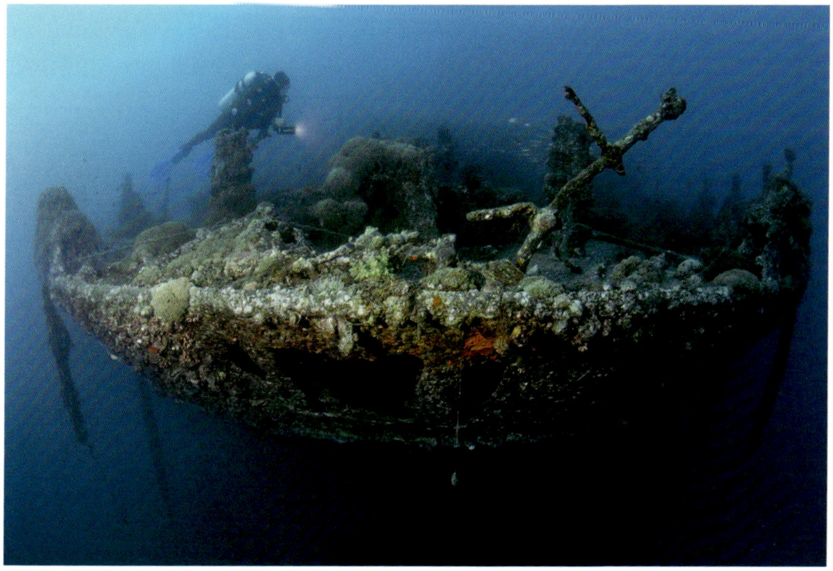

Views of the bow and stern of a shipwreck are usually the most photogenic

Canon EOS 5D Mark II • Canon 8–15mm fisheye lens • 1/160 s • f/8, ISO 200 and inner life of the ship between the bow and the stern, including the bridge, vents, instruments, or engine room. A wreck that is overgrown with coral makes for a truly great photo opportunity.

Fisheye lenses are often best for exterior photographs of wreck sites because they allow you to capture wider angles of view. Conversely, wide-angle lenses are ideal for interior photographs because they don't distort lines like fisheye lenses do, and they allow you to capture how the inner life of the sunken vessel actually looks.

Wrecks are often good candidates for breaking the rule of not photographing a subject from above. Sunken ships and airplanes are often located along a sandy stretch of ocean floor, which makes their dark elements stand out in stark contrast to the light background and makes for attractive photos.

A wreck can often serve as fruitful training ground for budding underwater photographers. A wreck won't swim away from you like a school of fish. You can analyze your work after a day of taking pictures, then go back the next day to work on improving your pictures of the same subject.

A wreck's interior is often rich with alluring subjects: old control panels, helms, and porcelain plates are among the treasures you can bring back to light by storing them on your memory card. With that said, though, there are strict safety precautions that you must follow when you explore the inside of a wreck. Only experienced divers and advanced photographers who can practically operate their equipment in their sleep should navigate the interior world of a wreck site. The risk is simply too great that an accidental kick of a fin may churn up all sorts of debris and make the exit route all but impossible to see. Never explore a wreck on your own. Always have someone with you who is familiar with the site. Such a diving partner is doubly useful because he or she can direct your attention to artifacts within the wreck that you might otherwise overlook.

Including another diver within your picture is a great way to convey the size of a sunken vessel. Another way to add depth to your images is to have your diving partner hold an additional source of light, such as a lamp or a slave flash. Positioning a model with a light source behind a

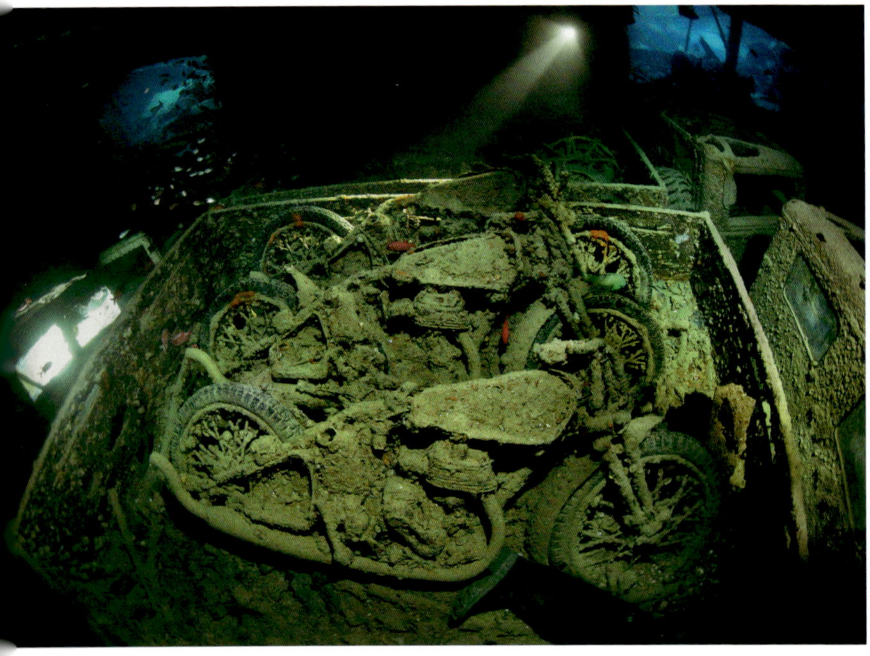

Cargo found within a wreck's interior is often unexpected and makes for a great subject. Several light sources help create the atmosphere and tone of this photo

Canon EOS 5D Mark II • Canon 8–15mm fisheye lens • 1/30 s • f/5.6 • ISO 3200

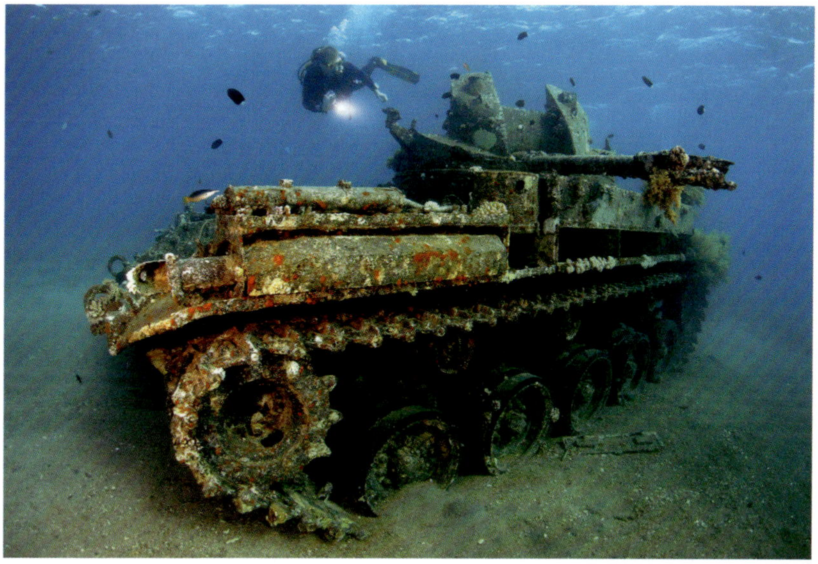

Though capturing a wreck in its entirety is rarely effective, this sunken tank off the coast of Jordan is an exception

Canon EOS 5D Mark II • Canon 17–40mm wide-angle lens • 1/125 s • f/8 • ISO 200

stairwell, at the end of a hallway, or above the bow can really take your wreck images to a new level.

Underwater photos of wrecks often lend themselves to black-and-white or sepia tones because they rely so much on natural lighting. It's often beneficial to boost the contrast during post-processing; try sliding the contrast control all the way to maximum and see what kind of effect it makes.

Using a red filter while you're shooting often yields good results, but you will need to disable—even better, remove—your flash units. Unless you can remove the filter while you're diving, there's no point in using flash because it elevates the red channel of your image too much. If you want to reproduce accurate colors, set your white balance manually when you reach your shooting location. (Read more about white balance in chapter 2.) Red filters will work properly between depths of 10 and 65 ft, depending on the ambient light. Working at other depths won't produce good results because the light and its red components will be too strong or too weak. Even the best red filters will be pretty much useless deeper than 65 ft.

Shooting wrecks is most successful when you've done some advance planning. In an ideal scenario you would meet with other divers and experts no later than the evening before the dive to discuss information about the wreck and potential photo opportunities. Also spend some time researching your dive before your trip. You can find images of most wrecks on the Internet, which can help to plan your work. You might even hunt down diagrams of the ship's deck and plan shots ahead of time.

When you explore wrecks with your camera, you absolutely must have your diving computer in plain sight because it's easy to lose track of time with all the wonderful opportunities around you. A meticulously planned excursion usually produces the best images because stress is often a barrier to creative and effective photography.

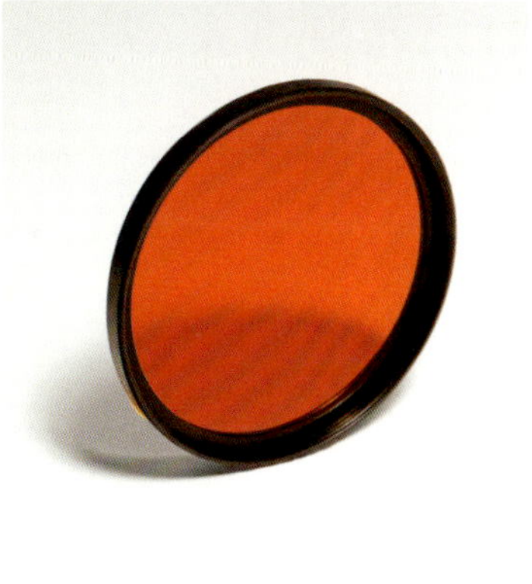

A typical red filter that can be attached to the front of a lens

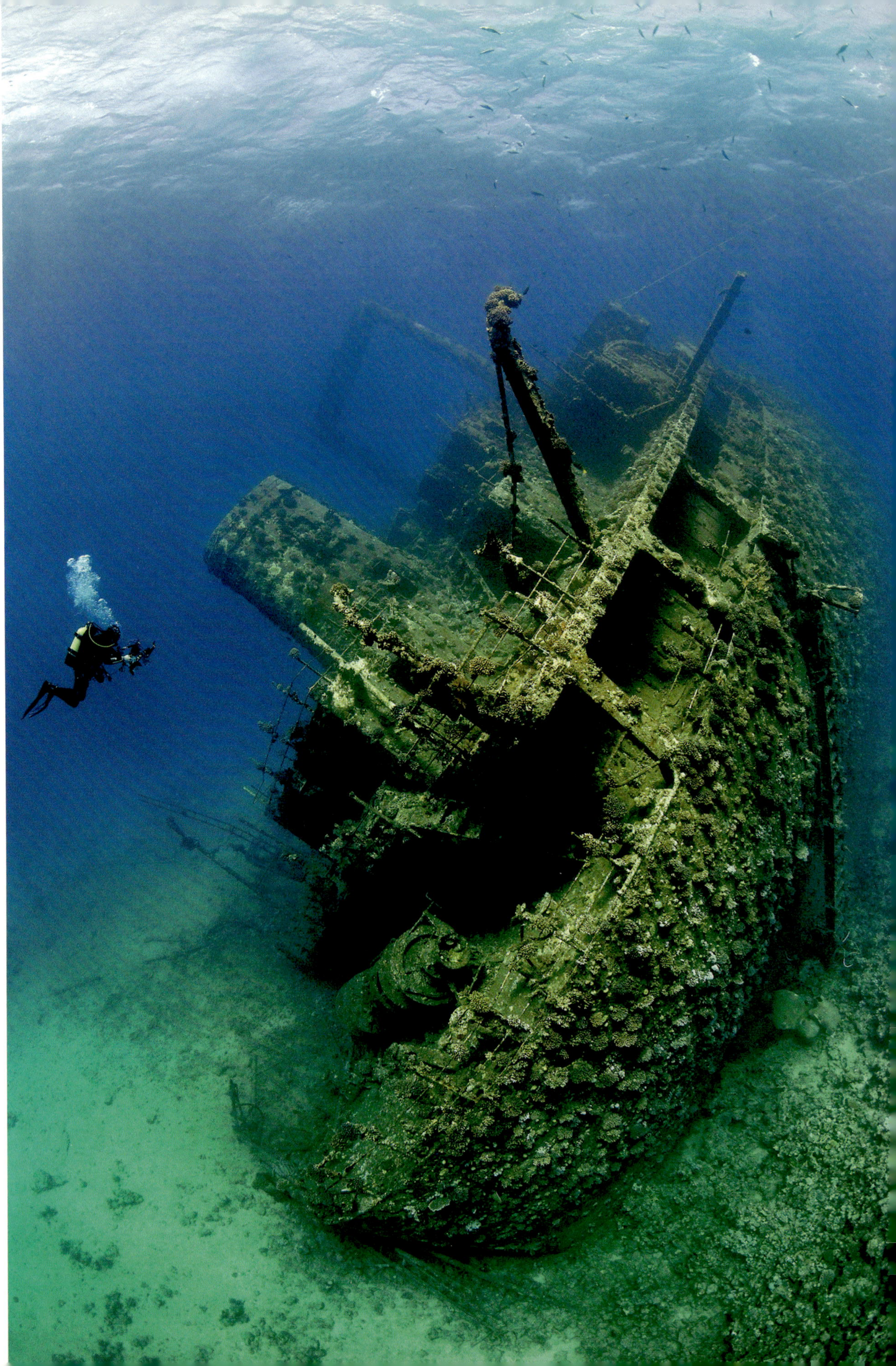

SUMMARY:

- Wrecks have interesting stories to tell; they are a favorite subject for underwater photographers.
- Spend lots of time at the wreck site and wait for the ideal lighting conditions.
- Stick to shooting the bow or stern; shots of the side are mostly not as attractive.
- Fisheye lenses are well suited for documenting wrecks.
- Exercise extreme caution while taking pictures inside wrecks. Safety always comes first!
- Images of wrecks lend themselves to black-and-white conversions.
- Red filters can make your images look even better, but they're effective only between depths of 10 and 65 ft.
- Research and planning before your dive will result in better photos.

Left page: When the lighting and visibility are good, red filters are particularly useful for photographing wrecks, as was the case here in the Red Sea in Egypt

Canon EOS 5D Mark II • Canon 8–15mm fisheye lens • 1/80 s, f/8, ISO 400

4.8 Split Waterline Photos

Pictures that feature elements both above and below the waterline are especially powerful for people who are not regular divers. These images reveal what's going on above the water and in the water at the same moment. They allow viewers to align the familiar surroundings above the water with the activity that occurs below.

Split waterline photos are particularly effective when the elements above the water continue under water, as shown in this photo of an iceberg in Greenland

Canon EOS 5D Mark II • Canon 8–15mm fisheye lens • 1/80 s • f/22 • ISO 100

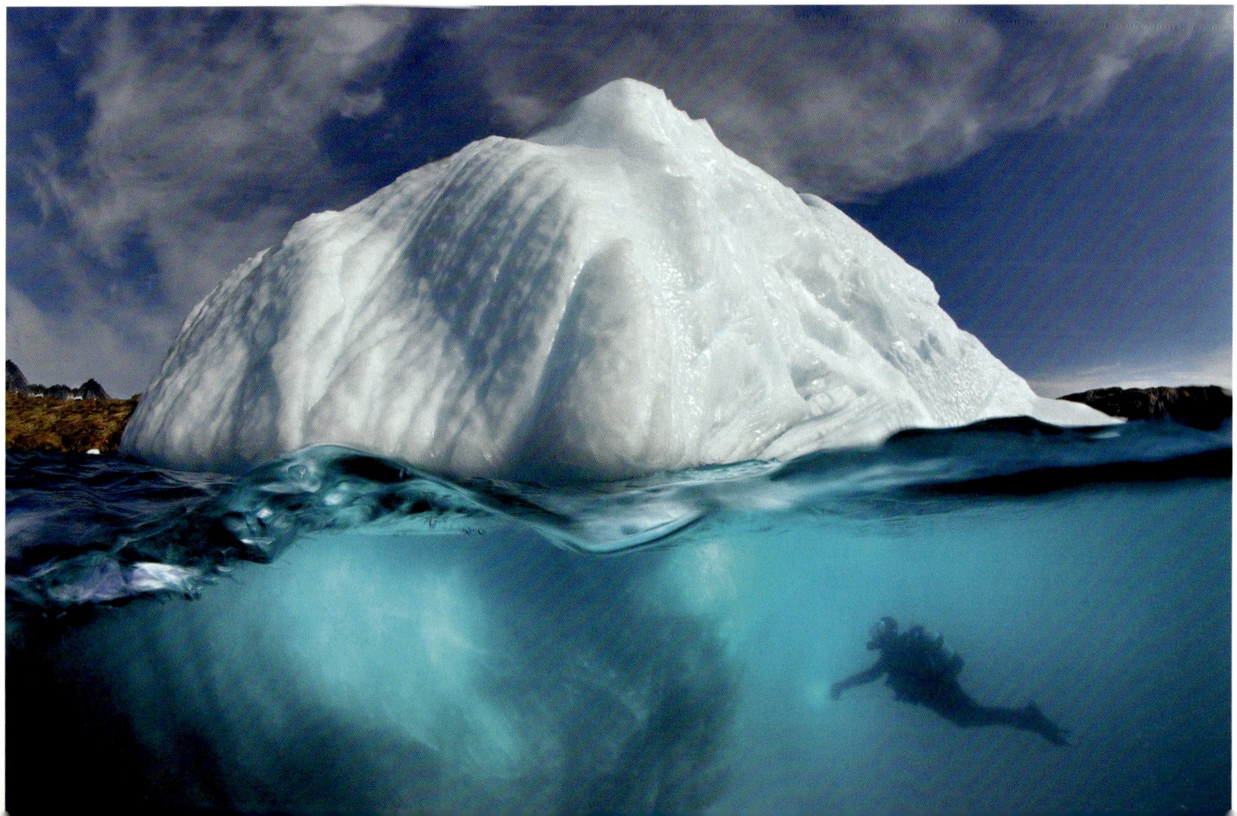

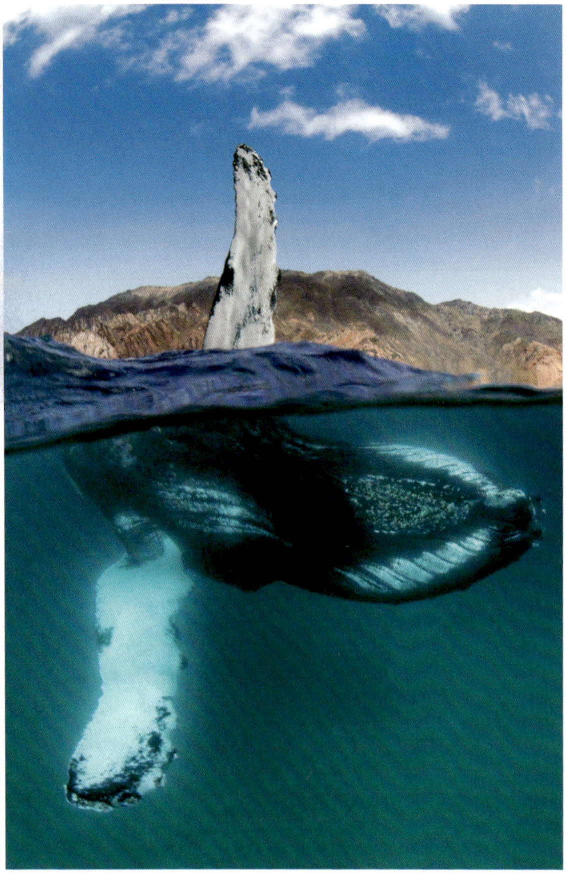

Various factors come into play when you try to create successful split waterline photos. The first concern is your equipment. Your lens needs to have the largest angle of view possible, which means that fisheye lenses are ideal. Furthermore, you need to use a dome port that has the largest diameter possible—the larger the diameter, the easier it will be to time your pictures with the waves. The usual goal with these types of photos is to have the waterline pass across the center of your dome port so equal portions of the image area will be devoted to what's above and what's below the waterline. Trying to accomplish this with a compact camera that has a lens diameter of less than an inch is extremely difficult.

After you've assembled all the necessary equipment, it's time to find an ideal location for your split waterline photo. This is no easy task because you need to find a site where both the above-water and below-water portions of the image have interesting subjects. Ideal conditions are difficult to come by, in part because coral tends to grow only deeper than 15 ft; shallower waters are often too warm to support them.

When the light and visibility are good, the below-water depth should be no greater than 15 ft. Ideally, the depth should be between 3 and 10 ft so the sun can take care of the lighting and you won't have to use your flash units.

As you can imagine, the lighting conditions above and below the water will be dramatically different, which makes it hard to get a good exposure. It helps to attempt this type of image only on sunny days and with the light at your back.

Unexpected moments sometimes force you to compose an image on the fly; the risk of failure sometimes gives way to particularly attractive pictures

Canon EOS 5D Mark II • Canon 8–15mm fisheye lens • 1/200 s • f/18 • ISO 800

Base the exposure on the top half of your photo. This will underexpose the underwater portion of your image, but you can fix this problem in post-processing. It's easier to make this kind of correction than to fix an overexposed sky.

Another challenge of split waterline photos is that optical distortions cause the above-water portion of the image to seem farther away. At an aperture of f/8, you might get either the under-water or the above-water portions of your image in focus, but not both. You can get most of the image area to be sharp by decreasing the aperture opening to f/16 or f/22, which increases the depth of field. This is another reason why fisheye lenses are practical for split waterline photos: they have an especially large depth of field. Focus on the elements below the waterline because the above-water elements can better tolerate blur.

Right page: What's happening above and below the surface of water? Split waterline photos reveal two worlds at once.

Canon EOS 5D Mark II • Canon 8–15mm fisheye lens • 1/800 s • f/16 • ISO 800

Set the ISO value as high as possible, but at the same time keep it as low as you can to avoid image noise. Increasing the ISO also allows you to use a

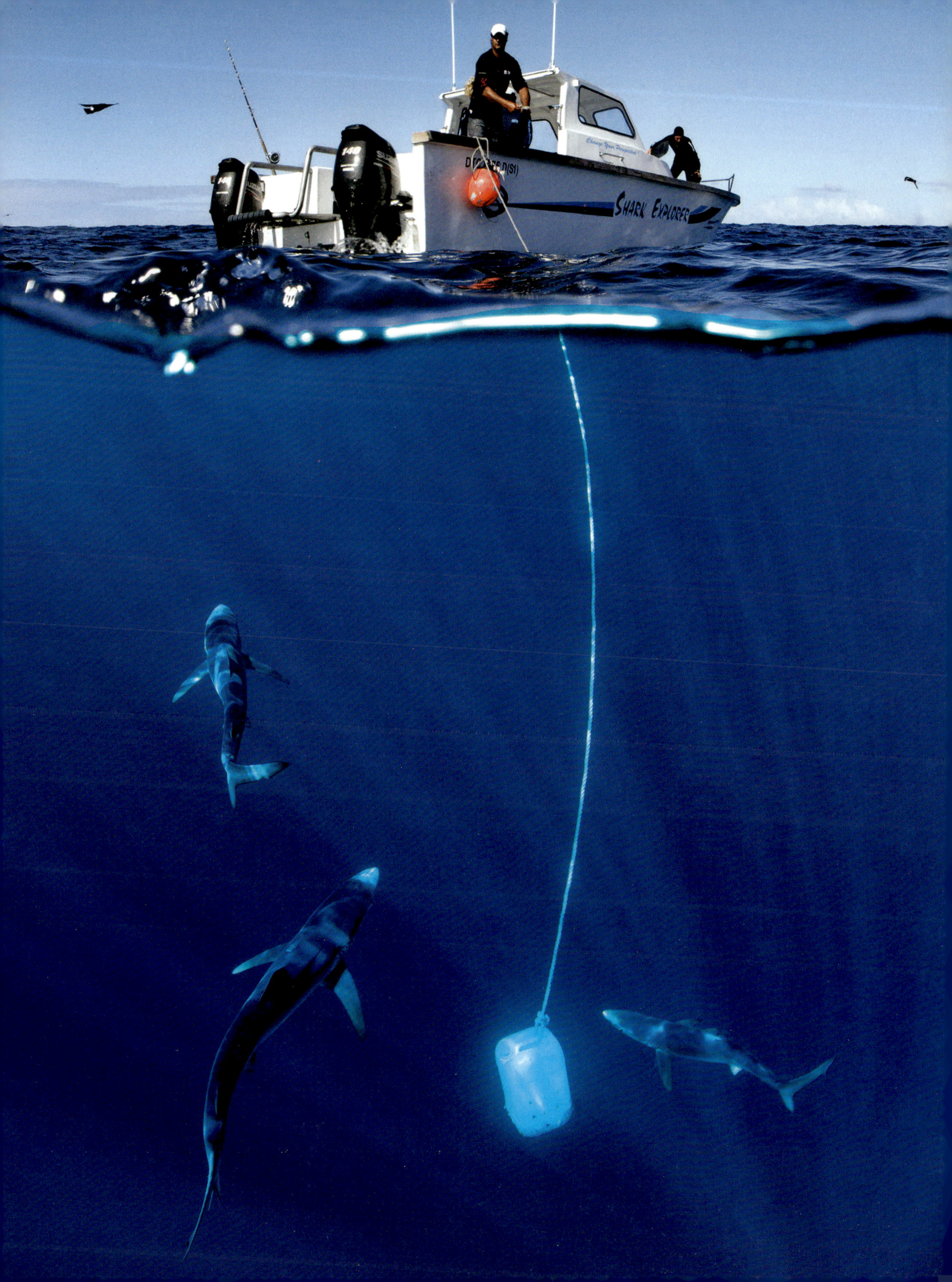
Shark Explorer

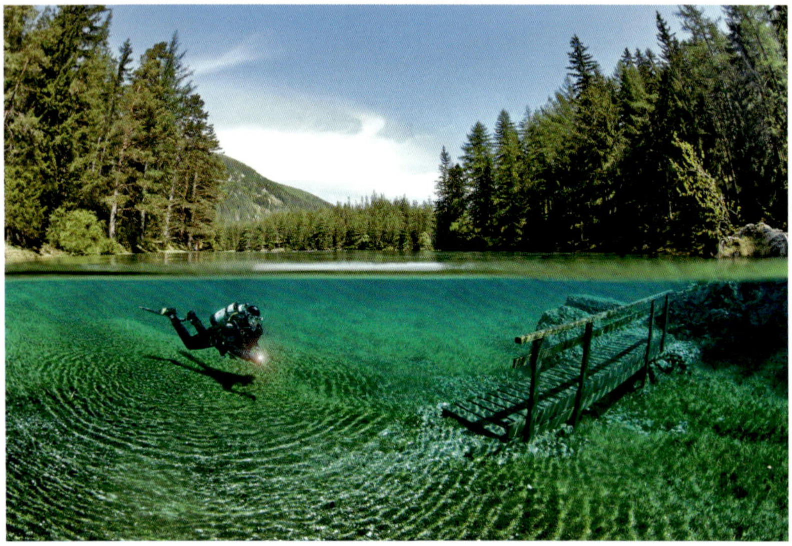

Still mountain lakes are ideal training grounds for practicing split waterline photos

Canon EOS 5D Mark II • Canon 8–15mm fisheye lens • 1/30 s • f/22 • ISO 400

faster shutter speed, which helps avoid camera shake. Use your camera's burst mode to quickly take a series of images. More exposures means a greater likelihood of obtaining at least one successful image.

There is no perfect solution for eliminating water droplets on the top half of your dome port. Products you can use on car windows to make water droplets roll off are only marginally helpful because they tend to quickly lose their effectiveness in water. Your best bet is to spread a bit of saliva on the top half of the dome port, then wash it off. Doing the same to a diving mask prevents fog from building up. You can also reduce the appearance of droplets by submerging your camera before your shot and then pulling it up right as you release the shutter. This actually results in a thin sheet of water covering the entire dome port, which will start to form droplets after only a few seconds.

If you attach a 45-degree angle viewfinder to your underwater camera housing, you can look down into your camera from above rather than at wave level. When you work like this, an inflated buoyancy compensator helps immensely to spare your calf muscles.

Practice makes perfect when it comes to split waterline photos. It is much easier to take this kind of picture in calm waters than in a choppy sea. Practicing with the glassy surface of a still lake is a good way to hone your technique.

SUMMARY:

- Split waterline photos attract viewers because the top part of the image is a familiar scene.
- Use a fisheye lens and a wide dome port for this type of photo.
- Both scenes—above and below the waterline—should be interesting.
- It's ideal to work on sunny days with the sun at your back.
- Use the smallest practical aperture (f/16 to f/22) to guarantee sharpness throughout your photo.
- Use a bit of saliva on the dome port to prevent water droplets from forming.
- A 45-degree viewfinder and an inflated buoyancy compensator are helpful.
- Wait for calm waters or practice in still lakes.

4.9 Large Sea Life

Photographing the ocean's giants is surely one of the most exciting tasks of an underwater photographer. Whales, sharks, and dolphins—all these animals impress with their sheer size. Sharks in particular, the predators of the sea, cause your adrenaline to spike, even though it's well known among divers that they are harmless. Nevertheless, these predators exude danger, even if that danger is only potential.

Keep a cool, level head when you have one of these exciting encounters so you can get the picture you came for. If you start fiddling with your gear, get overly excited, and double the air bubbles from your regulator, your chances of getting a successful picture are slim.

You need to effortlessly and accurately control your camera's settings, and you need to judge whether the animal—be it a shark, a Napoleon fish, or a dolphin—is actually worth pursuing. If an animal shows no interest in you, if it swims quickly past your diving group, or if it takes off at the first sight of air bubbles, continue with your dive and wait for the next opportunity. Always survey the situation and evaluate what's likely to happen, particularly when an animal demonstrates an interest in you, a strange object in the water. When an animal displays these signals, it's time to rely on your knowledge and experience to quickly find the correct settings on your camera. Can you predict where the animal is likely to head next? Can you set your camera ahead of time so you'll be prepared for the situation? How close will the animal come? Are the flash heads pointed in the right direction? There are lots of questions that you'll need to quickly consider.

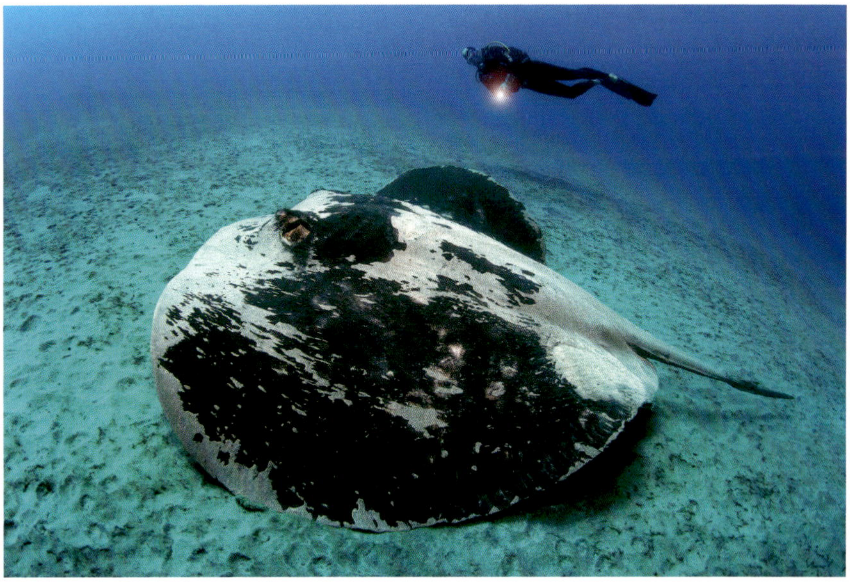

When you take a picture of a dramatic, large animal, including a diver in the image can be the icing on the cake

Canon EOS 5D Mark II • Canon 8–15mm fisheye lens • 1/250 s • f/9 • ISO 200

Finding a winning background is key to successfully creating pictures of large sea life. A rich blue backdrop, perhaps with some reef showing (or maybe not), is often an elegant way to isolate such magnificent creatures. Capturing large fish or mammals is easiest when your back is toward the reef. This minimizes the chances of ending up with a distraction in the background.

Diving in a group is usually not advisable when you're on the hunt for large game. To maximize your chances of encountering a large animal in waters that are

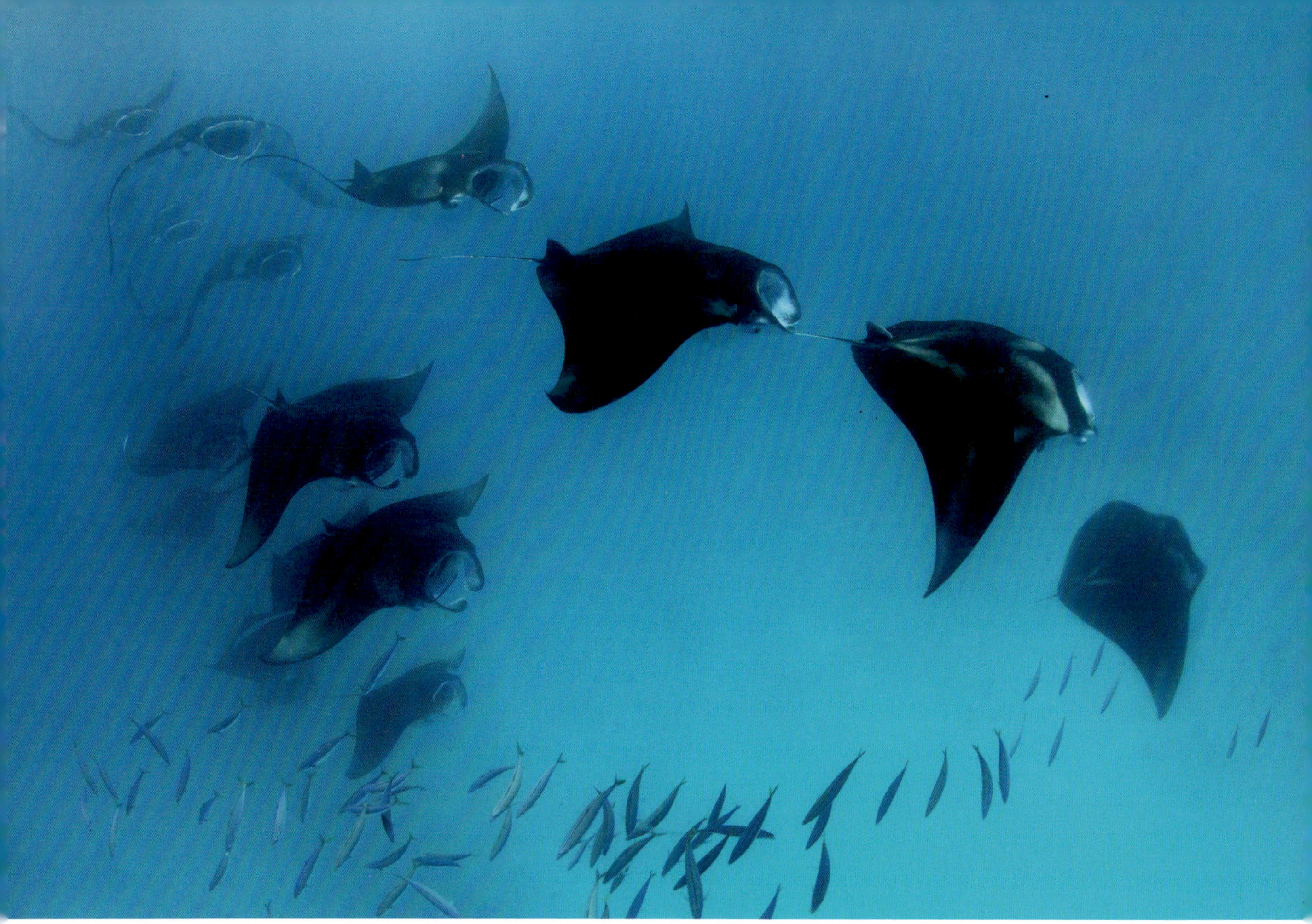

You will probably have to travel far and wide to have encounters with large marine life—and even then, luck plays a critical role

Canon EOS 5D Mark II • Canon 8–15mm fisheye lens • 1/125 s • f/16 • ISO 400

crowded with people, swim with one partner in the opposite direction of the rest of the divers. If you must be part of a group, position yourself either at the front or the back to increase the likelihood of getting a good shot. It's not likely that large sea animals will swim in the middle of a group of divers.

If you plan to snorkel with whales, dolphins, or whale sharks, don't bother with your flash units. The sunlight should be bright enough near the surface of the water to capture these animals in natural light. You'll be more agile and it will be easier to swim alongside these creatures without the extra gear.

In situations like this, it makes sense to increase your ISO setting as high as possible without sacrificing image quality. The faster your shutter speed is, the less likely your photos will be ruined by camera shake. This is also one of the few instances when it makes sense to use aperture-priority exposure mode. You set the ISO and the aperture, and the camera will automatically choose the correct shutter speed for the exposure. A modest underexposure of 1/3 stop is a good starting point.

You'll usually need to travel to have encounters with large sea animals. The likelihood of running across a great white shark in your local lagoon is not

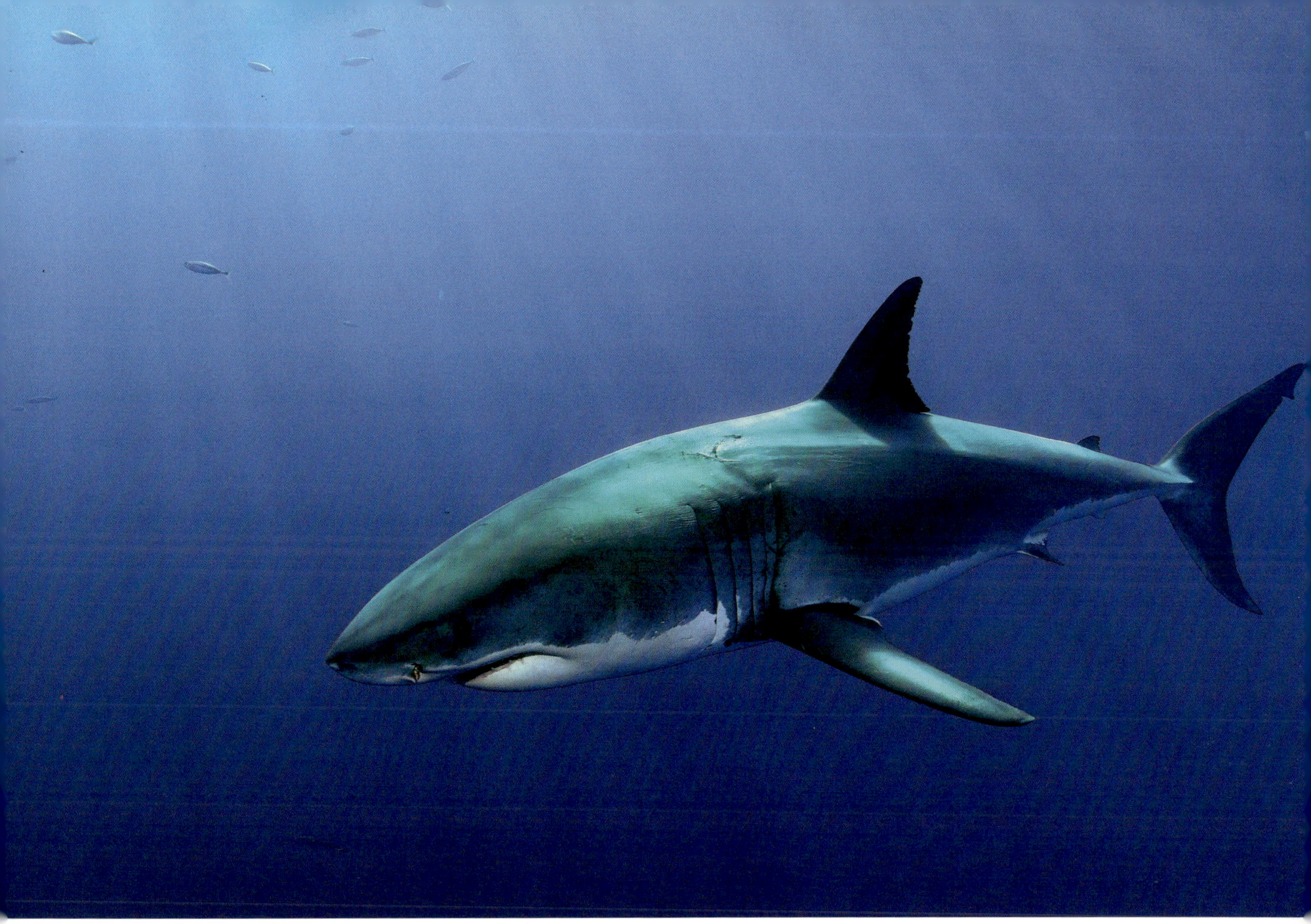

great. Visiting destinations such as the Bahamas, South Africa, French Polynesia, or Cocos Island will dramatically increase your chances of meeting the ocean's giants.

The great white shark is the most famous (and unjustifiably notorious) large fish in the world

Canon EOS 5D Mark II • Canon 8–15mm fisheye lens • 1/125 s • f/16 • ISO 400

SUMMARY:

- Photographing large sea life is exciting and requires a cool head.
- Survey the scene thoroughly to get good results.
- A large sea animal framed by blue water is a simple but attractive composition.
- You're more likely encounter large sea life when you dive with one partner rather than with a large group.
- The best way to photograph whales, dolphins, and whale sharks while snorkeling is without flash units mounted to your camera.
- Travel will likely be required to encounter and photograph the most majestic beasts of the sea.

4.10 Reefs

It's easy to learn how to photograph reefs. Because coral are sedentary creatures, you can be sure they'll hold still when you photograph them. Analyzing your photos after your dive can be a great way to get ideas, build motivation, and to improve using the same subject on the next day's dive.

A destination like Egypt, particularly Brother Islands, is optimal for reef photography because the coral gardens are so astounding. Raja Ampat in Indonesia also offers a huge diversity of coral, the likes of which can't be found anywhere else in the world.

Not every piece of coral or every reef is particularly photogenic. Does the gorgonian look a little battered? Is there an unsightly mass next to an attractive piece of coral? Is the surface of the coral garden simply too small? If you answer yes to any of these questions, it's time to look for another subject. The goal is to find a large area of brightly colored coral. Searching for such a garden can take a while, but your photos will be worth the effort.

The environment around the reef will determine the ideal perspective. Are you shooting a stretch of reef along the sandy bottom, or coral on a steep rock wall? The ideal position will depend on the subject. Good perspectives usually show the reef without distracting elements and with a significant swath of blue in the background. The general goal when you look for a good perspective is to keep moving until all the distractions are eliminated.

It's no simple task to find a stretch of reef that is mature and free of unsightly areas

Canon EOS 5D Mark II • Canon 8–15mm fisheye lens • 1/250 s • f/8 • ISO 400

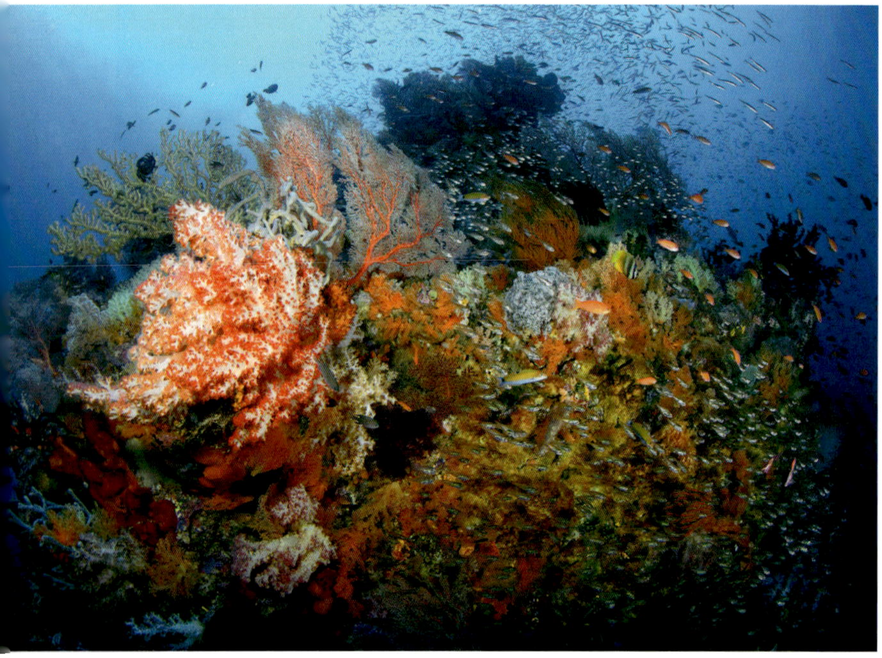

Huge gorgonians are usually best ignored because you have to move so far away to capture them in one image. Even with a fisheye lens, you'll end up with too much water between your camera and the subject, which results in a less than satisfactory result. You'll get better results if you find a medium-sized gorgonian amidst the coral, which allows you to get close enough and use your flash units to illuminate the scene. In most photos, it's impossible to tell whether a coral is 10 or 15 ft across anyway.

If you're shooting a particularly large reef, position your flash units away from your camera and set them to maximum power. Conversely, if you're shooting a single

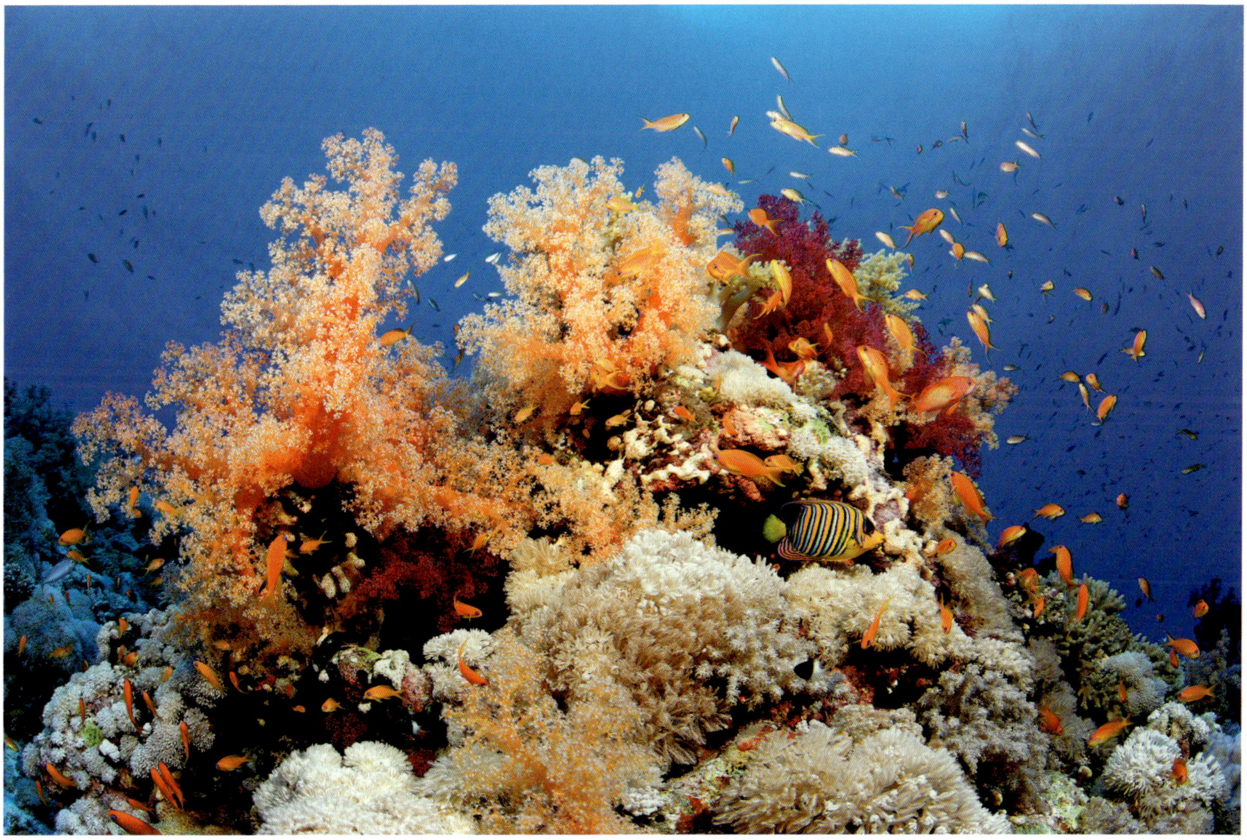

piece of soft coral, bring your flash units close to your camera and reduce their output accordingly.

It's often a good idea to use a model when you shoot reef landscapes. Divers function as an additional visual element, and they can be integrated into the picture without any stress or challenges. Divers can hold a strong light to illuminate a portion of the reef and add visual interest to the image.

If lots of fish are hanging out in the magnificent stretch of reef you plan to photograph, you'll have to consider their movements. Little reef fish often congregate in schools and rush out of the scene only to rush back in again. During this flurry is exactly when you want to take your shot because the fish will be lined up and visually coherent. Between these moments, the fish tend to crisscross the coral without any organization. Even larger fish, such as perch, can be cleverly photographed. Keep a close eye on your viewfinder to discern what parts of the image area contain movement. Perch tend to poke their heads around a corner to investigate what is paying so much attention to the reef. Keep everything under control so you can release the shutter at that precise moment.

Unusually beautiful coral gardens grow in Egyptian areas of the Red Sea

Canon EOS 5D Mark II • Tokina 10–17mm fisheye lens • 1/100 s • f/11 • ISO 100

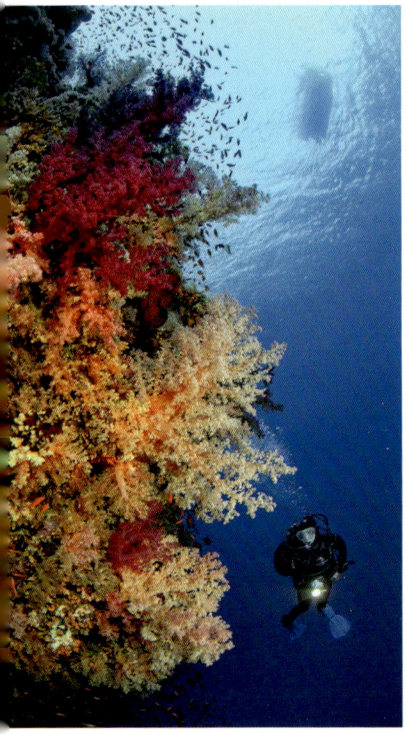

Photographing reef landscapes is an ideal time to practice working with models under water because it's easy to try many different positions

Canon EOS 5D Mark II • Canon 8–15mm fisheye lens • 1/40 s • f/8 • ISO 200

SUMMARY:

- It's relatively quick and easy to learn how to photograph reefs.
- Not all reefs are photogenic—you need to search for the most attractive ones.
- Setting an isolated patch of healthy coral against a large blue swath of water is an attractive composition for a photo.
- Ignore huge gorgonians and focus on medium-sized ones because they're easier to illuminate.
- When you shoot expansive reef landscapes, position your flash units away from your camera; when you shoot up close to coral, bring your flash units back in.
- Models are a nice complement to reef landscapes.
- Integrate reef fish into your images and capture their movements at ideal moments.

4.11 Close Range, Wide Angle

The photographic technique known as *close range, wide angle* (or close focus, wide angle) allows photographers to make relatively tiny subjects take up a significant portion of the image area and still clearly depict the background elements. For example, you can create a photograph of a small clown fish within its larger environment, a frogfish being inspected by a diver, or a detail of a wreck with the larger structures of the vessel behind it. Macro lenses let you make miniscule objects look big, but they don't let you include key portions of the background.

Close-range, wide-angle work generally requires a fisheye lens, which has a small range of minimum focusing distances. But the construction of a standard 7-inch dome port causes the focusing distances to artificially increase—the size of the lens in the port does not allow you to focus on close objects. Accordingly, you'll need to use a very small dome port in terms of diameter. This allows you to focus on objects that are mere inches from your housing.

When you compose an image using this technique, you will work with subjects that are at substantially different distances from your camera. To retain focus throughout the layers of your image, you need to reduce the aperture opening as much as possible—at least to f/16, if not smaller. The smaller aperture opening will require you to increase the ISO so the sensor can pick up enough ambient light and prevent the background from becoming too dark.

Two flash units can come in handy with this type of shot. Position one close to the camera so it can illuminate the foreground objects, and use the second one to illuminate the background. If you have only one flash unit, the elements in the foreground take priority.

The best perspective for a close-range, wide-angle shot is with your camera slightly below the subject and with a modest upward angle. Circumstances may make this perspective impossible when, for example, an animal is hiding behind some coral or is resting on the ocean floor. In that case you have no choice but to search for another subject. The ideal situation is when your subject is resting on an edge of some kind, or on top of a piece of coral, so you can position your camera slightly below it.

SUMMARY:

- The close-range, wide-angle technique is also known as close-focus, wide-angle photography.
- The combination of a fisheye lens with a very small dome port diameter makes it possible to compose images using extremely short focusing distances while still capturing a substantial backdrop.
- Set the aperture at f/16 or f/22 to ensure sharpness throughout the image.
- It's best to use two flash units: one for the foreground, the other for the background.
- The optimal perspective is slightly below the subject with a modest upward angle to isolate the subject against the background.
- If such a perspective is not possible, it's time to find another subject.

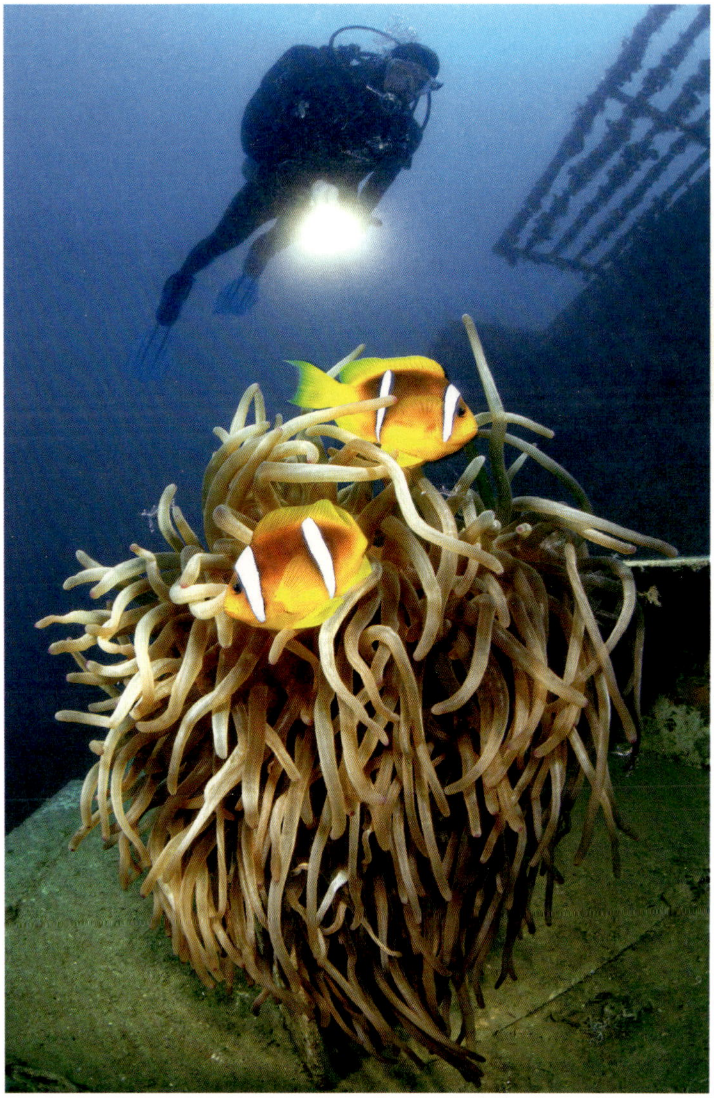

Close-range, wide-angle photography allows you to highlight small creatures in the foreground and include dramatic backgrounds

Canon EOS 5D Mark II • Canon 8–15mm fisheye lens • 1/60 s • f/20 • ISO 400

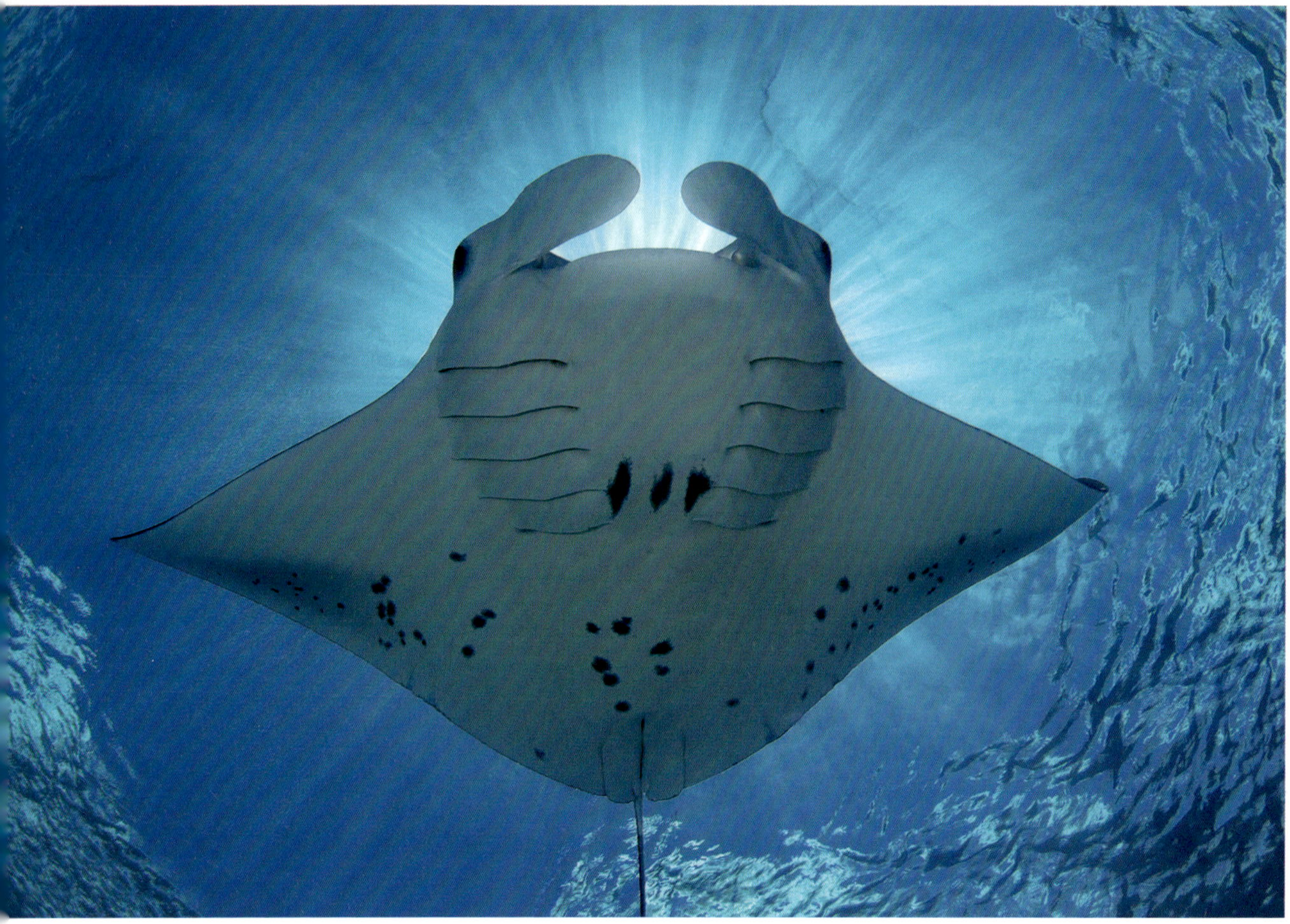

When the brightness of the midday sun is too overpowering, one solution is to set up your shot so the subject blocks it

Canon EOS 5D Mark II • Canon 8–15mm fisheye lens • 1/160 s • f/9 • ISO 50

4.12 Backlight

When you compose a photo that includes backlighting, it's almost always best to shoot at a time when the sun will be low in the sky—either early morning or late afternoon—so the light is not so intense. When the sun is too high in the sky, successful backlit photos are nearly impossible, except at great depths. Much of the sunlight at the crack of dawn or in the evening reflects off the surface of water, which makes backlit images easier to create.

One hallmark of successful backlit images is that they contain as few blown-out highlights near the light source as possible. Blown-out highlights occur where there is no visual information—all you can see is pure white. This is often the case right in the center of the sun.

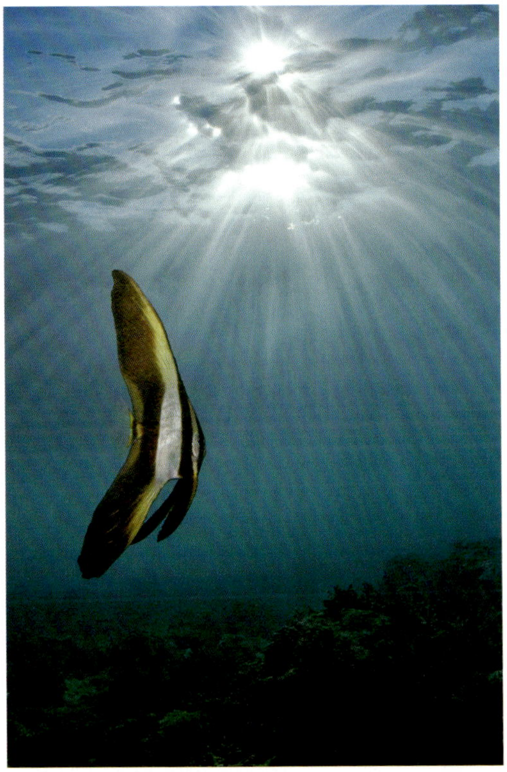

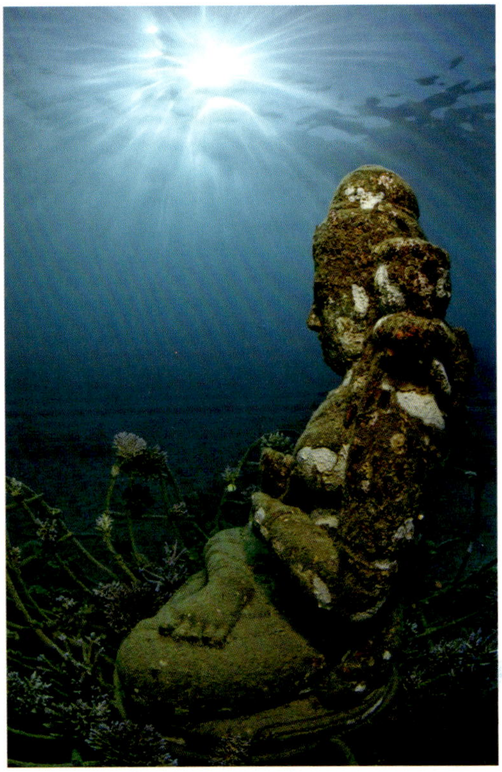

Even if you avoid blown-out highlights, the power of the sun is immense, so you need to let in as little light as possible. A good starting exposure might include a shutter speed of 1/200 second and an ISO setting of 100 or even 50. Make fine adjustments to the aperture; f/11 should be the absolute minimum, and you may need to stop down to f/16 or f/22. Your camera's histogram will reveal blown-out areas, so be sure to check it when you shoot a backlit photo.

If you need to add fill flash for the foreground, set your flash units to the maximum output and don't use diffusers. If your foreground is still too dark, try getting closer to your subject and bring your strobes in tighter.

There's a trick you can use if the sun's brightness is still too intense after you stop the exposure all the way down or if you're forced to shoot in the middle of the day: position a subject—maybe a fish, some coral, or your diving partner—in front of the sun. Whatever subject you choose needs to block the brightest part of the sun so that region can be properly exposed. Composing an image in this way also creates beautiful rays of sunlight around the subject that's blocking the light.

Backlit images demand a certain measure of patience and a passion for experimenting before you get consistent results.

In the early morning and late afternoon, when the sun is very low in the sky, you can create backlit images that don't suffer from blown-out areas

Canon EOS 5D Mark II • Canon 8–15mm fisheye lens • 1/250 s • f/22 • ISO 400

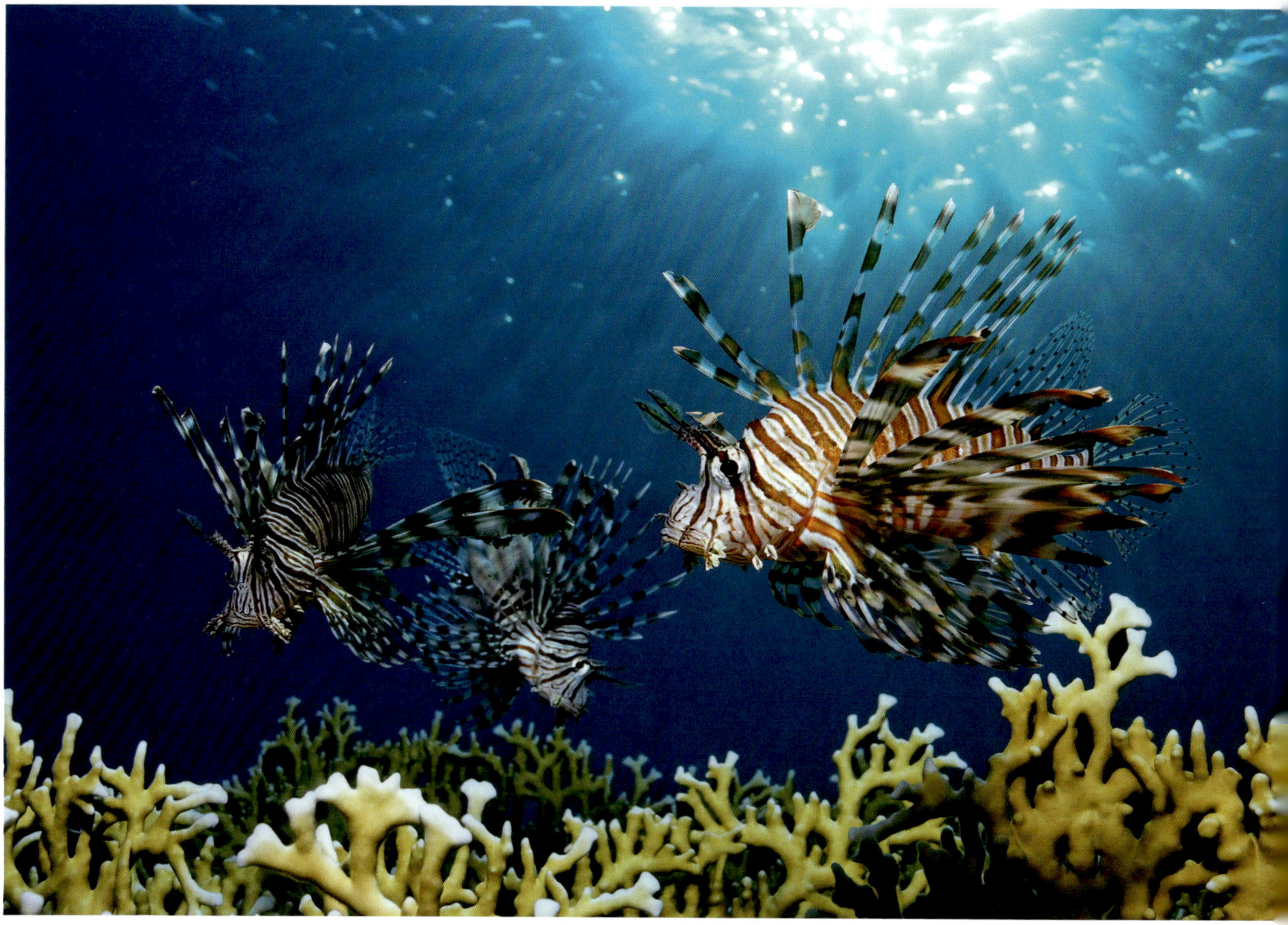

Backlit images require a fast shutter speed, a small aperture opening, and a bright flash

Canon EOS 5D Mark II • Canon 17–40mm wide-angle lens • 1/200 s • f/14 • ISO 400

SUMMARY:

- Plan your work around the position of the sun. It should be low in the sky, such as in the morning and evening.
- Your camera's histogram will reveal blown-out portions of your image.
- Minimize the amount of light that reaches the image sensor. Settings of 1/200 second, f/11, and ISO 100 are a good place to start.
- Set your flash unit output to the maximum, and place your camera close to the subject.
- Reduce the intensity of the sun by positioning a subject directly in front of it.
- Good backlit photos require patience and a passion for experimenting.

4.13 Models

The term *model* refers to any person that appears in an image, whether they are a professional model, a diving partner, or your own children. How effective a person is at modeling is based not only on what he or she does, it depends on making arrangements in advance and developing signals to ensure the photographer and the model can communicate effectively under water. In other words, success is not a matter of chance.

Photographers and models need to practice signals to indicate if the model should come closer or swim farther away, move higher or deeper, or improve his or her leg position. The longer a model and a photographer work together, the stronger their underwater communication will be and the less time they will spend trying to sort things out rather than taking pictures. Even agreeing on a few signals with the dive guide, who may never have been in front of a camera, can be extremely valuable so he or she doesn't end up fidgeting in the water.

The photographer's task is to direct the model to an attractive position near the primary subject. In most cases the model won't be the main subject but will be a secondary element to round out a composition or to provide a sense of scale. It's particularly effective when the position of the model forms a diagonal line relative to the image border and appears to be swimming into the picture. Make sure you don't crop off a fin when you take your picture; the goal is to isolate the model against a blue background as much as possible.

Including a model in your image is a good way to convey the size of a wreck

Canon EOS 5D Mark II • Canon 17–40mm wide-angle lens • 1/50 s • f/8 • ISO 200

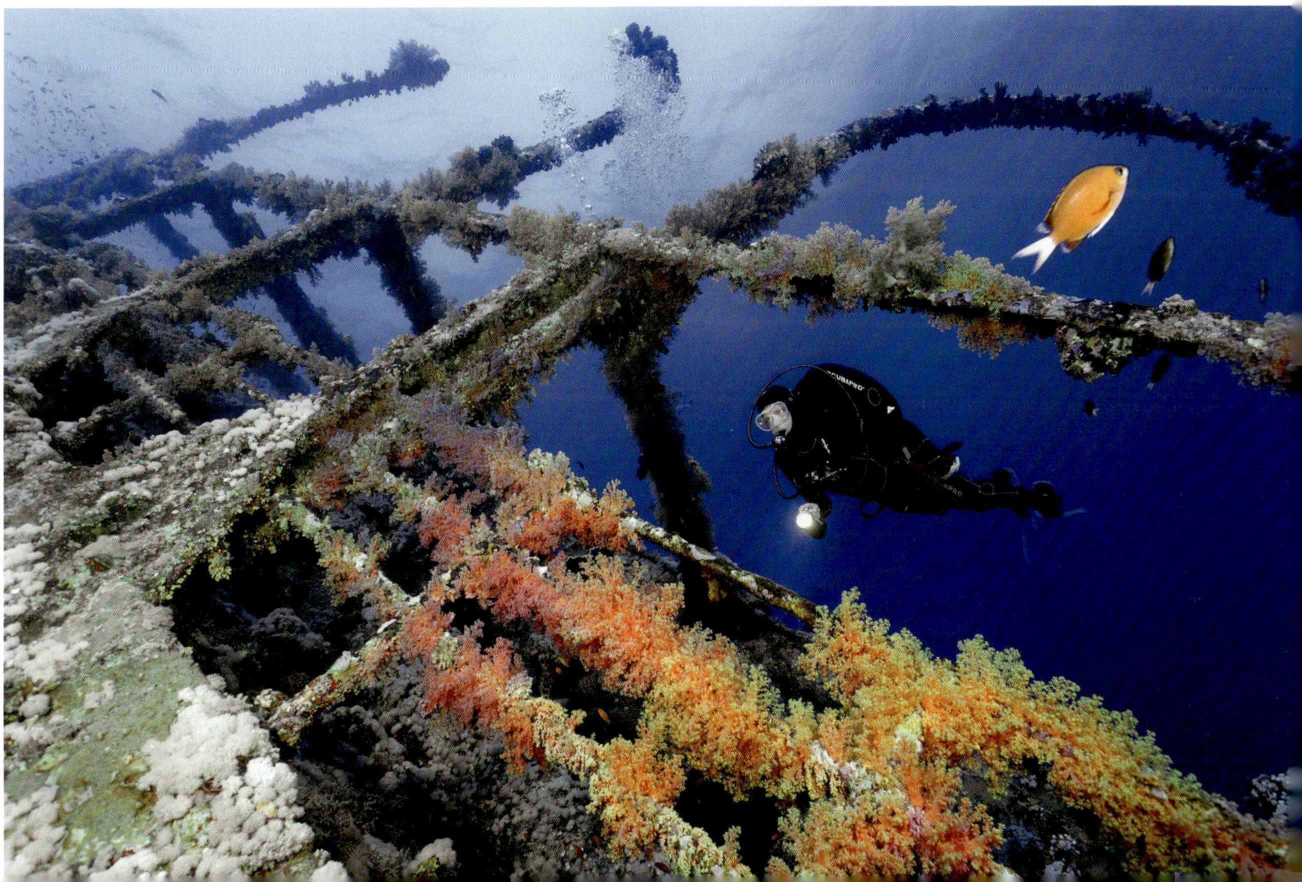

There are two opinions about how models should position their legs. Some photographers prefer a classic pose with the model's legs straight and parallel; others prefer the model to have slightly bent legs as though swimming. Regardless of which position you prefer, you probably don't want your model to angle anything other than the lower part of the leg. A model with their upper legs bent too much—as if on a bicycle—tends to look like an inexperienced swimmer.

For advanced photographers, working with a human model can be a welcome change from taking pictures of sea life

Canon EOS 5D Mark II • Canon 17–40mm wide-angle lens • 1/80 s • f/8 • ISO 400

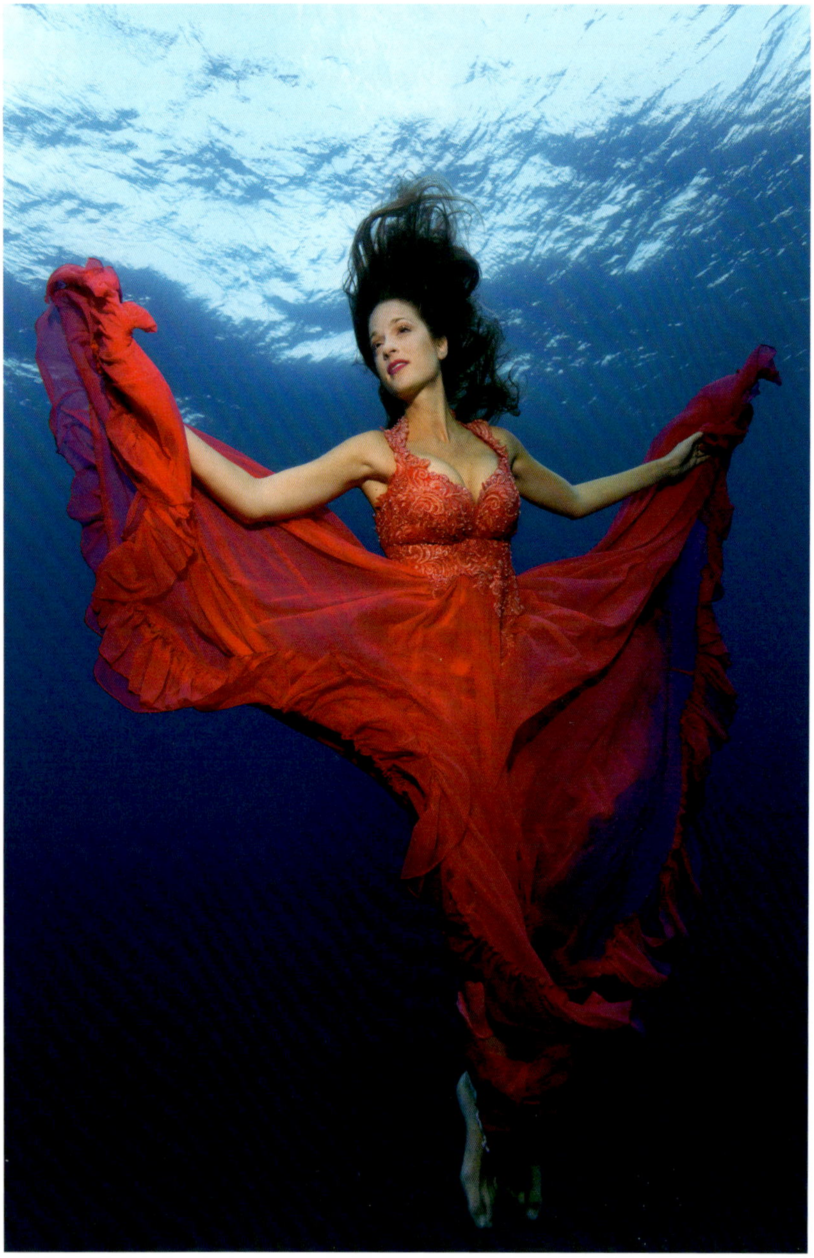

If you and your model have thoroughly prepared, the model will know exactly when to hold his or her breath. Air bubbles tend to be distracting in a photo and can conceal the model's face. Models should never hold their breath for too long, however, and they should not attempt to hold their breath at all as they go to deeper depths. Pay attention to when the model's breath pauses and quickly take the shot.

When you plan to shoot a model in front of a coral garden, program your exposure settings ahead of time. Then the model can come into the scene and take the agreed-upon position. Making preparations like this allows you to concentrate on the model without worrying about your exposure, provided the lighting conditions and the image area remain constant. One effective way to stage a model is to position the person slightly behind the main subject and out of the flash light's reach. This renders the model as a dark silhouette in a blue background. If the model is holding a lamp, it will give your photo a good point of interest and round out the composition.

It's more difficult to compose an image of a model along with another living creature, such as a dolphin or a whale. You must react quickly and intuitively when both subjects hit their marks. One particularly effective way

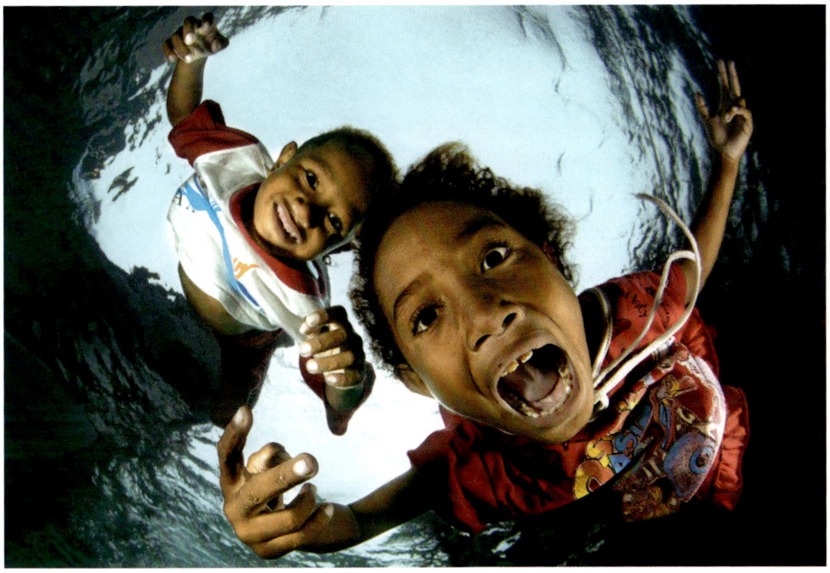

Even though models usually play a supporting role, sometimes they're the main attraction

Canon EOS 5D Mark II • Canon 8–15mm fisheye lens • 1/200 s • f/9 • ISO 100

to design an image is to capture a moment when the human model's form or position subtly echoes the shape of the surrounding landscape or the movement of the animal.

Instruct models to pay attention to whether or not they can see their own reflection in your dome port and if they can see the camera lens behind the port; if they can, they will know they are in the image area. If their entire form is reflected in the port, they can use it as a mirror to check their position.

When a model holds a lamp, the light beam functions as a useful attention grabber and directs the viewer's attention toward it. Make sure your model doesn't shine the lamp directly at you or your camera; the lamp—and the model's gaze—should be directed toward the main subject.

There are differing opinions about what sort of neoprene suit models should wear. Some photographers prefer bright yellow or green suits to contrast with the blue water, and others prefer the traditional look of a black suit with dark equipment. Variety is the key. It would be just as boring to view countless pictures of divers who look like tropical parrots as it would be to see the same black mass every time. A healthy variety of position, color, and distance will produce a rich and interesting portfolio. On a similar note, the best portfolios don't feature models in every picture—they frequently allow the beauty of nature to speak for itself without human distractions.

SUMMARY:

- Including a model in an image can often be the icing on the cake, but models should usually be secondary elements.
- Good communication before a dive and a system of signals make it easier to work under water.
- A standard composition shows the model in a slightly angled position in relation to the image border.
- Be ready for the moments when the model pauses breathing and gets his or her fins in the right position.
- Program your camera's exposure settings for the main subject before the model gets into place.
- One way to make a photo more interesting is for the model's body position to echo the shape of the surroundings or the movements of a nearby animal.
- The model can use a light to direct the viewer's attention toward the main subject.
- Models should rarely look directly at the camera.
- The color of a model's diving suit plays an insignificant role—be sure to include some variety in your photos.

4.14 Motion Blur

Razor-sharp images are the first goal of every underwater photographer. But intentional blur is sometimes intriguing in its own right. Images that feature motion blur can convey movement in a scene and elicit stronger responses from viewers.

The critical shutter speed limit of 1/30 second, which exists principally to *avoid* blur, needs to be bypassed for this technique. The goal is to show the foreground elements in sharp focus— likely your main subject—and to blur the background elements. How do you accomplish this? You can pivot or pan your camera to create blur. If you add flash, the main subject will stay sharp while the world around it starts to smear.

You can use a couple of techniques to introduce blur; each has a different effect. In any case, choose a small aperture—f/16 or f/20—and a shutter speed between 1/5 second and 1/15 second. Set the ISO relatively low to compensate for the slower shutter speed. Excessive sunlight can pose a challenge, so try to practice under overcast skies.

Position your flash units close to your camera and use their highest power setting. The goal is to illuminate the main subject rather than the background.

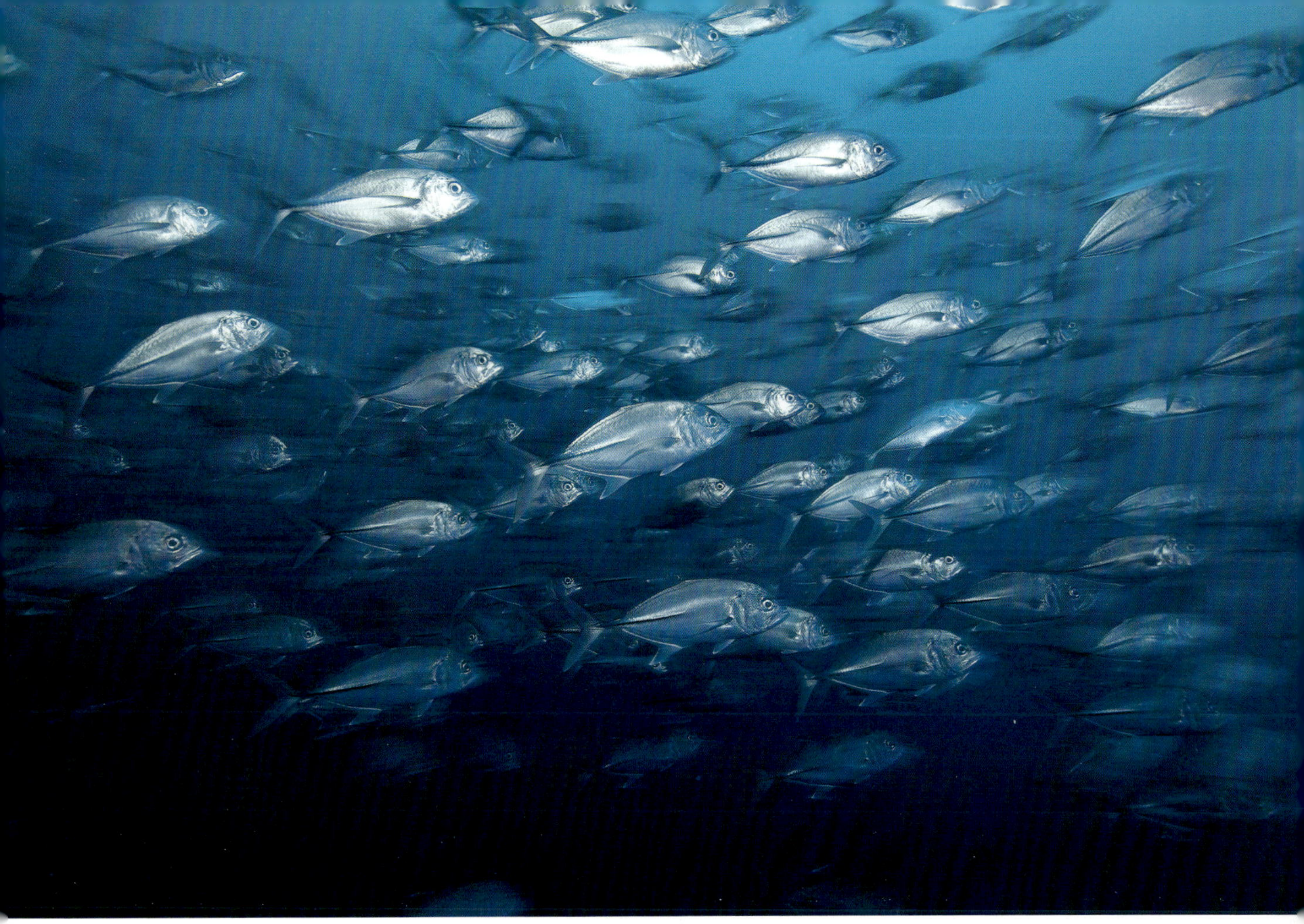

You can set your flash units to fire either as soon as the shutter opens or just before it closes. A flash synced with the first curtain freezes the beginning of the motion, and a flash synced with the second curtain freezes the end of the action. You can program the flash sync either on your camera or on the flash units. Some camera–flash combinations can be synced only with the first curtain.

The first technique is to track the motion of the subject with your camera. As a school of fish swims past, for example, you would pan your camera to follow its movement, which will emphasize motion. When you pan a shark, the intentional blur conveys its movement to the viewer. For schools of fish and large sea animals it's best to sync the flash to the second curtain so the motion isn't captured until the end of the exposure window.

The second technique involves pivoting the camera around its optical axis during the exposure, which produces a swirl effect around the main subject at the center of your image. A school of fish or a piece of coral that is relatively round are ideal candidates for this treatment, but individual animals and divers can also work well.

A school of fish lends itself to a composition with deliberate motion blur to convey movement

Canon EOS 5D Mark II • Canon 16–35mm wide-angle lens • 1/15 s • f/8 • ISO 400

▶ The effect of pivoting your camera is less visible when the background is even—
it's more effective to use a varied backdrop

Canon EOS 5D Mark II • Canon 17–40mm wide-angle lens • 1/5 s • f/22 • ISO 100

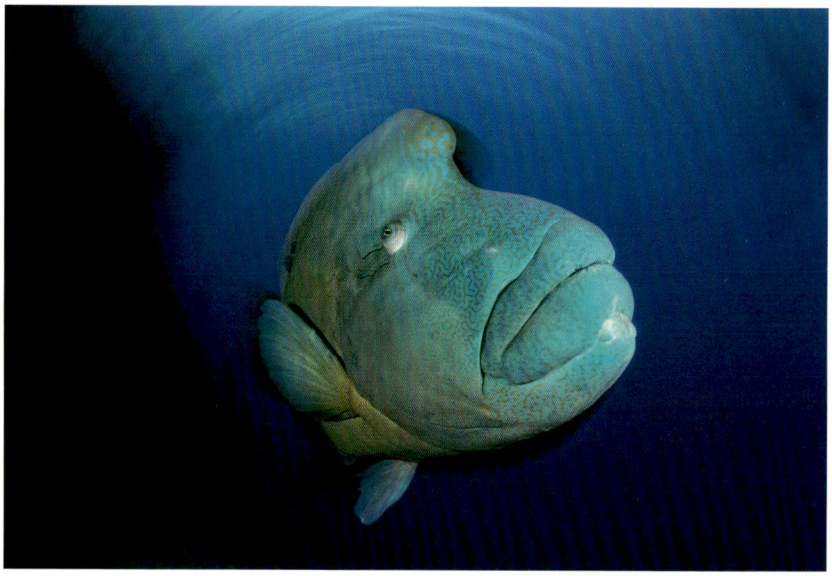

▼ It's easy to practice pivoting your camera with stationary subjects like wrecks and coral

Canon EOS 5D Mark II • Canon 8–15mm fisheye lens • 1/5 s • f/11 • ISO 100

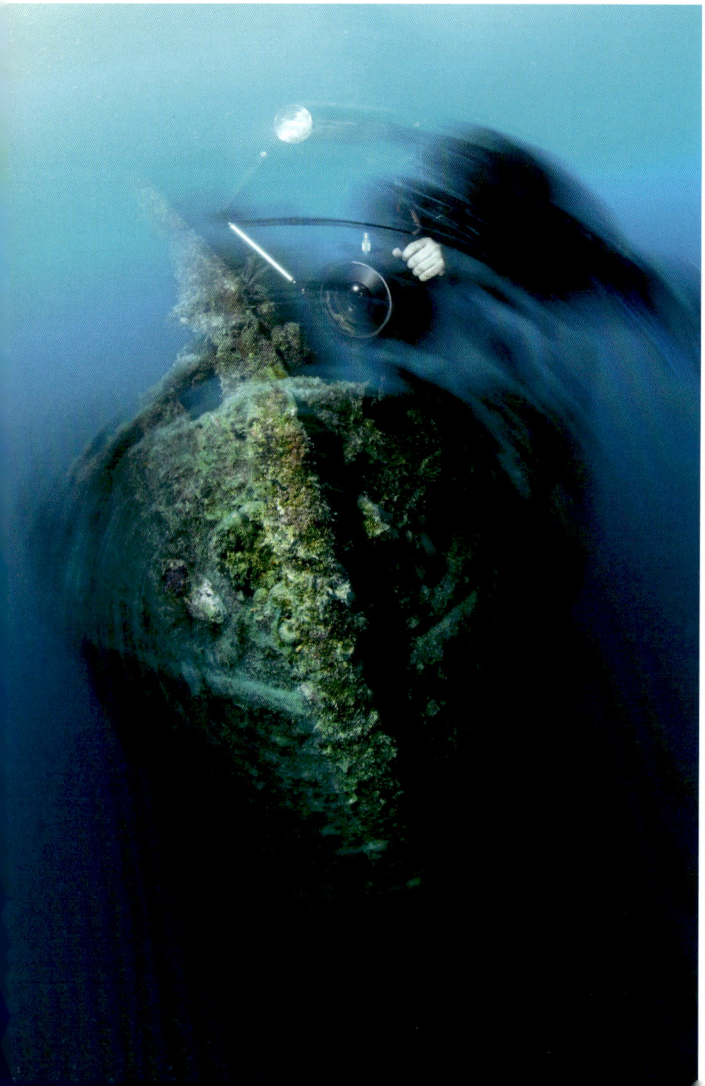

The background is critical for a pivot shot. If it is too uniform, such as an even swath of blue, the swirl effect may not be conspicuous enough to be effective. A background with structure and texture will result in a picture with a more dramatic and effective blur. It's difficult to look through the viewfinder when you take this kind of shot, so the photo will be more of an approximation than anything else. It's best to sync the flash with the first curtain because it's easier to guess your subject's position at the start of the exposure.

You can also use a zoom lens to create blur; just alter the focal length during the exposure. The result is a star-shaped zoom effect, like in sci-fi movies when spaceships enter warp speed. Timing the zoom while you release the shutter requires coordination and a lot of practice. One nice thing about this technique is that you can look through the viewfinder when you take the shot. First start adjusting the focal length, and then press the shutter button during the motion. Otherwise you run the risk of completely missing the motion and will fail to depict movement in your images. You'll need several tries and a lot of practice to master this technique.

SUMMARY:

- Images with motion blur feature areas that intentionally lack sharpness.
- Pan or pivot the camera, or zoom the lens, during the exposure to blur the background.
- Use flash so the main subject stays sharp and frozen in place.
- Exposure settings of f/16, 1/5 second to 1/10 second, and ISO 100 are a good starting point for creating images with blur.
- Position the flash units close to your camera and set them to their maximum output.
- Sync the flash with either the first or the second shutter curtain.
- Panning the camera and syncing the flash to the second curtain is an ideal technique for schools of fish and large sea life.
- Pivoting the camera produces attractive images of round subjects or coral.
- The background should have texture or obvious contrast to make the most of this technique.
- Adjusting the zoom during an exposure produces a star-shaped effect.

A touch of motion blur makes pictures of animals seem more dynamic

Canon EOS 5D Mark II • Canon 17–40mm wide-angle lens • 1/20 s • f/16 • ISO 200

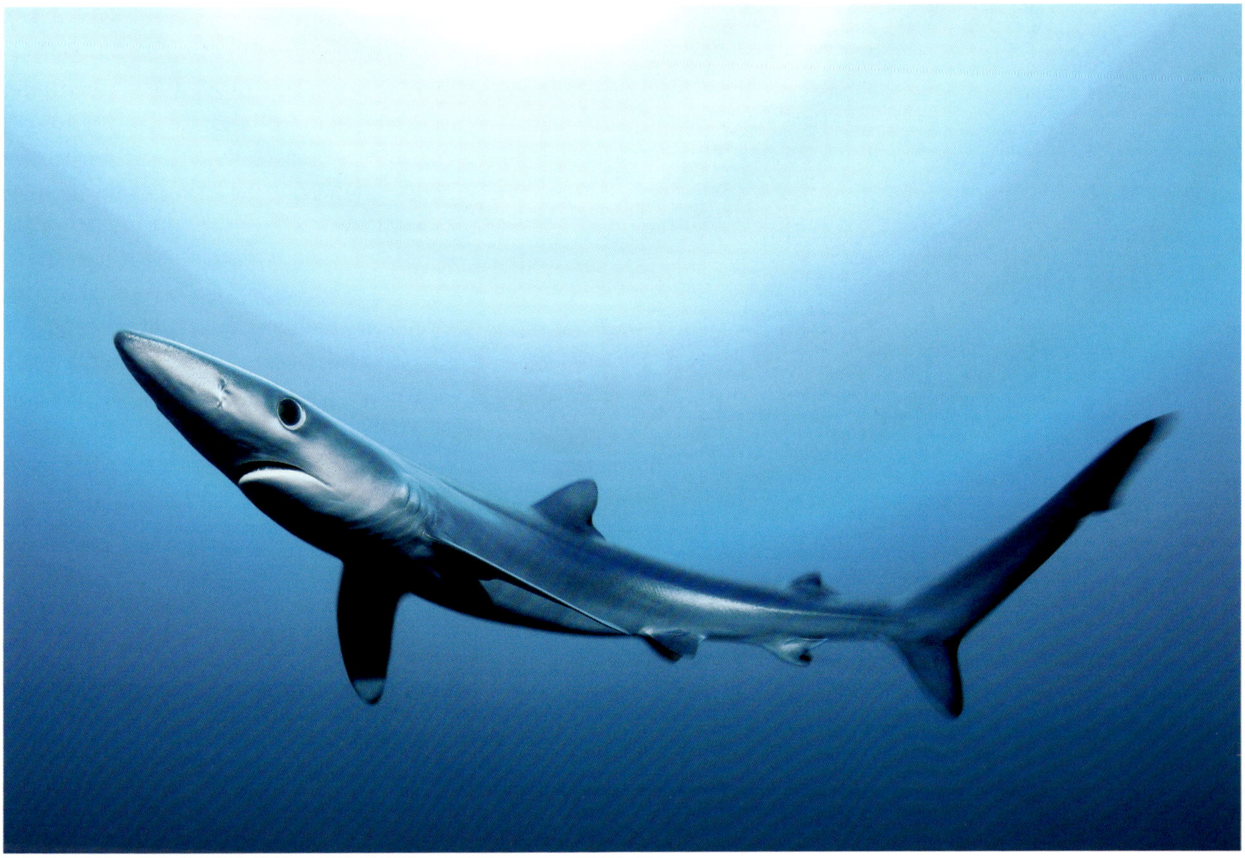

4.15 Recording Video

Video clips are effective in slide shows to convey movement in a way that still photos cannot. And the underwater world is rich with candidates for studying motion: schools of fish, dolphins, and rays are ideal. Recording video is a powerful and simple way to expand on your work.

Entire books could be written about the ins and outs of recording video under water, so it can't be covered completely in this book. Nevertheless, because recording video with a DSLR is getting easier and better, it makes sense to at least touch on some of the basics here. The goal is to give you basic knowledge and skills to capture some interesting video clips from your next dive.

The first decision you need to make is which format to use. Choose the setting that provides the highest resolution, which is probably 1920 × 1080 pixels. It's called *1080p* and is usually designated as *full HD* (high definition). Choose 1280 × 720 pixels only if your camera doesn't offer a higher resolution or if your computer at home can't play back higher-resolution formats.

The default aspect ratio for most DSLRs is 16:9, which corresponds to the aspect ratio of most televisions. When you record video with a DSLR, make sure you're using this format instead of a 3:2 aspect ratio. This can be tricky when you look at your LCD screen because often the aspect ratio won't switch to 16:9 until you press the record button, which results in cropping the frame and, in the figurative sense, cutting the subject.

Lamps designed for video are just as critical as flash units for still photography. You'll need two good lamps to illuminate the image area of a fisheye lens. Ask a trusted retailer to help you choose a lighting system that meets your needs.

One downside of using a DSLR to capture video—instead of a dedicated video recorder—is the absence of autofocus. Even when a DSLR comes equipped with such a system, it is often inadequate for underwater use. The problem is that your videos can be blurred if you change your perspective while you shoot. Using a fisheye or a wide-angle lens with a small aperture—f/8 or f/11 and smaller—will produce a sharp image throughout a large depth of field.

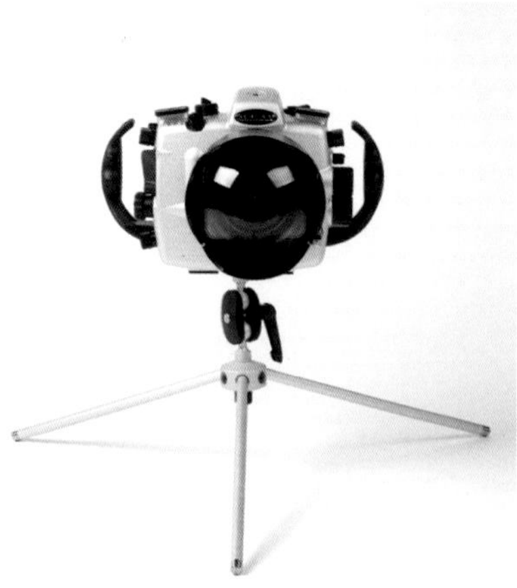

An underwater housing on a tripod (photo courtesy of SEACAM)

One trick is to first focus on the subject as though you are taking a still photo, then switch to recording video. After you start the video recording, make only minor adjustments to your position so your video stays in focus.

The shutter speed you should use depends on how many frames per second your camera captures during video recording. Generally speaking, you should double your frame rate to find your shutter speed. If your camera shoots 25 frames per second, set your shutter speed to 1/50 second. If your camera shoots 30 frames per second, 1/60 second is optimal. This rule of thumb produces a fluid, high-quality video. To adjust the exposure, change the aperture—or better yet, the ISO.

While you're shooting, hold your camera securely with both hands and try not to move the camera. Even the best image stabilization technology is powerless against jittery movements. Use a tripod to capture perfectly stable video; in the macro range, a tripod is a must because the depth of field is so minuscule that there's no other way to make sure your subject stays in focus.

Flecks and other blemishes in your images are not an insurmountable problem with still photographs because you can remove them in post-processing. They are more of a problem with video because it's nearly impossible to remove them. This is one reason to take good care of your dome port and have your camera sensor cleaned regularly.

It's also important to use a gray or white card to manually set the white balance for video shoots. Some video editing software allows you to adjust the white balance retroactively, but it's better to get it right before you shoot. The red filter guidelines for still photography apply to video: their functionality is limited to a maximum depth of 50 to 65 ft.

SUMMARY:

- Videos can be a valuable addition to your slide shows. They allow you to share the movement of the undersea world.
- Use the highest resolution possible—ideally full HD (1080p).
- Pay attention to the aspect ratio; a ratio of 3:2 might be converted to 16:9 and crop out the main subject.
- Fisheye and wide-angle lenses produce the best depth of field.
- You'll need two lamps to illuminate the full angle of view and bring rich colors into your video.
- It's best to focus your image first, then switch to video recording.
- Shoot steadily with both hands, and avoid sudden movements.
- Using a tripod is the only way to get perfectly stable video; it's mandatory for shooting in the macro range.
- Video is most effective when motion is a key characteristic of the subject.

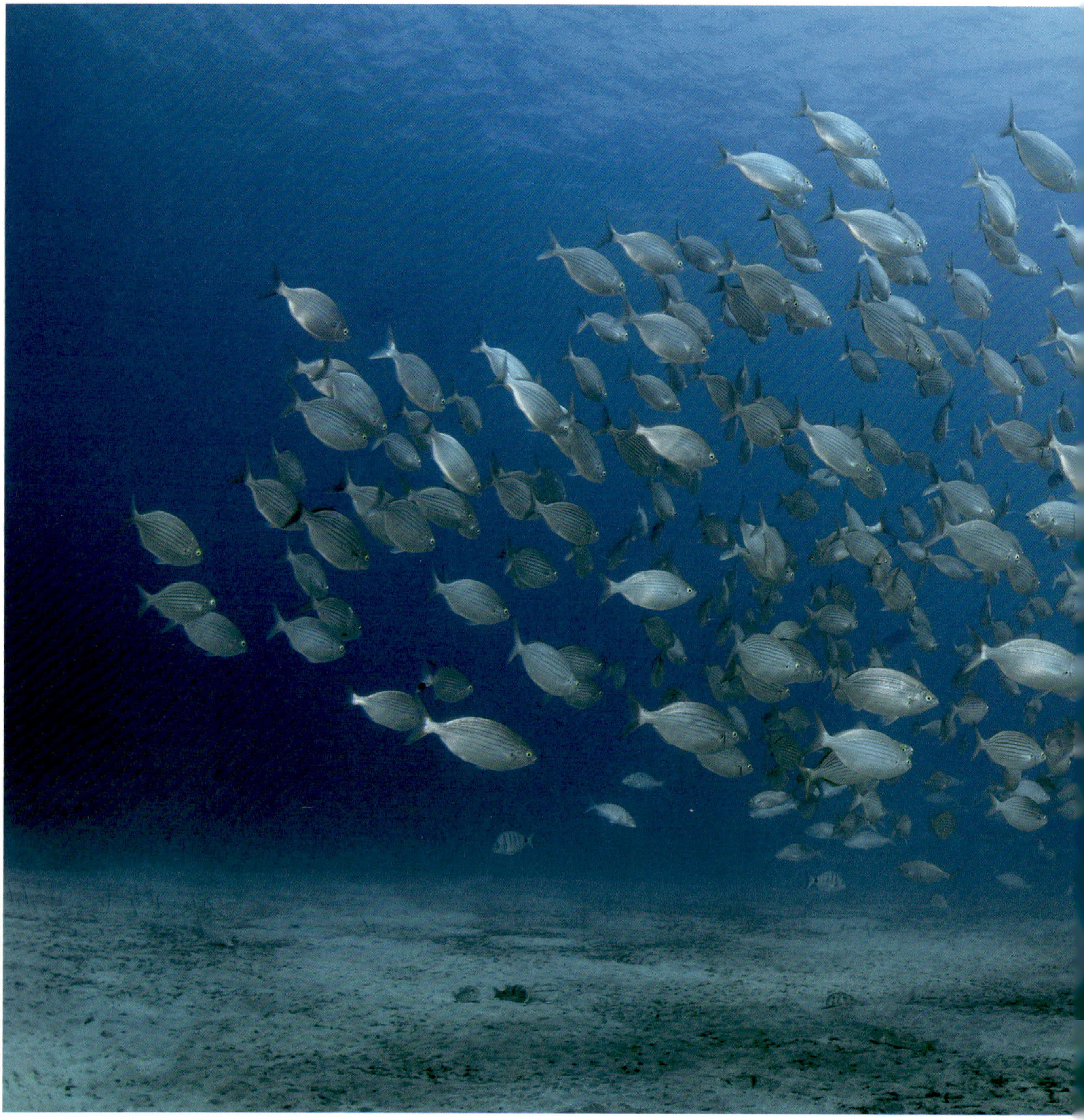

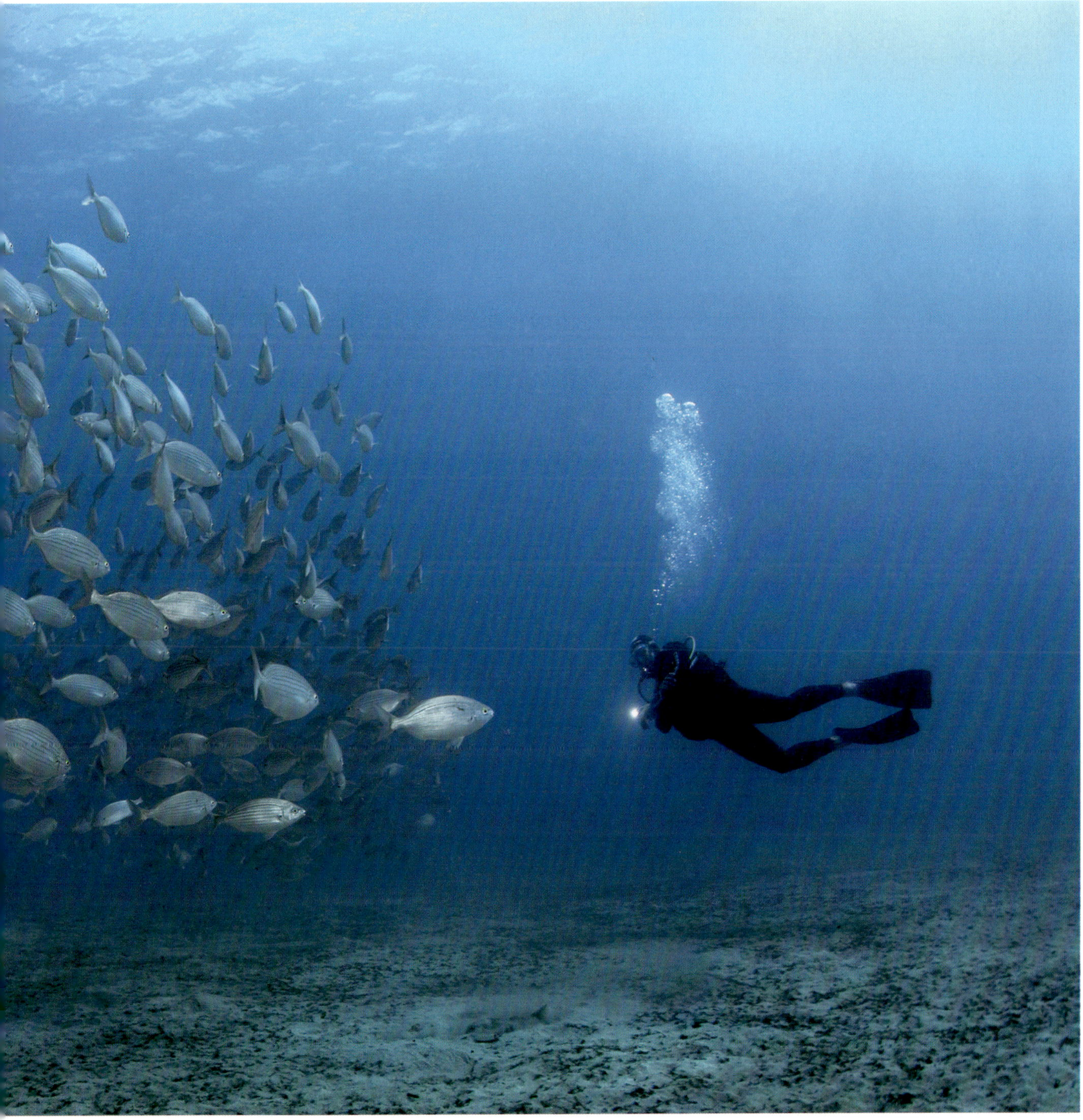

Some photos lend themselves to a panorama format adding to the expansive feel

Canon EOS 5D Mark II • Canon 8–15mm fisheye lens • 1/250 s • f/9 • ISO 200

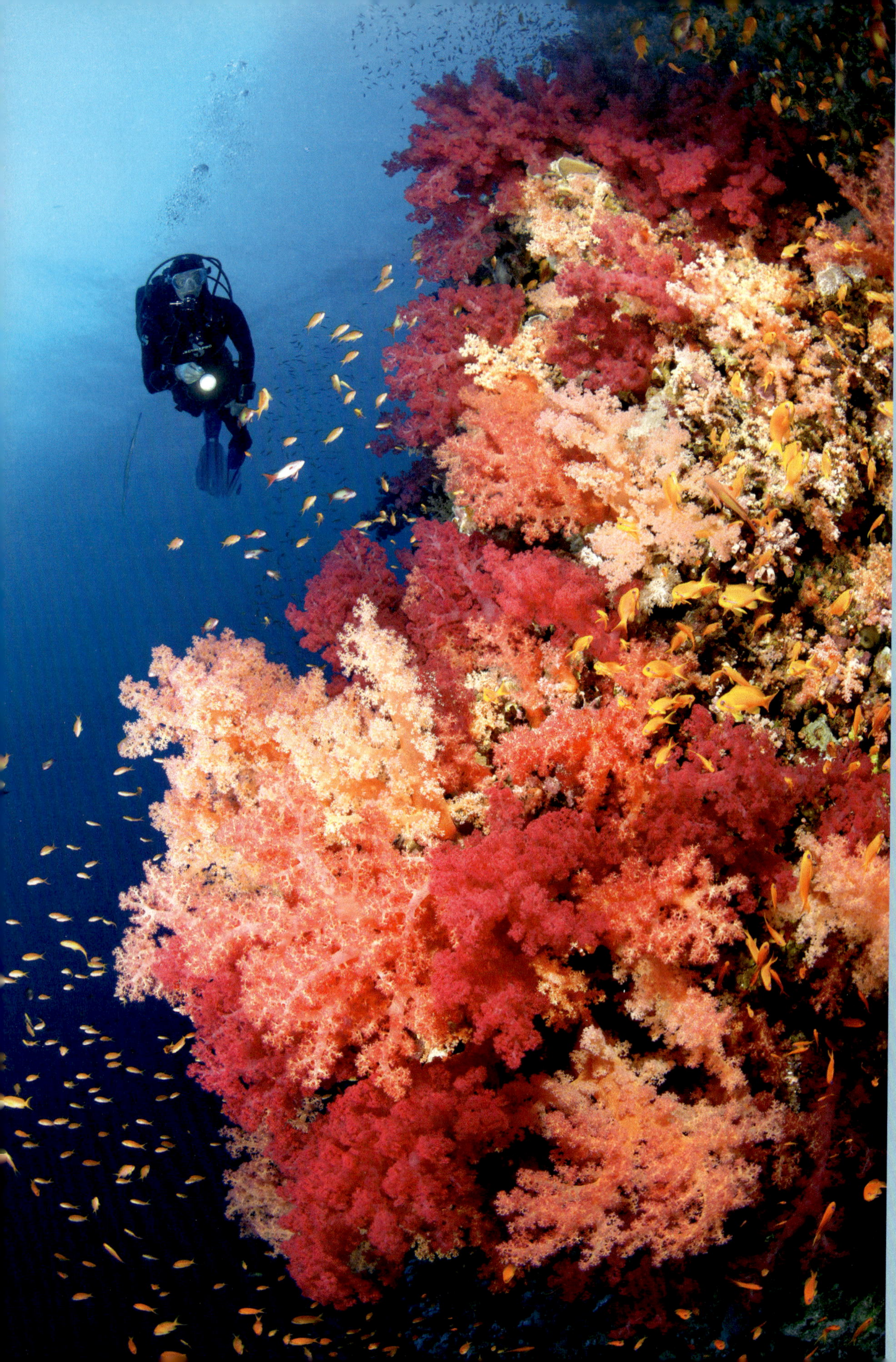

Case Study 5: Communal Living

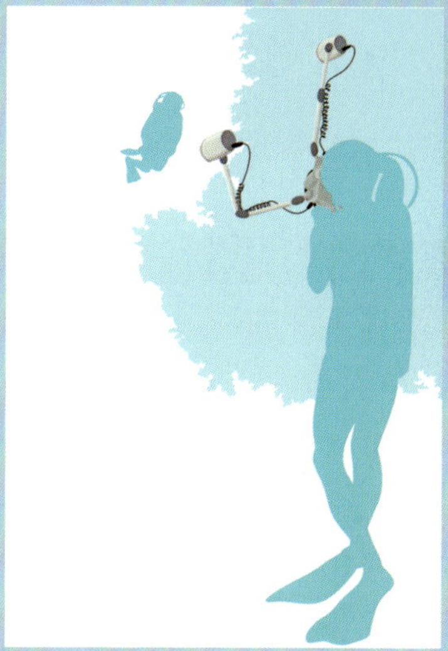

It's easy to feel grateful when you're taking pictures of reefs—they don't swim away from you, they don't turn to the side at the wrong moment, and they won't go blind even after the hundredth flash. You can have your diving partner swim around the reef searching for just the right spot as long as his or her air supply and patience lasts.

The challenge of reef photography is finding a worthy reef landscape and then figuring out how to illuminate it correctly. Not every reef is particularly photogenic. It's not easy to find a relatively large patch of densely grown coral that is also free from jutting stones and calcareous skeletons. There are only a few locations in the world where you can find large, healthy reef colonies—one such spot is Brother Islands in Egypt, where this photo was taken. Spectacular visibility conditions of 100 ft and more make the pictures look all the more brilliant.

Because I used a fisheye lens, I was able to swim very close to the under part of the soft coral, but I had to position my flash heads carefully. I brought one of them in tighter and pointed it toward the center, and I stretched the other flash arm out to illuminate the top part of the picture and to shine some light on the diver. I decided that the ideal position for my model was in the open space in the upper-left portion of the image. I had the diver hold a lamp as a final touch to solidify the composition.

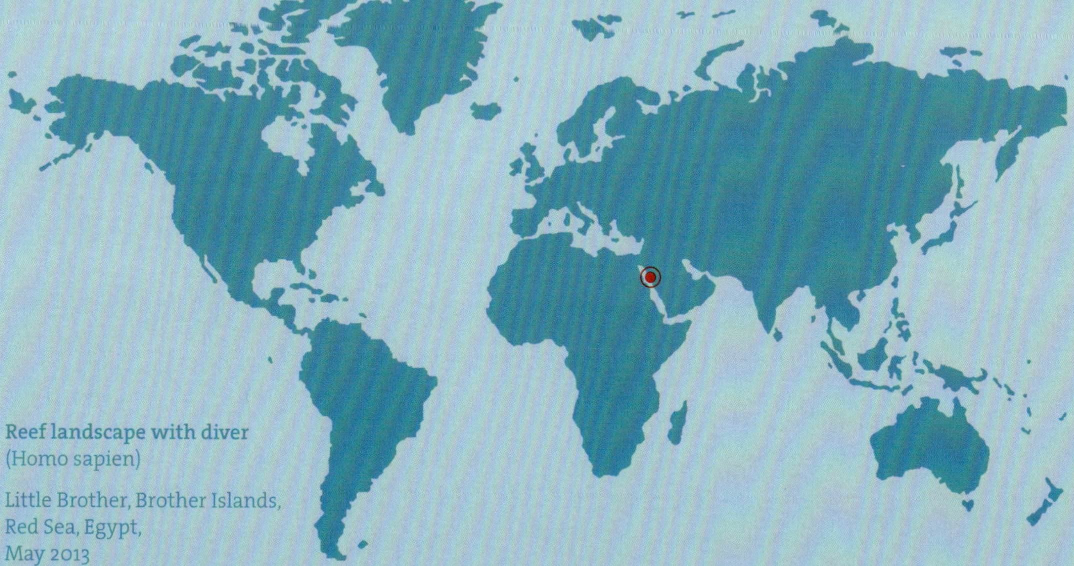

Reef landscape with diver
(Homo sapien)

Little Brother, Brother Islands,
Red Sea, Egypt,
May 2013

Canon EOS 5D Mark II • Canon 8–15mm fisheye lens • two SEACAM Seaflash 150D units • 1/125 s • f/10 • ISO 200 • TTL flash

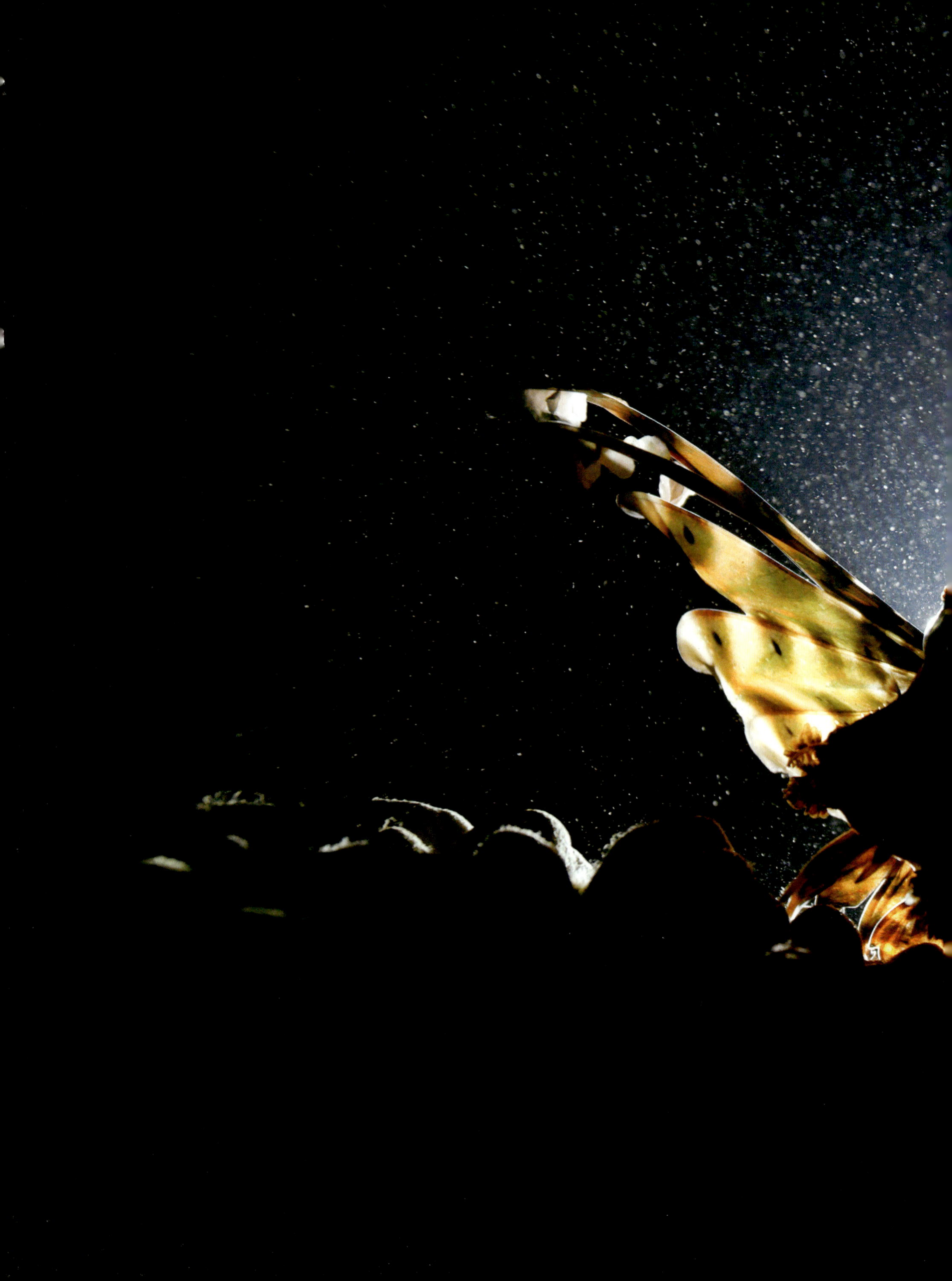

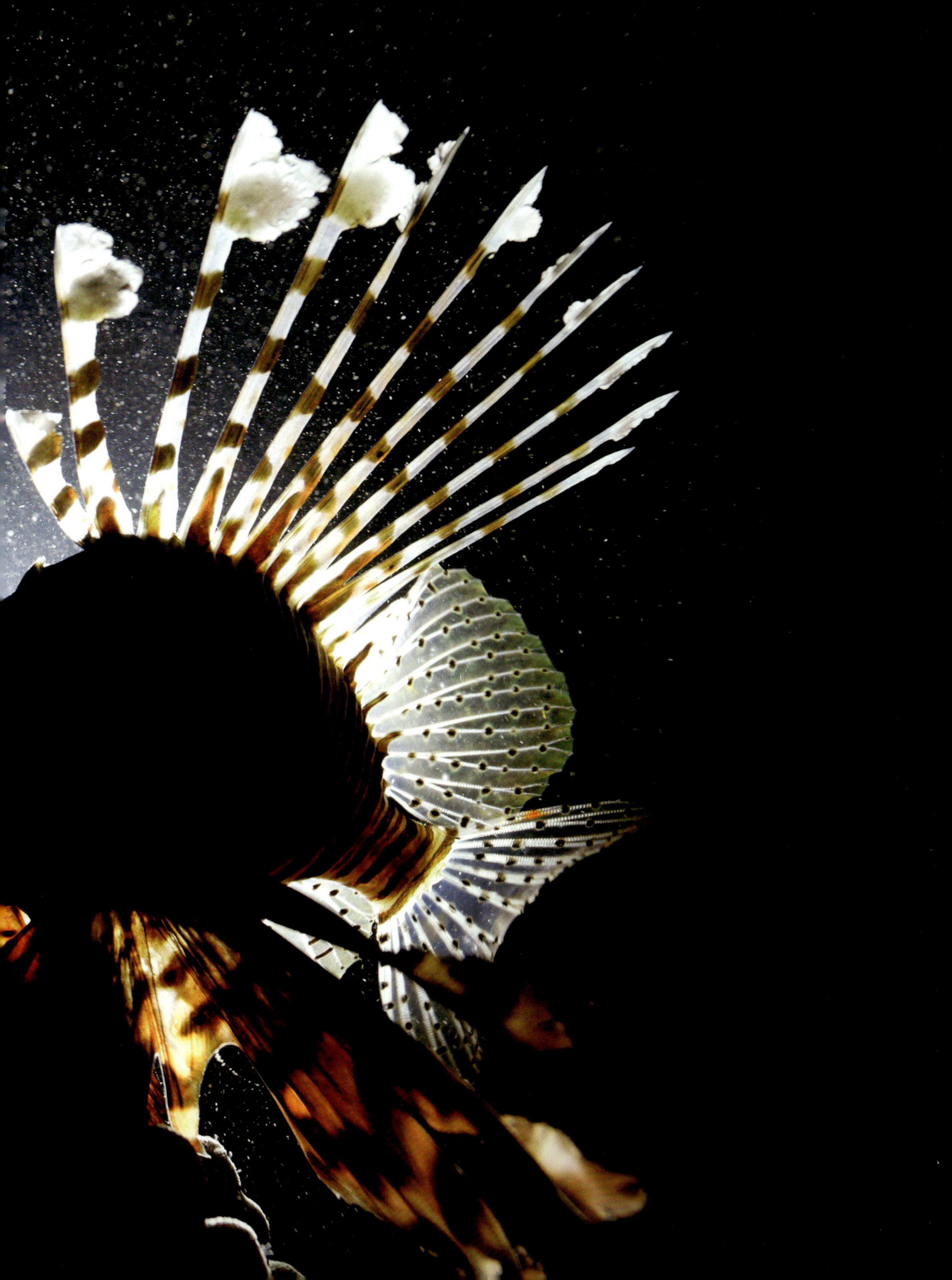

Case Study 6: Dive by Night

This photo is an ideal example of creative photography. I shot it during an underwater photography competition in which participants had three days to capture as many successful photos as possible. The contest took place in Eilat, Israel, which is on the Red Sea. The reefs aren't bad, but they are nothing like the spectacular coral formations a little farther south.

The challenge was to compose rather ordinary subjects to make them look extraordinary. Lionfish are natural subjects because they are fairly common in the area. Trying to compose a beautiful picture of this animal while including a nice background and during broad daylight is no easy task, so I had to venture

Canon EOS 5D Mark II • Canon 17–40mm wide-angle lens, no flash • 1/60 s • f/7.1 • ISO 1600

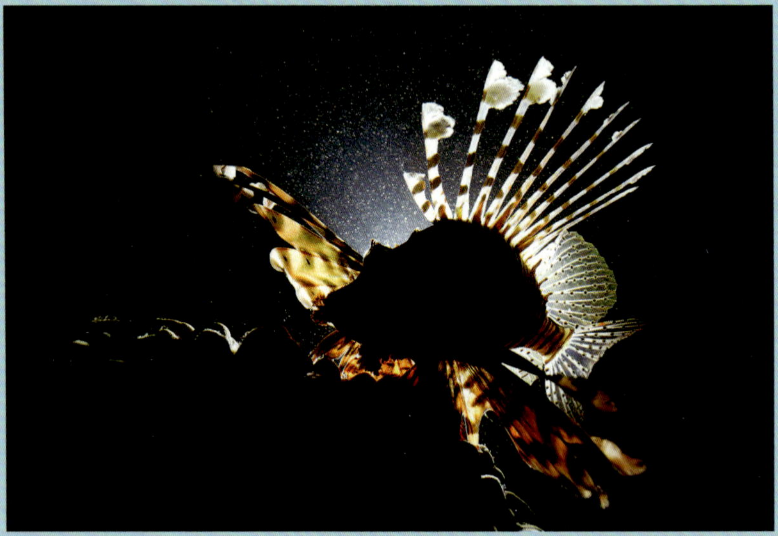

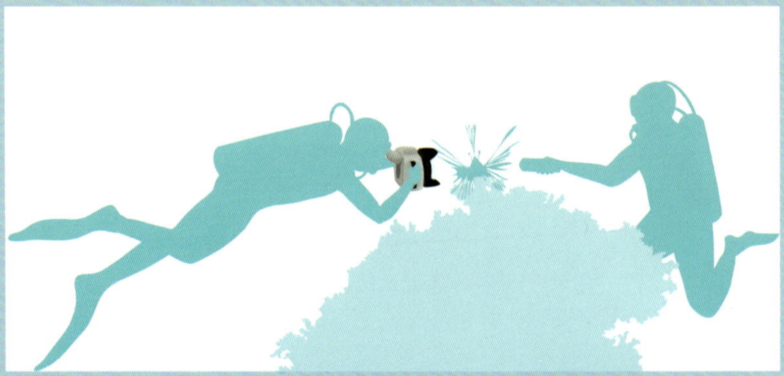

away from the popular areas. I planned something that is not common: a night dive with a wide-angle lens. This choice of lens is unusual because it's harder to see large sea life at night, and the lack of sunlight drastically reduces the appearance of depth, which is achieved by ambient light. Macro lenses are almost always the best choice for night dives.

When I was planning how to compose an image of a lionfish, I decided to use my wide-angle lens to capture the entire subject, which is relatively large. I could have used a macro lens, but it would have required more distance between my camera and the subject, and the volume of water would have reduced the image quality.

I decided to use backlighting to produce a silhouette and emphasize the animal's transparent fins. My diving partner and I talked about my strategy before the dive, so he knew what I had in mind and how he had to position the lamp for the desired effect.

For the exposure settings, I bumped the ISO way up because of the meager light. I couldn't open the aperture all the way because I needed to retain enough depth of field to keep the entire fish in focus. Finally, I set the shutter speed at 1/60 second to eliminate the chance of camera shake.

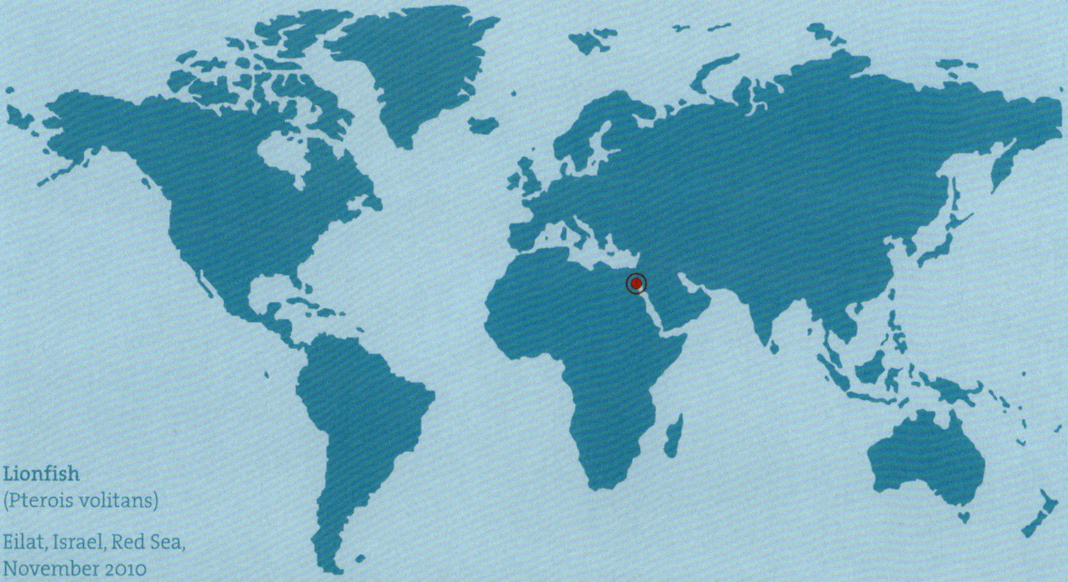

Lionfish
(Pterois volitans)

Eilat, Israel, Red Sea,
November 2010

5

Macro Photography

Macro photography lets you depict living creatures in a way that normally eludes the human eye. Some photographers devote their entire underwater craft to macro images, leaving their wide-angle lenses behind in pursuit of their true passion.

Wide-angle photography is generally capable of capturing and conveying more information and emotion, but macro photography is an easier first step into the world of aquatic photography. In contrast to wide-angle photography, the longer focal length of closeup lenses is tighter, which makes it easier to compose photos.

As with other types of underwater photography, patience plays a key role when you take macro pictures. When will the grouper finally open its mouth? Will the blenny pop out of its hole again? Will the sea horse turn toward the camera? Hours can pass while you wait for an animal to position itself perfectly for the image you envision. Patience pays big dividends in macro photography.

Things that make good macro subjects are easy to overlook. Sometimes the star of a macro photo is less than half an inch in size but is rich with detail.

Design guidelines like the golden ratio are just as applicable with a macro photo as any other image

Canon EOS 5D Mark II • Canon 100mm macro lens • 1/50 s • f/22 • ISO 400

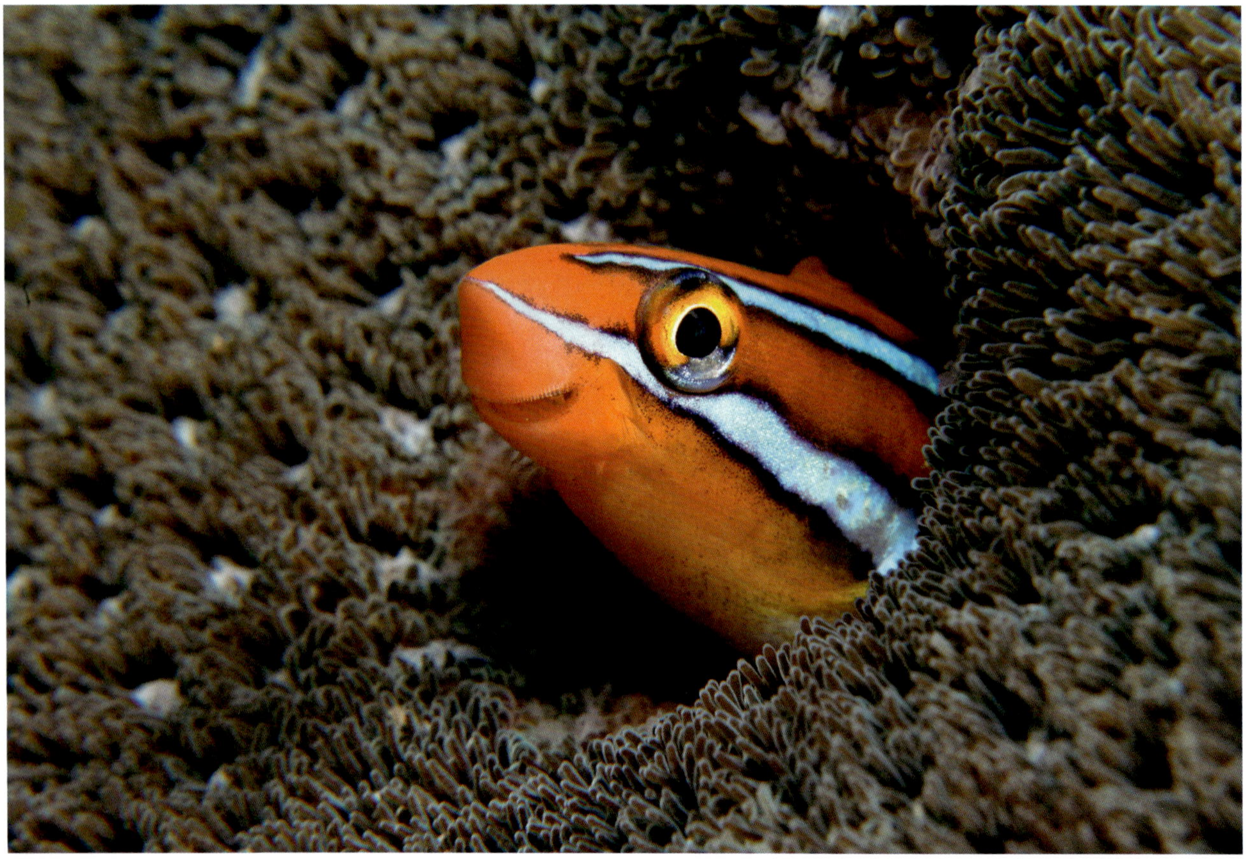

5.1 Lenses

The market is full of macro lenses that feature a broad range of apertures. It's difficult to keep track of what's out there. A macro lens with a 60mm focal length is a good place to start for a crop camera; for a full-format camera, 100mm makes a good first choice. This one basic lens is all you'll really need for the moment.

If photographing the tiny wonders of the sea has special importance to you, consider getting a macro lens with a shorter focal length. It will have a smaller minimum focus distance and will allow you to get even closer to subjects. These lenses can be challenging to work with for a couple reasons: first, you need to get so close to subjects that some of them will scurry away; and second, it's difficult to position the strobes with these lenses because the subject is often so close that you can't bring your flashes in tight enough.

Longer focal lengths in the 150mm to 180mm range are more practical for photographing skittish animals, but you'll have a greater minimum focus distance and therefore more water between you and the subject, which might result in a loss in clarity in your photo.

Most macro lenses have a fixed focal length and are particularly fast. Unfortunately you won't be able to use their maximum aperture, though; use an aperture number of f/8 or higher to preserve enough

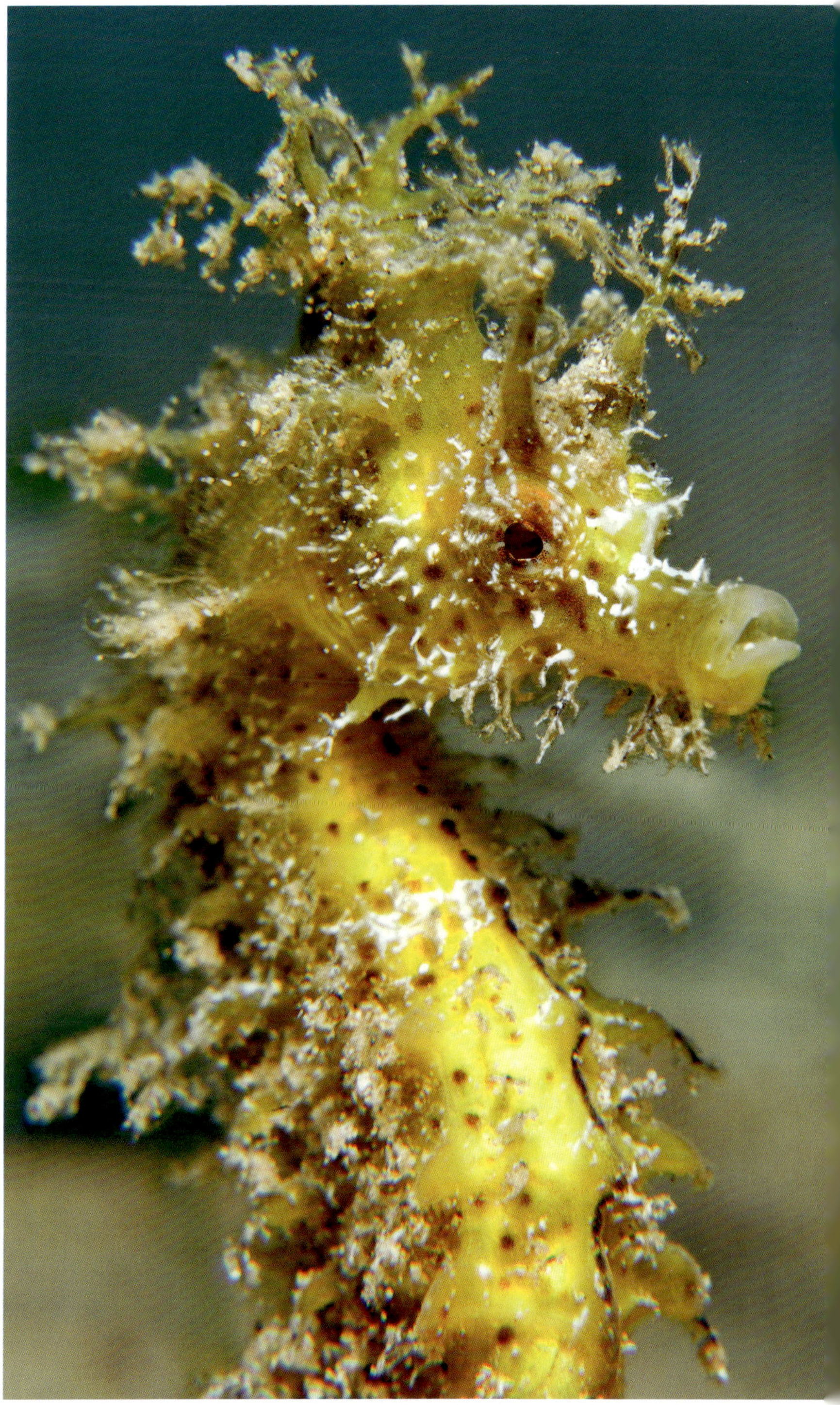

The sand behind this sea horse reflects enough light so the background isn't too dark, even with a small aperture opening

Canon EOS 5D Mark II • Canon 100mm macro lens • 1/100 s • f/20 • ISO 200

depth of field so the entire subject will be in sharp focus. Nevertheless, a professional lens, like the Canon L-series lenses, will provide higher image quality then a standard lens, even at higher f-stops.

A camera with a crop sensor is ideal for photographers who love shooting macro images because there is an even wider selection of lenses than for full-format cameras.

SUMMARY:

- The abundance of macro lenses can overwhelm buyers.
- A 60mm lens is an ideal starting point for a crop-sensor camera; a 100mm lens for a full-format camera.
- Shorter focal lengths allow for smaller minimum focus distances.
- Use longer focal lengths for especially shy animals.
- Macro lenses usually have fixed focal lengths and are very fast.
- There are more macro lenses available for cameras with a crop sensor than for full-format cameras.

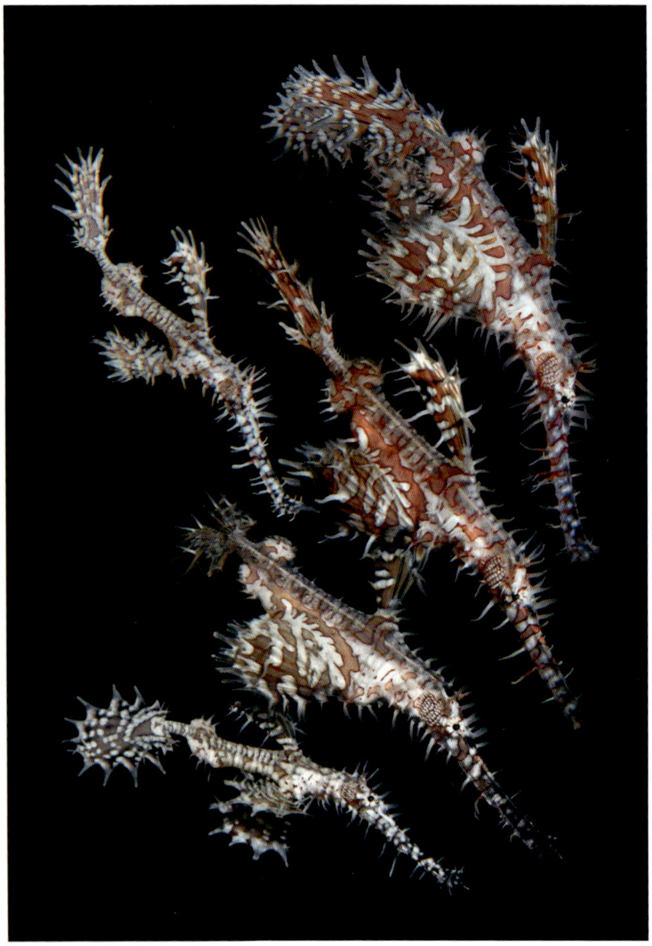

A family of ghost pipefish attempt to hide in some coral. A moment of inattention as they abandoned their camouflage provided a golden photographic opportunity.

Canon EOS 5D Mark II • Canon 100mm macro lens • 1/125 s • f/32 • ISO 200

5.2 Macro vs. Closeup

Photographers often distinguish between *macro* and *closeup* pictures based on the reproduction ratio. The key distinction has to do with the size of the subject on the sensor plane: either actual size (1:1), or larger or smaller. For example, if a subject that's 36mm (1.4 inch) big fills the entire image area on a full-format camera (with a 36mm sensor), the reproduction ratio is described as 1:1 (one-to-one). If the subject is half that size but still fills up the entire image area, the reproduction ratio is 2:1. Similarly, if the subject is twice as large, the reproduction ratio is 1:2 and the photo would be considered a *closeup* image.

To recap: an image that has a reproduction ratio equal to or greater than 1:1 is called a macro image; if the ratio is smaller than 1:1, it's a closeup image.

Many underwater photographers don't bother with this distinction; they refer to both types of images as macro. Nevertheless, it's important to be aware of the reproduction ratio so you can compare how it changes when you use teleconverters and different focal lengths.

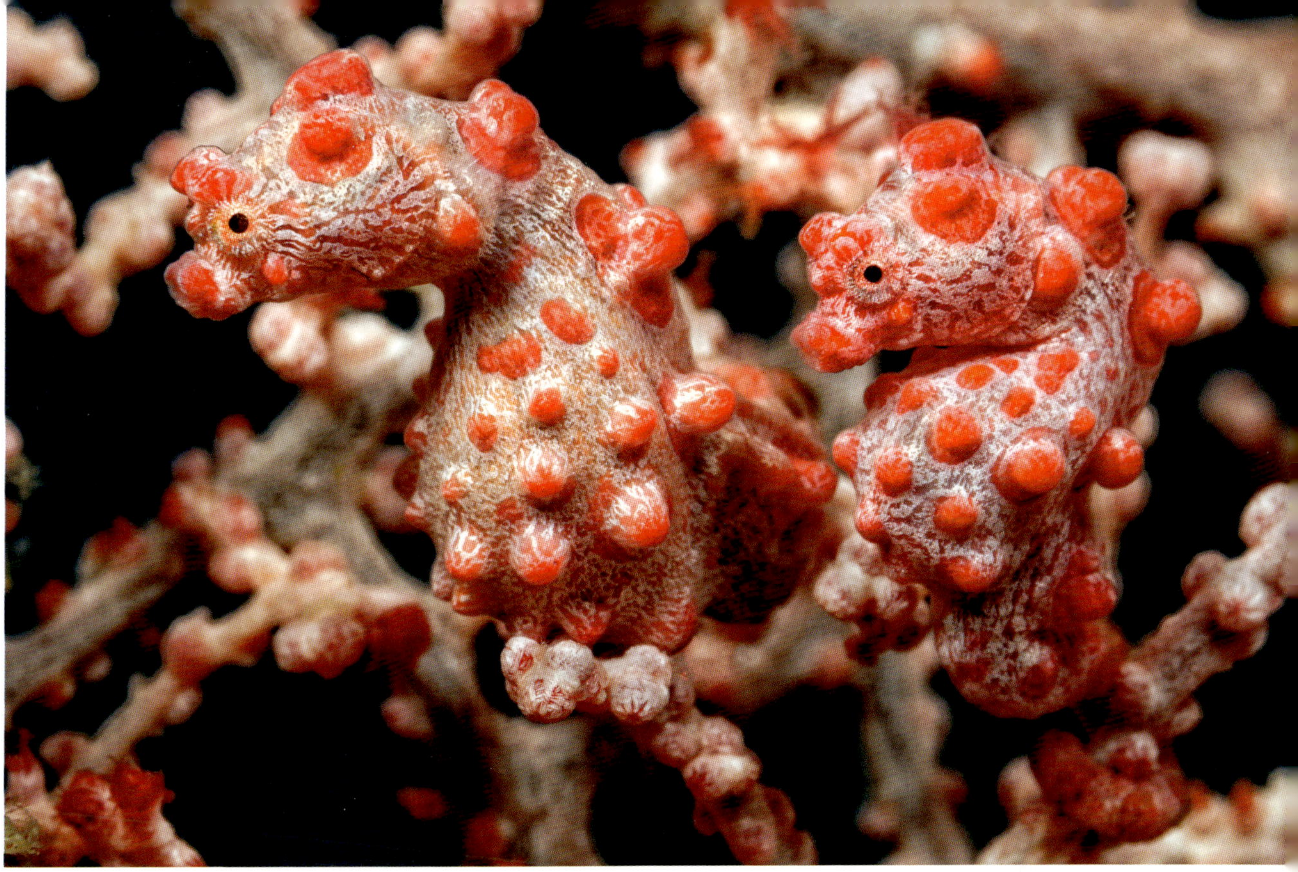

When you photograph pygmy sea horses, wait for them to turn toward the camera on their own rather than coaxing them

Canon EOS 5D Mark II • Canon 100mm macro lens • INON UCL-165 closeup lens • 1/125 s • f/16 • ISO 200

SUMMARY:

- A reproduction ratio of 1:1 means a subject is portrayed at actual size on the sensor plane.
- Images with a reproduction ratio of 2:1 are considered macro images.
- Images with a reproduction ratio of 1:2 are considered closeup images.

5.3 Settings

All successful underwater macro photos are taken with flash because the aperture opening needs to be small enough to create a sufficient depth of field. The small aperture prohibits most ambient light from reaching the sensor—a problem that can be overcome only by using artificial light.

Normally you should set your flash units at full power—or at least half power—if you are not using TTL metering.

To make sure the subject falls within the depth of field, start with an aperture of f/22 and fine-tune it from there. You can set the shutter speed at 1/160 second or 1/200 second because ambient light isn't a factor, and it will help avoid camera shake.

Depending on the power of your flash unit, set the ISO at 200 or 400. Modern DSLR cameras have such good performance at higher ISO settings that you can easily go up to ISO 800 without any problems.

Subjects that are obscured in shadows or hidden in dark areas require an additional focus lamp so the camera can automatically establish focus. The pilot light on some flash units can serve the purpose, or you can attach a separate auxiliary light to your camera (see section 1.4).

When you use artificial light exclusively for a macro photo, the image usually shows the subject isolated in front of a black background—often the open water, as long as it's not illuminated. Composing a photo to produce this contrast really emphasizes the subject and catches the viewer's attention, plus it eliminates the risk of distracting elements appearing in the background.

Once you get used to macro photography, you can try attempting more advanced techniques: during a dive with bright natural light, try using mixed light by opening your aperture as much as possible. An aperture of f/16 or f/11 and a shutter speed of 1/60 second or 1/30 second are good baseline settings. You can also increase the ISO to get the most out of whatever ambient light is available. If you manually control the intensity of your flash units, don't

Nighttime, when reef fish are sleeping, is the best time to photograph a fish's eye

Canon EOS 5D Mark II • Canon 100mm macro lens • 1/40 s • f/13 • ISO 200

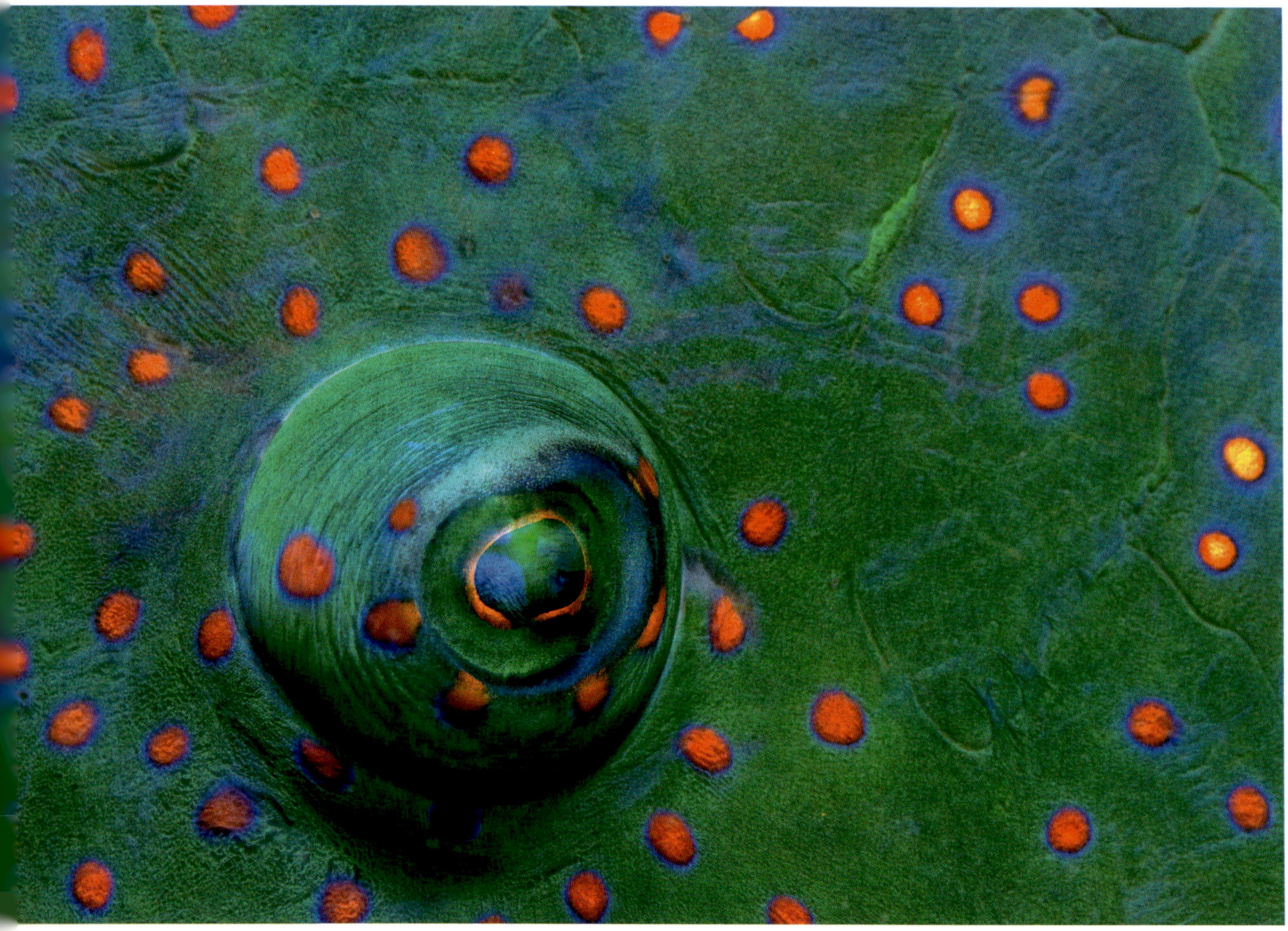

forget to reduce their power. With this setup you can compose a photo with the subject isolated in front of a stretch of ocean—try shooting with a slight upward perspective to produce a light background. If the water in your image is too dark or too bright, use small adjustments of the shutter speed, aperture, or ISO to fine-tune the exposure.

You can make a great macro photo of a small goby resting on a sea whip by isolating the subject. But be careful—the wider you open the aperture, the more difficult it is to control the focus.

The best way to compensate for poor underwater visibility is to use a lens with the smallest possible focal length and the minimum focus distance.

SUMMARY:

- Using a flash for macro photos is mandatory.
- An aperture of f/22 or f/32 will produce sharpness throughout your image.
- The exposure can be set at 1/160 second or 1/200 second.
- A focus lamp will aid your camera's autofocus system in dark areas.
- A closed aperture and fast shutter speeds block ambient light from coming through, which is why underwater macro images mostly have a black background.
- If you want to use both ambient and artificial light, open the aperture and decrease the shutter speed.
- If you use mixed lighting, shoot up toward the surface of water so your sensor receives as much natural light as possible.
- In poor visibility, use a lens with a small minimum focus distance.

5.4 Depth of Field

Sharp elements in an image command the viewer's attention. If the main subject in your image is not sharp, it can have a devastating effect on your photo. Successful images can be composed with the greatest area of sharpness running diagonally across the image, in the center only, or in the golden ratio, but it should not be too close to the edge of the picture.

When you photograph animals, make sure their eyes are in focus. Ideally photos should show their eyes and mouth in sharp focus, which you can usually accomplish by focusing on an area between them. If a limited depth of field makes this impossible, the eyes should always take priority.

Perspective influences how you establish sharpness in your photos. If a subject like a longnose hawkfish is perpendicular to your camera, most of its

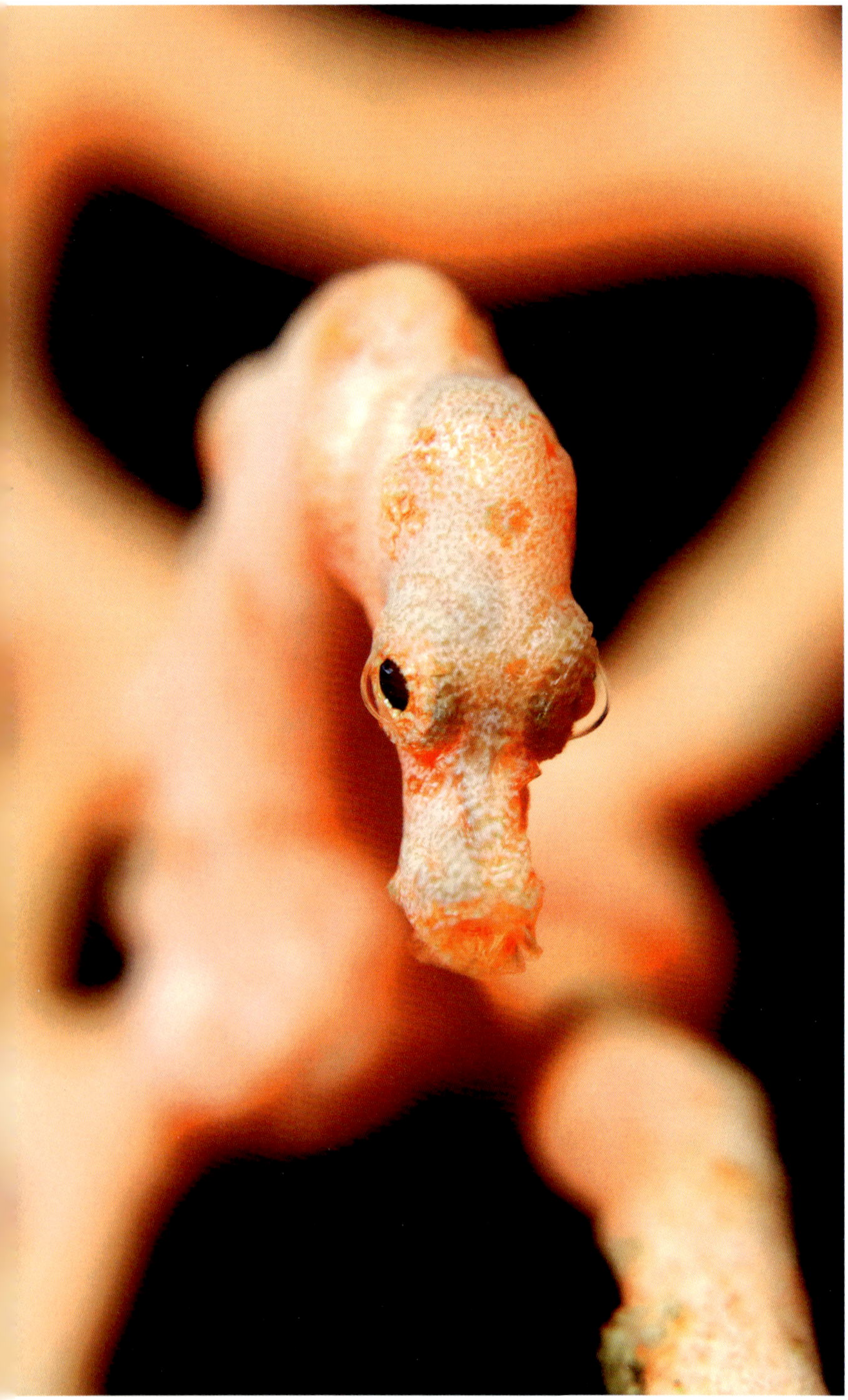

The wider the aperture, the narrower the depth of field

Canon EOS 5D Mark II • Canon 100mm macro lens • 1/40 s • f/10 • ISO 400

body will be sharp. If your camera is pointed toward it head-on, however, only a small portion of the picture will be in focus. Macro photographers have to be very conscious of how changes in perspective result in changes to the depth of field. The size of the area that appears sharp within an image depends on the aperture and the scale of the subject. Make the depth of field more shallow by choosing a wider aperture, such as f/16 or f/11; make it deeper by choosing a smaller one, such as f/32. As long as the scale of the reproduction stays constant, the sharpness won't change.

One situation that requires extra care is when you use a tiny aperture of f/22 or smaller with a subject that is extremely close to the lens—in other words, at the maximum possible reproduction ratio. In these circumstances your image can suffer from *diffraction blur*, which is a softening of the image that is apparent when rays of light bend around the edges of the tiny aperture. You can mitigate diffraction blur by opening the aperture slightly when you shoot at the maximum reproduction ratio. This will sacrifice some of your depth of field, but it's necessary to maximize image quality. Using a high-quality lens is another way to minimize this troublesome phenomenon.

SUMMARY:

- Sharpness is an integral part of image composition.
- When animals are the subject of a photo, their eyes should always be sharp.
- Perspective influences what appears sharp in your photos; objects that are perpendicular to your camera's optical axis are easiest to keep entirely in focus.
- Depth of field is influenced by aperture. The largest aperture opening produces the shallowest depth of field; the smallest aperture opening results in the largest depth of field.
- Shooting extremely close subjects with a miniscule aperture, such as f/32, can result in diffraction blur. Open the aperture a bit to fix it.

5.5 Flash Position

Deciding where and how to position your light sources is easier for macro photography than wide-angle photography because you're working with a significantly smaller area.

There are two points to consider when you decide how many flash units you'll need:

- First, think about if you want shadows to appear in your image. If you use a flash unit on each side of your camera, there will generally be no shadows. A single flash—positioned slightly above your camera housing, for example—will produce a hard shadow.
- Second, consider the overall power of your lighting setup. You can get by with only one flash unit if it has a guide number of at least 12 and if your camera performs well at higher ISO settings. But you'll need a second flash unit, or a more powerful one, if your first one has a guide number of less than about 12 or if your camera produces image noise at higher ISO settings.

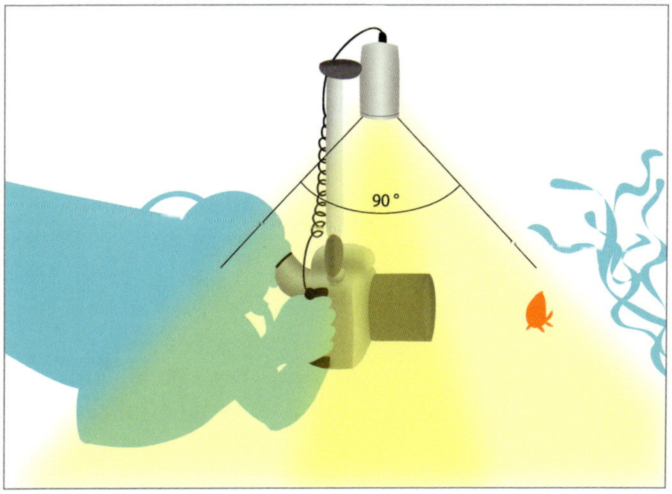

You can prevent unattractive backdrops from compromising your macro photos by positioning your flash unit directly above your camera, which will visually isolate the subject

The placement of your flash units depends on the subject. Position them based on how you want shadows to look in your picture. There is no right or wrong way; it just depends on the final effect and whether you like it or not. A good default position for your flash units is one on each side and slightly above your camera so they cast light at a slight downward angle.

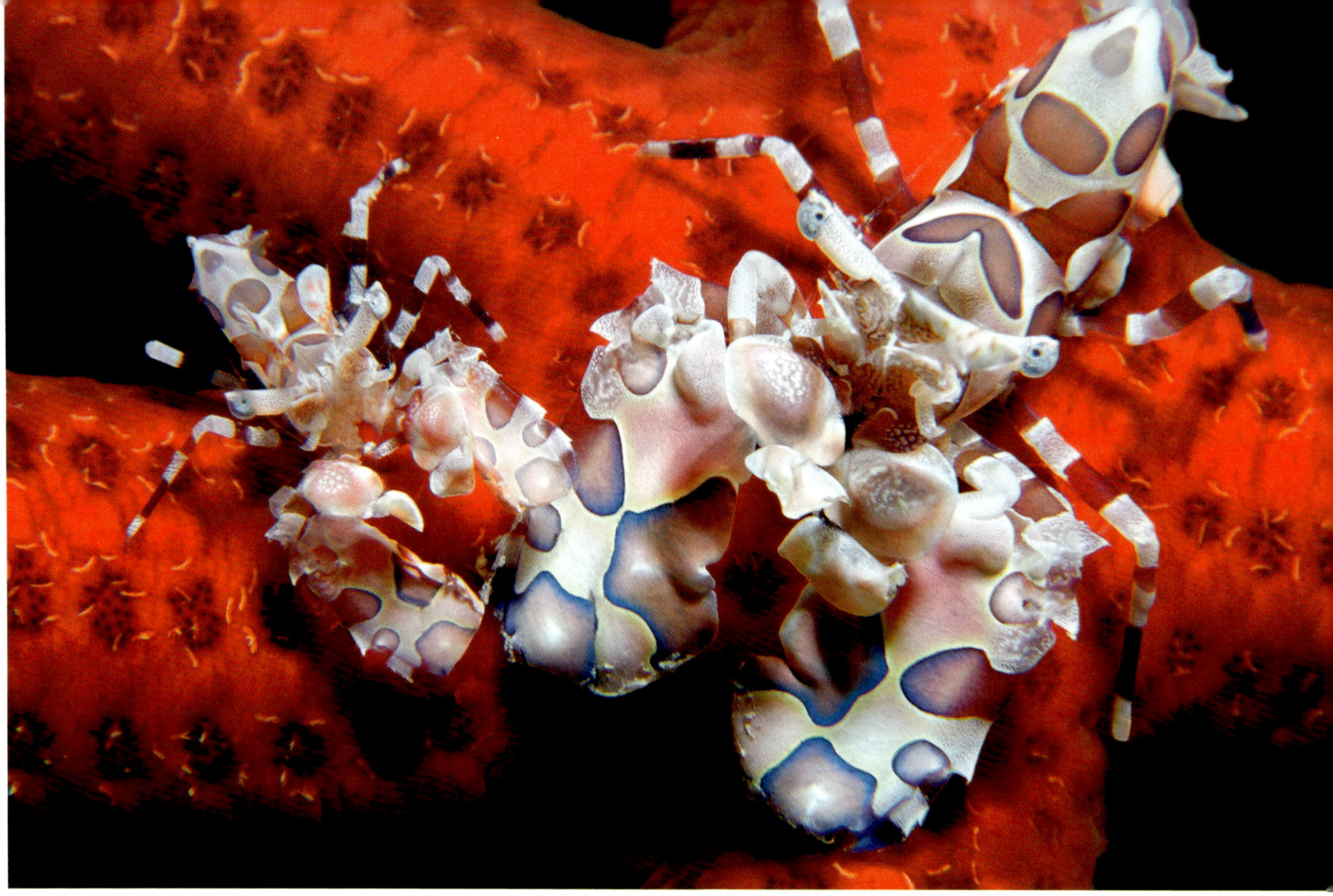

Don't snap your photos at the earliest convenience. Waiting until an animal changes its position to suit your composition can dramatically improve the quality of your photos.

Canon EOS 5D Mark II • Canon 100mm macro lens • 1/125 s • f/32 • ISO 400

The closer your subject is to your camera, the closer in your flash units should be. Conversely, for subjects that are farther away, move the flash units away from your camera to avoid capturing too much floating debris in the image.

When you're forced to shoot a subject against an unattractive background, position your flash units directly above—and even slightly behind—the subject instead of casting light forward. This will allow only the outside edge of the light cone to strike your subject, and the background will be left in dark obscurity. Finding the ideal angle may take a few practice shots (see the illustration on the previous page).

SUMMARY:

- Positioning your flash units is much less critical with macro photography.
- Use two flash units to eliminate most shadows.
- Make sure your flash units have enough power for macro photography.
- The ideal position for your flash units depends on the subject.
- As a default setup, position your flash units just above your camera.
- Casting light from above and slightly behind your subject can eliminate unsightly backgrounds.

5.6 Background

As with wide-angle photography, the background of a macro photo distinguishes good photos from great ones. Images with uniform or monochrome backgrounds have a calm feeling and encourage viewers to focus their attention on the main subject.

These images of a blue-ringed octopus illustrate this point. This animal is roughly 2 to 4 inches in size and it blends in with its surroundings extremely well—it barely stands out against a reef. This natural camouflage protects the small but highly poisonous animal from predators. Because the octopus is extremely rare, the first impulse is to snap a quick photo, regardless of what was behind it. This response is perfectly reasonable because you're sure to get the shot. But why stop there? Now is the perfect time to get serious. Think about what perspective would result in an ideal background. A low camera position could portray the animal in front of an attractive piece of reef, or it might isolate it against a background of water. Give this a try and you may get a much better photo that shows key details, like the octopus's arms, more clearly. It would be ideal to capture the animal swimming freely in the water where you would have a completely uniform background. But you should never remove an animal from a reef or try to make it swim in open water. Fortunately, most photographers follow this code of honor.

You can also create a uniform background by shooting with a wider aperture, such as f/11 or f/8, to intentionally reduce the depth of field. This will cause the background to fade into a blur and make the main subject even more prominent. If

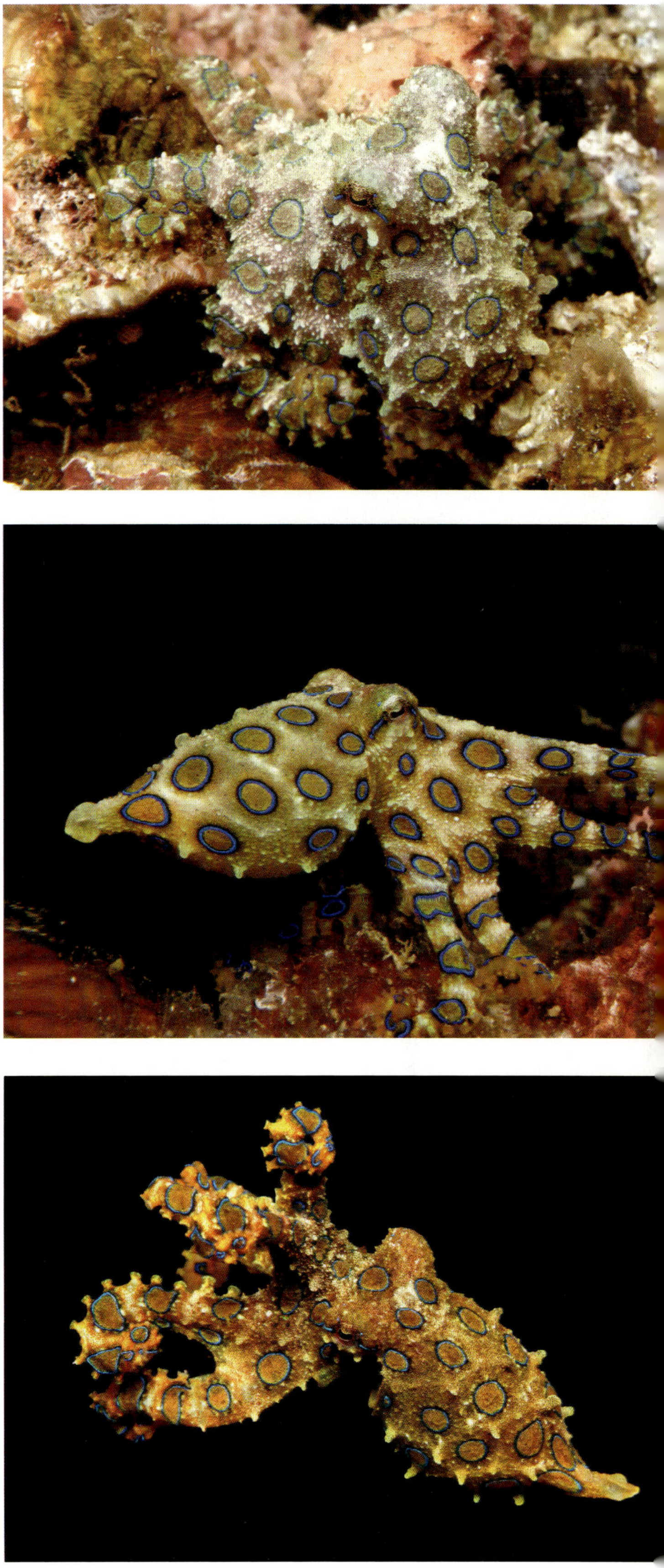

The little octopus is perfectly camouflaged on the reef and does not stand out at all (top). A lower perspective allowed for partial isolation of the animal against a less cluttered background (middle). Complete isolation, however, is ideal (bottom). Never force animals to move!

Canon EOS 5D Mark II • Canon 100mm macro lens • 1/100 s • f/16 • ISO 200

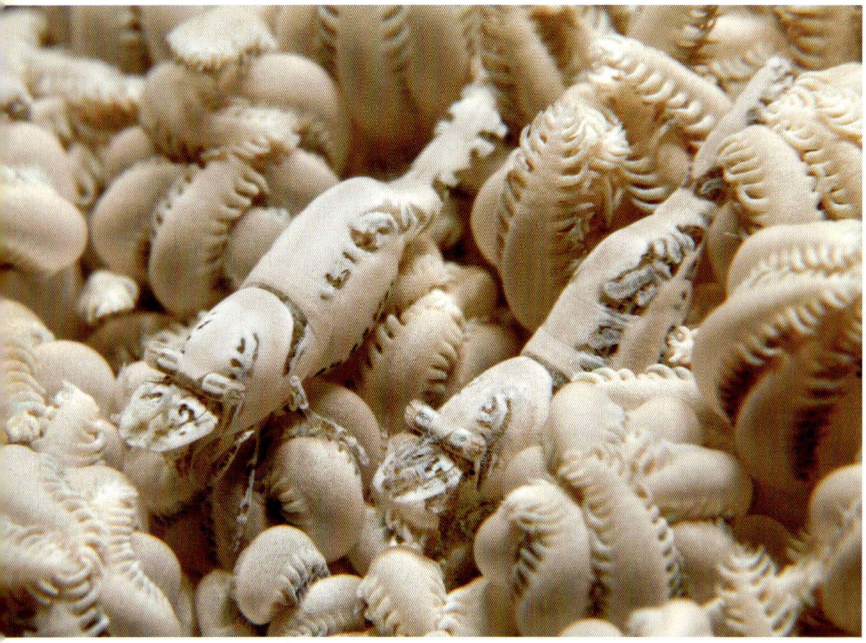

Photographing sea creatures against a similarly colored background illustrates how perfect camouflage can be

Canon EOS 5D Mark II • Canon 100mm macro lens • 1/100 s • f/16 • ISO 200

you use this approach, still search for the best perspective to eliminate any potentially distracting background elements. The farther away the background elements are, the more uniform the backdrop will appear.

Blurred areas of a photo are sometimes referred to as *bokeh*—a Japanese term that describes the aesthetic quality of blurry areas in the background. Setting your main subject in the golden ratio with attractive bokeh is an effective compositional technique. The blur fills up most of the image area and causes your viewers to pay attention to the main subject.

The bokeh doesn't have to be completely uniform; some successful photos have a pleasing, blurry background with recognizable secondary elements, such as a fish. Refracted rays of sunlight can be especially beautiful when they're captured like this. Allow your creativity free rein and experiment to get attractive results.

SUMMARY:

- The background plays a key role in the overall success of a photo.
- Subjects stand out better when they are isolated against the background.
- You can create a uniform background by artfully blurring parts of the image area.
- A blurry background is also referred to as bokeh.
- Bokeh can dramatically improve the attractiveness of an image when blur is used thoughtfully.

5.7 Focusing

When it comes to macro photography, correctly establishing the focus point is of the utmost importance. The tiniest error with image sharpness can dramatically impact even the most interesting composition. It's less than ideal to rely on automatic focus point detection. Instead, define a single focus point that will allow you to precisely control the sharpness in the image.

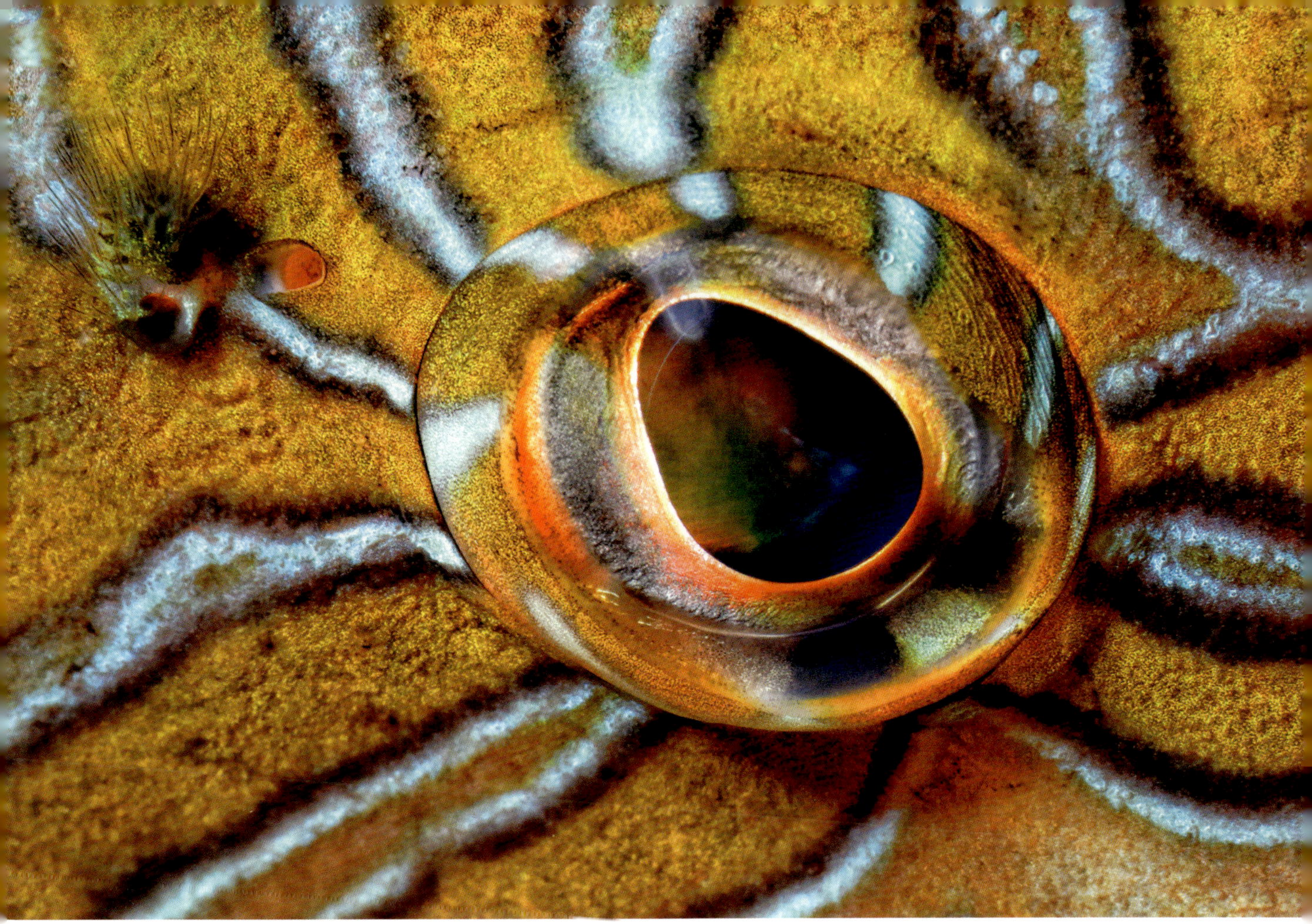

Photographers often use the central focus point. This is by no means a bad approach, especially when the subject is located in the center of the image area. But don't allow this tendency to become a habit that results in image after image with the subject in the center. Use other focus points to bring some compositional variety into your photos.

Many camera housings allow you to manually focus, which can produce highly accurate results but takes more time than using autofocus. If the subject is likely to move while you're working, or if you plan to shoot a variety of subjects, autofocus is often the way to go.

Autofocus allows you to press the shutter button halfway to lock in the focus, and then you can wait for the right moment to expose the image. This technique is particularly effective when you're shooting a clown fish because they move quickly and it's hard to focus fast enough to keep up with them. Focus on an attractive section of an anemone and then release the shutter when the clown fish moves into your image area.

You can also set the focus to a specific distance and then adjust how far your camera is from the subject. This technique is not practical for fish that move quickly, but it's great for slow or stationary subjects. It works well for

Attentive photographers home in on an animal's unique features. This photo highlights the interesting lines around the eye of a hawkfish.

Canon EOS 5D Mark II • Canon 100mm macro lens • 1/125 s • f/16 • ISO 400

super-macro photos because it's difficult to focus on those super small subjects.

After you take a macro picture, inspect it on your camera's LCD screen—ideally at an enlarged view—to see if it's sharp. Nothing is worse than having an otherwise amazing picture ruined by a lack of sharpness in a key area. Checking it during the dive means you will be able to repeat the shot, as long as the subject is still there.

SUMMARY:

- Choose a single focus point when you shoot macro photos.
- Mix up the position of your focus point for compositional variety.
- Manually focusing gives you more control, but it takes more time.
- Autofocus allows you to focus in advance and wait for the right moment to release the shutter.
- It's effective to set a fixed focal distance in advance when you shoot calm or stationary subjects.

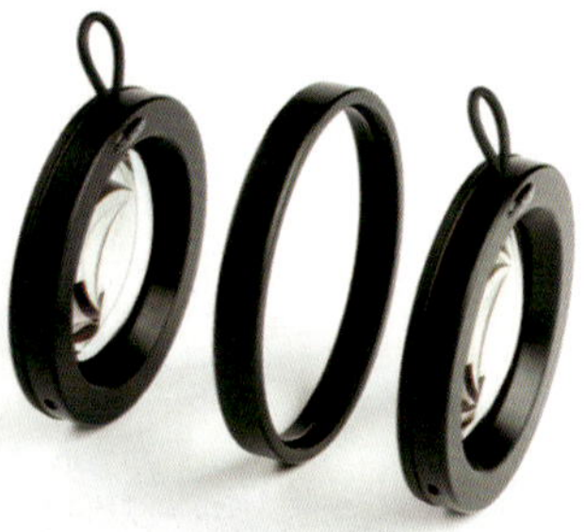

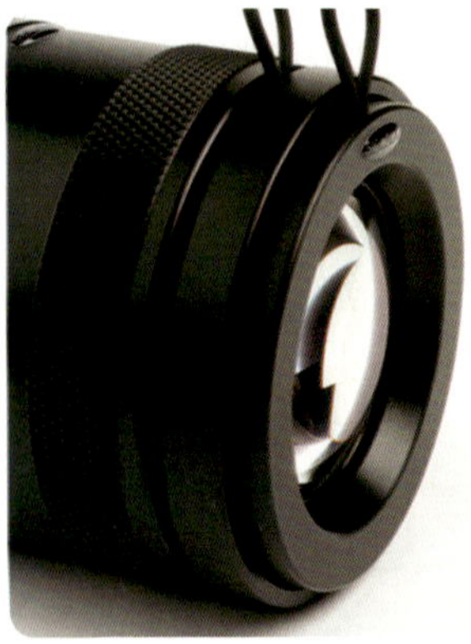

Closeup lenses (top) and shown attached to a macro port (bottom) (Photo courtesy of SEACAM)

5.8 Super Macro

Super macro photography is an advanced technique. Reproduction ratios of 2:1 and 3:1 are common because the subjects are so small. You need additional equipment to fill up the image area with these tiny wonders of the sea.

There are three main ways to capture super macro images. The first requires an extension tube, which simply increases the distance between the lens and the camera and reduces the minimum focus distance of the lens. You can't use autofocus with an extension tube, and you'll lose a full stop of light. If f/22 would produce a properly exposed image without an extension tube, you'll need to use f/16 with an extension tube. Of course, this adjustment also reduces the depth of field.

The second option for super macro photography is to use a teleconverter. This is an attachment that essentially increases the focal length of a lens and concentrates the light that enters the lens. You can still use the autofocus with a teleconverter, but the loss of light is significant. A 1.4x teleconverter results in a loss of one stop, a 2x teleconverter loses two stops, and a 3x teleconverter loses three stops.

The most commonly used tool for taking super macro pictures under water is a closeup lens, which works like a magnifying glass when you attach it to the plan port. A closeup lens gives you the most flexibility because you can attach it and remove it during your dive, and it loses only a small amount of light. The downside is it generates diffraction blur due to the minimal camera-to-subject distance. Because a closeup lens adds optics to the light path, it also degrades the image somewhat.

Getting the focus right for a super macro picture is especially difficult, but it helps to prepare. Manually set the focus to the minimum focus distance before you take a picture so you won't have to rely on autofocus. Instead, you can adjust the sharpness by slightly moving your camera.

Your diving buoyancy needs to be absolutely perfect when you shoot a super macro picture to avoid accidents that damage the underwater environment.

A large aperture and a slow shutter speed allow you to use natural light to create a harmonious blue background

Canon EOS 5D Mark II • Canon 100mm macro lens • 1/160 s • f/16 • ISO 400

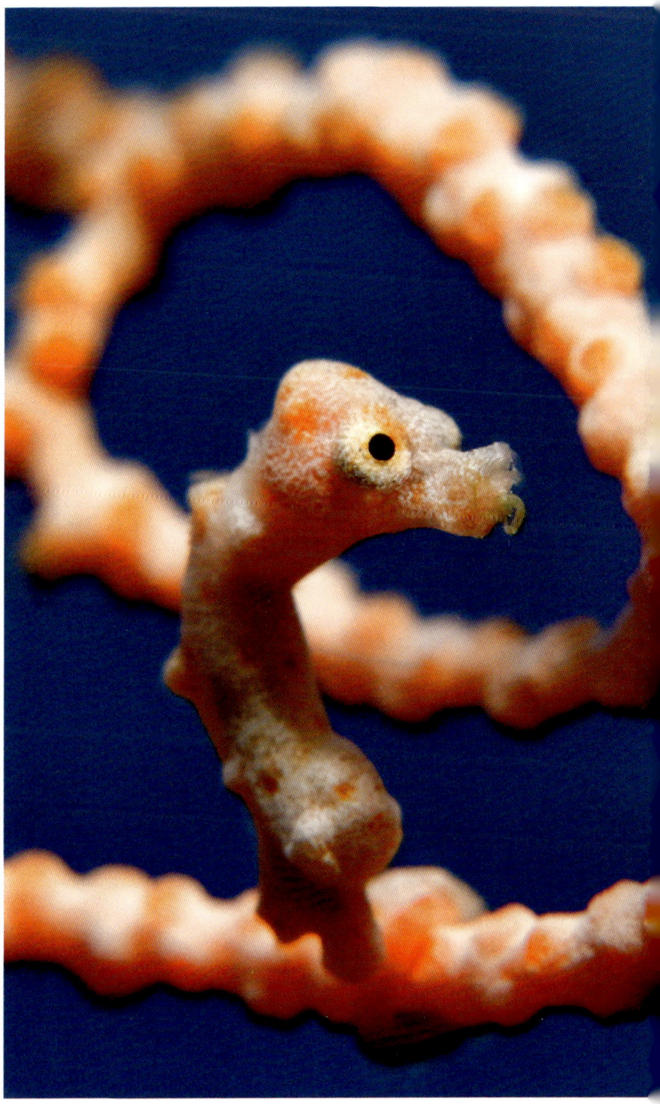

SUMMARY:

- Super macro photography involves large reproduction ratios.
- Extension tubes reduce the minimum focus distance, but you have to focus manually.
- Teleconverters increase the scale of your subjects, but they result in a loss of light.
- Closeup lenses work like a magnifying glass and have more advantages than disadvantages.
- It's easiest to work with a fixed focus distance when you shoot super macro images.

5.9 Subjects

The ideal subjects for macro photography are between 0.5 in and 5 in. If a subject is smaller, it's difficult to take a good picture. Larger objects require you to increase your distance from them, which results in a hazy or bluish appearance. You might, however, decide to zero in on a specific part of a larger subject, such as a carefully composed portrait of a grouper's head.

Having a good partner is indispensable to help you look for quality macro subjects. This could be your trusted diving partner of many years or a diving guide who knows the ins and outs of a particular dive spot. You will likely need the latter when it comes to searching for miniscule creatures that otherwise would be impossible to spot, even with a practiced eye. If your diving guide heads off to search for a pygmy sea horse in a huge gorgonian, it's best to find a nearby clown fish and continue taking pictures

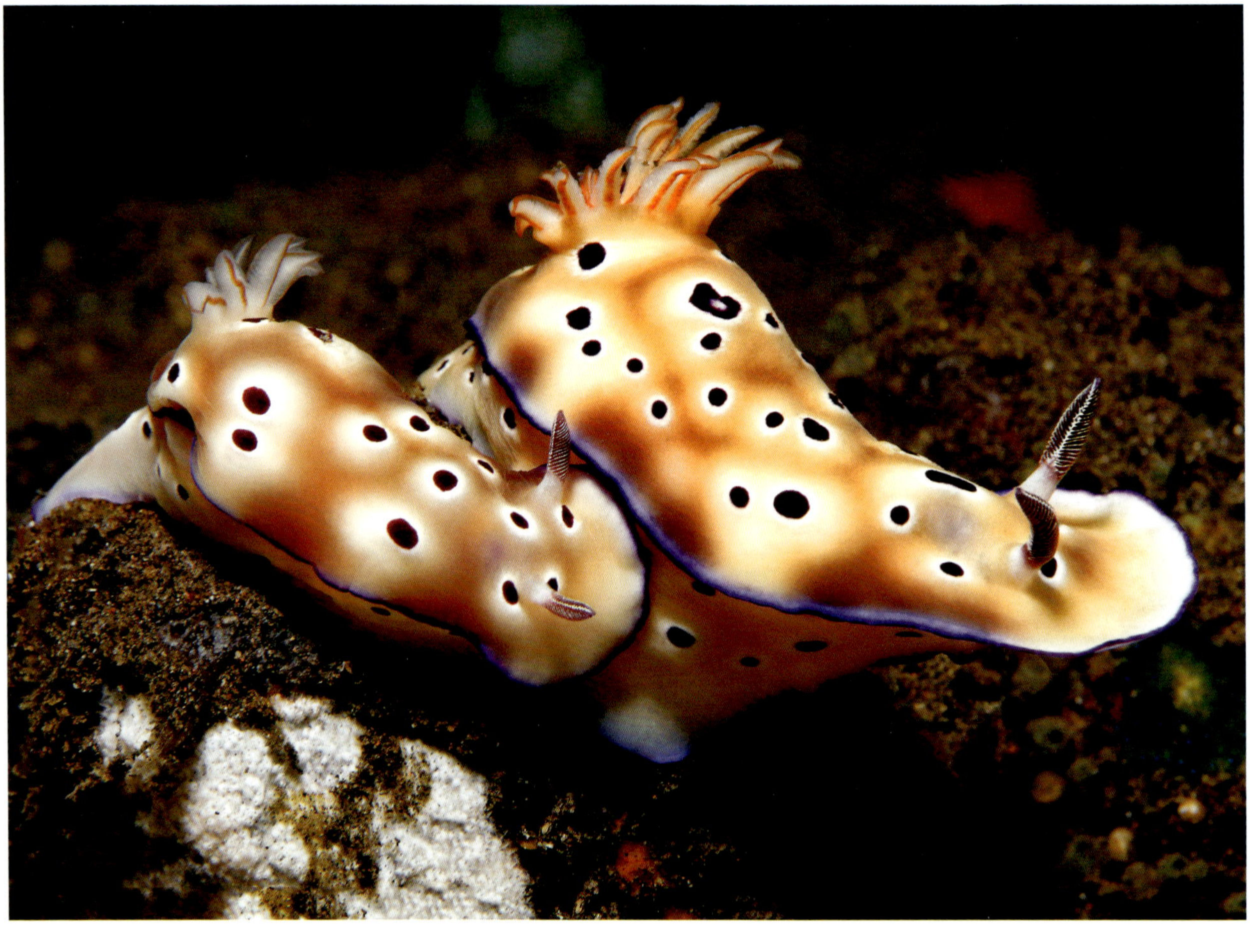

Nudibranchs are favorite subjects for macro images, and they are easy to photograph because they move slowly

Canon EOS 5D Mark II • Canon 100mm macro lens • 1/125 s • f/20 • ISO 200

rather than help with the search effort. Looking for a perfectly camouflaged creature is simply too difficult, and you'll risk wasting too much time.

As soon as a desirable target is located, make sure you can position yourself in a stable and secure manner for your shot. In an ideal situation, you would kneel on a patch of sand along the ocean floor and use both hands to operate your camera. That's not always possible, so you can use a muck stick to stabilize yourself. Rest the stick against a rock that juts out from the reef, but don't disturb coral or animal communities. If this is not an option and you have to shoot while freely suspended in the water, you need to be especially mindful of your buoyancy. It's better to abandon a photo if you're too unstable or if surges in the water make the situation too dicey. Don't risk striking a piece of coral with a fin, which is something that can happen to the most experienced divers. A mistake like this is too consequential and can usually be avoided when you are cautious.

SUMMARY:

- Look for subjects between 0.5 in and 5 in for your macro photos.
- A local diving guide is indispensable for finding rare, camouflaged sea life.
- Kneeling on a sandy stretch of ocean floor near the subject is the best way to position yourself.
- In tricky situations, use a muck stick to stabilize yourself against a rock—never against a piece of coral.
- It's difficult to take macro photos when you're floating freely.

5.10 Light-Shaping Tools

Light-shaping tools are nothing new—photographers have been using them for a long time to shape light in specific ways. Underwater photographers use a light-shaping tool known as a *snoot*. In simple terms, a snoot is an attachment that narrows the angle of light emitted from a flash unit so a clearly defined portion of the image area will be illuminated and the remainder will remain dark.

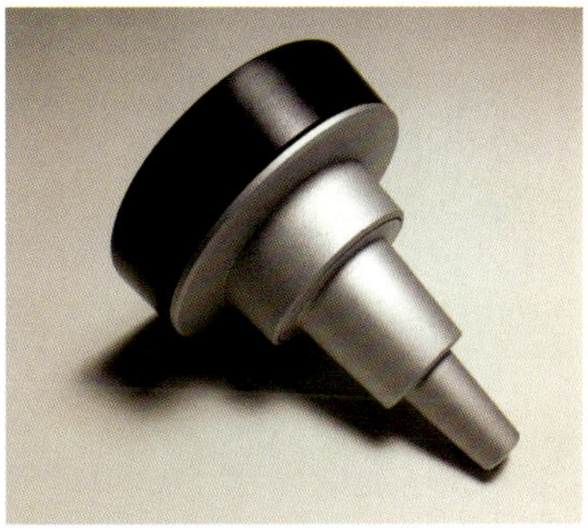

A SEACAM snoot designed for an underwater flash unit (Photo courtesy of SEACAM)

A snoot is commonly used to emphasize the main subject by eliminating unattractive elements or objects from the background. In other words, it can highlight a portion of your image. If you're taking a picture of a nudibranch on black sand, for example, a snoot lets you pare down your photo to the key elements and the rest of the background will fall into darkness. The effective use of a snoot often makes the difference between a mediocre photo and a good one.

The length of a snoot and the diameter of its opening determine how much of the image area will receive light. The longer and narrower the snoot, the smaller the area to be illuminated, and the closer you are to the subject, the more intense the light will be. To create the effect of a spotlight, the light source needs to be very close to the subject. That's easier said than done—the snoot needs to be pointed very precisely because the light is often only an inch or less wide. One way to deal with this problem is to have your diving partner hold the flash unit (disassembled from the housing) and direct it toward the subject. You can then alter the camera position without readjusting the flash.

Another thing that makes using a snoot so tricky is that it needs to be positioned so close to the subject. It's all too easy to get close to an animal and make it flee for safety. Approach sea life slowly and calmly to keep from scaring it away.

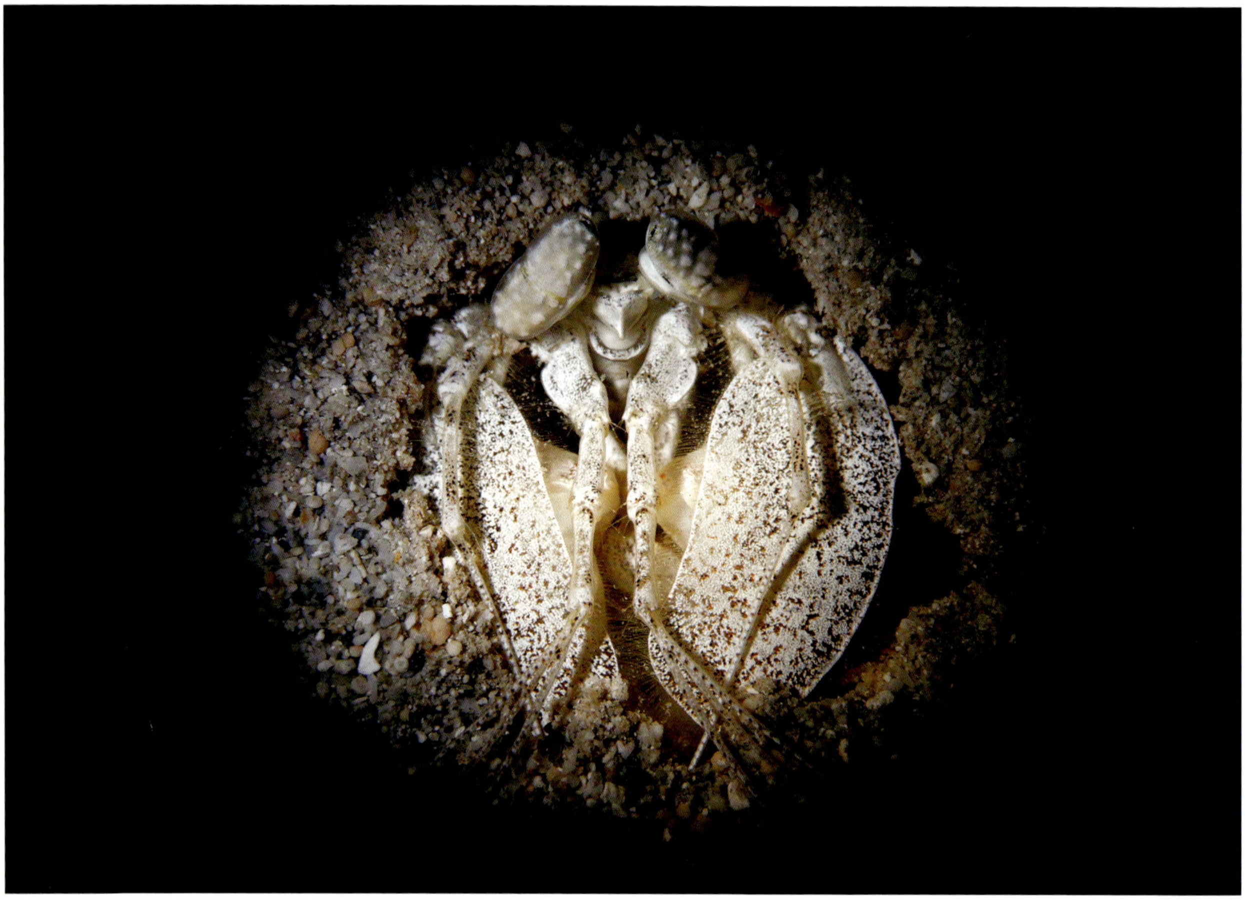

A snoot allows you to control which part of an image receives light, which directs the viewer's eye to a key element in the image

Canon EOS 5D Mark II • Canon 100mm macro lens • 1/125 s • f/10 • ISO 1600

As an alternative, you can set up a flash unit on a tripod, then you can direct the light toward the subject and not worry about it anymore—provided the subject isn't going anywhere.

Light-shaping tools also work great when you shoot with a wide-angle lens. You can draw attention to a subject, such as a piece of coral in a cave. By bathing only the coral in light, all the potentially distracting background elements go unnoticed.

Although this lighting technique is powerful and useful, don't overuse it. If all of your photos are created with a snoot, the effect will lose its impact. You'll know that you've taken a successful picture when viewers can't tell you used a snoot.

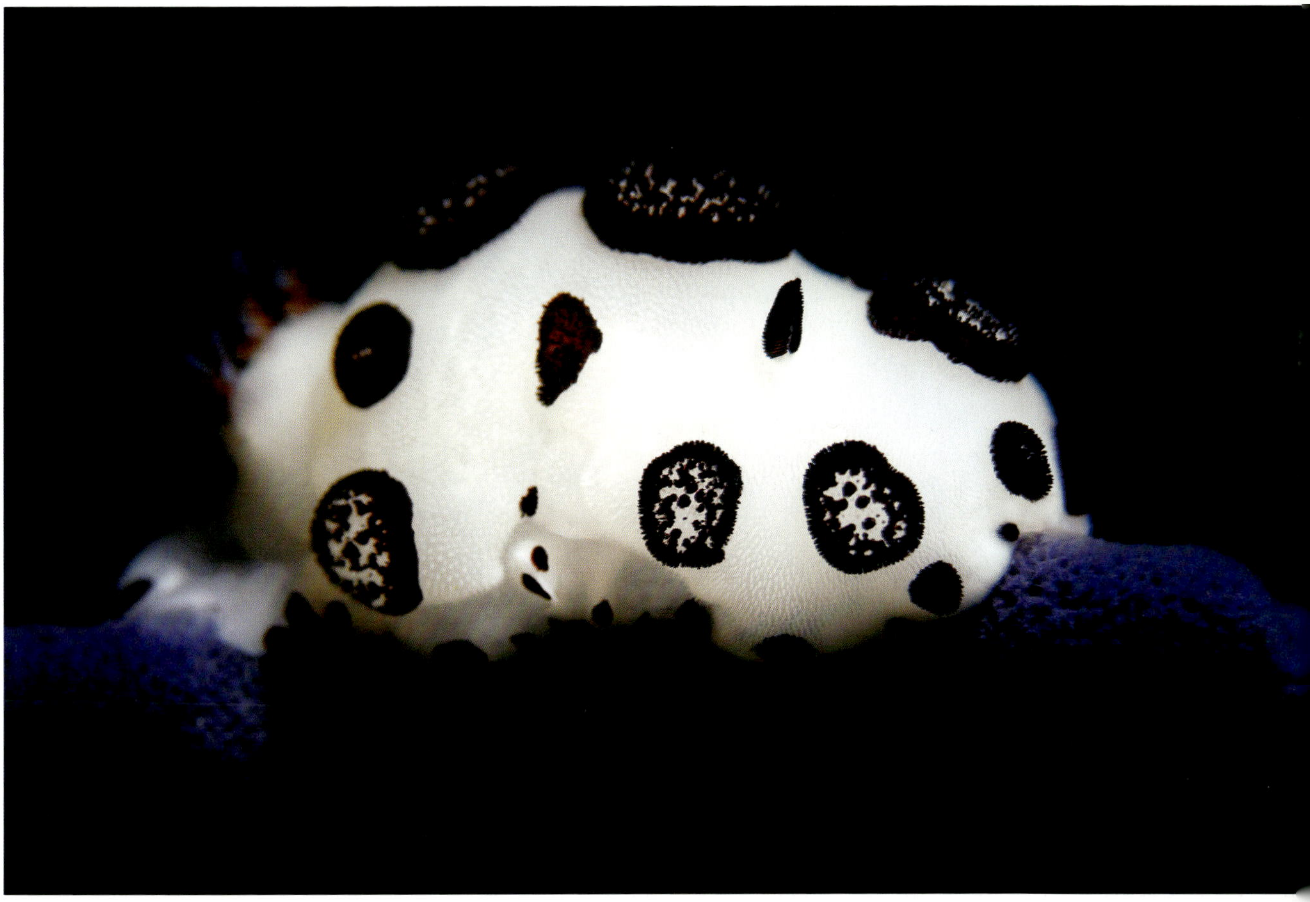

SUMMARY:

- A snoot is a light-shaping tool that is common in underwater photography.
- You can attach a snoot to your flash unit to control the width of the light beam and to highlight certain elements in the image area.
- To make it easier to use a light-shaping tool, take your flash unit off your camera and mount it on a tripod or have your diving partner hold it.
- Snoots are also useful for wide-angle photos because they allow you to emphasize a specific element.
- The best photos that were taken with a light-shaping tool don't hint at its presence.

Images that do not reveal the use of a snoot tend to be more appealing than those in which it's obvious

Canon EOS 5D Mark II • Canon 100mm macro lens • 1/125 s • f/4 • ISO 1600

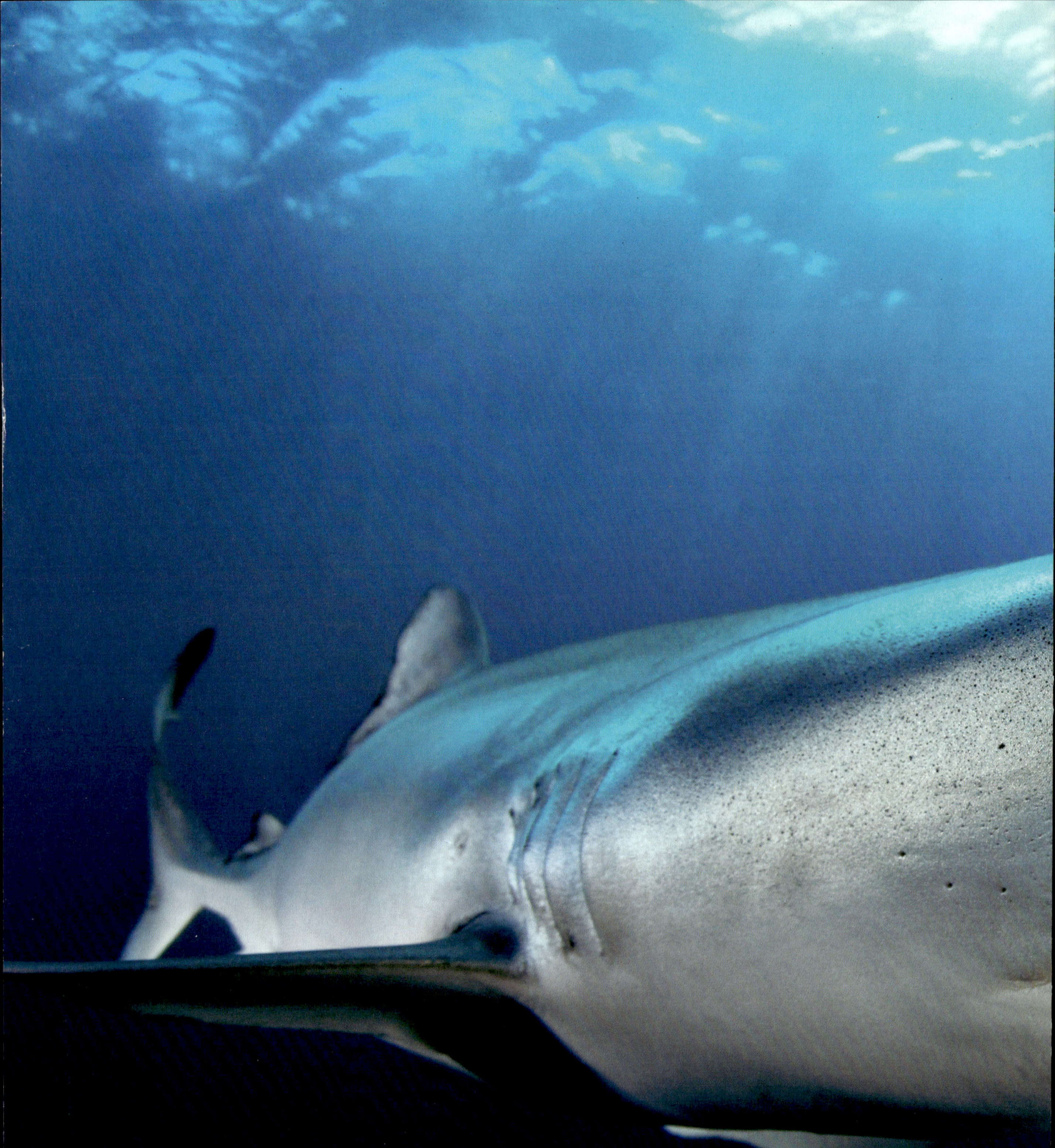

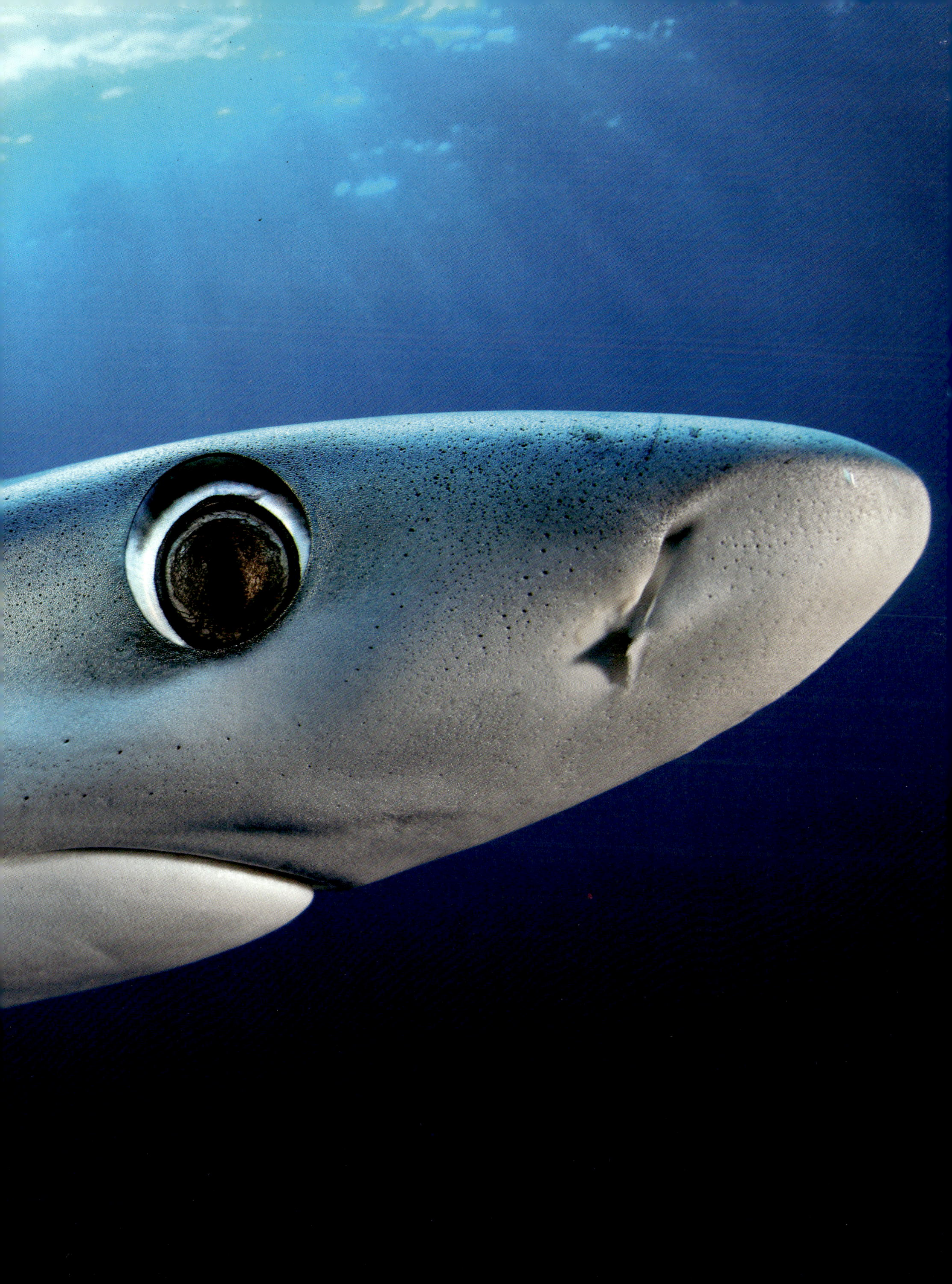

Case Study 7: Proximity Trigger

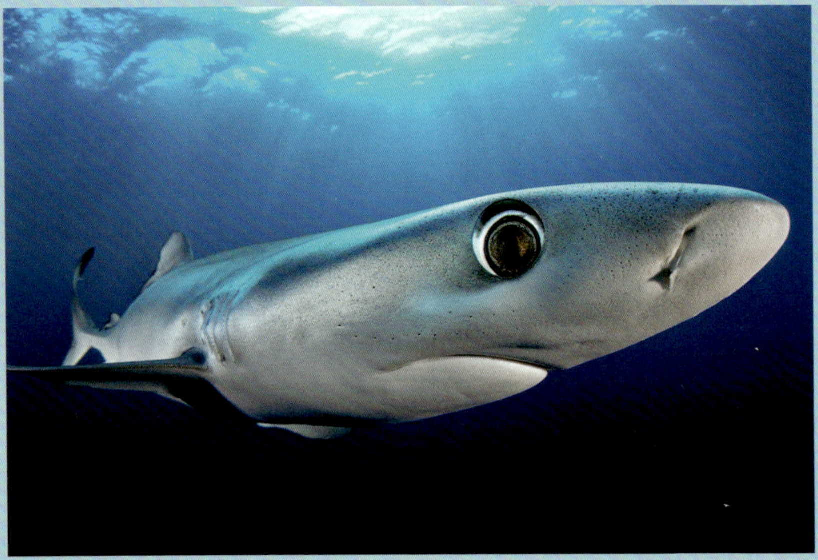

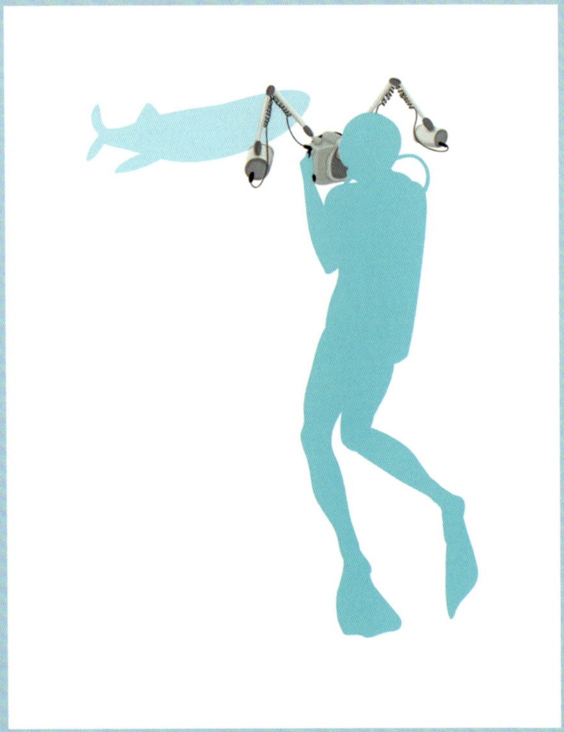

Canon EOS 5D Mark II • Canon 8–15mm fisheye lens • two Ikelite DS125 strobes • 1/125 s • f/10 • ISO 400 • manual flash at half power

Taking a good picture of a shark is not easy—unless you lure it with food. Offering a snack is a tried-and-true way to get close to these beautiful animals. Keep in mind that luring them with food is controversial because some believe that is interfering with nature.

I took this picture about 30 miles south of the Cape of Good Hope in South Africa. The warm Agulhas Current from the Indian Ocean flows through these waters, and blue sharks typically hang out at depths of more than 650 ft. They come to the surface only in search of food. Local dive operators know this and use bait to lure the animals up to shallower depths.

The beautiful predators are highly curious and approach divers to see what sort of strange creatures have come to visit them in their own element. Such conditions are optimal for taking closeup photos, where you can see the details in their skin.

I wanted to get as close as possible to the shark and to include an attractive background, including the sun's bright rays. I directed my camera toward the sun and waited for curious sharks. I had my two flash units about 20 inches out on either side of my camera and pointed slightly inward to make sure the shark's head got enough light. If the flash units had been pointed outward any more, they would have produced a shadow and obscured part of the shark's body. I used a fisheye lens because it allowed me to focus at a very small distance and guaranteed that I'd have a large angle of view. All that was left was to wait for a shark to find us and to take the picture at the right moment.

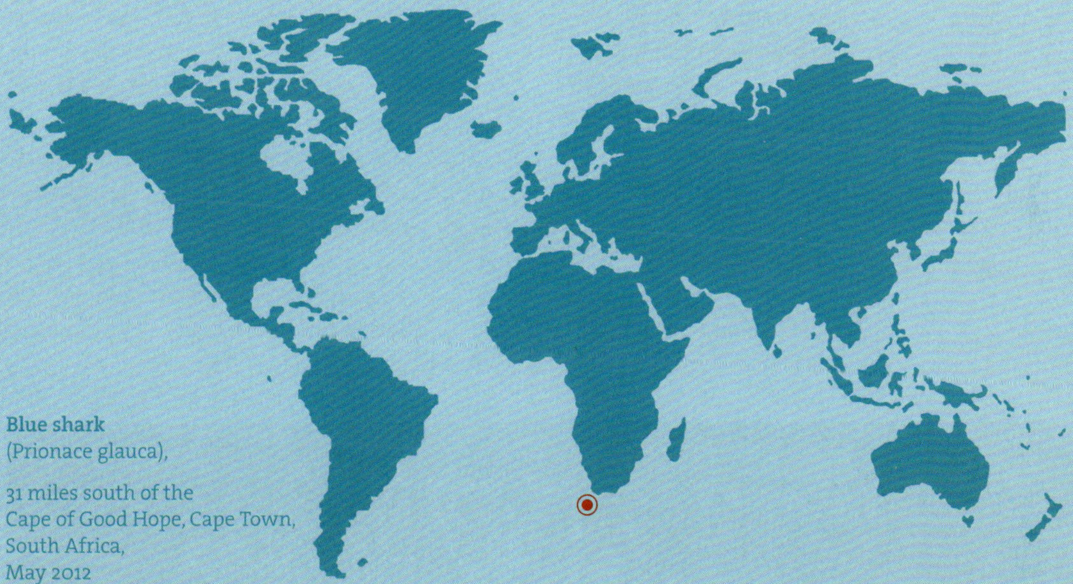

Blue shark
(Prionace glauca),

31 miles south of the
Cape of Good Hope, Cape Town,
South Africa,
May 2012

6

Image Editing

Image editing plays a huge role in the way most pictures turn out. In fashion photography image editing is an indispensable part of the process for creating top-flight photos. Image edits can be drastic, and the practice is hotly debated because the final result can be considered a distortion of the original image; many people consider such alterations to be a form of manipulating reality.

Drastic image editing has not been a problem in the world of underwater photography. Its foremost concern is capturing documentary images, so it should be as free of excessive alterations as possible. But where does optimizing end and manipulating begin? Is the removal of floating particles a form of manipulation? Is it acceptable to eliminate a stray fin that accidentally ended up in a photo? In general, as long as the overall content or message of a photo remains unchanged and no elements have been artificially added, it's fair to say the image has been optimized rather than manipulated.

Color corrections, contrast adjustments, and the elimination of floating particles are common editing steps for most underwater photographers. It's more questionable when an edit involves removing a diver who's in a less than optimal position in the background of an image. Is it acceptable to retouch the image to eliminate the diver and improve the photo? There are many strong opinions about such a practice; there will never be a universally accepted standard about what is right and what is wrong.

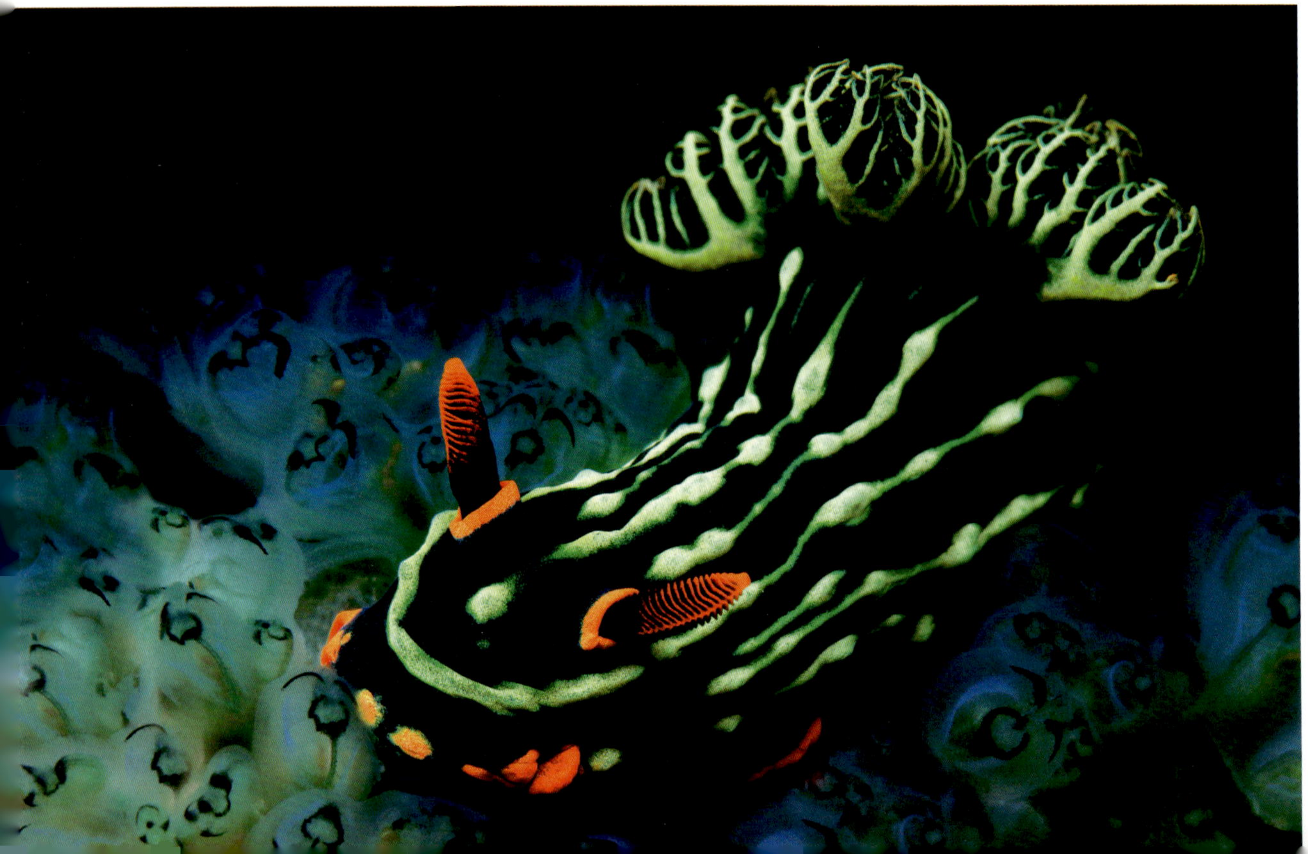

The play of colors at the bottom of the sea can be enhanced through image editing, but don't make them look artificial

Canon EOS 5D Mark II • Canon 100mm macro lens • 1/100 s • f/29 • ISO 100

Doubling an element in an image or combining multiple images into a montage and presenting it as a single photo, however, are absolutely out of the question. When you change a photo to this extent, you must reveal your methods and make it clear that the image is a montage. It's always better to plan and execute the photo the way you want it to appear instead of assuming you'll fix it later while post-processing.

When you take pictures under water, it can be exceedingly difficult to capture the ultimate image because so many factors influence what you can accomplish. You can see the full image area when you compose a picture only if you use a high-quality angle viewfinder. This limitation means you will probably need to crop your image during the editing stage. You can even convert a landscape-oriented photo to a portrait format. If edits like this improve the final result, then it's a legitimate approach, but you should still try to capture your photos in the desired orientation while you're shooting.

Edit your photos only to the extent required to get a pleasing result; one that you can share with a clear conscience. Does the picture reveal the scene as you saw it through your diving mask and viewfinder? Maybe you didn't see the errant fin in the background because the majestic manta ray commanded so much of your attention. Removing the fin in post-processing might be justified in this situation.

6.1 Workflow

Everyone who shoots with a digital camera has a preferred workflow. The process encompasses various tasks that start with downloading your images from your memory card and conclude with archiving your final files.

The purpose of developing a refined and thoughtful workflow is to ensure that you process all your images in a similar way. It allows you to process many images with the same corrections before you make detailed edits of each individual exposure. Even the shortest step—downloading your images to a computer—is the beginning of your workflow.

The more time you invest in processing images, the more involved your workflow will become. If you start out using basic software that can handle most processing steps, you might work in stages and use a RAW converter before you turn to more complex image editing software. The more often you execute your workflow, the more routine it will become.

A brief workflow makes sense for photographers who are not interested in a lengthy post-processing routine. Software like Apple Aperture or Adobe Lightroom might fill their needs.

If maximum quality is your primary concern, then using a RAW converter along with Adobe Photoshop is a good way to go. But this process will require significantly more time.

The steps of a typical workflow:

1. Download the images from your memory card to your computer, ideally with an image-editing program. It's enormously helpful if the software can rename your files during the transfer. Include your name, the date and time, the location, and the image number. When the download is done, save a copy of your images to an external hard drive, a server, or to the *cloud*.
2. Identify the best pictures from the entire collection. Don't select more than 30 to 50 photos per trip for your portfolio. The fewer pictures you choose, the higher quality your portfolio will be.
3. If you are using a RAW converter, import your selected photos then adjust the white balance, contrast, saturation, noise reduction, and other variables (see section 6.3).
4. Edit each image individually in a dedicated image-editing program (see section 6.4). This is when you will make specific corrections to individual pictures, such as eliminating floating particles.
5. Save your final files in a separate folder at maximum quality. You can also reduce the size of your images for online and e-mail use at this time and save multiple copies of each image at your desired sizes.
6. The last step should always be to back up your edited files (see section 6.5).

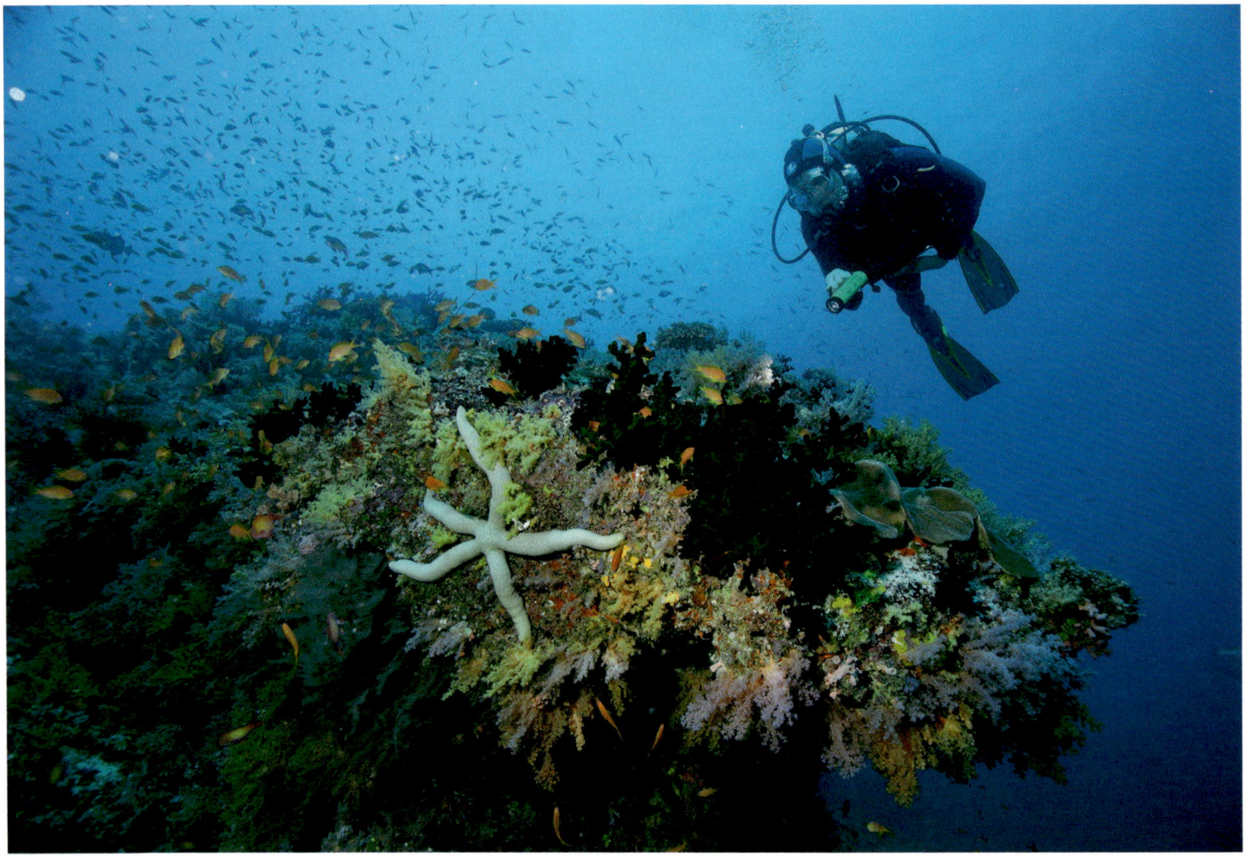

Take time to consider your personal workflow and alter these steps to suit your needs and preferences.

You should always back up your photos two or three times while you're traveling; it's a good idea to do this at least once a day. The originals can be on your laptop, and the copies can be stored on an external hard drive. Other backup options include burning your files to a DVD at the end of your trip or writing them to a separate memory card that won't be used for storing new pictures. Keep your backups in different pieces of luggage in case one of your bags gets lost.

SUMMARY:

- The word *workflow* refers to the various steps involved in editing a picture.
- Detailed image editing can be carried out in Aperture, Lightroom, or Photoshop.
- Renaming your files is a key step when you download your photos.
- While you're on the road, take time every day to create copies of your files.
- Save your backups in different pieces of luggage in case one of your bags gets lost.

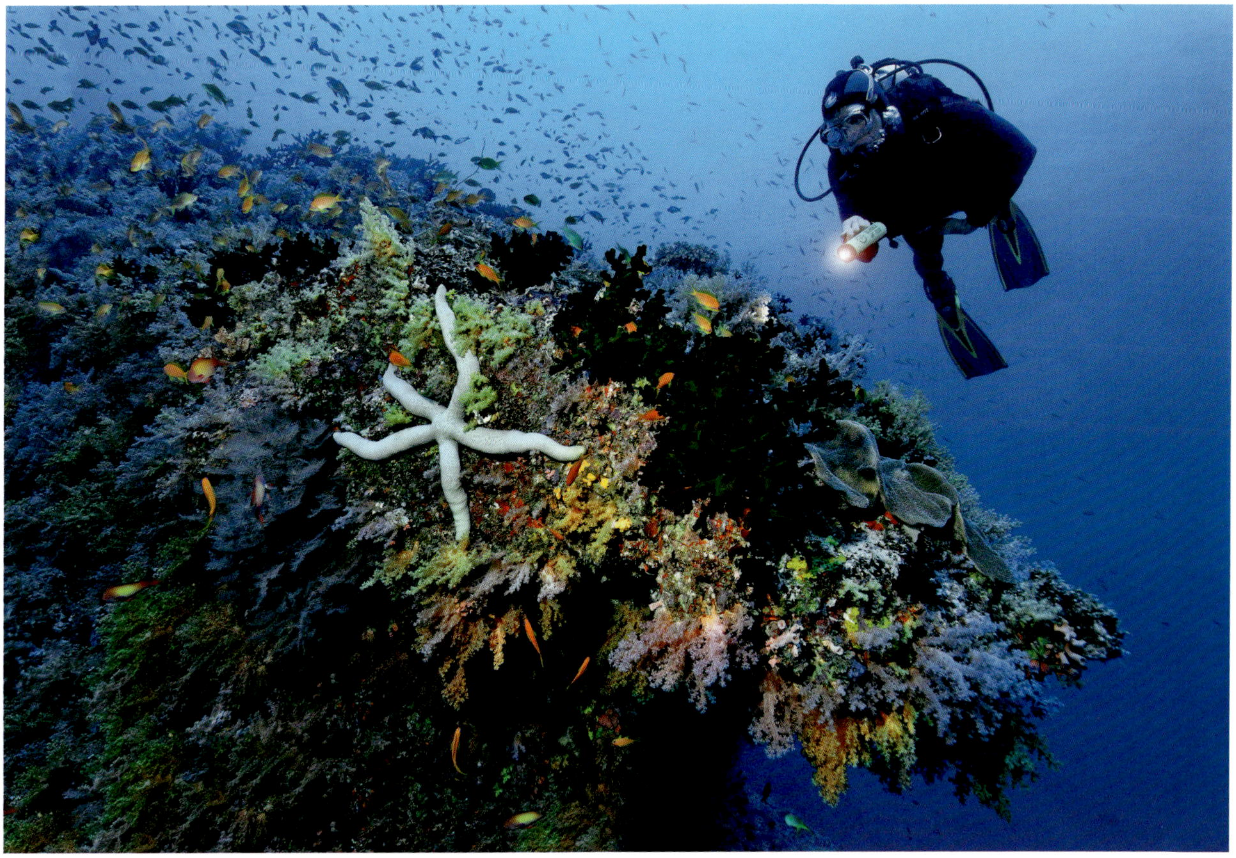

Slightly rotating the image and brightening the colors resulted in a much more vibrant and dynamic final picture (right) than the original unedited one (left). Since the diver's lamp appeared too weak, a light beam was added.

Canon EOS 5D Mark II • Canon 17–40mm wide-angle lens • 1/60 s • f/8 • ISO 400

6.2 Selecting and Evaluating Pictures

Sorting through your pictures and deciding which ones to add to your portfolio can be a difficult process, but a few self-imposed rules make it easier. The first step is to examine your photos on a computer screen. You can do this immediately after a dive, at the end of a day of shooting, or after you return home from your trip. Viewing your photos in an image viewing or editing program that allows you to rate each photo while quickly flipping through them makes this process easier. Adobe Lightroom and Apple Aperture offer this functionality.

When you're reviewing your pictures, use an external monitor that is properly calibrated. Calibration is critical because many monitors have a color cast, which makes it impossible to accurately evaluate and edit images. While you're traveling, a laptop will do the job, but after you get home you should take the time to look at all your photos again.

One way to evaluate your photos is to make several passes. Use an evaluation system with ratings from one (the lowest level) to five (the highest), and assign the lowest score to all the photos you like during the first pass. From this selected group take another pass and apply the next higher rating to the ones you like. Repeat this process on and on until you end up with only a few images with the highest rating. However you decide to rate your images, you need to have a defined and thorough process.

When you have several pictures of the same subject, select only the single best image—skip any others that resemble it too closely. Even if the blue-ringed octopus continued to display fantastic poses and you have several great shots of it, people can get tired of seeing the same subject several times in your portfolio.

Try to analyze your photos without emotion. It's easy to remember how much effort went into taking a particular shot—perhaps you took a lengthy detour to visit a remote location—but what matters is how the end result stacks up against your other photos. Is it better than the rest?

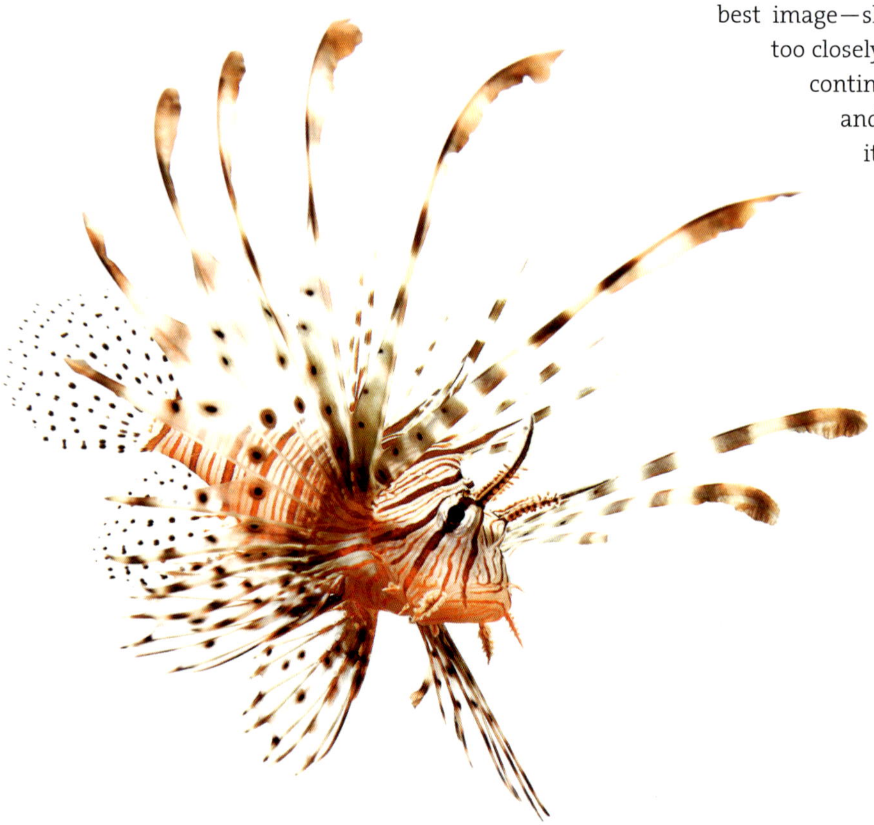

This lionfish was not isolated in an image-editing program; instead, a plastic sheet was positioned behind it during the exposure

Canon EOS 5D Mark II • Canon 17–40mm wide-angle lens • 1/125 s • f/8 • ISO 100

Evaluating your photos objectively is critical because viewers—and jurors at photo competitions—don't factor in the technical prowess and physical effort that went into your photo. You may be proud of a photo you took when you encountered a hammerhead, but if the shark is too far away and the image has a blue haze, it shouldn't be included in your best photos.

After you have settled on your best images, ask yourself if the collection is a good summary of your trip and experiences. If not, you can sneak another image into your portfolio, even if it wouldn't have made the cut on its own merits. When you include photos like this among your best images, they can play an important role in rounding out your portfolio.

A good rule of thumb is to select 15 to 20 pictures per week of travel. A limit in this range will prevent your post-processing work from getting out of hand and will mean that viewers will see only the highlights from your trip. The more strict you are with your inclusion criteria, the fewer pictures you will share with others, which results in a higher-quality portfolio. Less is indeed more.

SUMMARY:

- A few rules make selecting and evaluating photos easier.
- Evaluate your images in a peaceful setting, ideally on an external calibrated monitor.
- An image viewing program simplifies the evaluation process, especially if it features a rating system.
- Evaluate your photos by making several passes through them to make sure you single out the best ones.
- Don't let emotion cloud your evaluation process; remain objective.
- The final selection of photos should be a good representation of the location you visited.
- Select 15 to 20 photos per week of travel. Less is more.

6.3 RAW Conversion

RAW converters allow you to develop pictures from the files you saved in RAW format. It's important to understand that a RAW file contains only data about an image and cannot be read on all devices. RAW converters are provided either as standalone software or in a comprehensive image-editing program.

The biggest advantage of working with RAW files is they give you more flexibility when you post-process your images. For example, you can adjust the exposure by several stops or change the white balance. You can make a wide range of edits that are not possible when you work with a JPEG file.

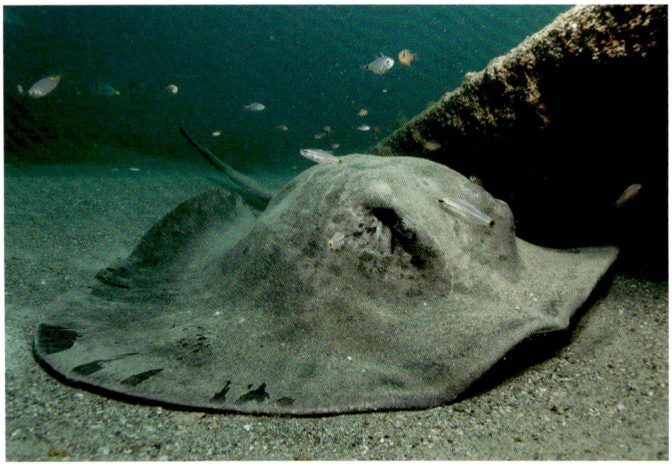

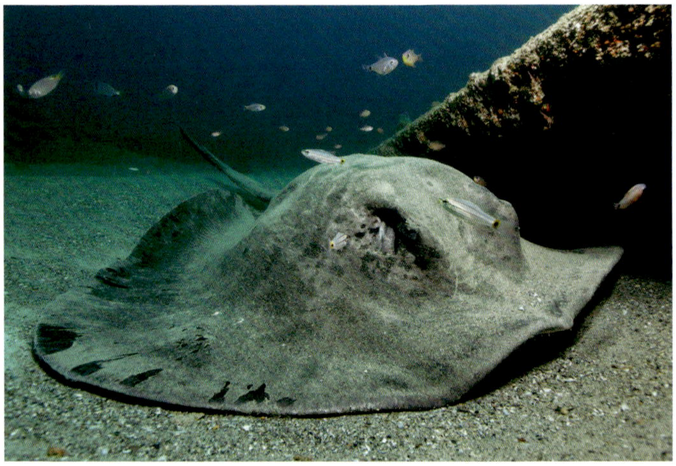

Shifting the white balance to a cooler temperature causes water with a green tint (left) to take on an attractive blue tone (right)

Canon EOS 5D Mark II • Canon 17–40mm wide-angle lens • 1/60 s • f/8 • ISO 400

RAW files can be saved with a color depth of 10, 12, or 14 bits, and JPEGs offer only 8-bit color. RAW files, in other words, contain much more color and brightness information, which is particularly advantageous for reproducing rich blue gradients in water.

Some common adjustments that you can make in a RAW converter include sharpening, setting the white balance, and correcting the exposure. In some cases RAW converters allow you to rescue images that you thought were hopelessly flawed because of overexposure in some areas. The larger the adjustments you make, the more the overall quality of the image suffers. This is apparent in digital image noise, which is comparable to the coarse graininess you can sometimes see in film photography. Once again, try to expose the image as effectively as you can when you release the shutter, but know that you can make fine adjustments during post-processing.

Many RAW converters allow you to make automatic corrections that minimize image noise, correct vignetting (darkness around the edges of an image), and remove chromatic aberrations (color fringing) before you have to manually adjust a single setting. Decide for yourself which processes you want your software to execute automatically; many of them are very useful.

RAW converters can also correct line distortions that can be caused by shooting with fisheye or wide-angle lenses. The adjustment is minor for wide-angle lenses, but it can even restore a natural look to distorted fisheye exposures.

You may also want to crop an image in the RAW converter (e.g., to get rid of distortions that get stronger toward the edges of the frame), because the RAW converter can calculate (interpolate) the resolution to the original size of the photo. The smaller the crop section you choose, the greater the drop in image quality. Some RAW converters are very good at this process, however, and the loss of quality is barely noticeable.

RAW converters can also modulate saturation, tonal values, and contrasts, or you can make these corrections later in image editing software.

For every edit you make to a RAW file, the converter will save a new file so the edit is fully documented. This means you can continue to revise your edits without losing image quality, and the original file is always available.

After you finish working with the RAW converter, you can save your image either as a JPEG, which will cause a slight loss of image quality, or a lossless TIFF. JPEGs have significantly smaller file sizes, so they take up much less storage space. A TIFF file saved with LZW compression is totally lossless, but it will take up less space than a TIFF with no compression.

SUMMARY:

- RAW converters develop the unfinished raw data captured by the camera.
- A RAW file can be substantively edited with a large degree of flexibility.
- RAW converters allow you to adjust the white balance and correct overexposed or underexposed areas of an image.
- Automatic RAW processes are very helpful as a first post-processing step.
- Every edit you make to a RAW picture is saved in a new file, and the unaltered original image is always available.
- Lossless file formats include TIFF and TIFF with LZW compression.
- Saving pictures as JPEGs results in a slight loss of quality, but they take up less storage space.

6.4 Detailed Image Editing

The technical and creative possibilities offered by today's image editing programs are nearly inexhaustible. Many of their features are of great use to underwater photographers, but it can be difficult to know where to get started with the various options. This section will give you a good overview of the most critical editing features.

Remove all floating particles and incidental blemishes to produce a clean image. View your photo at full size (100 %) so you can see all the distracting elements. When you examine your pictures at full size, you'll discover that eliminating blemishes is a large undertaking, so you can take the view down to 50 % if you can live with a few flaws in your final image.

When you're ready to start eliminating particles from your picture, use the editing tools like the Photoshop's Clone Stamp or Spot Healing Brush. Activate

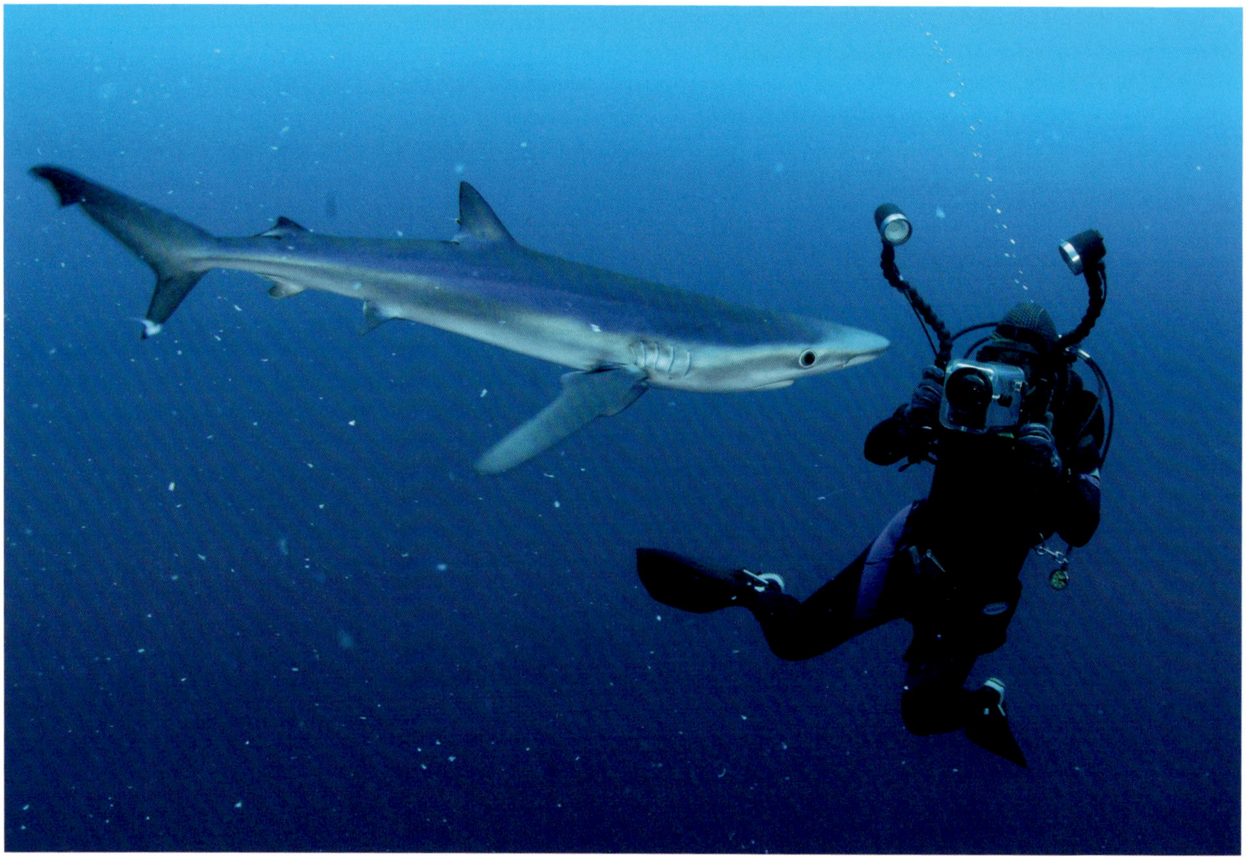

Even when you use the best possible technique with artificial light, floating particles inevitably show up. Fortunately, image editing can take care of this problem.

Canon EOS 5D Mark II • Canon 8–15mm fisheye lens • 1/50 s • f/10 • ISO 400

the tool, and then point the tip of the cursor at the blemish to make the artifact disappear with a single click. The software replaces the fleck with color information from the surrounding area. Other image editing programs offer similar functions. When you're done removing particles, begin working on the colors.

A quick way to adjust colors is to use your software's automatic color and tone correction features. The software will analyze the picture's histogram and make targeted corrections on its own. The resulting edits are often too strong, but you can specify how aggressive you want the automatic correction to be. You can also make these corrections manually, which often produces the best results. When you access the Levels dialog box in Photoshop—or a similar option in other software—an RGB (red, green, blue) histogram pops up. An ideal histogram displays a mountain-shaped graph with values decreasing on both sides. The values should not extend beyond the right and left limits of the graph area. If there's a gap between the end of the values and the edge of the graph area, move the slider to the right or left so the edge of the graph aligns with the values. This increases the color contrast and produces fresher and

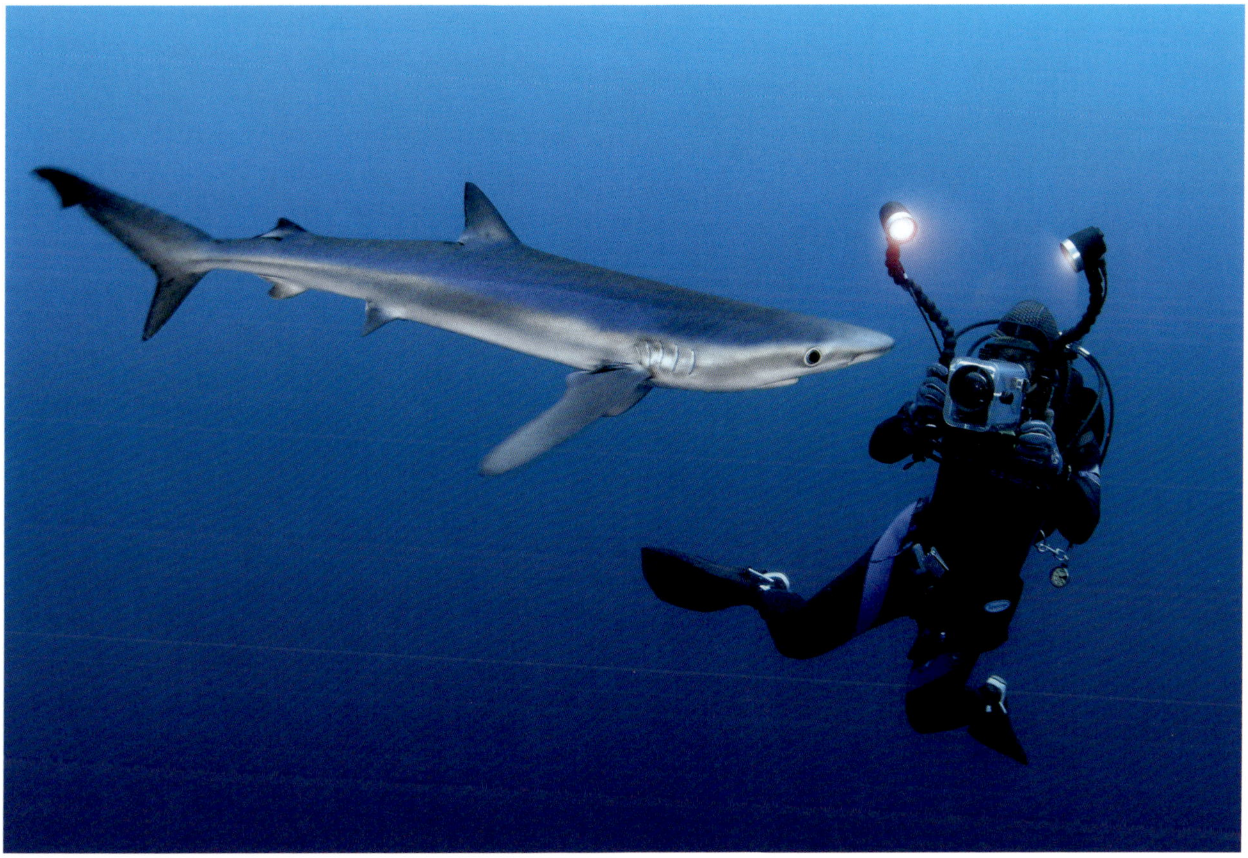

more saturated colors. Play around with the sliders a bit until you are satisfied with the result.

Overly saturated colors can make a picture look gaudy and artificial. It's better to modestly accentuate the colors with the goal of subtly enhancing the result while retaining a natural look.

Use the shadows and highlights control in your image editing software to correct the exposure in problematic areas. Undertake this correction carefully, though, because significant changes result in a loss of image quality and can cause your picture to seem unnatural. Overcompensation will produce digital image noise.

Split waterline photos often require an additional editing step because the underwater portion is often too dark. Brightening the bottom half of these images usually makes them better. Photoshop's Quick Selection Tool makes these edits easy. You can select entire areas, and then edit them separately. After you adjust the water portion of your image, you can invert the selection and optimize the rest of the photo.

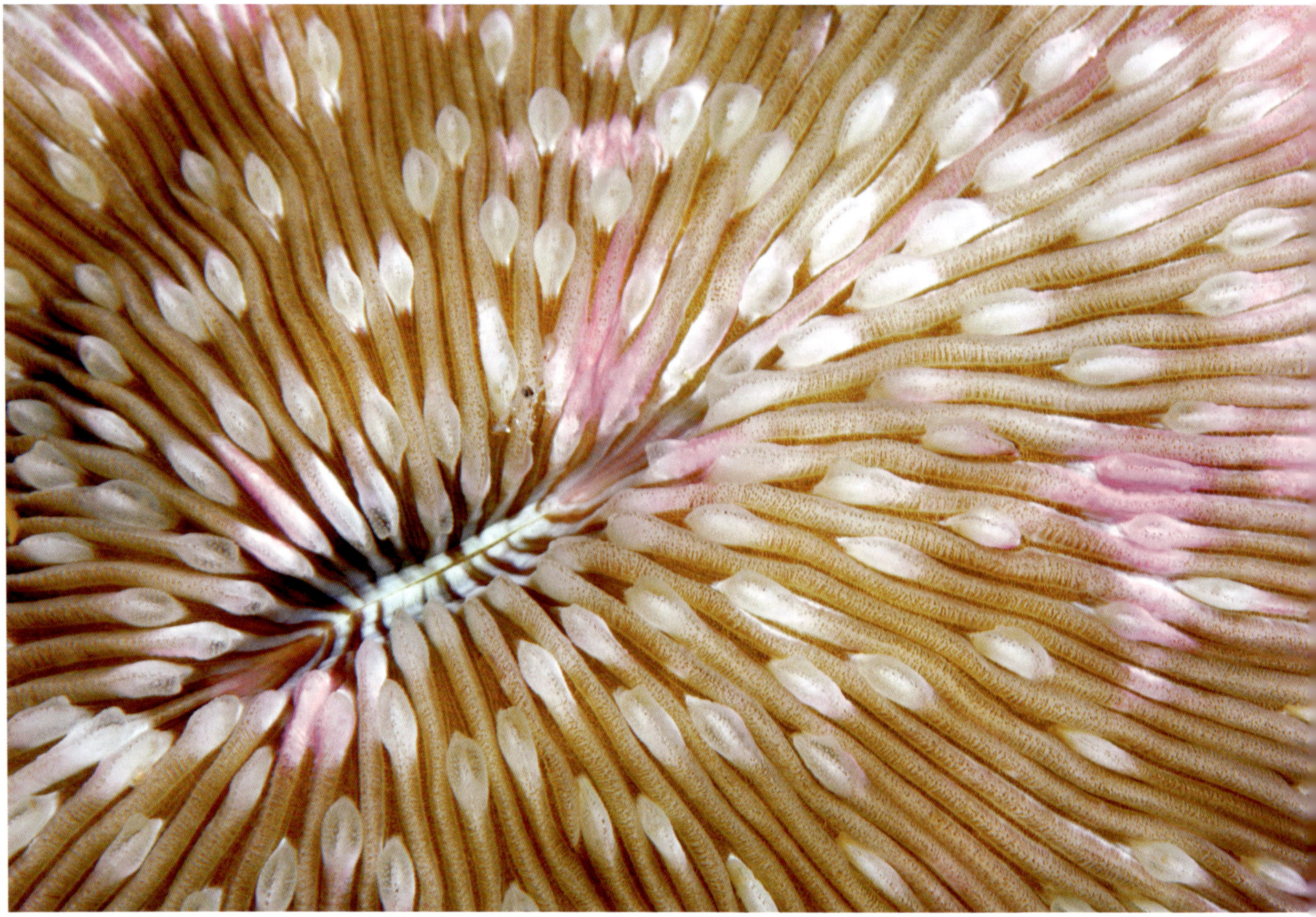

Detailed depictions of simple structures and patterns are often fascinating

Canon EOS 5D Mark II • Canon 100mm macro lens • 1/125 s • f/22 • ISO 100

Sharpening is an excellent way to make your photos look more brilliant, but be careful not to overdo it. Over-sharpening will make your picture seem grainy and fake.

If you plan to print your pictures, use your software's color management tools. They allow you to preview how your pictures will appear given the limitations of your printer. For example, a printer's color palette is more limited than what your monitor can display. If your picture has areas with color values that your printer can't render, you might want to adjust the saturation before you print.

It's helpful to store metadata tags with your pictures as you edit them so you can catalog your photos. This will save you time and effort when you need to find a specific picture or review what you have in your files. For example, an effective metadata tagging system can allow you to bring up all clown fish pictures at once.

SUMMARY:

- View your pictures at 100 % to edit out floating particles and other blemishes.
- The shadows and highlights feature of image editing software allows you to correct areas that are too dark or too bright.
- Automatic tone correction will result in brighter, fresher images, but it's better to make these corrections manually.
- Avoid oversaturated colors to keep your photos from looking artificial.
- Edit each half of a split waterline photo separately.
- Sharpening makes images more brilliant, but don't overdo it.
- Store metadata tags with your pictures to make searching easier.

6.5 Archiving

An effective process for archiving your files is more important now than ever before—modern digital cameras produce a vast amount of data, and it all has to be backed up safely and effectively. Saving your files in a minimum of two places is absolutely necessary to avoid losing critical photos. The more backups you have, the less likely you will suffer devastating losses.

The first step is to transfer your image files from your memory card to your computer hard drive. An internal hard drive usually works perfectly well as the first location for storing your files. If your files are so massive that they exceed the memory capacity of your computer, you'll have to look for external solutions.

The easiest options are portable hard drives, which nowadays offer tremendous capacity at reasonable prices. These drives can be the second location for your files. If you transfer your files to an external drive and delete them from their original location, you'll need to employ another backup system so you always have at least two copies of your files.

A RAID 1 system makes an ideal external storage device because it features two separate internal hard drives: the content of one is mirrored on the other. If one drive fails, the other serves as a backup until the damaged drive can be replaced. Investing in a RAID 1 system is a good investment if you're just getting started. But keep in mind that a backup is only truly secure if it is kept at a location that is off site from where the original files are kept.

Another option is a server, which operates like a normal computer but can be shared by multiple computers on a network. For example, you could access your photos from your main computer and from other computers and devices, depending on how you have your network configured. Setting up a system like

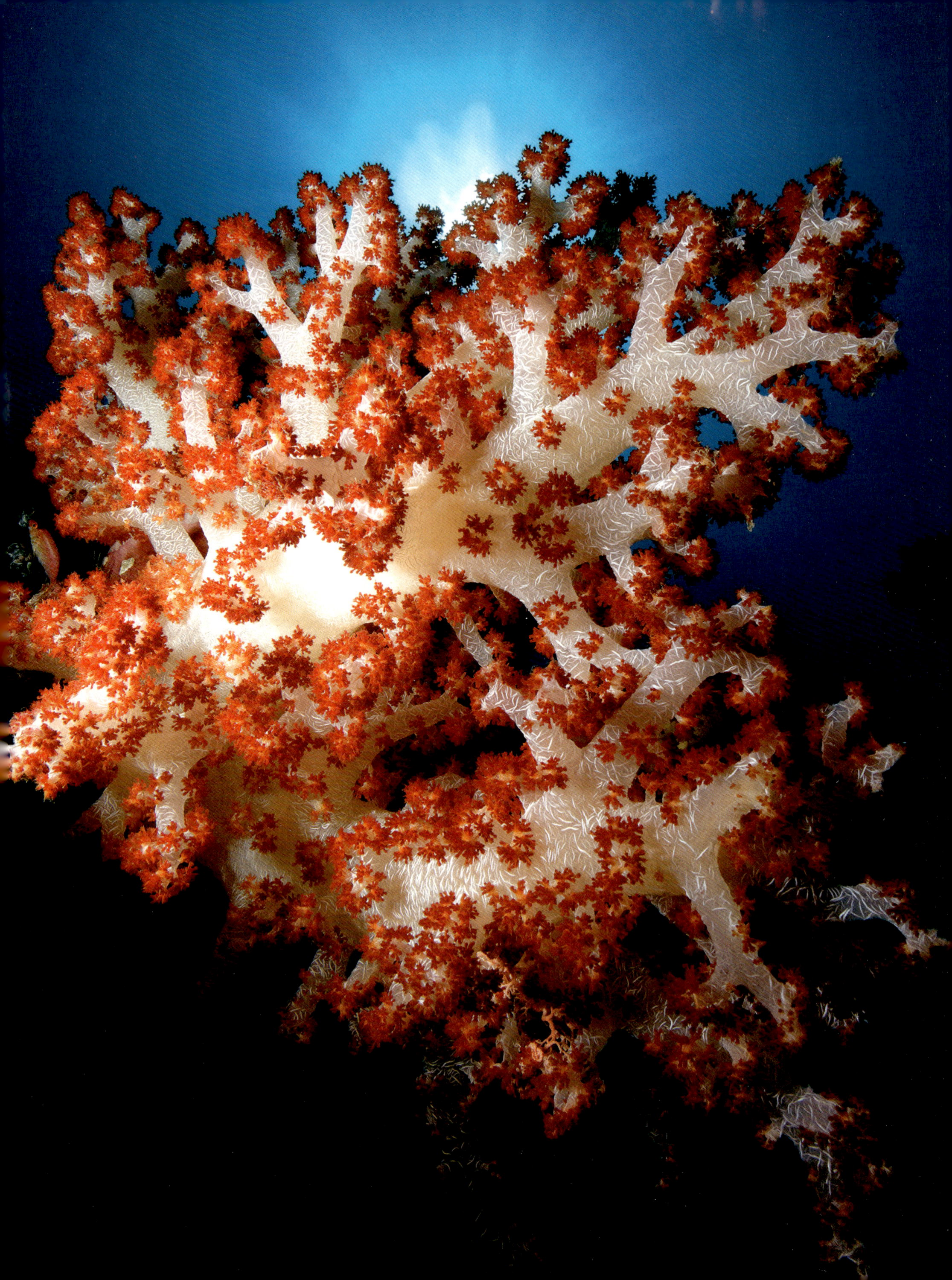

this requires a fair amount of computer know-how and may require the help of an information technology professional.

The *cloud* is a modern way to back up your data. When you use a cloud service, you upload your files to a server on the Internet that secures them and protects them from malicious access. These services are sometimes plagued by slow access and are often fairly expensive.

Creating secure backups of your files means you'll regularly transfer large amounts of data, so you'll need fast connectivity between your devices. Many gigabytes of data can quickly push the limits of a USB 2.0 connection; a USB 3.0 connection is more useful, as is the Thunderbolt interface from Apple.

SUMMARY:

- It's absolutely necessary to archive at least two copies of your images.
- Additional backups will protect you even more.
- The most simple backup system includes your computer's internal hard drive and an external storage device.
- RAID 1 systems mirror data on two drives. If one drive fails, your data will still be on the other drive.
- A server allows you to share data across several devices on the same network, but it is relatively complicated to set up.
- It's convenient to archive images in the cloud, but connectivity is sometimes slow and the service is often costly.
- Connections to external hard drives should be as fast as possible because of the amount of data you'll need to transfer.

After distractions have been eliminated, a minimalist composition is more powerful than an cluttered one

Canon EOS 5D Mark II • Canon 17–40mm wide-angle lens • 1/200 s • f/22 • ISO 200

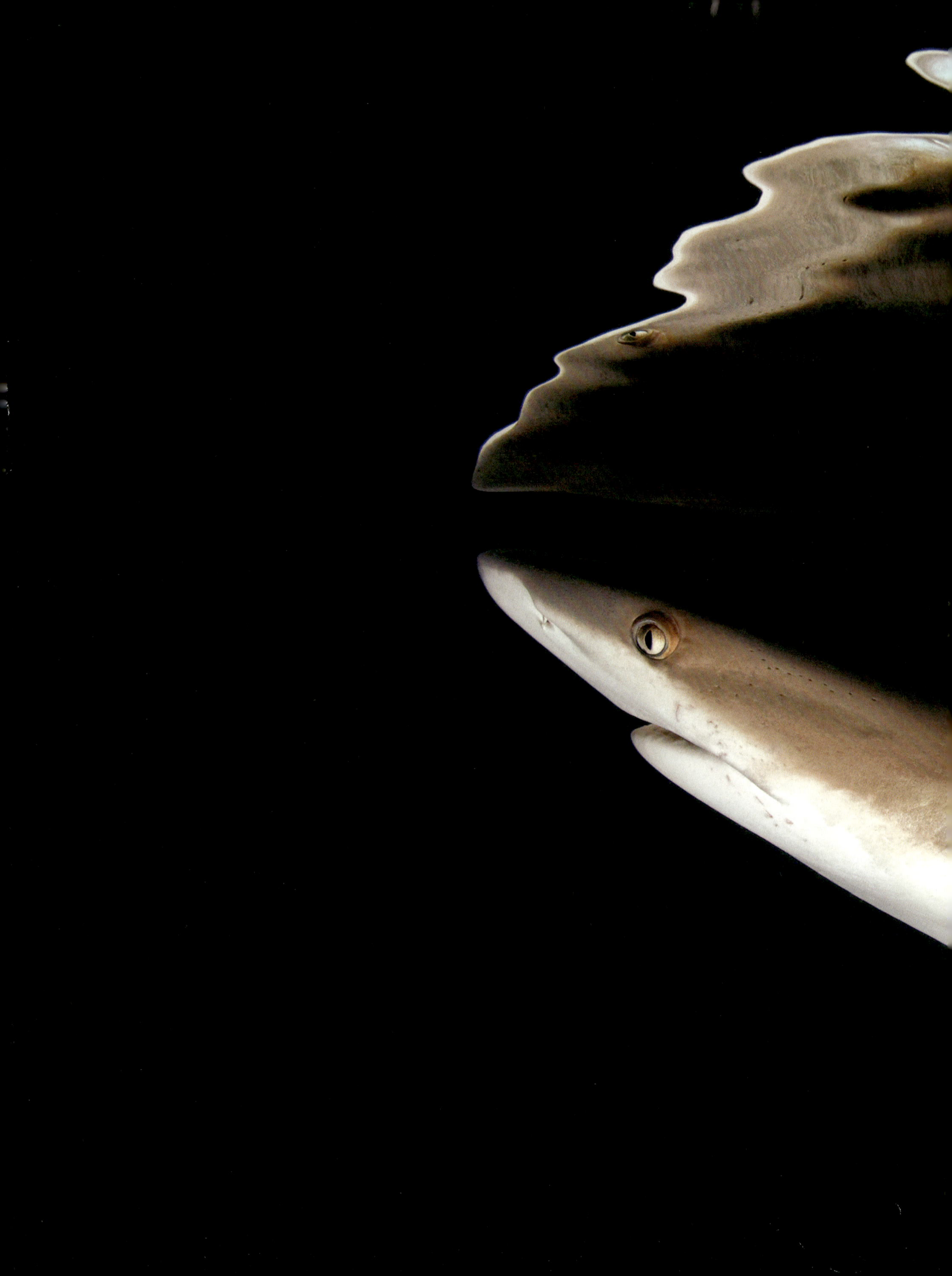

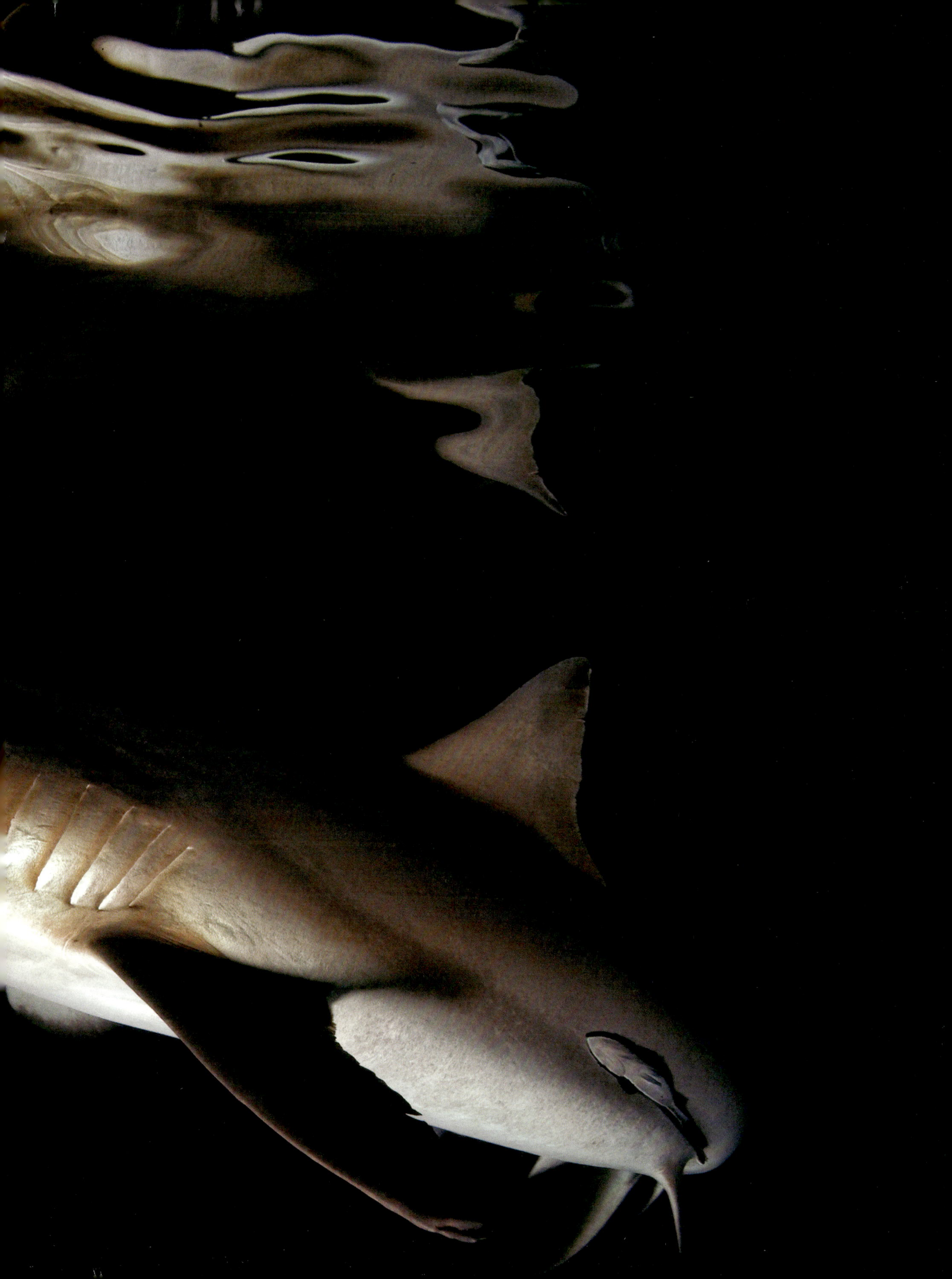

Case Study 8: The Dark Knight

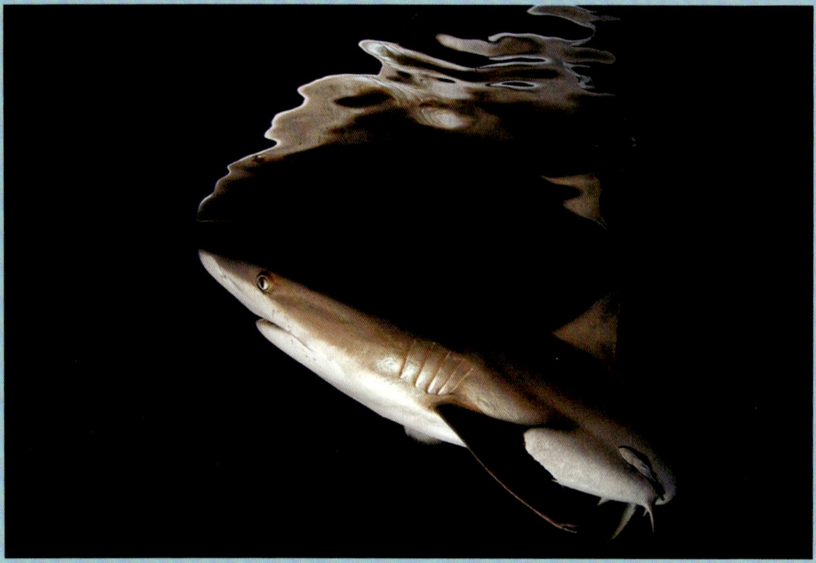

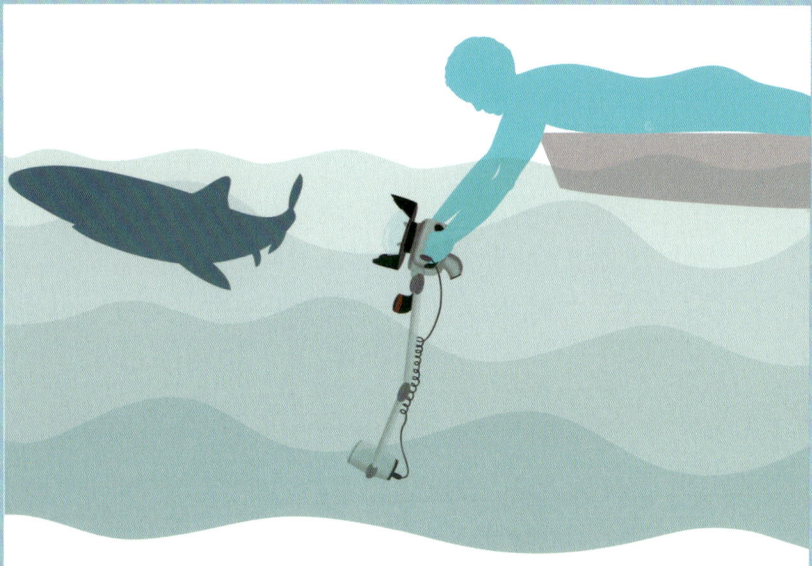

Canon EOS 5D Mark II • Canon 17–40mm wide-angle lens • one Ikelite DS125 strobe • 1/200 s • f/9 • ISO 400 • manual flash at half power

The saying "Beggars can't be choosers" suits this photo perfectly. A faulty diving mask made me cut my night dive short. During my ascent, a couple of gray reef sharks started swimming near the boat. I was disappointed about the dive, and when I was back on board I could still see the sharks hanging out near the surface of the water. In an effort to salvage the evening, I decided to try photographing the sharks in the dark. I waited until all the divers were out of the water, then the sharks came even closer while they hunted squid in the light from the diving deck.

Instead of going back into the water and probably scaring away the sharks, I lay down on my stomach a couple inches above the surface of the water, inverted my camera, and stuck it in the water. My flash arm extended deep into the water, allowing me to illuminate the shark from below. The angle of light created the shark's reflection on the surface of the water. The drawback was that I couldn't see what I was photographing and I had to rely on my intuition. I used a strong focus lamp to ensure that the autofocus would work.

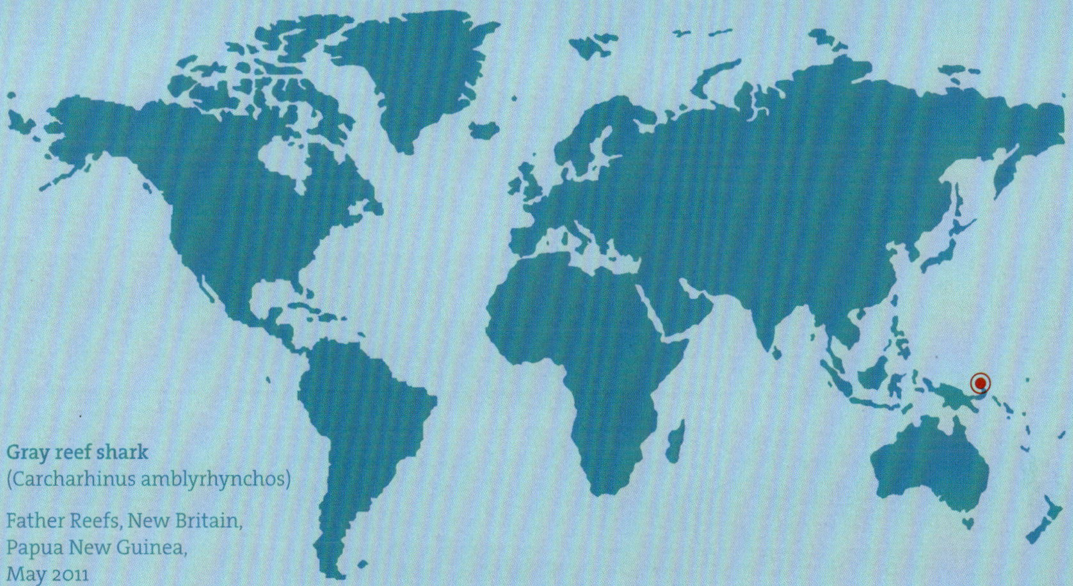

Gray reef shark
(Carcharhinus amblyrhynchos)

Father Reefs, New Britain,
Papua New Guinea,
May 2011

7 Appendix

7.1 Behind the Scenes

Tobias Friedrich has visited many countries searching for photographic stories and travel essays to bring home. Here are a few behind-the-scenes pictures showing the life of an underwater photographer.

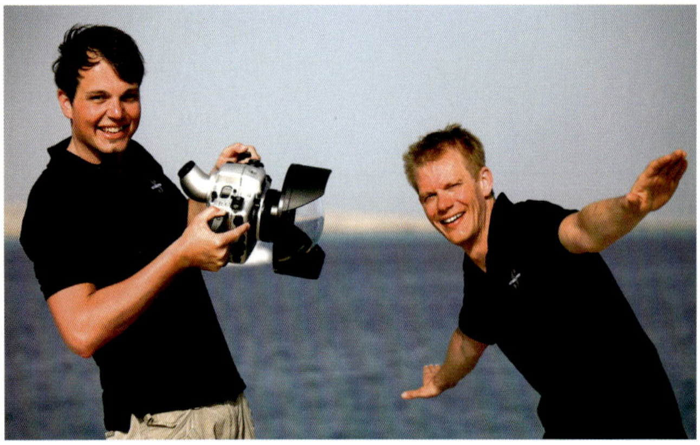

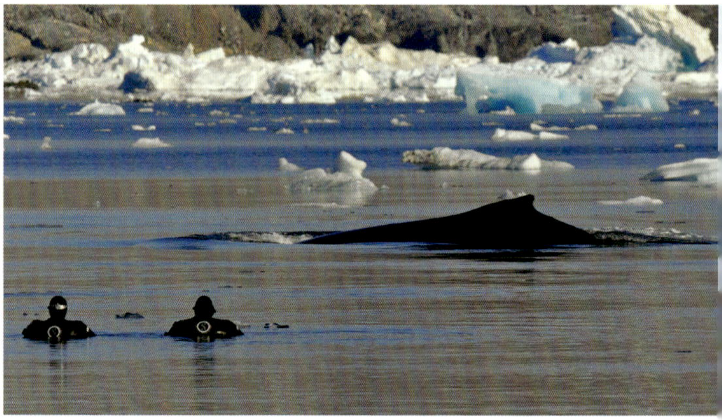

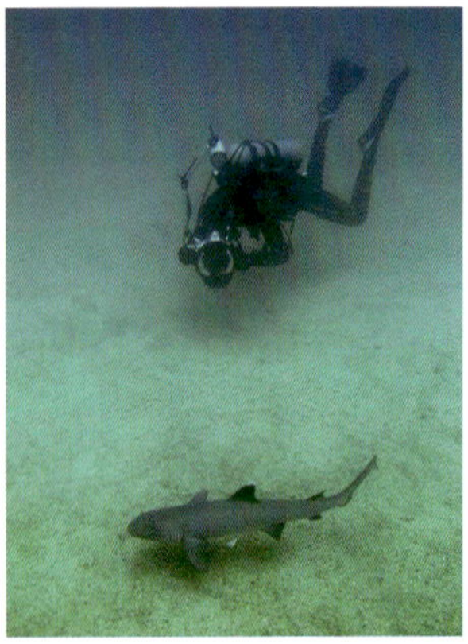

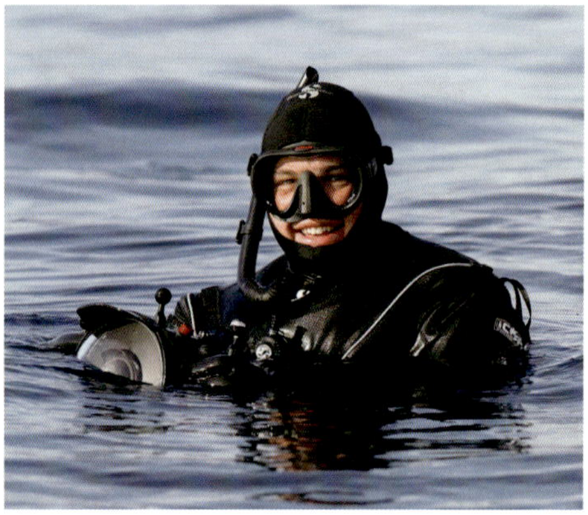

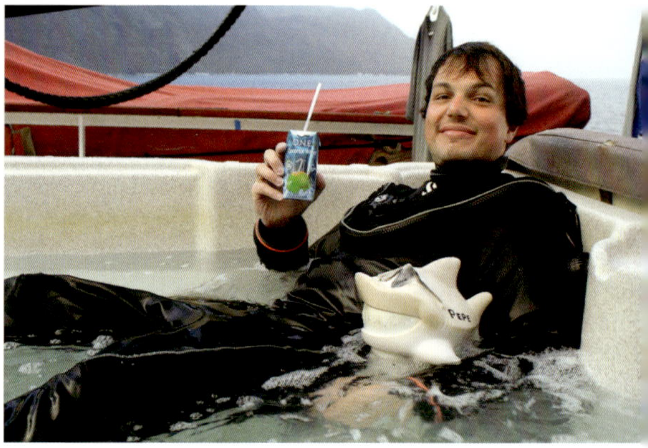

7.2 Acknowledgements

A book doesn't write itself. The author's subjective opinions make it impossible to evaluate the content and the quality of the message. Only through the opinions and feedback of others does the writing become consistent.

I would like to thank Gerhard Rossbach, the publisher of Rocky Nook (and dpunkt.verlag in Germany), for the confidence he placed in me and the encouragement he provided along the way.

I am particularly grateful for the commitment of my diving partner, Thomas Fiebig, who I hope will stick with me for many years and will continue to follow my sign language for hundreds of corals to come.

Thanks to Linus Geschke for editing the original German manuscript and for passing along tips that constantly reminded me that writing is an art form too. Thanks also to David Hettich and Tino Brandt for their suggestions and comments about where to add explanations, as well as to Frank Dornberger who double checked the video part.

I am extremely grateful to the five photographers who have generously allowed their images to appear in the gallery section of this book: Ernie Brooks, Alex Mustard, Imran Ahmad, Richard Salas, and Eric Cheng. Their beautiful images show us a vast variety of styles and approaches that may be used to create outstanding underwater photos.

Lastly, I'd like to thank all the people over the years who shared tips and secrets with me and encouraged me to write this book.

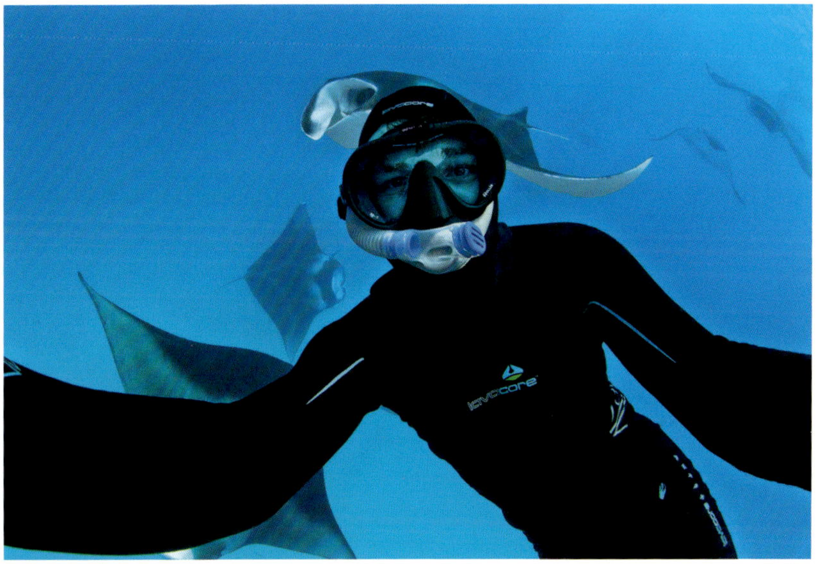

7.3 Travel Checklist

Go through this list at least two times before you travel and check off each item only after you have packed it.

DIVING EQUIPMENT

- ☐ Diving suit
- ☐ Regulator
- ☐ Jacket
- ☐ Diving computer
- ☐ Logbook
- ☐ Lycra shirt
- ☐ Fins
- ☐ Neoprene socks
- ☐ Masks
- ☐ Snorkel
- ☐ Current certificate
- ☐ Booties
- ☐ Ice vest
- ☐ Replacement straps for masks
- ☐ Gloves
- ☐ Writing board
- ☐ Replacement straps for fins
- ☐ Reef hook
- ☐ Diving wheel
- ☐ Pointer
- ☐ Buoy
- ☐ Muck stick

PHOTOGRAPHY EQUIPMENT

- ☐ Camera body
- ☐ Standard zoom lens
- ☐ Telephoto lens
- ☐ USB cable
- ☐ Second camera body
- ☐ Fisheye lens
- ☐ Teleconverter
- ☐ Camera belt
- ☐ Camera batteries
- ☐ Wide-angle lens
- ☐ Memory cards
- ☐ Camera charger
- ☐ Macro lens
- ☐ Tripod

UNDERWATER PHOTOGRAPHY EQUIPMENT

- ☐ Housing
- ☐ Dome port
- ☐ Zoom ring for fish-eye lens
- ☐ Flash unit
- ☐ Replacement flash batteries
- ☐ Red filter
- ☐ Locking strap
- ☐ Replacement O-rings
- ☐ Macro port
- ☐ Zoom ring for wide-angle lens
- ☐ Second flash unit
- ☐ Focus lamp
- ☐ Allen wrench
- ☐ Light-shaping tool/snoot
- ☐ Viewfinder
- ☐ Port extension for fisheye lens
- ☐ Focus ring for macro
- ☐ Flash arms
- ☐ Silicone lubricant
- ☐ Screwdriver
- ☐ Sync cable and replacement
- ☐ Port extension for wide-angle lens
- ☐ Flash diffuser
- ☐ Flash arm clamps
- ☐ O-ring removal tools
- ☐ Screw wrench

ELECTRONICS

- ☐ Computer
- ☐ External hard drives
- ☐ Eyeglass wipes
- ☐ Computer charger
- ☐ Microfiber cloth
- ☐ Card reader
- ☐ USB cable
- ☐ Tablet/e-reader
- ☐ Power strip
- ☐ Cell phone
- ☐ Cell phone charger
- ☐ Tablet charger
- ☐ Power converter

GENERAL TRAVEL

- ☐ T-shirts
- ☐ Shorts
- ☐ Socks
- ☐ Underwear
- ☐ Sweater
- ☐ Rain jacket
- ☐ Rain pants
- ☐ Pants
- ☐ Hiking pants
- ☐ Flip-flops
- ☐ Second pair of shoes
- ☐ Swimsuit
- ☐ Hand towels
- ☐ Toothbrush
- ☐ Toothpaste
- ☐ Deodorant
- ☐ Medicines
- ☐ Shower gel/soap
- ☐ Face lotion
- ☐ Nail clipper
- ☐ Nasal spray
- ☐ Earplugs
- ☐ Band-Aids
- ☐ Hats
- ☐ Backpack
- ☐ Mosquito repellant
- ☐ Sunscreen
- ☐ After-sun lotion
- ☐ Pen
- ☐ Wet bag
- ☐ Sunglasses
- ☐ Paper
- ☐ Passport (still valid?)
- ☐ Travel documents
- ☐ Visa for foreign country, if needed

Personal Notes

7.4 Predive Checklist

Print this list, laminate it, and keep it with your underwater equipment so it's always handy.

- ☐ Are the O-rings lubricated?
- ☐ Are the camera and flash batteries charged?
- ☐ Have you removed the lens cap?
- ☐ Is the zoom ring installed, and did you check that everything is working?
- ☐ Is the camera set to autofocus?
- ☐ Is there enough space on your memory card?
- ☐ TAKE A TEST PHOTO!!!
- ☐ Are the flashes working properly?
- ☐ Program your baseline exposure settings:
    - Wide-angle: 1/125 second, f/8, ISO 200
    - Macro: 1/160 second, f/22, ISO 200
    - Split waterline: Aperture priority, f/22, ISO 400
    - Close range, wide angle: 1/60 second, f/16, ISO 400
    - Backlight: 1/200 second, f/13, ISO 100
    - Motion blur: 1/10 second, f/22, ISO 100
- ☐ Submerge the housing in a tub and look for bubble formation.
- ☐ Turn the camera and the flash units off.
- ☐ Attach the protective cap for the dome or macro port.
- ☐ Store your equipment in a safe place out of direct sunlight.

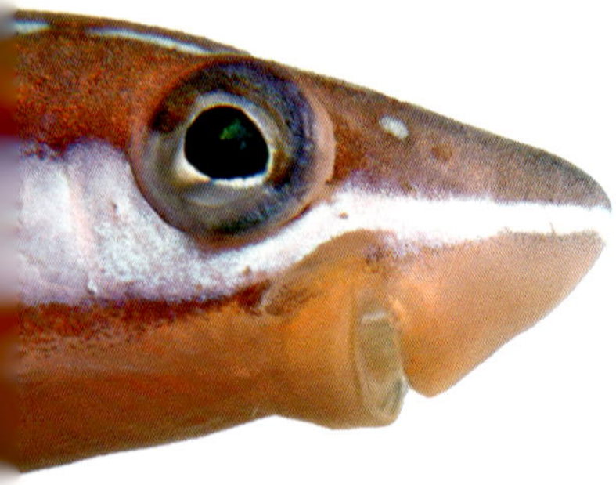

Creativity and a calculated perspective allowed me to perfectly isolate this saber-toothed blenny

Canon EOS 5D Mark II • Canon 100mm macro lens • 1/160 s • f/16 • ISO 400

7.5 Ready, Set, Go

Wide-Angle

Settings:	Shutter speed	Aperture	ISO	Exposure style
	1/125 second	f/8	200	Single shot
Lens:	Wide-angle or fisheye			
Flash units:	• One unit: Position the unit above the camera at a minimum distance of 20 in, pointed forward. • Two units: Spread the units along a horizontal axis as far away from the camera as possible, pointed forward.			
Tips:	• Always adjust the flash units for each subject. • To produce a rich blue tone for the water, narrow the aperture by one stop based on the open water.			

Macro

Settings:	Shutter speed	Aperture	ISO	Exposure style
	1/160 second	f/22	200	Single shot
Lens:	60mm for crop-sensor camera; 100mm for full-format camera			
Flash units:	• One unit: Position the unit above and close to the housing, pointed forward. • Two units: Position the units on either side of the camera, close to the housing.			
Tips:	• The closer the subject is, the closer your flash units should be to the camera housing. If the subject is farther away, you can move the flash units out. • Open the aperture and use a longer shutter speed to capture ambient light. • For a super-macro shot, focus manually at the minimum focus distance.			

Split Waterline

Settings:	Shutter speed	Aperture	ISO	Exposure style
	Automatic	f/22	400	Continuous shooting
Lens:	Fisheye			
Flash units:	None			
Tips:	• Use the largest dome port possible. • Set the focus based on the objects under water. • Adjust the exposure 1/3 stop downward. • Wait for the right moment between waves. • Inflate your buoyancy compensator.			

Close Range, Wide Angle

Settings:	Shutter speed	Aperture	ISO	Exposure style
	1/60 second	f/16	400	Single shot
Lens:	Fisheye			
Flash units:	• One unit: Position the unit above the camera close to the housing, pointed forward. • Two units: Position one unit above the camera and directed at the foreground; use the other unit for the background.			
Tips:	• Use the smallest dome port possible (a mini dome). • Get as close as you can to the subject. • Position the camera so it is angled slightly upward at the subject. • Set the focus point on the macro subject. • Increase the ISO or decrease the shutter speed to capture more ambient light.			

Backlight

Settings:	Shutter speed	Aperture	ISO	Exposure style
	1/200 second	f/13	100	Single shot
Lens:	Wide-angle or fisheye			
Flash units:	• One unit: Position the unit above the camera at a medium distance from the housing, pointed forward. • Two units: Spread the units along a horizontal axis at a medium distance from the camera, pointed forward.			
Tips:	• Shoot in the morning or afternoon. • If you shoot in the middle of the day, position the subject in front of the sun. • Set your flash units to maximum power. • Swim close to the subject. • Control the ambient light by adjusting the aperture.			

Motion Blur

Settings:	Shutter speed	Aperture	ISO	Exposure style
	1/10 second	f/22	100	Single shot
Lens:	Wide-angle or fisheye			
Flash units:	• One unit: Position the unit above the camera at a medium distance from the housing, pointed forward. • Two units: Spread the units along a horizontal axis at a medium distance from the camera, pointed forward.			
Tips:	• Overcast skies are ideal. • Pan the camera with the movement of the subject. • Sync the flash with the first or second curtain. • Practice zooming and rotating your camera in advance.			

7.6 Index